Portfolio
Performance
Measurement
and
Benchmarking

JON A. CHRISTOPHERSON

DAVID R. CARIÑO

WAYNE E. FERSON

New York   Chicago   San Francisco   Lisbon
London   Madrid   Mexico City   Milan   New Delhi
San Juan   Seoul   Singapore   Sydney   Toronto

1 2 3 4 5 6 7 8 9 0   DOC/DOC   0 1 0 9

ISBN   978-0-07-149665-0
MHID   0-07-149665-3

This publication is designed to provide accurate and authoritative
information in regard to the subject matter covered. It is sold with the
understanding that the publisher is not engaged in rendering legal,
accounting, or other professional service. If legal advice or other expert
assistance is required, the services of a competent professional person should
be sought.

*—From a declaration of principles jointly adopted by a committee of the
American Bar Association and a committee of publishers.*

McGraw-Hill books are available at special quantity discounts to use as
premiums and sales promotions, or for use in corporate training programs.
To contact a representative please visit the Contact Us pages at
www.mhprofessional.com.

CONTENTS

Chapter 6

Comparing Two Portfolio Returns   47

Chapter 7

Some Foundations   57

Chapter 8

Estimating the Elements of the CAPM   67

Chapter 9

What Is Risk?   79

Chapter 10

Risk-Adjusted Return Measures   93

PREFACE

The efficient use of capital and the effective allocation of scarce resources among economic enterprises improve the overall economy. Improving the financial security of people requires that investment management be carried out as efficiently and effectively as possible. Therefore, each generation of students, scholars, and business people in this field should obtain a thorough understanding of the financial world around them. We hope that this book contributes to this effort.

We have sought to assemble state-of-the-art methodology in the areas of performance measurement that we cover. This book assembles and integrates our own work with the work of many contributors to provide a uniquely comprehensive view of benchmark construction and philosophy. We take some deliberately firm stands on the philosophy and construction of equity indexes and we hope that our positions will enhance the conversation in this field.

This book began with the intention of setting down information that the authors have found useful in their careers. Each of the authors has colleagues who have contributed a great deal of knowledge to them. In the same way that each of us has experienced the generosity of our teachers and colleagues who shared their knowledge with us, it is incumbent upon us to pass on that knowledge to other colleagues and students.

We would like to take this opportunity to express our appreciation to the many colleagues at Russell Investments who contributed directly and indirectly to the content and quality of this book. We specifically thank those colleagues who have generously allowed us to use their previous work and who took the time to review chapters of this book: Kelly Haughton, Lori Richards, Tom Monroe, Tom Goodwin, Grant Gardner, Steve Murray, Rolf Agather, Ernie Ankrim, George Oberhofer, Leola Ross, Dave Brunette, Dave Hintz, Matt Dmytryczyn, Wenling Lin, Barry Feldman, Erik Anderson, Artemiza Woodgate, Mahesh Pritamani, and John Stannard.

Jon Christopherson and David Cariño would also like to thank Ron Kahn of Barclays Global Investors, Ted Aronson of Aronson+Johnson+ Ortiz, the staff of the U.S. Equity Research group at Russell, the Capital Markets Research group at Russell, the Russell Index group, and the leadership of Russell Investments who encouraged and supported the creation of this book, including Tom Hanly, Pete Gunning, Tim Hicks, Dave Grieger, and Ron Bundy. Of course, this book would not exist without the entrepreneurial leadership of George F. Russell Jr. and Mike Phillips who built Russell Investments into the platform from which this book could be launched. Peter O. Dietz, Russell's first Director of Research, set the standard in research for all of us who have followed.

Jon Christopherson would also like to thank those to whom he feels special debt: namely, Peter O. Dietz for hiring him; Andy Turner for sharing his knowledge; Kelly Haughton who championed the index business; and Dennis Trittin, Nola Kulig, Tom Monroe, and Paul Greenwood who shared their knowledge of equities. He learned a great deal from these mentors and colleagues over the years.

David Cariño would also like to thank Peter O. Dietz, Kelly Haughton, Andy Turner, Don Ezra, Grant Gardner, and Steve Fox, whose influences are reflected in this work. He is also grateful for the help of many associates in performance measurement, investment operations, and support roles who have generously explained many aspects of their work.

Wayne Ferson would like to thank his colleagues at Russell, especially Jon Christopherson, for teaching him many practical things and would like to acknowledge support from the Ivadelle and Theodore Johnson Chair in Banking and Finance at the University of Southern California.

We would like to dedicate this book to our families, without whose love, support, and encouragement this work would have never been started, much less completed: Patricia Christopherson, Katherine Christopherson, and Anna Christopherson, Florence R. Cariño, Gail Fitz Cariño, and Nancy Ferson.

Finally, the statements and opinions expressed in this book are the authors' and not the opinions of Russell Investments or the University of Southern California. Any mistakes are the authors' responsibility.[1] We hope you find this book useful.

Jon A. Christopherson
David R. Cariño
Wayne E. Ferson

---

[1] Comments, criticisms, errors or suggestions should be directed to David R. Cariño at e-mail address: DCarino@russell.com.

CHAPTER 1

What Is Performance and Benchmarking?

THE BASIC ISSUE: HAS YOUR WEALTH INCREASED?

If we receive a $5,000 bonus check because we sold more widgets than our competitors did, we can either spend the money now or we can defer spending it now and let it grow in an investment. Say we had invested our $5,000 in a certificate of deposit (CD) and our account grew to $5,050 over a period of three months. We earned $50 on a $5,000 investment or 1 percent over three months, or about 4 percent per year on our investment. If we think that the $50 earned on a $5,000 investment is not a reasonable return, then we might be inclined to spend $5,000 and not invest it or look for an alternative higher-paying investment.

To make investment choices we must have the proper data and information about the return on investments and the risk of not being paid. This relatively simple notion of performance measurement and evaluation is basic to all investments. The decision to consume today or defer consumption by investing for tomorrow is absolutely fundamental to all economic activity. Economic growth depends on investors deferring consumption so that the money can be invested for the future. No factory is built, no new company is capitalized, and no economic growth is possible without this deferred consumption.

The confidence that people have that their investments will earn sufficient compensation in the future is critical to justifying their deferring consumption today. Hence, it is fundamental to any economic system.

Instances of hyperinflation such as in Zimbabwe in 2007, Argentina in the 1990s, or Germany in the early 1930s create very challenging environments for economic activity. Investors ask themselves why anyone would put money in a bank, buy a stock, buy a bond, or invest in anything if the payoff cannot be expected to exceed the very rapid rise in prices. Being able to reasonably anticipate the payoff we will receive for investing is absolutely critical.

The institutions that gather money from investors and distribute it to users of capital make up the financial system. The more efficient and effective the collection and distribution of capital, the more efficient the economy will be. Essential to this operation is the ability to correctly assess the performance of various investment alternatives. New companies or companies seeking to expand attempt to raise capital by persuading potential investors that their investment will be rewarded. If investors are unable to calculate before or after the fact whether the promises or expectations of an investment were met, they will not invest. This flow of information is fundamental to the efficient allocation of capital within an economy toward productive activities and enterprises that increase wealth and away from activities and enterprises that are less productive. In this sense, anything investors can do to improve the performance evaluation techniques and methods that they use makes a positive contribution by helping the economic system to more efficiently allocate their savings (i.e., capital) and thereby maximizing economic growth.

WAS THE CHANGE IN WEALTH WORTH THE RISK?

If investors want their investments to grow more than in a savings account, then they are going to have to invest in enterprises whose outcomes are uncertain. Most investors comparing alternatives that provide the same return, the same promised payoff, will choose the alternative that is less risky. If a company's management wants investors to invest in its enterprise but the outcome of the enterprise is not certain, the company has to offer a higher return potential than comparable less risky investments.

This leads to the second dimension of the investment problem—risk. When we calculate our growth in wealth, we want to balance that knowledge with an assessment of the risk we undertook to achieve that wealth. The problem with the term *risk* is that it's not easy to measure in a way that satisfies all investors. In this book we will examine various definitions and measures of risk.

The preceding considerations lead us to this definition of *performance measurement*:

> Performance is the return or the increase in wealth over time of an investment relative to the amount of risk the investor is taking; that is, performance measurement provides a risk-adjusted return assessment.

So the first central problem in performance measurement is to assess the increase in wealth over a given time frame. Then we must view this return in terms of some measure of the risk we took to obtain it. If we have more than one investment opportunity, we will want to compare these investments in terms of their reward relative to their risk. In the first part of this book we focus on calculating different measures of wealth growth and different measures of risk calculation. The objective is to provide tools for calculating risk-adjusted return.

COMPARING RETURN WITH ALTERNATIVE INVESTMENT RETURNS

After we have calculated our growth in wealth and have assessed the risk we took to gain that wealth, the next logical question is, How large was the risk-adjusted return compared with the risk-adjusted return achieved with alternative investments? We ask ourselves whether we could have obtained the same return at less risk by following an alternative strategy.

This leads to the discussion of benchmarking. *Benchmarking* is the process of finding a quantifiable standard against which to measure one's performance. Benchmarking seeks to determine whether the performance of our investment is better than what we could have obtained using a simpler or less costly investment plan. The subject consumes a large portion of the latter half of this book.

The notion of benchmarking the performance of investment strategies is a relatively new phenomenon. As recently as the 1960s, large sophisticated investors were comparing their growth of wealth to T-bills or government bonds on an absolute basis. Investors thought the comparison that mattered was absolute return relative to zero—loss was all that mattered. Zero return is still the first fundamental level of performance evaluation. However, managers of complex funds also wanted to know how various segments of their plans, such as stocks, performed relative to some alternative.

Until about the 1980s, if investors wanted to know how well their stocks performed relative to other stocks, the primary equity indexes available in the United States were the Dow Jones Industrial Average and the S&P 500. This was the extent of equity benchmarking. Much has changed since then. A wide variety of equity benchmarks have been created. A hierarchy of comparisons has been developed to allow investors to understand how well their equity investments are doing. Analysts also noted that if the benchmark selected was inappropriate, then the analyst would obtain a useless or even perverse result and make erroneous evaluations and decisions. For example, if you hold a selection of small company stocks in your portfolio during a period when most small stocks went down while large company stocks went up, it makes little sense to benchmark your selection of small stocks by comparing your returns to those of large stocks in the S&P 500. It would be better to compare your returns to a portfolio of all the small stocks that you might have reasonably chosen among.

ACTIVE INVESTING VERSUS PASSIVE INVESTING

During the 1970s and 1980s, portfolios based on the list of securities in an index led to the creation of index funds, which in turn led to the growth of a huge industry that provides passive alternative investment vehicles based on all sorts of benchmarks. These inexpensive to manage passive index funds provide investment vehicles for investors who want exposure to the average risk and returns of an asset class without having to select individual securities.

One of the first questions modern investors face is that of whether they should undertake "active management of assets" or invest in an index fund, that is, engage in "the passive management of assets." When investors purchase a stock or a bond and do not purchase others in the same class, they presumably do so because they have some information that persuades them that the stock or bond they purchased will provide higher payoffs than the other stocks and bonds available. This is *active management*. *Passive management* refers to the purchase of a share in an index fund or a group of assets chosen with no information about their prospective payoffs other than the asset type to which they belong. Passive investing is a "no information" or "naïve investment" strategy because no specialized knowledge is needed to execute the investment strategy. For example, "buy all stocks in the market and weight each by its float-adjusted capitalization weight" is a strategy that anyone who knows the basics of investments can do.

Unfortunately for active management, passive strategies can perform quite well. Investors, who have been in the markets for many years and have seen up markets and down markets, know that it is difficult for most active investors to outperform the return of a naïve passive index. In fact there are some who would argue that passive investing is the only sensible way for the majority of people to invest.

PERFORMANCE ATTRIBUTION

Once the investor has calculated return on a risk-adjusted basis and compared it to an appropriate benchmark, the next natural question is, Where did the return come from, or to what "market forces or factors" can we attribute the return? The investigation of the sources of return leads to the field called *performance attribution*. The objective of attribution analysis is to break out the performance that emerged among various factors in the marketplace and the decisions the investor made.

Our objective in this book is to provide the reader with fundamental knowledge about measuring return and risk and how to use this fundamental information to accurately evaluate the performance of investment strategies. As we cover the mathematics underlying each of the methods, we also try to explain what they mean in simple terms.

CHAPTER 2

Asset Class Return Expectations

To understand performance measurement it is useful to begin with some knowledge of what investors can expect when they invest. The objective of this review is to provide a background for the performance measurement discussion. The first observation is that there is a variety of opportunities for investing.

THE EXPECTED RANGE OF RETURNS FROM DIFFERENT KINDS OF INVESTMENTS

Intuitively we know that different kinds of investments have different kinds of risks and potential payoffs. The payoff for buying a winning lottery ticket is much greater than the interest received on a savings account; however, the probability of payoff is quite a bit smaller—usually close to zero. Choosing among different asset class investment alternatives is always a choice among return expectations, each of which is associated with a risk of payoff.

Understanding the range of values you are likely to encounter for different asset classes is useful for practical reasons. It has been said that there are "good data," "bad data," "funny looking numbers," and "ugly data." Good data are data in which you have confidence. Bad data are data that are obviously wrong and in which you cannot have confidence. Funny looking numbers are data that intuitively just do not look correct but might be. Ugly data are data that you believe are accurate but do not meet your expectations.

To avoid errors in performance evaluation it is useful to be able to intuitively identify each of these kinds of data.

For analytical purposes professionals in the investment community classify different investment opportunities into groups called *asset classes*. The savings account or CD we have mentioned previously is classified as a member of the *fixed-income* asset class. Common stocks are grouped into the asset class called *equity*. In performance evaluation, the best way to guard against errors in calculation and interpretation is to recognize "funny looking" numbers when you see them. To accomplish this you must have an expectation of what the numbers should be.

WHAT RANGE OF VALUES IS LIKELY TO BE ENCOUNTERED?

Generally speaking, the expectation for each asset class tends to change with recent experience. During the 1970s a leading business magazine asked whether equities were dead as an investment class because the deep recession of 1972–1976 had caused stocks to decline so much that no one could see stocks ever returning 20 percent a year again—but they did in the 1990s. Conversely, when stocks did so well in the 1990s, there were those who claimed a new model of economic development had occurred and stocks would continue to perform well indefinitely. They asked why anyone would ever invest in bonds again—then there was a 20 percent correction in stock prices in 2000.

Any assumptions made about the performance of asset classes should have a long-run perspective—for example, that true values are not known for the next quarter, next year, or even five years. Return expectations, whenever made, often seem quite heroic. Recent history has been hard on equities and favorable for most bonds. However, no matter when such expectations are written down, recent historical events will color investors' expectations.

Return expectations should be based on the long-term analysis of these asset class returns, and the investor should bear in mind that optimizers are generally very sensitive to the forecast value of the spreads between all asset returns. For the spread between U.S. equities and bonds a forecast of between 2 and 6 percent is reasonable. This level of forecast spread is in line with postwar capital market history and within the range shown as reasonable in academic studies.

Generally, the more risky the asset, the higher the expected return, so equities return more than fixed income. This raises the issue of the expectation for hedge funds, which seem to have far greater return prospects than their claimed risk attributes would suggest. However, recent academic work suggests the risks of hedge funds are probably higher than many have believed.

Obviously, short-term forecasts of the asset class returns will be different than longer-term forecasts because analysts can see what is going to happen in the next six months much more clearly than what is going to happen in the next five years.

Expectations are always debatable, and different investment analysts will surely advocate different return and risk expectations, but these numbers and principles are a place to begin.

The efficient markets hypothesis argues that all relevant information is publicly available, is widely disseminated among all market participants, and is reflected in current security prices. Yet a casual observer can see that there is considerable variability in interest rates and security market performance around the world due to different economic systems, different economic prospects, and different levels of inflation. These differences are also affected, if not controlled, by the differences in the political systems governing these different market environments. Since the U.S. economy is one of the strongest in the history of the world and U.S. equities are one of the largest asset classes in the world, we will spend a little time looking at the expected returns to U.S. stocks over time.

Equities: Stocks in the Long Run

Jeremy Siegel[1] examines U.S. stock behavior over nearly two centuries and finds that while stocks are certainly riskier than bonds on a day-to-day basis or in the short run, over long windows

---

[1] Jeremy Siegel, *Stocks for the Long Run*, 2d ed. (New York: Basic Books, 2002).

(5-, 10-, and 20-year periods) stock returns are so stable that stocks are actually less volatile over 20 years than either government bonds or Treasury bills. This is a quite astounding statement, but Siegel backs it up with a thorough statistical analysis.

The consistency of stock returns, after inflation, is exceptional. Siegel believes that fixed-income assets pose higher risks for the long-term investor because investors holding bonds can never be compensated for unexpected inflation while those holding stocks can. He maintains that stocks perform better than bonds and cash because it is more rewarding to own a profitable business (own stock) than to lend money (own bonds or be a cash investor).

Since 1871, stock returns have been higher than cash and bond returns in every rolling 30-year period. The overall span of Siegel's study was 190 years. The world and U.S. economies have undergone massive changes over this time. To find such consistency suggests that the return comes from the fundamental structure of the economy rather than accidentally.

Siegel found that stocks provided returns at least 5 percent higher than inflation and higher than cash or bonds in 99.4 percent of the rolling 30-year periods from 1802 through 1992. For Siegel, the term *stocks* refers to those in the S&P 500, or the nearest equivalent proxy for the overall stock market for the years prior to the inception of the S&P 500, while *bonds* means long-term investment-grade bonds. For *cash* he used U.S. Treasury bills.

Siegel also found that even if a person invested in stocks at the worst possible time, investing just before the 1929 crash, stocks still outperformed cash or bonds by the end of 1950. For the 30 years 1929–1958, the average returns on stocks were 6.8 percent per year more than inflation, 5.1 percent per year more than bonds, and 7.5 percent per year more than cash.

The world today is much different from what it was in the time period covered by Siegel. There is no guarantee that the U.S. economy will continue to flourish over the next 200 years like it has over the last 200 years. Even in the United States, over fairly long time spans we have seen very different market conditions. The bull market of the 1950s started in mid-1949 when the cash dividend for stocks in the Dow Jones Industrial Average (DJIA) was 7 percent, while U.S. Treasury bonds were paying a low interest of only 2.5 percent. In 2006, the relative values of stocks and bonds were exactly the opposite.

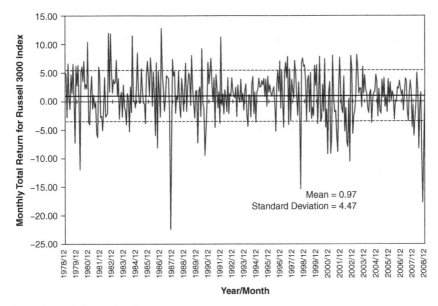

Source: Russell Index Database.[2]

Figure 2.1 Monthly return of the Russell 3000 Index

In January 2006, the DJIA was around 10,000, and its aggregate cash dividend was only about 2.5 percent while the interest on intermediate Treasury bonds was over 5 percent.

Figure 2.1 shows monthly returns for the Russell 3000 from January 1979 to December 2008. The arithmetic average monthly return over this period was 0.97 percent with a standard deviation of 4.47 percent. Notice the number of positive returns greater than one standard deviation as compared with the number of returns lower than negative one standard deviation. There are a few big spikes on the downside with many more, albeit smaller, positive spikes on the upside. The overall annualized geometric average return is 10.9 percent—about what we would expect given Siegel's research.

---

[2] Prices for the Russell 3000 can be found at http://finance.yahoo.com/q/hp?s=^RUA.

Bonds: Ibbotson and Sinquefield

An alternative perspective on return expectations can be obtained from the classic work by Ibbotson and Sinquefield,[3] which reviews a variety of asset classes in the United States from 1926 to 1987. Table 2.1 shows their return expectations for the various asset classes. Note that these values are also based on historical analysis. For example, they report a historical geometric return for long-term government bonds of 4.3 percent.

T A B L E 2.1

Annual Returns from 1926 to 1987

Series Name	Geometric Mean (%)	Standard Deviation (%)
Common stocks	9.90	21.10
Small company stocks	12.10	35.90
Long-term corporate bonds	4.90	8.50
Long-term government bonds	4.30	8.50
Intermediate-term government bonds	4.80	5.50
U.S. Treasury bills	3.50	3.40
Inflation rate	3.00	4.80

Source: Roger C. Ibbotson and Rex Sinquefield, *Stocks, Bonds, Bills, and Inflation: Historical Returns (1926–1987)* (Chicago, IL: Dow Jones-Irwin, 1989), p. 14.

---

[3] Roger C. Ibbotson and Rex Sinquefield, *Stocks, Bonds, Bills, and Inflation: Historical Returns (1926–1987)* (Chicago, IL: Dow Jones-Irwin, 1989).

CHAPTER 3

Returns Without Cash Flows

The performance of an investment is measured by *return*. In common usage, the return of an investment refers to the *change in wealth created by holding the investment*. However, there are several common ways of calculating a return with similar-sounding names: holding period return, cumulative return, annualized return, continuously compounding return, time-weighted return, internal rate of return, and so on. Analysts and users of returns data typically use returns that have been previously calculated and stored in databases. In order to evaluate performance correctly, an analyst must understand how the various types of return are defined. This chapter and Chapters 4 and 5 review the various calculations.

We assume, in this chapter, that there are no cash flows into or out of the portfolio during the time interval over which return is measured. This assumption allows return to be calculated from beginning and ending market values, as explained in the following. We describe how to measure return in the presence of cash flows in Chapter 5.

PORTFOLIO MARKET VALUE

A prerequisite for calculating return is a measurement of portfolio *market value*. The *holdings* of a portfolio at a particular time consist of a list of the asset identifiers and the respective quantities of the assets held. The security *prices* are typically merged with the portfolio holdings by the account record keeper and multiplied by the quantities to produce market values of the holdings.

Market value, rather than cost or book value, is used because it measures the value at which the portfolio may be traded for other assets at that time. Book values depend on when assets were bought and may not accurately measure the investor's economic wealth. Accordingly, market value should include all receivables and payables belonging to the portfolio: accrued interest on fixed-income assets, assets traded but not yet settled, and so on. The details of valuation procedures vary by asset type. If a market price is not available, for example, in the case of an illiquid security, then the valuation process should attempt to estimate what the market price would be if the security were traded.

Although exchange ticker symbols are commonly used by broker-dealers to identify securities, back office operations typically rely on security identifier numbering systems—CUSIP, SEDOL, or ISIN codes, for example—to facilitate trading and record keeping. Analysts also can use these identifiers in accessing other databases of reference data related to the holdings, such as security characteristics, industry membership, and accounting data.

Although, in principle, price quotes may be obtained at any time while markets are open, portfolio valuation is typically done using prices at the close of a trading day. The close of trading depends on the particular market in which a security is traded and, given global markets, some securities in a portfolio might be priced at different times than others. This consideration might affect intraday studies and studies using daily data, but it is rarely important for longer-horizon returns.

HOLDING PERIOD RETURN

A return measures the change in value over a *holding period*, which is an interval between two points in time. Calendar units such as years, quarters, months, or days are commonly used to measure the length of a period. If returns are measured monthly, for example, then the portfolio values at month-ends are required. Because the last trading day of a month might not coincide with the last calendar day, the length of time spanned by a "monthly return" might differ from month to month. For most purposes, this consideration is of minor importance and a monthly holding period is a familiar time unit for measuring returns.

If, over a given holding period, there were no cash flows into or out of the portfolio, then a *holding period return* can be calculated from the beginning and ending values of the portfolio. By "no cash flows" we mean that no external funds were added to nor internal funds withdrawn from the portfolio and that income or dividends received from the investments were reinvested. This assumption is critical, and we address cash flows fully in Chapter 5. Setting the cash flow issue aside for now, the ratio of the portfolio ending market value (EV) to the beginning market value (BV) is the relative value, which we call the *return relative* for the holding period:

$$\text{Return relative} = \frac{\text{EV}}{\text{BV}}.$$

From the return relative, the *holding period rate of return, r,* can be calculated by subtracting 1:

$$r = \frac{\text{EV}}{\text{BV}} - 1 = \frac{\text{EV} - \text{BV}}{\text{BV}}. \tag{3.1}$$

As seen, the holding period return can also be calculated as the change in value over the period divided by the beginning value. The result is usually expressed as a percentage by multiplying by 100. Returns that are less than 1 percent are often expressed in *basis points* (abbreviated as *bps*), or hundredths of a percent. For example, given a beginning value of 5,000 and an ending value of 5,048, we can calculate a return of

$$r = \frac{5,048 - 5,000}{5,000} = 0.0096$$

$$= 0.96\%$$

$$= 96 \text{ bps}$$

LINKING RETURNS

A return over a longer holding period, such as a year, can be calculated in the same way, from beginning and ending values (still assuming no cash flows). Alternatively, if subperiod returns have already been calculated, then the longer-period return can be calculated from the subperiods. Suppose month-ends are indexed by $t = 0, 1, 2, \ldots, 12$, where $t = 0$ denotes the beginning of the first month. Given the portfolio values V_t, the return relative for the year can be written as the product of the monthly return relatives

$$\frac{V_{12}}{V_0} = \frac{V_1}{V_0} \times \frac{V_2}{V_1} \times \cdots \times \frac{V_{12}}{V_{11}}$$

because the intermediate values $V_1, V_2, \ldots, V_{11}$ cancel in the expression on the right-hand side. Substituting the monthly holding period returns $V_t / V_{t-1} = 1 + r_t$ into the preceding expression leaves

$$\frac{V_{12}}{V_0} = (1 + r_1)(1 + r_2) \cdots (1 + r_{12}).$$

In general, if $r = (V_T / V_0) - 1$ is the return over T periods, then r can also be calculated from the *linking formula*

$$r = (1 + r_1)(1 + r_2) \cdots (1 + r_T) - 1. \tag{3.2}$$

For notational convenience, the product operator $\prod(\bullet)$ is often used to denote the product of terms. With this notation, the linking formula is written as

$$r = \prod_{t=1}^{T} (1 + r_t) - 1.$$

This formula is also known as *chain-linking returns* or *geometric compounding*. In this context, in which a return over multiple periods is calculated from individual period returns, the result is called the *cumulative return*. The associated return relative $V_T / V_0 = 1 + r$ is the amount of ending wealth per unit of market value invested at the beginning.

Given the flexibility of linking returns over any number of periods, portfolio analysis systems are often designed to calculate and store returns (or return relatives) over sufficiently short holding periods such as monthly or daily. A typical analysis begins by pulling returns from the database and linking them over the desired time interval.

RULE OF 72

There is a handy formula that gives the approximate number of periods for an investment to double in value given a constant rate of return per period. The formula is

$$\text{Number of periods to double in value} = \frac{72}{\text{rate per period in percent}}.$$

The rate must be expressed as a percentage. For example, an investment that returns 8 percent per year doubles in value in about $72/8 = 9$ years. Using the linking formula, the exact number is the value of T for which $(1+r)^T = 2$, which is $T = \ln(2)/\ln(1+r)$. Although the exact number can easily be computed, the *rule of 72* is useful for a "back of the envelope" calculation and gives reasonable results for rates up to about 20 percent or so.[1]

---

[1] See "Rule of 72," *Wikipedia, The Free Encyclopedia*, http://en.wikipedia.org/w/index.php?title=Rule_of_72&oldid=236462557 for more information, including a historical reference to the rule by Fra Luca Pacioli (1445–1514) in *Summa de Arithmetica* (Venice, 1494, fol. 181, n. 44).

CHAPTER 4

Average Returns

Averaging provides a way to summarize returns over time. Two methods of averaging, geometric and arithmetic, give different results and are useful for different purposes. We review these two methods in this chapter.

AVERAGE RETURN PER PERIOD

The linking formula [Equation (3.2)] combines shorter holding period returns into a longer holding period return. Now consider the converse. Suppose we have the cumulative return (or return relative) over T periods and want to calculate an equivalent return per period. By equivalent, we mean the constant return per period that would produce the same cumulative return.

Using the linking formula on both sides, we want to find the value of r_G that satisfies

$$(1+r_G)^T = \prod_{t=1}^{T}(1+r_t).$$

Solving for r_G gives the formula for *geometric average return*:

$$r_G = \left(\prod_{t=1}^{T}(1+r_t)\right)^{1/T} - 1. \qquad (4.1)$$

The ordinary average of a collection of returns is the *arithmetic average return*

$$r_A = \frac{1}{T}\sum_{t=1}^{T} r_t \tag{4.2}$$

where $\Sigma(\bullet)$ denotes the sum of terms. Both the geometric and arithmetic average returns are useful concepts, and we have much more to say about them in Chapter 6. Here, we note the fact that

$$r_G \leq r_A.$$

That is, the geometric average is less than or equal to the arithmetic average. We can show this fact by taking logarithms:

$$\ln(1+r_G) = \ln\left[\left(\prod_{t=1}^{T}(1+r_t)\right)^{1/T}\right]$$

$$= \frac{1}{T}\sum_{t=1}^{T}\ln(1+r_t)$$

$$\leq \ln\left(\frac{1}{T}\sum_{t=1}^{T}(1+r_t)\right)$$

$$= \ln(1+r_A)$$

where the inequality follows from concavity of the logarithm function. Strict inequality holds if not all the r_t are equal. The amount by which the geometric average is less depends on the volatility—the greater the volatility of the returns, the greater the difference between the two averages. A good approximation of the difference can be calculated from

$$r_G \cong r_A - \frac{1}{2}\sigma^2$$

where σ is the standard deviation of the returns r_t.[1] For example, given the data

$$r_A = 2.8\%$$
$$\sigma = 5.8\%$$

the geometric average return is approximately

$$r_G \cong 0.028 - (0.5)(0.058)^2$$
$$\cong 0.026$$

or $$r_G \cong 2.6\%.$$

ANNUALIZED RETURN

These formulas can be generalized to calculate the return per year, assuming annual compounding, that would produce the same ending relative value as a sequence of shorter holding period returns. If the holding period of the return r_t is $1/n$ years (where $n = 12$ corresponds to monthly, for example), then T periods span T/n years. The *annualized geometric average return* is

$$r_G^{\text{ann}} = \left(\prod_{t=1}^{T} (1 + r_t) \right)^{n/T} - 1. \tag{4.3}$$

This return is also commonly called *compound annual return* or simply *annualized return*.

The arithmetic average return [Equation (4.2)] can be annualized by multiplying by n, giving the *annualized arithmetic average return*

$$r_A^{\text{ann}} = \frac{n}{T} \sum_{t=1}^{T} r_t. \tag{4.4}$$

---

[1] More precisely, if returns are independent and lognormally distributed, then $E[\ln(1 + r_t)] = \ln[1 + E(r_t)] - (1/2) \, \text{Var}[\ln(1 + r_t)]$.

Ordinarily, averages should be annualized only if the number of periods T exceeds n. If T is less than n, then the returns span a period of less than a year. An average "per year" in this case might be misleading.

Given the different ways of "annualizing," users of returns data should take note of what a data provider or performance reporter means by an "annualized return."

COMPOUNDING FREQUENCY

Annual compounding is ordinarily assumed in calculating the annualized geometric average return. However, other compounding frequencies are possible, which give slightly different numbers. When banks pay interest on term deposits, the compounding frequency must be specified. Conventionally, the *nominal rate*, stated in annual terms, is the periodic rate multiplied by the number n of compounding periods per year. Thus, the nominal rate i of interest paid n times per year that would give the annual return r satisfies

$$1+r = \left(1+\frac{i}{n}\right)^n.$$

The compounding frequency, in principle, can be taken to the limit, called *continuous compounding*. For a given nominal rate, as the compounding frequency gets large, the annual return approaches a limit

$$\lim_{n\to\infty} \left(1+\frac{i}{n}\right)^n = e^i$$

where e is the base of the natural logarithm, a constant approximately equal to 2.718. Conversely, for a given annual return r, the nominal rate $i = \ln(1 + r)$, if compounded continuously over a year, produces the return relative $1 + r$.

The holding period of the return r is immaterial to this relation. Consequently, the logarithm $\ln(1 + r)$ of a return relative is called a *continuously compounding return*. For example, Table 4.1 shows the nominal rates at different compounding frequencies that give the same annual return.

TABLE 4.1

Nominal Rates at Different Compounding Frequencies

Compounding Frequency	Annual	Quarterly	Monthly	Weekly	Continuously
Periods per year	1	4	12	52	Infinite
Nominal rate (%)	12.00	11.49	11.39	11.35	11.33

Although the interpretation of continuous compounding justifies the terminology, the use of logarithms can also be thought of as simply a transformation. A useful property of logarithms is the fact that the logarithm of a product is equal to the sum of the logarithms of the individual terms. The linking formula, for example, can be written as

$$r = \exp\left(\sum_{t=1}^{T} \ln(1 + r_t) \right) - 1$$

where $\exp(\bullet)$ is the exponential function. Computationally, it is sometimes convenient to calculate sums of terms instead of products.

Using logarithms also reveals a useful interpretation of the geometric average return r_G defined earlier. Taking the logarithm of $1 + r_G$,

$$\ln(1 + r_G) = \frac{1}{T} \sum_{t=1}^{T} \ln(1 + r_t).$$

In words, the logarithm of 1 plus the geometric average return is the average of the logarithms of the periodic return relatives. Statistically, if the returns r_t are assumed to be lognormally distributed, that is, if $\ln(1 + r_t)$ are normally distributed, then $\ln(1 + r_G)$ is a simple estimate of the mean of $\ln(1 + r_t)$. Because the normal distribution is symmetric, $\ln(1 + r_G)$ is also an estimate of the median of the distribution of $\ln(1 + r_t)$. Further, because the logarithm function is monotonic, the median of the distribution of $\ln(1 + r_t)$ maps into the median of the distribution of r_t. The geometric average return r_G is therefore an estimate of the median of the lognormally distributed returns r_t.

EXPECTED RETURN

In order to form useful assumptions about future returns, statistical models might be employed. A very common modeling assumption is that future returns will be independent draws from some probability distribution—an assumption known as *independent, identically distributed* (i.i.d.) returns. If an initial wealth amount V_0 grows by simple compounding of the periodic returns,

$$V_T = V_0(1+r_1)(1+r_2) \cdots (1+r_T),$$

then the independence assumption enables us to calculate the expected wealth $E(V_T)$ by replacing the returns in the preceding formula by their expected values. If the expected value of the identically distributed returns is $E(r_t) = m$, then the expected wealth can be calculated as

$$E(V_T) = V_0(1+m)^T. \tag{4.5}$$

This formula looks suspiciously similar to the formula for ending wealth, given the geometric average of *past* returns:

$$V_T = V_0(1+r_G)^T.$$

Perhaps because of this similarity, an analyst might think that the geometric average return r_G is a good estimate of the expected value m. Unfortunately, this is not the case. The arithmetic average return is a better statistic to use as an estimate of m, because it is unbiased in the sense that $E(r_A) = (1/T)\sum_{t=1}^{T} E(r_t)$ is equal to m. As shown in the preceding, the geometric average return is less than or equal to the arithmetic average return by an amount that depends on the volatility.

Because the geometric average return is influenced by volatility, comparisons of portfolios with differing volatilities should be interpreted carefully. To illustrate, we simulated two series of returns using random numbers. Summary statistics of the two return series are shown in Table 4.2.

TABLE 4.2

Summary Statistics of Randomly Generated Returns

	Asset A	Asset B
Standard deviation (%)	5.82	10.12
Arithmetic average return (%)	2.78	2.87
Geometric average return (%)	2.62	2.38

Note that the arithmetic average returns are very similar, while asset B has substantially larger volatility. Consequently, the geometric average return of asset B is *less* than that of asset A, although its arithmetic average return is slightly *greater*.

We further created portfolios of the two assets and calculated summary statistics of the resulting portfolio returns. A graph of the results, with average return plotted against standard deviation of return, is shown in Figure 4.1.

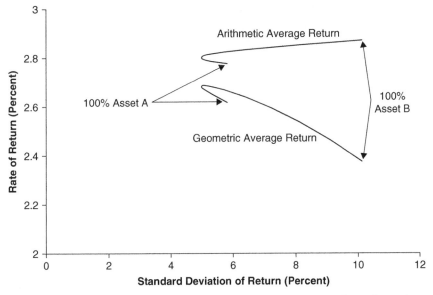

Figure 4.1 Arithmetic and geometric average returns plotted against standard deviation

The graph of the arithmetic average return resembles a typical efficient frontier, showing the reduction in volatility achieved by combining two volatile assets in a portfolio. Moving from 100 percent in asset B toward asset A reduces volatility to a point, with a continuous reduction in arithmetic average return. This result is a basic lesson of portfolio theory.

The graph of the geometric average return, however, suggests an unusual result. Moving from asset B, the geometric average return *increases* while the standard deviation *decreases*. Interpreting this result as a possible return benefit from diversification, however, would be erroneous. As shown in Equation (4.5), the expected future wealth of the portfolio is related to the arithmetic average return, not the geometric average. The fact that the geometric average increases with decreasing volatility does not imply that expected wealth also increases. If the geometric average return is plotted in a graph of this sort, volatility affects *both* axes of the graph. To keep the concept of expected return separate from volatility of return, an arithmetic average should be used for the return axis of this graph.

As a result, when we want to depict expected values of *future* returns by calculating statistics of *past* returns, the arithmetic average return is the better choice. We caution, however, against simply using historical averages as estimates of expected returns. Given the amount of volatility in typical asset returns, many observations are required to reduce statistical error to acceptable levels, often far more than can reasonably be obtained.[2] Additional modeling techniques or assumptions must supplement historical averages in order to increase confidence in expected returns.

---

[2] David G. Luenberger (in *Investment Science*, New York: Oxford University Press, 1998, p. 212) calls this phenomenon the "blur of history."

CHAPTER 5

Returns in the Presence of Cash Flows

In previous chapters we have assumed that there were no external cash flows into or out of the portfolio. Naturally, transactions may occur from time to time that result in funds being added to or withdrawn from the portfolio. With cash flows, simply dividing the ending value by the beginning value of the portfolio over a holding period would give a distorted measurement of performance. For example, if we started the year with $100 in a bank account paying 1 percent interest and then added $100 late in the year, we might have about $201 in the account at the end of the year. But a return calculated as $(201 - 100)/100$, or 101 percent, would not be a meaningful measure of the interest paid by the bank. In this chapter, we describe a meaningful measure of performance with cash flows.

CASH FLOWS

By *cash flow*, we mean a transfer of value into or out of a portfolio. By convention, an inflow is considered a positive flow and an outflow is a negative flow. The sum of cash flows is therefore the net cash flow into the portfolio.

Cash flows may arise, for example, from contributions by the plan sponsor or payments to beneficiaries, in the case of a pension fund, or from deposits and withdrawals by investors, in the case of a mutual fund or a personal portfolio. The decision to make a cash flow of this sort is generally not under the control of the portfolio manager. If a return is sensitive to cash flows, it would be difficult to compare meaningfully one portfolio's performance with another. In order to measure the decisions of the portfolio manager, the return should be unaffected by cash flows.

Portfolio transactions such as purchases, sales, or income received generally do not create cash flows into the portfolio. Ordinarily, transactions of this sort create flows between assets within a portfolio. These flows may be regarded as *internal* cash flows, as distinct from the *external* cash flows described previously. In many contexts, we may want to measure the performance of sub-portfolios or *segments* of an overall portfolio—equities, bonds, and so forth, or sectors and industries, for example. In this case, where the performance of a segment is to be measured, transactions may create cash flows that are external to the segment but still internal to the overall portfolio. The internal cash flows—transfers of value between segments—are the cash flows of interest when measuring the performance of segments.

Although internal cash flows may be under the control of the portfolio manager, segment portfolio performance is commonly measured using identical methods to those at the total level. Methods for measuring the impact of the manager's decisions resulting in internal cash flows are described in Chapters 17 and 18.

Usually, purchases, sales, or income transactions create flows between the relevant assets and a segment of the portfolio invested in short-term cash assets, which may be called the *liquidity reserve*. If the performance of portfolio segments is measured, the liquidity reserve should be treated just as any other segment, accounting for flows between it and other segments.

UNIT VALUE METHOD

A measure of return that is independent of cash flows follows naturally from the process by which gains are divided among investors in a mutual fund or other fund in which the assets of multiple investors are commingled. In a mutual fund, investors may purchase or sell shares, or *units*, of the fund at any time. The *net asset value* (NAV) of a unit of the fund is the total market value V of the portfolio divided by the number of units U existing at the time of valuation:[1]

$$NAV = \frac{V}{U}.$$

When an investor deposits or withdraws money, the number of units of the fund changes. If V' is the market value of the portfolio immediately after the cash flow, then the new number of units U' is calculated from the NAV at that time:

$$U' = \frac{V'}{NAV}.$$

For example, consider the data in Table 5.1. At the end of December, the market value of the fund was 213. The NAV at the start is immaterial for this discussion and is set to 1; therefore, the number of units on December 31 was 213. On January 10, there was a net cash flow of 20. The value of the fund before adding the cash flow was 228, which, divided by 213 units, gives an NAV of 1.0704.

T A B L E 5.1

Example Data for the Unit Value Method

Date	Market Value	Units	NAV
December 31	213	213.00	1.0000
January 10 before cash flow	228	213.00	1.0704
January 10 after cash flow	248	231.68	1.0704
January 31	254	231.68	1.0963

---

[1] Net asset values of mutual funds also account for management fees and expenses. The impact of fees, sales charges, and taxes on return is important in many contexts but is beyond the scope of this book. For a thorough discussion, see "Adjusting Returns for Impact of Fees, Taxes, and Currency" in Bruce J. Feibel, *Investment Performance Measurement* (Hoboken, NJ: Wiley, 2003), chap. 6.

The new number of units after the cash flow was therefore 231.68. Note that the NAV does not change because of the cash flow—the number of units adjusts to maintain the identity $NAV = V/U$.

Now consider the return r for the month calculated from the NAV:

$$r = \frac{NAV_{31}}{NAV_0} - 1 = 1.0963 - 1 = 9.63\%.$$

If we were to split the month into two subperiods, before and after the date of the cash flow, then we could calculate the return from each subperiod and link the results:

$$
\begin{aligned}
r &= \left(\frac{NAV_{10}}{NAV_0} \times \frac{NAV_{31}}{NAV_{10}} \right) - 1 \\
&= \left(\frac{1.0704}{1.0000} \times \frac{1.0963}{1.0704} \right) - 1 \\
&= (1.0704 \times 1.0242) - 1 \\
&= 9.63\%
\end{aligned}
\tag{5.1}
$$

which produces the same return because the NAV_{10} cancels out. The *unit value method* of calculating returns effectively controls for cash flows—which is the basic goal of the method, producing an equitable division of investment gains among the investors.

TIME-WEIGHTED RETURN

Consider each of the subperiod returns in Equation (5.1). Substituting the identity $NAV = V/U$ into the formula for the first subperiod return relative, for example, gives

$$\frac{NAV_{10}}{NAV_0} = \frac{V_{10}/U_{10}}{V_0/U_0}.$$

Now, if the value V_{10} is taken *immediately before the cash flow*, then the number of units U_{10} is equal to U_0 and may be canceled from the expression on the right-hand side.

Similarly, for the second subperiod,

$$\frac{\text{NAV}_{31}}{\text{NAV}_{10}} = \frac{V_{31}/U_{31}}{V_{10}'/U_{10}'}.$$

Here, if the value V_{10}' is taken *immediately after the cash flow*, then the number of units U_{10}' is equal to U_{31} and may again be canceled from the expression.

For the data in Table 5.1, we can calculate the return for the month as

$$r = \left(\frac{V_{10}}{V_0} \times \frac{V_{31}}{V_{10}'} \right) - 1$$

$$= \left(\frac{228}{213} \times \frac{254}{248} \right) - 1$$

$$= 9.63\%$$

which gives the same return as the unit value method, without the intermediate step of calculating the numbers of units.

Generalizing this idea, we can calculate a return that is neutralized for cash flows if we have the market values of the fund immediately before and after each cash flow. Assuming that cash flows occur exactly at the ends of periods, we can express the return over T periods as

$$r = \left(\frac{\text{EV}_1}{\text{BV}_1} \times \frac{\text{EV}_2}{\text{BV}_2} \times \cdots \times \frac{\text{EV}_T}{\text{BV}_T} \right) - 1,$$

where EV_t is the value *immediately before the cash flow at t* and BV_t is the value *immediately after the cash flow at $t - 1$*, that is, *at the beginning of period t*. Note that the value BV_t at the beginning of a period need not equal the ending value EV_{t-1} of the previous period and therefore does not cancel in the preceding expression. It is natural, however, to define a holding period return as $r_t = \text{EV}_t/\text{BV}_t - 1$ and to calculate the return over T periods by linking:

$$r = (1 + r_1)(1 + r_2)\cdots(1 + r_T) - 1. \tag{5.2}$$

This return, calculated from valuations at each cash flow, is called the *time-weighted rate of return*.[2] We will explain the meaning of the term *time-weighted* shortly.

If there are no cash flows, then, of course, the formula for time-weighted return is identical to Equation (3.2) introduced in Chapter 3. Also, all the calculations of Chapter 4 are applicable— compounding, geometric and arithmetic averages, annualization, and so on. The notion of cumulative return, now, can be interpreted as the *growth of a unit value*, rather than the literal growth of the total value of the portfolio, which is affected by cash flows.

In application, if a portfolio is not unitized as a mutual fund, then the performance measurer must make assumptions about exactly when the cash flows occur in relation to the valuations of the portfolio. If the cash flows occur on a given day, it might be unclear whether the flow occurred at the beginning, at the end, or at some other point during the day. Although end-of-day and beginning-of-day assumptions are common, another possibility is to assume that inflows occur at the beginning of the day and outflows occur at the end of the day. Doing so allows a return to be calculated from the first to the last days of a portfolio's existence, when the true beginning and ending values are zero. By assuming inflows occur at the beginning of the day, the denominator of the return formula is not zero on the first day, but is instead the cash flow in for the day. Similarly, by assuming outflows occur at the end of the day, the return on the last day need not equal negative 100 percent.

Depending on the size of the cash flows, the calculated returns can be significantly affected by these assumptions. For example, consider the data in Table 5.2. The market values at the end of the day are given, but the timings of the cash flows on day 1 are unknown. Assuming the cash flows occur at the end of the day, the market value immediately before the cash flows would be $168 - 30 + 10 = 148$. The return for the day would be $148/140 - 1 = 5.71$ percent.

---

[2] Peter Dietz called this method the "average return method" in "Pension Fund Investment Performance—What Method to Use When," *Financial Analysts Journal*, January/February 1966. The term "time-weighted" appeared in the first major study of performance measurement in *Measuring the Investment Performance of Pension Funds: For the Purpose of Inter-Fund Comparison*, by Kalman J. Cohen, Joel Dean, David Durand, Eugene F. Fama, Lawrence Fisher, Eli Shapiro, and James H. Lorie (Park Ridge, IL: Bank Administration Institute, 1968).

T A B L E 5.2

Example Cash Flow Data

Day	Cash Flow In	Cash Flow Out	Market Value at End of Day
0			140
1	30	10	168

Now assume that the cash flows occur at the beginning of the day. The beginning market value immediately after the cash flows would be 140 + 30 − 10 = 160. The return with this assumption would be 168/160 − 1 = 5.00 percent. Finally, suppose we assume that the inflow occurred at the beginning and the outflow occurred at the end. The beginning value immediately after the inflow would be 140 + 30 = 170, while the ending value immediately before the outflow would be 168 + 10 = 178. With this assumption, the return would be 178/170 − 1 = 4.71 percent. The calculated return in this example clearly depends on the timing assumption. Whatever assumption is used, it should be used consistently. Changing the assumption after calculating the returns may be misleading.

Even if the timing of the cash flows is known, a drawback of the unit value method and time-weighted returns is that a portfolio valuation must be available at every cash flow. The data and resources required to value a portfolio may be too expensive or simply unavailable at every cash flow. Nevertheless, a true time-weighted return is regarded as the exact measure of performance when cash flows are not under the control of the investment manager. When valuations at cash flows are unavailable, other methods can be used to calculate an approximate time-weighted return. We discuss these next.

LINKED INTERNAL RATE OF RETURN

The *internal rate of return* (IRR) is a rate of return that can be calculated from the beginning and ending values of the portfolio together with the timing and magnitudes of the cash flows. Suppose that market value grows at a constant rate r over a period for which we have the beginning value BV and ending value EV. If a net cash flow C occurred midway through the period, then the values would be related by

$$EV = BV(1 + r) + C(1 + r)^{0.5}.$$

If there were multiple cash flows C_k, $k = 1, \ldots, K$, this expression generalizes to

$$EV = BV(1+r) + \sum_{k=1}^{K} C_k(1+r)^{W_k} \qquad (5.3)$$

where W_k is the fraction of the period over which the cash flow applies, namely,

$$W_k = \frac{TD - D_k}{TD} \qquad (5.4)$$

where TD is the total number of calendar days in the period and D_k is the number of days since the beginning of the period. This *day-weighting* fraction assumes end-of-day cash flows. For beginning-of-day cash flows or other timing assumptions, the fraction should be adjusted accordingly. For example, assuming beginning-of-day cash flows, we would use $TD - D_k + 1$ in the numerator.

The IRR is the rate r that satisfies Equation (5.3). Unfortunately, there is no closed-form formula for the IRR and it must be calculated by an algorithm. This fact is rarely a problem because many spreadsheet programs and financial calculators have IRR functions. A possible problem arises, however, because for some patterns of cash flows, there are multiple values of r that satisfy Equation (5.3), and some solutions might even be complex (not real) numbers. For cash flows that are small relative to the beginning and ending values, however, an IRR can usually be found.[3]

Notice that the IRR does not require valuations at the times of cash flows, only at the beginning and at the end of a period. Of course, if there are no cash flows over a period, then the IRR gives exactly the same result as the familiar holding period return.

---

[3] See David G. Luenberger, *Investment Science* (New York: Oxford University Press, 1998), p. 35, for a basic algorithm.

An approximation of a true time-weighted return can therefore be calculated as follows:

1. Divide the overall period into subperiods based on the times of valuation. For example, if the portfolio is valued monthly, then a subperiod is a month.
2. For each subperiod, calculate the IRR for the subperiod. This step requires the times and amounts of cash flows in addition to the valuations at the beginnings and ends of subperiods.
3. Link the results.

This method is called *linked internal rate of return.*[4]

As an approximation, the resulting return is reasonably insensitive to cash flows, but the approximation degrades as the magnitudes of the cash flows increase. In a study by the Bank Administration Institute,[5] the authors recommended that if a cash flow exceeds 10 percent of the portfolio value, then the portfolio should be revalued to improve the accuracy of the performance measurement.

For example, suppose we have the valuations in Table 5.1 at the ends of the months, but not on the day of the cash flow. The available data are shown in Table 5.3.

TABLE 5.3

Example Market Values and Cash Flows

Date	Cash Flow	Market Value
December 31		213
January 10	20	
January 31		254

---

[4] This method is the second of two approximations suggested by Cohen et al. in *Measuring the Investment Performance of Pension Funds,* p. 5. Their first approximation, called the *regression method,* is less well-known. The linked internal rate of return method is sometimes called the *BAI method.*

[5] Ibid.

The internal rate of return for the month is the rate r that solves

$$254 = 213(1 + r) + 20(1 + r)^{(31 - 10)/31}$$

which is 9.28 percent.

THE DIETZ METHOD

The idea of calculating an approximation over periods between valuations and linking the results was developed by Peter O. Dietz in his Columbia University doctoral dissertation entitled "Evaluating the Investment Performance of Noninsured Pension Funds," from which three publications appeared.[6]

Dietz proposed a simpler calculation than the IRR, one that also assumes a constant rate of growth over a period between valuations. The idea is to split the cash flow into two parts and assign the pieces to the beginning and to the end of the period. In the original *Dietz method*, the timing of the cash flows is not required as they are assumed to occur midway through the period. Thus, half of the cash flow is added to the beginning value and half is subtracted from the ending value. The *midpoint Dietz formula* is

$$r = \frac{EV - C/2}{BV + C/2} - 1,$$

where C is the sum of all the cash flows during the period. Equivalently, this formula can be written as

$$r = \frac{EV - BV - C}{BV + C/2}.$$

If the timing of the cash flows is available, then the formula can be modified to use the times of the cash flows. The *modified Dietz formula* is

---

[6] Peter O. Dietz, *Pension Funds: Measuring Investment Performance* (New York: The Free Press, 1966), republished by TSG Publishing, Somerset, NJ, 2004; "Pension Fund Investment Performance—What Method to Use When," *Financial Analysts Journal*, January/February 1966; "Components of a Measurement Model: Rate of Return, Risk and Timing," *Journal of Finance*, May 1968.

$$r = \frac{EV - BV - \sum_{k=1}^{K} C_k}{BV + \sum_{k=1}^{K} W_k C_k} \qquad (5.5)$$

where W_k is the fraction of the period over which the cash flow applies given by Equation (5.4). This formula is also called the *day-weighted Dietz formula*.[7]

In the modified Dietz formula, the denominator consists of the beginning value plus the sum of cash flows weighted by the lengths of time over which the flows were in the portfolio. The weighted cash flows $\sum_{k=1}^{K} W_k C_k$ comprise a *beginning adjustment*, from which an *adjusted beginning value*

$$ABV = BV + \sum_{k=1}^{K} W_k C_k \qquad (5.6)$$

can be calculated. Similarly, by calculating a corresponding *adjusted ending value*

$$AEV = EV - \sum_{k=1}^{K} (1 - W_k) C_k, \qquad (5.7)$$

the modified Dietz formula can be written as

$$r = \frac{AEV}{ABV} - 1 = \frac{AEV - ABV}{ABV},$$

completely analogous to the holding period return formula [Equation (3.1)] introduced in Chapter 3.

Using data from the example in Table 5.3, the calculations are as follows:

Beginning value	213
Beginning adjustment	13.55
Adjusted beginning value	226.55

[7] Peter O. Dietz and Jeannette R. Kirschman, "Evaluating Portfolio Performance," in John L. Maginn and Donald L. Tuttle, eds., *Managing Investment Portfolios: A Dynamic Process* (Boston, MA: Warren, Gorham & Lamont, 1983). Second edition published in 1990.

Ending value	254
Ending adjustment	6.45
Adjusted ending value	247.55

The modified Dietz return calculated from these values is 9.27 percent, which is comparable to the IRR value of 9.28 percent. Both of these values are approximations of the true time-weighted return of 9.63 percent calculated from Table 5.1. The modified Dietz formula is much easier to calculate than the IRR because it does not require an iterative algorithm.

Because the Dietz formulas effectively assume a constant return over a period, similar to the IRR, the Dietz formulas also degrade in accuracy from a true time-weighted return as the magnitudes of the cash flows increase. A threshold of 10 percent of the beginning value is commonly used as a trigger to revalue a portfolio in order to improve the accuracy of the measured performance.

The *linked modified Dietz method* and the linked IRR method are standard in the investment industry when valuations at the times of cash flows are not available. If valuations are available, then true time-weighted return is the preferred method.

SUBPORTFOLIO RETURNS AND CONSISTENCY

A portfolio might be segmented by asset class—stocks, bonds, and so on—or by sector and industry, or in other ways. Each segment can be regarded as a subportfolio for which returns can be calculated. Time-weighted returns or an approximation can be used. If segment performance is calculated for the purpose of calculating contributions to return (Chapter 17) or performance attribution (Chapter 18), then the associated weights of the segments must also be calculated. For such purposes, it is crucial that the weights and returns for any period be internally consistent. By internally consistent, we mean that the weights sum to 1 and that the weighted sum of the segment returns equals the total portfolio return.

With true time-weighted returns, internal consistency is ensured if valuation of the segments coincides with valuation of the total portfolio. For example, suppose a portfolio is divided into two segments, stocks and bonds. A valuation at the beginning of a period gives $BV = BV_S + BV_B$ (where the subscripts S and B denote stocks and bonds, respectively) and at the end $EV = EV_S + EV_B$. The portfolio return relative can be written as

$$
\begin{aligned}
\frac{EV}{BV} &= \frac{EV_S + EV_B}{BV} \\
&= \frac{BV_S}{BV}\frac{EV_S}{BV_S} + \frac{BV_B}{BV}\frac{EV_B}{BV_B}
\end{aligned}
\tag{5.8}
$$

Consequently, the beginning weights $w_S = BV_S/BV$ and $w_B = BV_B/BV$ are consistent with the segment returns $r_S = (EV_S/BV_S) - 1$ and $r_B = (EV_B/BV_B) - 1$. Equation (5.8) can be rewritten as $r = w_S r_S + w_B r_B$.

   If there are cash flows without portfolio valuations, then an approximation (modified Dietz, IRR, etc.) must be used for the portfolio return. If similar approximations are made for the segment returns, will the beginning weights still be consistent with the returns? Unfortunately not, in general. However, in the Dietz method, weights calculated from the adjusted beginning market values *are* consistent with the returns.

   To see this, we first note that the cash flow C of a segment is equal to

$$C = P - S - I$$

where P = value of purchases

   S = value of sales

   I = value of income from assets in the segment.

Income appears with a negative sign, as does sales, because both income and sales represent market values that can be used either for purchases within the segment or for transfers to other segments (or withdrawal from the total portfolio). For a given segment, the net value of purchases less sales less income equals the cash inflow to the segment.

   Now, a cash flow between two assets creates flows at the segment level of equal magnitudes and opposite signs—a sale of one asset creates a purchase of another asset (into the liquidity reserve, perhaps), for example. If all flows are correctly accounted for, then the sum of cash flows over all segments equals the cash flow at the total portfolio level. That is, for a portfolio segmented into stocks and bonds, if ΣC_S and ΣC_B are the sums of all cash flows at a given time into the stock and bond segments, respectively, then the cash flow into the overall portfolio is $C = \Sigma C_S + \Sigma C_B$. Consequently, the adjusted beginning value [Equation (5.6)] and the adjusted ending value [Equation (5.7)] can be segmented, respectively, as ABV = $\text{ABV}_S + \text{ABV}_B$ and AEV = $\text{AEV}_S + \text{AEV}_B$. As shown by Equation (5.8), the weights $w_S = \text{ABV}_S/\text{ABV}$ and $w_B = \text{ABV}_B/\text{ABV}$ are consistent with the returns $r_S = (\text{AEV}_S/\text{ABV}_S) - 1$ and $r_B = (\text{AEV}_B/\text{ABV}_B) - 1$. This consistency of weights and returns is a valuable feature of the Dietz method.

TIME-WEIGHTED VERSUS MONEY-WEIGHTED RETURNS

A common description of the distinction between the internal rate of return and time-weighted return is that the IRR "measures the performance of the fund rather than the performance of the fund's manager."[8] In some settings the IRR is called a "personal" rate of return.[9] Because the time-weighted return controls for cash flows, it is a better measure to use when comparing the performance of different managers.

The IRR is often called a *money-weighted* (or *dollar-weighted*) return. This terminology should be understood as a general characterization, not as a specific prescription, because the "money-weighting" only holds approximately. In what sense is either time or money weighted in calculating returns? An author of the 1968 BAI study, Lawrence Fisher, explained the term in an appendix titled, "Proof That the Internal Rate of Return is a 'Dollar-Weighted' Rate of Return."[10] We review that proof here.

For motivation, consider the data in Table 5.4. The portfolio returned 5 percent in the first year and 20 percent in the second. The geometric average return was therefore $\sqrt{1.05 + 1.20} - 1 = 0.1225$, or

---

[8] Cohen et al., *Measuring the Investment Performance of Pension Funds*, p. 4.

[9] David Spaulding, *The Handbook of Investment Performance: A User's Guide* (Somerset, NJ: TSG Publishing, 2005), p. 18.

[10] Lawrence Fisher, Appendix IV in Cohen et al., *Measuring the Investment Performance of Pension Funds*.

TABLE 5.4

Market Values and Cash Flows of a Portfolio

Year	Cash Flow at Beginning	Beginning Value	Ending Value	Annual Return (%)	Continuously Compounding Annual Return (%)
1	100	100	105	5.00	4.88
2	100	205	246	20.00	18.23
		Arithmetic average		12.50	11.56
		Time-weighted rate of return		12.25	11.56

12.25 percent per year. In the geometric average, each term is given equal weight, because the two periods are of the same length. If the annual returns are expressed as continuously compounding returns $\ln(1 + r)$, as shown, then the familiar arithmetic average can be used to arrive at the same result. The average continuously compounding return is $(0.0488 + 0.1823)/2$, or 11.56 percent. The weighting in this averaging is what the "time-weighted" aspect of time-weighted returns refers to.

In light of the preceding, the original concept of "time-weighted return" referred to the geometric average or compound annual return. In current usage, the term refers to linked returns in general, where the periodic returns are calculated from valuations at the times of each cash flow.

Now consider the internal rate of return, which is the rate i satisfying the equation $100(1 + i)^2 + 100(1 + i) = 246$. The rate is 14.62 percent per year, which can be calculated by a spreadsheet function or financial calculator. Expressed as a continuously compounding rate, the rate is $\ln(1.1462) = 0.1365$, or 13.65 percent per year. Suppose we were to weight the annual returns by the principal amounts invested, as shown in Table 5.5.

The numerators in the weights are the cumulative sums of all cash flows, or the principal values, invested at each point. This is 100 for the first year and $100 + 100 = 200$ for the second year. The denominator for each period is the sum of the numerators across the periods, so the weights are normalized to sum to 1. Year 1 has a

T A B L E 5.5

Money-Weighted Return Calculations for the Example

Year	Weight	Annual Return (%)	Continuously Compounding Annual Return (%)
1	100/300	5.00	4.88
2	200/300	20.00	18.23
	Weighted average	15.00	13.78
	Internal rate of return	14.62	13.65

weight of 1/3, while year 2 has a weight of 2/3. The weighted sum of the annual returns is therefore 15 percent. This number is close to the annually compounding internal rate of return (14.62 percent). Similarly, the weighted sum of the continuously compounding returns is 13.78 percent, which is close to the continuously compounding internal rate of return (13.65 percent). In this sense, the internal rate of return is approximately a money-weighted average of the periodic rates of return.

Note that the internal rate of return, 14.62 percent in this example, is greater than the time-weighted geometric average rate of return, 12.25 percent. This result can be understood in light of the money weighting. The amount invested during the second year was substantially greater than that invested during the first year, due to the additional cash flow. The internal rate of return gave more weight to the second year, when the investment return also happened to be greater.

These concepts can be generalized to subperiods of unequal length, for which we need more notation. Consider a period split into K subperiods defined by the times of the cash flows. The cash flows C_j are indexed by $j = 0, 1, 2, 3, \ldots, K-1$. For notational convenience, C_0 represents the beginning value of the portfolio. The Kth subperiod extends from the last cash flow to the end of the overall period.

Let TD be the total number of days in the period and assume that cash flow C_j occurs at the end of day D_j, where $D_0 = 0$ and $D_K = $ TD.

Let $L_k = (D_k - D_{k-1})/TD$ be the length of subperiod k, as a fraction of the total length of the period, and let $W_j = (TD - D_j)/TD$ be the fraction of the period remaining after the time of cash flow j. Note that $W_0 = 1$, $W_K = 0$, and $W_j = \sum_{k=j+1}^{K} L_k$. Incidentally, $\sum_{k=1}^{K} L_k = 1$, which is immaterial to the following discussion.

Assuming that valuations are available at the times of all cash flows, the subperiod returns r_k can be calculated. Unlike the usual calculation, however, we state all returns as rates *compounding per overall period* instead of rates *compounding per subperiods*. That is, if V_k is the value before the cash flow at k and if V'_{k-1} is the value *after* the cash flow at $k - 1$, then we define the subperiod return relative as $1 + r_k = (V_k / V'_{k-1})^{1/L_k}$. For example, if the overall period length is one year, then the subperiod returns are annualized returns. *Note:* Annualizing a single return spanning less than one year is done here for analytical purposes and is not recommended for reporting purposes.

With returns stated as compound returns as in the preceding, the time-weighted return r for the overall period is calculated by linking the subperiod returns, written as

$$(1+r)^{L_1 + L_2 + \cdots + L_K} = (1+r_1)^{L_1}(1+r_2)^{L_2} \cdots (1+r_K)^{L_K}.$$

The time-weighted return r is the weighted geometric average of the subperiod returns. In this form, the subperiod lengths L_k serve as weights in the geometric average.

In continuously compounding form,

$$\tilde{r} = \frac{\sum_{k=1}^{K} L_k \tilde{r}_k}{\sum_{k=1}^{K} L_k} \tag{5.9}$$

where $\tilde{r} = \ln(1+r)$ and $\tilde{r}_k = \ln(1+r_k)$. The returns $\tilde{r}_k$ are weighted by the respective fractions $L_k / \sum_{k=1}^{K} L_k$ of the overall period length. The time-weighted sum of returns is clear.

Now consider the internal rate of return for the overall period. Let $\tilde{i}$ denote the continuously compounding internal rate of return.

That is, if i is the internal rate of return, then $\tilde{i} = \ln(1+i)$. The rate $\tilde{i}$ satisfies the equation

$$EV = C_0 \exp(W_0\tilde{i}) + C_1 \exp(W_1\tilde{i}) + \cdots + C_{K-1}\exp(W_{K-1}\tilde{i}) \quad (5.10)$$

where EV is the ending value given by

$$
\begin{aligned}
EV = \; & C_0 \exp(L_1\tilde{r}_1 + L_2\tilde{r}_2 + \cdots + L_K\tilde{r}_K) \\
& + \; C_1 \exp(L_2\tilde{r}_2 + L_3\tilde{r}_3 + \cdots + L_K\tilde{r}_K) + \cdots \\
& + \; C_{K-1}\exp(L_K\tilde{r}_K)
\end{aligned}
\quad (5.11)
$$

Next, apply the approximation, $\exp(x) \cong 1 + x$, that is, the first two terms in the series expansion of $\exp(x)$. This approximation is accurate for small enough values of x. Substituting the approximation into Equation (5.10) gives

$$EV \cong \sum_{j=0}^{K-1} C_j(1 + W_j\tilde{i})$$

and substituting the approximation into Equation (5.11) gives

$$EV \cong \sum_{j=0}^{K-1} C_j\left(1 + \sum_{k=j+1}^{K} L_k\tilde{r}_k\right).$$

Equating these two expressions for EV gives

$$\sum_{j=0}^{K-1} C_j(1 + W_j\tilde{i}) \cong \sum_{j=0}^{K-1} C_j\left(1 + \sum_{k=j+1}^{K} L_k\tilde{r}_k\right).$$

Substituting $W_j = \sum_{k=j+1}^{K} L_k$ and solving for $\tilde{i}$ gives

$$\tilde{i} \cong \frac{\displaystyle\sum_{j=0}^{K-1} C_j \sum_{k=j+1}^{K} L_k\tilde{r}_k}{\displaystyle\sum_{j=0}^{K-1} C_j \sum_{k=j+1}^{K} L_k}.$$

Switching the order of the summations leaves

$$\tilde{i} \cong \frac{\sum_{k=1}^{K} \left(L_k \sum_{j=0}^{k-1} C_j \right) \tilde{r}_k}{\sum_{k=1}^{K} L_k \sum_{j=0}^{k-1} C_j}. \tag{5.12}$$

The returns $\tilde{r}_k$ are weighted by $L_k \sum_{j=0}^{k-1} C_j / \sum_{k=1}^{K} L_k \sum_{j=0}^{k-1} C_j$. Compare Equation (5.12) for the continuously compounding internal rate of return to Equation (5.9) for the continuously compounding time-weighted return. Doing so completes the proof of Fisher's theorem:

> *Fisher's Dollar-Weighted Return Theorem*   Assume continuous compounding. The internal rate of return $\tilde{i}$ for a time period can be approximated by Equation (5.12), which is similar in structure to Equation (5.9) for the time-weighted rate, but includes the additional "dollar-weighting" terms $\sum_{j=0}^{k-1} C_j$.

In words, the internal rate of return is approximately the weighted sum of the subperiod returns, where the subperiod weight is given by the product of the subperiod length and the accumulated cash flow up to the beginning of the subperiod. Allowing for the approximation, the internal rate of return is, in fact, *both* a time-weighted *and* a money-weighted rate. In current usage, the internal rate of return is simply known as a money-weighted return, which, as we have seen, is a general characterization, not an exact algorithm.

As demonstrated by the preceding example, the approximation also works if we assume annual compounding and use annually compounded returns and the annually compounded internal rate of return.

By comparison, Equation (5.9) is a time-weighted rate. As currently used, the term "time-weighted return" refers to linked returns in general, not necessarily annualized, in which valuations at the times of all cash flows are used in calculating the returns. The linked modified Dietz and linked IRR methods, being approximations of true time-weighted returns, are usually also presented as time-weighted returns, to distinguish the overall approach from money-weighted returns.

In summary, the internal rate of return takes into account the amounts of market value in the portfolio over periods of time and summarizes, in a single number, the growth of the value of the portfolio, giving more weight to periods with more principal invested. In contrast, the time-weighted rate of return summarizes the growth of a unit of initial value of the portfolio. This growth comes from investments and is not affected by cash flows.

The internal rate of return may be appropriate for measuring growth, if the cash flows are under the control of the decision maker. Because cash flows are usually not under the control of a manager of a fund, the time-weighted rate of return is the appropriate measure for comparing the performance of investment managers.

CHAPTER 6

Comparing Two Portfolio Returns[1]

When evaluating the performance of a portfolio, analysts usually compare the return to some reference point. The reference point may be a cash return, for example, which might be regarded as risk-free; in this case the comparison would measure the additional return obtained from investing in risky assets. Most often, the reference point is provided by another portfolio, one that may be constructed in a particularly simple fashion and thought to provide a baseline for the comparison; in this case, the comparison would measure the additional return obtained from active management of the portfolio. In any case, the reference portfolio against which a portfolio is to be compared is a *benchmark portfolio*. We discuss benchmark portfolio construction beginning with Chapter 20.

Comparing a portfolio's return to a benchmark return yields *excess return*—the additional return the portfolio creates in excess of the benchmark portfolio. How should we calculate excess return? It seems simple on the surface, but, in fact, there are different ways to calculate excess return for different settings and they do not all yield the same excess return.

For a single holding period of, say, one month or one year, it is common to subtract the benchmark return from the portfolio return and call the difference *excess return*. This simple excess return is readily understood as the difference in end-of-period wealth, assuming reinvested gains, expressed as a percentage of beginning wealth.

---

[1] We thank Tom Goodwin for contributing to this chapter.

However, problems arise when one wants to summarize performance over multiple periods. The operations of compounding and averaging cause problems for simple differences between holding-period returns, which cannot be compounded over time in the usual way.

To contend with the issues, excess return over multiple periods may simply be calculated as the difference between two average, or mean, returns. Sometimes analysts calculate the difference between arithmetic means, while at other times they calculate the difference between geometric means. There is a third method—we call it *compound excess return* or *geometric excess return*—that precisely maintains the intuitive link between excess return and excess wealth when assessing past performance.

Why maintain the link to excess wealth? The benchmark represents an investor's opportunity cost. The investor is interested in the portfolio's wealth at the end of the period—and how that wealth compares with the wealth that would have been earned if the benchmark portfolio had been chosen. Excess return should be a measure that intuitively and precisely maps into the investor's excess wealth.

EXCESS RETURNS OVER A BENCHMARK—
PAST PERFORMANCE

Recall from Chapter 4 that the geometric average return is a direct transformation of the growth of a unit of wealth invested in the portfolio. Conversely, given the geometric average and the number of periods, the cumulative return of a portfolio can be recovered. No analogous calculation can be performed with the arithmetic average return to recover the cumulative return. Consequently, we might think that comparing two geometric averages would give a meaningful comparison of the growth in value of two portfolios. It turns out that the result depends on what is meant by "comparing two geometric averages."

Consider the returns data in Table 6.1 for a portfolio and a benchmark. The table shows three months of returns, with geometric and arithmetic average returns calculated using Equations (4.1) and (4.2), respectively, of Chapter 4. Also shown are the cumulative returns for the two portfolios, calculated using the linking formula (Equation 3.2, Chapter 3).

It seems certain that our "active" portfolio underperformed the "benchmark" portfolio during this period, but by how much?

T A B L E   6.1

Monthly Returns of a Portfolio and a Benchmark

	Portfolio Return (%)	Benchmark Return (%)	Difference (%)
Month 1	19.2	−2.0	21.2
Month 2	−2.6	9.7	−12.3
Month 3	−15.6	−3.1	−12.5
Geometric mean	−0.67	1.37	−2.04
Arithmetic mean	0.33	1.53	−1.20
Cumulative return	−2.01	4.17	−6.18

Two common ways of calculating average excess returns are to take the difference between the arithmetic mean returns—which we call *arithmetic mean excess return*—or to take the difference between the geometric mean returns—which we call *geometric mean difference*. The arithmetic mean excess return is 0.33 percent minus 1.53 percent, which equals −1.20 percent, and the geometric mean difference is −0.67 percent minus 1.37 percent, or −2.04 percent. Neither of these two measures is ideal for assessing past performance because neither one can reproduce the investor's excess wealth.

Assuming an initial portfolio value of $100, the ending wealth of the active portfolio is $100(1 − 0.0201), or $97.99. The benchmark portfolio's ending wealth is $104.17, so the excess wealth is −$6.18. This value may also be calculated from the cumulative return difference,[2] −2.01 percent minus 4.17 percent, or −6.18 percent, indicating a loss of $6.18 per $100.00 of initial investment.

Given the arithmetic mean excess return of −1.20 percent per month, it is tempting to simply multiply by 3 to get −3.60 percent for the period, or an apparent loss of $3.60 on an initial investment of $100.00. This conclusion is incorrect because ending wealth cannot be recovered from the arithmetic mean.

---

[2] Arguably, the cumulative return difference is the only concept deserving the label "excess return." Because we have seen the term used in many ways, we recommend being explicit.

In fact, it is not possible to recover ending wealth from the simple return differences month by month. The return differences for the three months, respectively, are 21.2, –12.3, and –12.5 percent. Given these three simple excess returns, compounding them in the usual way yields

$$(1 + 0.212)(1 - 0.123)(1 - 0.125) - 1 = -6.99\%,$$

which is obviously incorrect.

Given the geometric mean difference of –2.04 percent, it may also be tempting to compound this return over three months to try to obtain the excess wealth, using the usual compounding calculation:

$$(1 - 0.0204)^3 - 1 = -6.00\%.$$

This suggests a loss of $6.00 on the initial investment of $100.00. This conclusion is also incorrect.

An alternate way to calculate excess return focuses directly on ending wealth. The investor wants to know how the active portfolio's wealth at the end of the period compares with the wealth that would have been earned if the benchmark portfolio had been chosen. The ratio of those two wealth positions, the terminal wealth relative, is a meaningful basis for calculating excess return. The monthly excess return that is consistent with these two terminal wealth positions is

$$\left(\frac{\$97.99}{\$104.17} \right)^{1/3} - 1 = -2.02\% \qquad (6.1)$$

Neither the arithmetic mean excess return (–1.20 percent) nor the geometric mean difference (–2.04 percent) is equal to –2.02 percent. Given this value, a cumulative excess return over three months can be calculated from

$$(1 - 0.0202)^3 - 1 = -5.94\%,$$

indicating a loss of $5.94 per $100.00 of *ending* wealth of the benchmark portfolio, or a final excess wealth of

$$\$104.17(-0.0594) = -\$6.18.$$

Note that –$6.18 is the difference between the ending wealth of the active and benchmark portfolios, $97.99 minus $104.17.

We would not expect the arithmetic excess return to be a properly compounding return because it is the difference between two uncompounded returns. But that we cannot simply link the geometric mean difference is perhaps more surprising, because it uses two properly compounding returns in its calculation. To be fair, it does come close in this example. Unfortunately, the difference between two geometric mean returns is not itself a geometric mean return.

COMPOUND EXCESS RETURN

Algebraically, let V_0 be the beginning value of the active portfolio and V_{P1} be the value one month later. The beginning and ending values of the benchmark portfolios are V_0 and V_{B1}, respectively.

Assuming there are no flows into or out of the portfolios, the portfolio return r_P and benchmark return r_B are defined in terms of relative values by $1 + r_P = V_{P1}/V_0$ and $1 + r_B = V_{B1}/V_0$. So, by defining *compound excess return* r_X in terms of the ending portfolio-to-benchmark wealth relative, we have the relation

$$1 + r_X = \frac{V_{P1}}{V_{B1}} = \frac{V_{P1}/V_0}{V_{B1}/V_0} = \frac{1 + r_P}{1 + r_B}.$$

The compound excess return r_X is also known as *geometric excess return*. Observe that the compound excess return is related to the arithmetic excess return $r_P - r_B$ by

$$r_X = \frac{1 + r_P}{1 + r_B} - 1 = \frac{r_P - r_B}{1 + r_B}. \tag{6.2}$$

Whereas the arithmetic excess return $r_P - r_B$ is the excess value of the portfolio relative to the benchmark as a fraction of *beginning* value, the compound or geometric excess return r_X is the excess value as a fraction of *ending value of the benchmark*. Rewriting the preceeding relation as

$$r_P - r_B = r_X + r_B r_X,$$

we can see that the two types of excess return differ by the interactive term $r_B r_X$. If both r_B and r_X are small, then the two types of excess return can be close. Note that the arithmetic excess return can be either greater than or less than the compound excess return, depending on the sign of the interactive term $r_B r_X$.

The compound excess return can be linked (geometrically compounded) over time, just like ordinary returns. By calculating the geometric mean over three months, we obtain the correct mean monthly excess return:

$$\left[\left(\frac{1+r_{P1}}{1+r_{B1}}\right)\left(\frac{1+r_{P2}}{1+r_{B2}}\right)\left(\frac{1+r_{P3}}{1+r_{B3}}\right)\right]^{1/3} - 1$$

$$= \left[\left(\frac{1+1.192}{1-0.020}\right)\left(\frac{1-0.026}{1+0.097}\right)\left(\frac{1-0.156}{1-0.031}\right)\right]^{1/3} - 1$$

$$= -2.02\%$$

This is the compound monthly excess return implied by the terminal wealth positions of the investor in Equation (6.1). In fact, the relationship between compound excess return and geometric mean returns is readily written:

$$r_{XG} = \frac{1+r_{PG}}{1+r_{BG}} - 1 \tag{6.3}$$

where r_{PG} and r_{BG} are the geometric mean returns of the portfolio and the benchmark, respectively. In the example the gap between the geometric mean difference (–2.04 percent) and the exact compound excess return (–2.02 percent) is relatively small. The discrepancy arises from taking the arithmetic difference between the two geometric means instead of calculating the ratio of return relatives. The error tends to get smaller as the frequency of compounding increases. As shown in Chapter 4, the continuously compounding return is the logarithm of the return relative. Therefore, $\ln(1 + r_X) = \ln(1 + r_P) - \ln(1 + r_B)$, which means that the approximation error disappears altogether with continuous compounding.

However, one should not be complacent about using either the geometric mean difference or the arithmetic excess return as an approximation to the compound excess return—especially because most excess returns are reported on an annualized basis.

SITUATIONS WHERE THE ARITHMETIC EXCESS RETURN IS THE APPROPRIATE CHOICE

The previous section demonstrates that the arithmetic excess return can be misleading when evaluating past performance. Yet there are settings where the arithmetic average is the appropriate choice. These tend to be situations where the statistical properties of returns, either total or excess, play an important role.

Expected Return

In Chapter 4, we showed that the geometric mean return is less than or equal to the arithmetic mean return, by an amount that depends on volatility. When modeling expected values of *future* returns, the arithmetic mean is "unbiased" in the sense that the expected value of the arithmetic mean is equal to the expected value of the returns, if the returns are mean-stationary, or have a well-defined expected value. As a result, when we want to depict expected values of *future* returns by calculating statistics of *past* returns, the arithmetic mean return is the better choice.

A similar analysis of excess returns would show that the compound excess return [in Equation (6.3)] is affected by the volatilities of the portfolio and benchmark returns. Arithmetic excess return, in contrast, is not affected by volatility.

Sometimes uncoupling the measurement of excess returns from the measurement of tracking error is useful. The following are several of the most important cases where the arithmetic excess return is the appropriate choice.

Information and Sharpe Ratios

The information ratio IR is a measure of risk-adjusted returns that calculates the amount of excess return per unit of active risk (tracking error). The IR is the mean excess return ER_A over a benchmark divided by tracking error ω, where the tracking error is usually defined as the standard deviation of simple return differences:[3]

$$IR = \frac{ER_A}{\omega}$$

where $ER_A = r_{PA} - r_{BA}$ is the difference between arithmetic mean returns of the portfolio and the benchmark. We discuss the information ratio and the closely-related Sharpe ratio in Chapter 10.

Hypothesis Testing—On the Significance of Excess Returns

Working with the arithmetic mean has some statistical advantages. The central limit theorem states that as long as the individual returns have a mean and a variance, and the returns are independent (or not too dependent) and identically distributed, the arithmetic mean becomes normally distributed if the sample is large enough.[4] The central limit theorem applies to the arithmetic mean of excess return. This allows for the formulation of hypothesis tests using the mean excess return. Accounting for sampling variation in the tracking error (standard deviation of excess returns) leads to t-tests on the significance of excess returns using the information ratio

$$\sqrt{T}IR = \sqrt{T}\frac{ER_A}{\omega} \sim t_{T-1}$$

where T = number of time points
ER_A = arithmetic mean excess return

ω = standard deviation (tracking error) of simple return differences.

---

[3] Thomas Goodwin, "The Information Ratio," *Financial Analysts Journal*, July/August 1998, pp. 34–43. Also published as a *Russell Research Commentary*, (Tacoma, WA: Russell Investments, November 1997).

[4] Morris DeGroot, *Probability and Statistics*, 2d ed. (Reading, MA: Addison-Wesley, 1996), p. 275.

RECOMMENDED PRACTICE

It is apparent that one should use the term *excess return* very carefully, as it can be used to refer to very different calculations. Analysts would be well advised to always disclose the specific calculation used when reporting measures of excess return. And users of excess returns should seek to understand how a reported measure was calculated.

We have given several examples where particular measures are more meaningful than others. When summarizing past performance, statistical issues aside, we prefer the compound excess return to the geometric mean difference or the arithmetic excess return. Neither of the latter two measures (the differences in means) gives an accurate indication of the excess wealth over multiple periods. Annualization magnifies the approximation error.

When summarizing statistical properties of returns, as for expected return or information ratios, we prefer arithmetic mean returns and arithmetic excess returns. Arithmetic means provide estimates that are independent of volatility, when returns are normally distributed.

Finally, we summarize the two measures of mean returns, the four measures of excess return, and the appropriate settings discussed previously in Table 6.2. The formulas are annualized for a T-period series of n-frequency returns r_{Pt} of an active portfolio and r_{Bt} of a benchmark portfolio (i.e., assuming there are T/n years of data).

TABLE 6.2

Measures of Average Returns and Excess Returns

Arithmetic mean return: $$r_{PA} = \frac{n}{T}\sum_{t=1}^{T} r_{Pt} \quad \text{and} \quad r_{BA} = \frac{n}{T}\sum_{t=1}^{T} r_{Bt}$$	The appropriate choice when statistical analysis is involved. It is preferred when both mean return and standard deviation of return are displayed such as a scatterplot of risk and return or an efficient frontier.
	(continued)

T A B L E 6.2

Measures of Average Returns and Excess Returns (*continued*)

Geometric mean return: $$r_{PG} = \left[\prod_{t=1}^{T}(1+r_{Pt})\right]^{n/T} - 1$$ and $$r_{BG} = \left[\prod_{t=1}^{T}(1+r_{Bt})\right]^{n/T} - 1$$	The appropriate choice for summarizing past performance of a portfolio with a single number. Because it maps uniquely to ending wealth, it accurately reflects the effect of compounding, that is, the reinvestment of gains in a portfolio.
Simple excess return/cumulative return difference: $$\prod_{t=1}^{T}(1+r_{Pt}) - \prod_{t=1}^{T}(1+r_{Bt}) = (1+r_{PG})^{T/n} - (1+r_{BG})^{T/n}$$	The appropriate choice when the meaning is clear, but it cannot be linked over multiple periods with Equation 3.2. The cumulative return difference directly expresses the difference in ending wealth as a percentage of beginning wealth.
Annualized compound excess return: $$r_{XG} = \left[\prod_{t=1}^{T}\left(\frac{1+r_{Pt}}{1+r_{Bt}}\right)\right]^{n/T} - 1 = \frac{1+r_{PG}}{1+r_{BG}} - 1$$	The most appropriate choice for assessing past performance because it is an accurate measure of the excess wealth that has been produced by active investment. It measures this as a fraction of ending wealth if invested in the benchmark. It can be linked over multiple periods and annualized in the usual way.
Arithmetic mean excess return: $$ER_A = \frac{n}{T}\sum_{t=1}^{T}(r_{Pt} - r_{Bt}) = r_{PA} - r_{BA}$$	The appropriate choice for information ratios, Sharpe ratios, hypothesis testing, and risk-return analysis, where statistical inferences are involved.
Geometric mean difference: $$\left[\prod_{t=1}^{T}(1+r_{Pt})\right]^{n/T} - \left[\prod_{t=1}^{T}(1+r_{Bt})\right]^{n/T} = r_{PG} - r_{BG}$$	The approximation to compound excess return, but it can be a poor and misleading one. It is a biased estimator of expected excess return. The geometric mean difference is inappropriate for any setting.

CHAPTER 7

Some Foundations

For many years, academics have wrestled with fundamental questions of how prices of assets are determined. The theory of asset pricing provides a foundation for the evaluation of financial assets—asset pricing models. In this chapter, we cover some basic elements of the theory in order to provide background for evaluating the techniques and methods described later on and to place the return expectations in context. Many of the performance evaluation techniques that we review flow from asset pricing models, so understanding them should prove beneficial.

THE RISK-FREE RATE

We begin with a discussion of the *risk-free rate,* usually symbolized as R_f. This rate represents the minimum an investor could expect for investing in the most secure investment. The safest investment is an investment guaranteed by an agent who has a probability of defaulting on the promised payoff close to zero. Two such agents are the governments of the United States and United Kingdom. Between them, these governments have long histories of economic stability. They have never missed an interest payment on their debt obligations, and their currencies are and have been among the most stable in the world.

The safest U.S. asset would be a U.S. government Treasury bill. The return of the short-term bills is often used as the risk-free rate. However, there are other governments in this world that are just as safe a bet as that of the United States and Britain—such as

those of Germany, Japan, and Switzerland. These safe-bet governments provide financial instruments that are the backbone of the
global financial community. These are often referred to as the
"reserve currencies."

An examination of the guaranteed returns on short-term
investment instruments offered by these reserve currency governments reveals a variety of different returns. The three-month government bill yield as of January 3, 2007, for the United States was
4.875 percent, while the U.K. yield was 5.04 percent, the German
government yield was 3.59 percent, and the Japanese instruments
yield was 0.46 percent.[1] Why was there a discrepancy among these
rates? The answer to this question is beyond the scope of this book,
but simply stated it is a function of the supply and demand of currency and the economic health of the countries involved. A U.S.
investor investing in the United Kingdom, for example, has an investment not only in the U.K. government, paying off in pounds sterling,
but also an investment in the currency—the British pound itself.

A crucial variable is inflation expectations. The higher the
inflation rate expected in the country, the higher the fundamental
returns will have to be to attract investors. Given this logic, inflation
in the United States was expected to be higher than inflation in
Germany, which was expected to be higher than the inflation
in Japan. The U.S. investor may earn a low return in yen, but the
return on the yen itself when translated back into U.S. dollars was
expected to make up much of the difference.

The casual observer looking at the interest rates for risk-free
assets in the United States, such as the 90-day T-bill, will also notice
that this rate changes over time. Sometimes that change can be quite
dramatic in a relatively short period of time. The outbreak of war,
the collapse of a large financial institution, or any number of other
political, military, or economic events can dramatically affect short-
term interest rates.

If you buy a Treasury bill on January 1 that promises to pay $100
on March 31, and you pay $99.40 for that bill, the expected return
over that three-month interval is 0.60 percent. The U.S. treasury

---

[1] The source for these data is Bloomberg www.bloomberg.com/markets/rates/
index.html.

auctions off bills every month. If a dramatic event happens in January and we seek to buy another bill in February, the implied interest rate on that bill is likely to be quite different. If you want to sell the T-bill in January when it still has two months left until maturity, you will receive more or less than the $99.40 you paid for the bill to reflect what happened during January. Therefore you arrive at this fundamental observation—there is no completely risk-free rate. All investment has some level of risk, even government securities. If you were certain that you would not want to sell the bill before March 31, you might think of it as risk free. However, there is still uncertainty about what inflation will be between now and March 31, so there is still real risk to the investment.

MARKET EQUILIBRIUM

In markets, there is always a variety of viewpoints about what the price of an asset should be. Those who think the price is too high will not buy the security and may in fact want to sell it. Those who think the price is too low will be happy to pay the "low" price. At some price the amount that buyers are willing to buy just equals the amount that sellers are willing to sell. At this point the price is said to be in equilibrium. The price of an asset is exactly what that "marginal" investor will pay you for it—not a penny more or less. Those who say things like "The true value of this asset is . . . " are usually saying that they expect the price of the asset to adjust to a new price different from the current market price.

This raises the issue of the information used by investors to gauge the "true value" of an asset. Information is critical. Why do different people have different opinions about an asset's future prospects? One explanation for this has to do with different investors having different levels of information and different skill sets for handling and evaluating that information. Added to this, investors have different time horizons, from five minutes (or a "New York minute") to 20 years, over which they expect to sell the asset and the payoff to emerge.

Eugene Fama[2] makes an argument in favor of what is known as the "efficient markets hypothesis," which argues that current

---

[2] Eugene F. Fama, "Efficient Capital Markets: A Review of Theory and Empirical Work," *Journal of Finance*, vol. 25, 1970, pp. 383–417.

prices reflect the efficient processing by market participants of information about the prospects of a security. He outlines three forms of efficient markets.

1. The "weak form" argues that all past market prices and returns data are fully reflected in securities prices. If true, then technical analysis is of little use.
2. The "semi-strong form" argues that all publicly available information is fully reflected in securities prices. If true, then fundamental analysis will not provide excess returns.
3. The "strong form" argues that all information is fully reflected in securities prices. If true, then even insider information is of no use.

The research on the efficiency of markets is inconclusive as to the level of market efficiency. The evidence has shown that, with some exceptions or "anomalies," form 1 generally holds and form 2 is often reasonable to assume. If level 2 market efficiency holds, then information is freely available and arrives in a timely manner and most investors can process the information correctly to arrive at the correct value for an asset. In such a world all assets are correctly priced most of the time. The main driver of changing prices is the arrival of new, unexpected information. The arrival of this information can be considered to be random. The effect of this random information on the price is also assumed to be random. Therefore, the assets prices are set correctly and random changes in prices are driven solely by the random arrival of new information. The unexpected change in the price is driven by random events.

Given these assumptions and observations, we may conclude that information arriving randomly results in price changes randomly distributed around an average price change. Each month in the future we can expect that the average return may move up or down and that the standard deviation of the return distribution may also increase or decrease.

THE CAPM OF SHARPE, LINTNER, AND MOSSIN

If asset prices are determined by market equilibrium, what is the relationship between return and risk? The capital asset pricing model (CAPM) of Sharpe, Lintner, and Mossin was developed around 1965.[3] The central idea of the CAPM is that the expected return for an asset above the risk-free rate is equal to some average for the market to compensate for risk that cannot be diversified away, scaled by the sensitivity of the asset to the return of the market. The expected return of a risky asset like a stock must be above the risk-free rate, otherwise investors would have no incentive to invest in it. The general movement of the prices of all securities is captured in a single index factor called the market portfolio. These ideas are captured in the following equation:

$$E(R_i - R_f) = \beta_i E(R_m - R_f) \tag{7.1}$$

where

R_i = stock i return

R_f = risk-free return

$E(\bullet)$ = market's expectation of $(\bullet)$

R_m = market portfolio return

β_i = stock i sensitivity to changes in market portfolio.

The sensitivity of the asset to movements in the market is called beta (β_i). Beta is unique to each asset and is assumed to be constant for the holding period. Beta can be viewed as the universal measure of risk because it captures the risk of each asset relative to the market. It is also called the systematic risk of the asset. If the market has on average a 16 percent annualized standard deviation and a particular stock has a beta of 0.5, then we can expect the part of the annualized standard deviation of that stock that is due to market risk to be about 8 percent or about half as risky as stocks in general. A beta of 1.5 means that the security has a standard deviation of market-related return of about 24 percent annualized, considerably higher than the market. The desirable property of beta is

---

[3] William Sharpe, "Capital Asset Prices: A Theory of Market Equilibrium Under Conditions of Risk," *Journal of Finance*, vol. 19, no. 3, September 1964, pp. 425–442. Jan Mossin, "Equilibrium in a Capital Asset Market," *Econometrica*, vol. 34, no. 4, October 1966, pp. 768–783. John Lintner, "The Valuation of Risk Assets and the Selection of Risky Investments in Stock Portfolios and Capital Budgets" *Review of Economics and Statistics*, vol. 47, February 1965, pp. 13–47.

that it is a single number that measures the market-related riskiness of stocks and is comparable across stocks. Stocks, of course, also have nonmarket or security-specific risks in addition to market-related risk, but the CAPM views these as unimportant for assessing the expected returns.

The beta of an individual security is equal to the covariance of the security's returns with a market return adjusted by the market standard deviation σ_m:

$$\beta_i = \frac{\text{Cov}(R_i, R_m)}{\sigma_m^2}. \tag{7.2}$$

The CAPM also applies to portfolios, which are weighted combinations of assets. The market portfolio is the capitalization weighted portfolio of all assets. The beta of the market with itself is 1.0 because $\sigma_m^2 = \text{Cov}(R_m, R_m)$. Thus, the systematic risk for asset i is $\beta_i \sigma_m$ and, according to the CAPM [Equation (7.1)], the market price of risk (the amount of return you can expect per unit of systematic risk), is

$$\frac{E(R_m - R_f)}{\sigma_m}. \tag{7.3}$$

The numerator of Equation (7.3) is the expected return to the market minus the risk-free rate, otherwise known as the market risk premium.

The Security Market Line

In Figure 7.1 we show the relationship between beta and the expected return for a security according to CAPM. This graph is called the security market line. When beta equals 1.0, the expected return is the market return. When beta is zero, the expected return is the risk-free rate. Beta has no upper limit but is typically greater than zero.

In the framework of the CAPM, if we can estimate the beta for an individual security, we know what its expected return should be. Our empirical problem then reduces to the problem of how to estimate beta accurately. We will turn to this issue in Chapter 8.

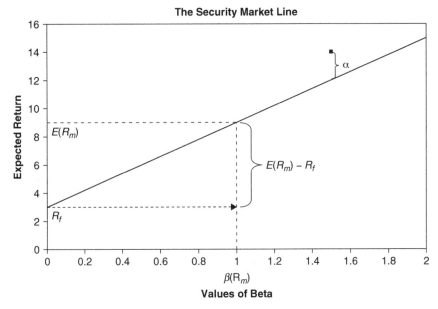

Figure 7.1 The security market line relating expected return and asset beta

Alpha as Risk-Adjusted Excess Return

Admitting that the CAPM is only a model, we can define alpha relative to the CAPM as

$$\alpha_i = E(R_i - R_f) - \beta_i E(R_m - R_f).$$

That is, alpha is the difference between the expected return and what the CAPM says it should be. The CAPM offers a useful baseline or consensus expected return.

Alpha, in the upper right of Figure 7.1 just above the security market line, can be viewed as a risk-adjusted excess return because it is the average return above the return that one would expect to receive for an asset given its beta. In this example the beta is 1.5 and the asset return is 14 while the expected return for most stocks with a beta of 1.5 is 12. So the alpha is 2 percent.

Active investing can be viewed as the search for a positive alpha above and beyond what one would expect for a stock or portfolio of stocks with the given level of beta.

Assumptions Associated with the Capital Asset Pricing Model

There are various assumptions associated with the capital asset pricing model. The first and foremost is that all investors are wealth-seeking, risk-avoiding rational investors. There are other assumptions as well, such as all investors have the same information, desire to hold the same efficient portfolio, and have the same time horizon. The theory also assumes that there are no taxes or other costs in buying and selling securities and that, in fact, you can buy and sell as much of a security as you wish and borrow at the risk-free rate as much as you want. None of these assumptions strictly holds true in practice, but they are assumed in the model so that one can see the behavior of the interesting variables.

In terms of risk avoidance, all investors are seen as mean-variance optimizers; that is, they seek to maximize return while minimizing variance through exploitation of asset covariance. The most difficult assumptions to accept are ones like all investors analyze securities in the same way, share a common economic view of the world, and have identical expectations about the probability distribution of the returns among the available securities. In other words, they have homogeneous expectations or beliefs that would seem to be inconsistent with the existence of a stock market. Lintner developed versions of the CAPM that allowed for differences in investor's beliefs.[4]

Generally, historically calculated betas do not predict out-of-sample returns very well. There are other factors that the model ignores such as the liquidity premium for shares that are difficult to trade.[5] However, the model captures the basic financial behavior surprisingly well and there is no alternative model that is as universally accepted or used as the CAPM. The CAPM provides a useful base for understanding the relationships between return and risk.

---

[4] John Lintner, "Security Prices, Risk and Maximal Gains from Diversification," *Journal of Finance*, vol. 20, no. 4, December, 1965, pp. 587–615.

[5] For a discussion of the calculation of the illiquidity premium, see Zvi Bodie, Alex Kane, and Alan Marcus, *Investments*, 5th ed. (New York: McGraw-Hill, 2002), pp. 283–285. Chapter 9 of this book has an excellent review of CAPM, and see chapter 11 for a review of the APT.

ARBITRAGE PRICING THEORY (APT) AND OTHER ASSET PRICING MODELS

There are of course other models that have been proposed for capital asset pricing. Investors and researchers have noted that there are characteristics about securities or factors in the marketplace that have been rewarded over time such as low price/book securities and small-cap securities. The rewards to some of these factors seem episodic—their rewards can persist for several time periods. These rewards can also be viewed as sources of return variation and can be called sources of risk. When these risks are rewarded, it is said that these risks are "priced" by the market. These observations have given rise to the development of multiple-factor models of asset returns. A theory that takes into account multiple factors that are priced and rewarded is called arbitrage pricing theory (APT) developed by Stephen Ross.[6]

An arbitrage exists when you can construct a zero investment portfolio that will yield a sure profit, such as purchasing an oil option for $60 a barrel when you know you can sell the oil for $65 a barrel for a guaranteed profit of five dollars with no risk to you. The same is true when a stock is traded in two different markets for two different prices. If one can put together a portfolio of one or more securities that mirror the return of another security (with identical growth prospects and dividend payouts) that has a price that is less than the current price of the security, then an arbitrage opportunity exists. One buys the portfolio of underpriced securities and shorts the overpriced securities to pocket the difference as profit.

In a market where all investors are able to form such portfolios and all investors have the information necessary to form such portfolios, stocks whose prices are too high offer arbitrage opportunities and their prices must fall. When all the trading is finished and the market has settled into equilibrium, the prices for all securities will offer no more arbitrage opportunities.

---

[6] Stephen A. Ross, "The Arbitrage Theory of Capital Asset Pricing," *Journal of Economic Theory*, vol. 13, 1976, pp. 341–360. A critique of APT can be found in Christian Gilles and Stephen F. LeRoy, "On the Arbitrage Pricing Theory," *Economic Theory*, vol. 1, no. 3, 1991, pp. 213–229.

The APT model portrays the return of a security as equal to an expected return plus the return attributable to the asset's sensitivities to all factors that are priced in the marketplace plus specific risk:

$$R_i = E(R_i) + \sum_{k=1}^{K} \beta_{ik} F_k + \varepsilon_i \qquad (7.4)$$

where

R_i = return of security i

$E(R_i)$ = the expected return of security i

β_{ik} = exposure or sensitivity of security i to changes in factor k

F_k = unexpected shock to factor k

ε_i = asset-specific return unrelated to any of the factors.

The APT concludes that to avoid arbitrage,

$$E(R_i) \approx R_f + \sum \beta_{ik} \lambda_k$$

where

R_f = risk-free return

λ_k = the expected risk premium of a unit exposure to factor k.

That is, the expected return of an asset is approximately a linear combination of the risk-free return and the expected risk premia of the factors. The approximation reflects the idea that there may be deviations in expected returns from the arbitrage relation, but they can't be too large and they must average out to zero.

This model is analogous to the CAPM and produces the same kind of risk adjustment as the CAPM where there is only one factor, the market portfolio. Most commercial factor models such as the Barra factor model, which we will review later, use a variation of Equation (7.4).

CHAPTER 8

Estimating the Elements of the CAPM

Given the central importance of the capital asset pricing model (CAPM) in finance theory and its general utility, a great deal of time and effort has been spent over the years trying to devise methods for calculating accurate alphas and betas for assets. Of course, the model talks about beta in the future; that is, beta measures the comovement of future returns and is thus related to the alpha or return tomorrow. Unfortunately, when we estimate beta, all we have to work with is theory and past data. Typically, estimates of beta are obtained by running a regression model on past data. There are a variety of practical considerations when estimating beta that if not dealt with properly can lead to wildly incorrect beta estimates. Some of the questions include: What do we use for the market proxy R_m? How long should the return holding period be? How many observations are required? But there are other problems as well. This chapter attempts to provide guidance on these problems.

THE CAPM WITH CONSTANT ALPHA AND BETA OVER TIME

Consider a market model regression equation, with returns in excess of the risk-free rate:[1]

$$r_{pt} = \alpha_p + \beta_p r_{bt} + \varepsilon_{pt},$$ (8.1)

---

[1] As discussed in Chapter 6, the term *excess return* is often used loosely. In this chapter it refers to the arithmetic excess return over the risk-free rate.

where for portfolio p over time $t = 1, \ldots, T$ we have

r_{pt} = portfolio return R_{pt} net of the risk-free rate R_{ft}, or $r_{pt} = R_{pt} - R_{ft}$

r_{bt} = return R_{bt} of a benchmark portfolio net of the risk-free rate, or $r_{bt} = R_{bt} - R_{ft}$

α_p = unconditional alpha

β_p = unconditional beta

ε_{pt} = regression error or residual otherwise known as specific return.

This model says essentially that the return for an asset or portfolio is equal to an alpha component, plus beta times the return on the benchmark, plus a specific return that is unique to the portfolio and presumably unique to the assets that compose the portfolio. *It is assumed that the alpha and beta are constant over the entire time, which may or may not be true.* Chapter 12 addresses time-varying alphas and betas.

Selecting a Market Proxy

If the benchmark is regarded as the market portfolio, then the regression gives direct estimates of a portfolio's alpha and CAPM beta. The first problem is selecting a market proxy for R_m. This is not as easy as it appears. What is the market? In the CAPM theory, the market consists of all assets globally. Practitioners usually adapt the theory to a single equity market such as the U.S. stock market, for example. The CAPM "market portfolio" is now a "benchmark portfolio." There is considerable debate about what the proper benchmark for even a single equity market should be. The consensus of most practitioners and theorists is that the proper one is a capitalization-weighted benchmark that includes all the assets that are likely to be chosen, with each asset weighted by the market value of that asset relative to the total value of the market. This is usually called a capitalization-weighted index. Broad market indexes like the Russell 3000 or Wilshire 5000 are more representative of the U.S. equity market than more narrowly defined indexes. We discuss benchmarks extensively beginning in Chapter 20.

Equation (8.1) is specified in excess returns, so we also need to choose the risk-free rate. Typically, a rolling 90-day T-bill rate or some other equivalent for risk-free investment is used. Note that the choice of a proxy for the risk-free rate might make a difference, although usually a very small one for common stocks. The reason that the estimated betas are similar is that the variance over time of most risk-free proxies is miniscule compared to the variance of common stocks.

PROBLEMS WITH THE USE OF INAPPROPRIATE BENCHMARKS

If you choose the wrong benchmark, very bad results can occur. As Richard Roll said, "Econometric difficulties may be encountered when attempting to fit the static equilibrium Sharpe model to time series. A major difficulty is due to measurement error in the 'riskless' and 'market' returns explanatory variables of the model."[2] He says further in 1978,

> To consider the beta as an attribute of the individual asset alone is a significant mistake. For every asset an index can be found to produce a beta of any desired magnitude however large or small. Thus, for every asset (or portfolio) judicious choice of the index can produce any desired measured "performance" (positive or negative), against the security market line.[3]

These are pretty strong words.

Alpha Is Ambiguous

When the benchmark is inappropriate, a regression on historical data will provide an analyst with alphas that are clearly incorrect. However, the more subtle problem is how you interpret alpha when the benchmarks are slightly different. For example, in Table 8.1 we show the annualized regression alpha for three stocks calculated against different indexes for the 232 months from 1987 through December of 2006. These alphas are the monthly alpha annualized.

---

[2] Richard Roll, "Bias in Fitting the Sharpe Model to Time Series Data," *Journal of Financial and Quantitative Analysis*, vol. 4, no. 3, September 1969, p. 278.

[3] Richard Roll, "Ambiguity When Performance Is Measured by the Securities Market Line," *Journal of Finance*, vol. 33, September 1978, p. 1056.

T A B L E 8.1

Annualized Alpha for Stocks versus Indexes

	GE	GM	XOM
R3000 alpha (%)	5.70	−1.19	9.83
S&P 500 alpha (%)	5.65	−0.85	9.82
R2000 alpha (%)	10.25	1.13	11.78

Source: http://finance.yahoo.com/q/hp?s=GE, GM and XOM. The data reflect price change only, ignoring dividends and other income.

Note that the S&P 500 and the Russell 3000 provide similar alpha estimates. The Russell 2000 on the other hand provides much higher and different alpha estimates. The three stocks GE, GM, and XOM are large-cap stocks, for which the small-cap Russell 2000 index is an inappropriate benchmark. An observant analyst might ask why the alpha for the S&P 500 relative to these very large cap stocks is different from the alpha against a broader Russell 3000. We will delve into these issues later, but suffice it to say the S&P 500's weighting of the securities is quite different from the Russell 3000 weighting for these securities in the index. The point here is that the alphas are different, and it is not obvious which is more accurate.

Beta Could Be Useless

As Roll points out, the alpha and beta that an analyst obtains are intimately bound up with the index they choose to represent the market. We just saw that three very large stocks have slightly different alphas relative to three well-known indexes. Therefore, it is highly likely that they will have different betas relative to those same indexes. Table 8.2 bears this out.

Could an analyst have guessed the beta from the alpha? You would have guessed that the large-cap indexes would have approximately the same betas but not what those values would be. The betas for the large-cap stocks are lower against the Russell 2000 than they are against the S&P 500 and the Russell 3000. This reflects the fact that the Russell 2000 has small highly volatile stocks.

TABLE 8.2

Beta for Stocks versus Indexes (Monthly Price Return Data)

	GE	GM	XOM
R3000 beta	1.0754	1.0801	0.5301
S&P 500 beta	1.1171	1.0774	0.5491
R2000 beta	0.5476	0.7479	0.3020

Source: http://finance.yahoo.com/q/hp?s=GE, GM and XOM. The data reflect price change only, ignoring dividends and other income.

OTHER ESTIMATION PROBLEMS

Window Length

When one computes regressions, one of the obvious questions is, How many observations do you need to arrive at the correct precision? In the previous examples we used 232 months of observations. Most analysts would argue that this is too long. The standard normally used is 60 months or five years. A 60-month window length is thought to roughly correspond to a typical business cycle—from the top of the market to the next top of the market. However, there is nothing in theory to specify exactly what the length of that window should be.

Let us examine the behavior of alpha and beta for the relationship between General Electric and the Russell 3000 to obtain an idea of how the alpha and beta change with different window lengths.

Table 8.3 is based on 60-month rolling windows of the regressions of the General Electric price returns on the Russell 3000 price returns. There are 173 windows beginning in August of 1992 and ending in December 2006. The statistics in the table reveal considerable variability in the alpha and beta estimates. The alphas range from –0.44 percent to a positive 1.43 percent, while the betas range from 0.738 to 1.325. Any other broad market index would have produced similar results. The conclusion is that the alphas and betas are probably not constant over time. However, note that the average standard error of the beta estimates and the variation of the window estimates are similar, which could suggest that the "true" beta is actually constant over time. The same argument could be made for the alpha estimates. Also be aware that the sample variance and

T A B L E 8.3

Statistics for 60-Month Regressions of General Electric Against Russell 3000

	Alpha	Beta	SE-alpha	SE-Beta	R^2
Minimum	−0.44	0.738	0.45	0.100	0.225
Maximum	1.43	1.325	0.82	0.182	0.705
Average	0.58	1.099	0.62	0.149	0.484
Standard deviation	0.46	0.143	0.12	0.015	0.098

Source: http://finance.yahoo.com/q/hp?s=GE, GM and XOM. The data reflect price change only, ignoring dividends and other income.

standard deviation are biased due to the autocorrelation induced in the estimates because of the overlapping windows.

In Figure 8.1 we show graphically the relationship between the alpha and beta for these regressions for General Electric. The graph shows that there can be considerable variability in alpha and beta.

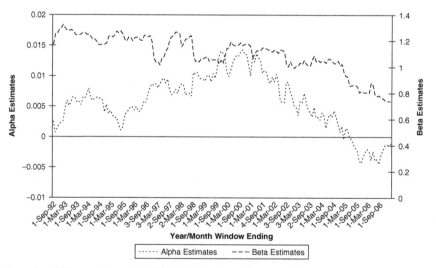

Source: http://finance.yahoo.com/q/hp?s=GE. The data reflect price change only, ignoring dividends and other income.

Figure 8.1 Alpha and beta estimates from regressions of General Electric against the Russell 3000 index using 60-month windows

If you change the windows to shorter intervals such as 24, 36, or 48 months, you will obtain results that are similar but not the same. As the window length becomes shorter, the volatility in the alpha and beta estimates increases as does the variability in R^2.

There is no theoretical reason why any one window length is superior to another. As we mentioned most analysts use the 60-month window that is thought to coincide with a five-year economic cycle. However, if you have reason to believe that the portfolio or the assets you are analyzing have changed their character more recently, you may want to choose a shorter window.

Another alternative is to weight each of the observations by giving greater weight to more recent observations and less weight to more remote observations. Exponentially declining weights are often chosen, but linear declining weights could be used equally well. The real question is how quickly an analyst believes the information in current data decays. In any case, shortening the window or down-weighting the distant observations will increase the volatility of the alpha estimates, beta estimates, and R^2. A generalized (weighted) least squares regression weights the observations inversely to the absolute value of the specific risk (the residual in the regressions) in each period; this may be useful if specific risk is thought to vary a lot over the sample period, because times with low specific risk are times when the regression relation may be measured more accurately.

Meaning of the Coefficient of Determination R^2

If a regression line passes exactly through every point on a scatterplot, it would explain all the variation. The further the line is away from the points, the less it is able to explain. The coefficient of determination R^2 gives the proportion of the variance or fluctuation around the mean of one variable that is predictable (i.e., determined) by the variations around the mean of another variable. It is also a measure that tells us how certain we can be in making predictions from a regression model because it tells us how well the regression line represents the data.

In Table 8.3, the quality of the fit of the regressions, given by R^2, varies from a low of 22.5 percent to a maximum of 70.5 percent with the average being about 48.4 percent—not once does it come close to 1.0.

The R^2 is the ratio of the explained variation to the total variation or

$$R^2 = 1 - \frac{\text{SSE}}{\text{SST}},$$

where SSE equals the residual sum of squares not explained by the regression equation and SST equals the total sum of squares. It is a proportion but is normally presented as a percentage.

The coefficient of determination lies in the range $0 < R^2 < 1$. Pearson's correlation coefficient between two variables x and y is usually noted as r_{xy}. The two measures of correlation are related, since $r_{xy} = \sqrt{R^2}$; thus if $r_{xy} = 0.922$, then $R^2 = 0.850$, which means that 85 percent of the total variation in y can be explained by the linear relationship between x and y (as described by the regression equation). The other 15 percent of the total variation in y remains unexplained.

Multiple Meanings of a Low Beta Value

The relationship between R^2 and beta is often underappreciated by analysts. As we saw earlier for the three large-cap stocks regressed against the Russell 2000, the betas were all much lower than they were against the Russell 3000 or the S&P 500. Analysts talk about low beta managers, but they rarely accompany the discussion with any information about the R^2.

One should bear in mind the following observation: when the relationship between two variables breaks down, empirically two things happen simultaneously (1) the R^2 of the fit of the two variables approaches zero and (2) the beta on the explanatory variable also approaches zero.

This means whenever you are examining a beta and hence the alpha associated with it, you must remember that the low beta may not be due to low risk but may be due entirely to the absence of the fit between the two series. When viewing estimated betas as measures of risk, one should not forget this—an absence of high R^2 does not mean a strategy is riskless. Furthermore, as the beta and R^2 approach zero, alpha approaches the mean of the dependent variable and can become quite large. Therefore, an analyst should report alpha, beta, and the coefficient of determination R^2.

Finally, an analyst should also remember that when a relationship is not strong, the slope of the regression line can be driven quite easily by a few outlier observations.

The bottom line is an analyst cannot view estimated alpha and beta without also paying close attention to the coefficient of determination. How high does the R^2 have to be? There is no perfect answer.

"Intervailing" Effects and Nonsynchronous Trading in Beta Estimates

The estimates of beta depend on the horizon of the returns used in the regression. For example, daily returns, monthly returns, and annual returns can give different beta estimates over the same historical time period. These differences in beta estimates are called *intervailing effects*.[4] Unfortunately, theory does not say what the "right" interval should be. Many analysts use monthly returns, as we have, but daily returns are also often used to estimate betas (e.g., Merrill Lynch data services).

When daily data are used, it is important that the stocks are frequently traded. If they are not, then even if the market index on the right-hand side of the regression is frequently traded, beta estimates will be biased. Essentially, this is because part of the return measured on the portfolio may be "stale." Scholes and Williams[5] suggest including the lagged value of the market index being used on the right-hand side of the regression to control for stale returns, on the left-hand side, and then adding up the two slope coefficients to get an adjusted beta. Asness et al.[6] show that this idea produces very different estimates of betas for hedge funds, which are thought to report "smoothed" or stale returns. If the market index itself has

---

[4] These effects are studied, for example, by Kalman J. Cohen, Steven F. Maier, Robert A. Schwartz, and David K. Whitcomb, "An Analysis of the Economic Justification for Consolidation in a Secondary Security Market," *Journal of Banking and Finance*, vol. 6, 1982, pp. 117–136.

[5] Myron Scholes and Joseph Williams, "Estimating Betas from Nonsynchronous Data," *Journal of Financial Economics*, vol. 5, 1977, pp. 309–327.

[6] Clifford Asness, Robert Krail, and John Liew, "Do Hedge Funds Hedge?" *Journal of Portfolio Management*, Fall 2001, pp. 6–19.

stale prices, Dimson and Marsh[7] suggest including future values of the measured index return as well.

Beta Corrections

In the early 1970s, Blume and Levy observed that sample betas tended to regress toward the mean of 1.0[8]; that is, betas below 1.0 moved upward toward 1.0 and betas above 1.0 moved downward toward 1.0. Blume's empirical examination of the data led to the heuristic that sample betas regress toward the mean in the following way:

$$\beta = 0.343 + 0.667\beta_{36 \text{ month}}.$$

Vasicek's Correction

An alternative adjustment method proposed by Vasicek in 1973 suggested a Bayesian method for adjusting betas. Vasicek's Bayesian beta correction is

$$\beta_i = \frac{\dfrac{\beta_p}{\sigma_p^2} + \dfrac{\beta_\beta}{\sigma_\beta^2}}{\dfrac{1}{\sigma_p^2} + \dfrac{1}{\sigma_\beta^2}},$$

where

β_i = Bayesian adjusted beta estimate asset for portfolio i

β_p = best estimate of beta for the portfolio using regression data

---

[7] Elroy Dimson and P. R. Marsh, "Sizing Up Stock Market Indices," *Investing*, vol. 4, no. 3, 1990, pp. 52–59.

[8] M. E. Blume, "On the Assessment of Risk," *Journal of Finance*, vol. 26, 1971, pp. 1–10; M. E. Blume, "Betas and Their Regression Tendencies," *Journal of Finance*, vol. 30, 1975, pp. 785–199; R. A. Levy, "On the Short Term Stationarity of Beta Coefficients," *Financial Analysts Journal*, vol. 27, 1971, pp. 55–72. A useful review of the problems involved in estimation of alpha and beta can be found in Elvis Jarnecic, Michael McCorry, and Roland Winn, "Periodic Return Time-Series, Capitalization Adjustments, and Beta Estimation," February 1997, at SIRCA.org.au/papers/1997001.pdf.

β_β = market average of betas. Usually this is 1.0, but it could be based on an analyst's prior knowledge and differ from 1.0. It represents the "prior" estimate of what the beta was before we look at any data.

σ_p^2 = estimated variance of beta estimates from regression output stock i

σ_β^2 = estimated variance of market betas taken across sample of all stocks. This measures our uncertainty about the prior estimate.

The market average of betas and σ_β^2 in particular requires a great deal of calculation. For these reasons, the Vasicek correction is normally obtained from a commercial vendor. The larger the standard error of the regression estimate of beta, the lower weight it will be given relative to the overall market average beta.[9]

Bid-Ask Bounce

Roll suggested that liquidity traders trading randomly against the bid-ask spread should produce negative autocorrelation in transaction price changes.[10] In a market with equally likely buy and sell orders, this bias and price change obviously affects the estimation of beta. It can also bias estimates of return volatility and thus information ratios. The bias is more pronounced in daily data than in monthly data, more pronounced in thinly traded or small-cap stocks, and small for very large cap stocks that trade frequently. The bias is worse for equal-weighted indexes and is small for market capitalization weighted indexes.[11]

[9] Oldrich Vasicek, "A Note on Using Cross-Sectional Information in Bayesian Estimation of Security Betas," *Journal of Finance*, vol. 28, 1973, pp. 1233–1239.

[10] See Richard Roll, "A Simple Implicit Measure of the Effective Bid-Ask Spread in an Efficient Market," *The Journal of Finance*, vol. 39, no. 4, September 1984, pp. 1127–1139.

[11] Marshall Blume and Robert Stambaugh, "Biases in Computed Returns: An Application to the Size Effect," *Journal of Financial Economics*, vol. 12, 1983, pp. 387–404.

CHAPTER 9

What Is Risk?

A fundamental assumption in financial analysis is that it is "irrational" for investors to engage in risk taking if investment is not rewarded with a return that is above the risk-free rate or the fundamental time value of money. Implicit in this idea is that all investment has risk for which investors deserve compensation. However, there are different kinds of risks. There is the risk of losing all your money. There is the risk that your wealth will fall below a specified level. There is the risk that you will not be able to liquidate your investments at a time of your choosing for a reasonable price. There is the risk that the owner or manager of the asset you buy will default on his or her promises or contracts.

TYPES OF RISK

Economic "risk factors" such as business cycle risk, default risk, and volatility risk will cause asset prices to change by varying amounts as the factor changes. Each of these kinds of risks is uniquely different and applies to some asset classes more than to others.

Table 9.1 lists a variety of risks that can be identified when investing. This list is not completely exhaustive for every asset class, and not every asset is exposed to each risk, but the list provides a range of the risks that might be encountered.

TABLE 9.1

Types and Nature of Various Financial Risks

Type of Risk	The Nature of the Risks Involved
Credit	The risk that borrowers will not be able to pay their loans on time or they might declare bankruptcy
Default	The risk that a financial entity will default on the terms of the obligation by not making payments or reneging on other contract terms
Business cycle	The risk that the economy or area of business of an entity will fail to be profitable
Interest rate	The risk that interest rates in the marketplace will rise or fall, affecting the value of the investment
Exchange rate	The risk that foreign exchange rates will rise or fall thereby changing the economic terms of the entity's business and/or the value of the investment in terms of the investor's home currency
Liquidity	The risk that investors will not be able to buy or sell securities when they choose at reasonable prices
Volatility	The risk that the historic volatility or variability of outcomes in financial markets will change thereby increasing or decreasing the riskiness of financial asset prices
Political	The risk that the environment for business will change dramatically due to governmental action or political instability
Market	The risk that asset prices will appreciate or fall due to general overall asset market moves
Legal	The risk that legal actions will impair the value of the investment
Operational	The risk inherent in a business that the physical operations (e.g., manufacturing processes) will be impaired
Settlement	The risk that the terms of a financial obligation will be unsuccessfully met due to a financial system operation that is less efficient than expected

The methods for measuring all these risks are beyond the scope of this book.[1]

---

[1] A general book that focuses on S&P's methods for risk assessment is Arnaud de Servigny and Olivier Renault, *The Standard & Poor's Guide to Measuring and Managing Credit Risk* (New York : McGraw-Hill, 2004). A comprehensive statistical and mathematical treatment of risk measurement can be found in Philippe Jorion, *Financial Risk Manager Handbook,* 4th ed. (Hoboken, NJ: John Wiley & Sons, 2007). This is the main text for the Global Association of Risk Professionals (GARP) Financial Risk Management program. For short explanations, see also http://en.wikipedia.org/wiki/Liquidity_risk and follow the threads to other kinds of risk. Also see Les A. Balzer, "Measuring Investment Risk: A Review," *The Journal of Investing,* vol. 3, no. 3 (Fall), 1994.

A BASIC MEASURE OF RISK AS
VOLATILITY IN RETURNS

The most common measure of risk is the volatility of return. Following Eugene Fama, we consider here that returns for all practical purposes are approximately normally distributed on a monthly basis.[2] This assumption is highly useful. It should also be pointed out that if the returns are substantially nonnormal, some of the methods we review in this section may not accurately measure volatility.

Stand-Alone Variance and Standard Deviation

Volatility is measured by the standard deviation of a return distribution. The standard deviation is the square root of the variance, which is the expected squared deviation of return from the mean. Analyzing one set of returns without considering their correlations with other returns is sometimes referred to as the "stand-alone" standard deviation.

Standard deviation has useful statistical properties. For example, if returns are normally distributed, then we would expect about 68 percent of the return observations to fall within the range of plus or minus one standard deviation from the mean, about 95 percent to fall within plus or minus two standard deviations, and about 99.7 percent to fall within plus or minus three standard deviations.

Armed with a standard deviation and knowledge of the normal distribution, we can make probability statements about how often good or bad events occur. For these reasons the standard deviation is a fundamentally useful measure of risk for a distribution of asset returns.

To estimate the standard deviation σ from a sample of N returns, the formula is

$$\sigma = \sqrt{\frac{1}{N-1}\sum_{i=1}^{N}(R_i - \bar{R})^2},\qquad(9.1)$$

---

[2] Eugene F. Fama, *Foundations of Finance* (New York: Basic Books, 1976), p. 43.

where

R_i = return for observation i

$\bar{R} = \dfrac{1}{N}\displaystyle\sum_{i=1}^{N} R_i$, the mean return

N = number of returns in the sample.

The denominator, $N - 1$, is used in Equation (9.1) to correct for bias when the mean $\bar{R}$ is estimated, because the sum of squares around the estimated mean will be smaller in a sample than the sum of squares around the true mean. The formula using $N - 1$ is called the unbiased or sample standard deviation. If the mean is assumed to be known with certainty, then the sum of squared deviations would be divided by N. The formula using N in the denominator is called the population standard deviation.

Table 9.2 shows an example of how these numbers are calculated. In this example we have chosen three years of quarterly returns for the Russell 3000 from March 2003 to December 2005. We calculate the standard deviation of this short time series of returns.

The mean of this sample is 12.82 percent (very high by historical standards). The table also shows the deviations from the mean. The average of the squared deviations is about 239 percent-squared, and the square root of that is the population standard deviation of 15.45 percent. The sample standard deviation is 16.13 percent.

Statistical tables tell us that about 68 percent of the observations should fall within plus or minus one standard deviation of the mean. In the right hand column of the table, we have noted whether the value falls within this range. We would expect about 8 out of 12 quarters to fall within this range, and we observe 9.

Annualized Standard Deviation Based on Periodic Returns

To compare returns over different time periods we usually convert them to a standardized measure such as annualized returns. It is therefore useful to be able to convert a standard deviation computed for one holding period length to an annualized number. Equation (9.2) demonstrates how to calculate this:

$$\sigma_{\text{annualized}} = \sigma\sqrt{n}, \tag{9.2}$$

TABLE 9.2

Standard Deviation of Russell 3000 Quarterly Returns

Date	R3000 Quarterly Return (%)	Deviation (%)	Within ±1σ
Mar-03	−24.66	−37.48	No
Jun-03	0.77	−12.05	Yes
Sep-03	25.92	13.11	Yes
Dec-03	31.06	18.25	No
Mar-04	38.19	25.38	No
Jun-04	20.46	7.65	Yes
Sep-04	14.26	1.45	Yes
Dec-04	11.95	−0.87	Yes
Mar-05	7.09	−5.73	Yes
Jun-05	8.05	−4.77	Yes
Sep-05	14.57	1.76	Yes
Dec-05	6.12	−6.70	Yes
Mean	12.82%	0.00%	
Population Standard Deviation	15.45%		
Sample (Unbiased) Standard Deviation	16.13%		

Source: Russell research database.

where n is the number of holding periods in a year ($n = 4$ corresponds to quarterly and $n = 12$ corresponds to monthly, for example) and σ is the standard deviation calculated for the given holding period.

The standard deviation of returns of the Russell 3000 normally ranges between 16 and 20 percent annually. In the example in Table 9.1, the standard deviation of the Russell 3000 quarterly returns was 16.13 percent. Given $n = 4$, the annualized standard deviation would be

$$\sigma_{annualized} = 16.13\% \times \sqrt{4} = 16.13\% \times 2 = 32.26\%.$$

This sample period had double the volatility that we normally see due to the large positive and negative deviations in the first few quarters of this time period.

This annualization calculation assumes there is no correlation among the periodic return values over time and holds exactly for continuously compounded returns. The formula is often applied to discretely compounded returns and returns that may have correlation, as a convenient approximation.

MEASURING BAD VARIATION

When talking about risk earlier, we pointed out that there are many ways to define risk. The standard deviation treats upside deviations from the mean the same as downside deviations. From a wealth maximization point of view we might view upside variation as good variation and downside variation as bad variation. We might also consider return values below a given target as undesirable. We could say for example that we do not like any returns below 2 percent. Harry Markowitz in his classic book *Portfolio Selection*[3] devotes a chapter to semivariance, and the risk measure has been applied in various settings.[4] The concept is particularly useful either if the return distribution is asymmetric, as can happen in certain asset classes or portfolio strategies with option-like characteristics, or if a return target is of particular importance to the investor.

---

[3] Harry M. Markowitz, *Portfolio Selection: Efficient Diversification Investment* (New Haven, CT: Yale University Press, 1959), chapter 9, pp. 188–201.

[4] See V. S. Bawa and E. B. Lindenberg, "Capital Market Equilibrium in a Mean-Lower Partial Moment Framework," *Journal of Financial Economics*, vol. 5, 1977, pp. 189–200; W. V. Harlow, "Asset Allocation in a Downside Risk Framework," *Financial Analysts Journal*, Sept–Oct 1991; B. M. Rom and K. Ferguson, "Post-Modern Portfolio Theory Comes of Age," *Journal of Investing*, Winter 1993; D. R. Cariño and Y. Fan, "Alternative Risk Measures for Asset Allocation," *Gestion Collective Internationale*, no. 2 (July/August) 1993, pp. 47–51; F. A. Sortino and L. N. Price, "Performance Measurement in a Downside Risk Framework," *Journal of Investing*, vol 3., 1994, pp. 50–58; L. Balzer, "Measuring Investment Risk: A Review," *Journal of Investing*, vol. 3., no. 3 (Fall) 1994, pp. 47–58; D. R. Cariño and A. Turner, "Multiperiod Asset Allocation," in *Worldwide Asset and Liability Modeling*, ed. by W. T. Ziemba and J. Mulvey, Cambridge University Press, 1997.

Target Semivariance and Downside Risk

The concept of semivariance is analogous to variance, but instead of squaring all deviations from the mean, we square only negative deviations from the mean. The square root of semivariance is called semideviation. The concept is further generalized by introducing a return target, or minimal acceptable return (MAR). Instead of measuring deviations below the mean, we measure deviations below the target. *Target semivariance* is the expected squared deviation below the target, and *target semideviation* is the square root of target semivariance. Target semideviation is often simply called *downside deviation* or *downside risk*.

A more general methodology for dealing with downside variation is called lower partial moments (LPM). The formula for target semideviation is a special case of LPM. The LPM methodology also uses a downside return target or MAR, τ. Below this point any return is assumed to be a bad variation. Typical targets are the mean, the risk-free rate, or zero.

The formula for computing the lower partial moment of degree p, given a target τ, is

$$\text{LPM}_p = \sum_{i=1}^{N} w_i d(i)(R_i - \tau)^p, \tag{9.3}$$

where

$d(i)$ = function that returns 1 or 0, $d(i) = \begin{cases} 1 & \text{if} \quad R_i \leq \tau \\ 0 & \text{if} \quad R_i > \tau \end{cases}$

$R_i - \tau$ = return observation i minus the target τ

τ = target return or MAR

p = power to which to raise the deviation, that is, for semivariance, $p = 2$

w_i = weight applied to each return. For an equal-weighted sample of returns, $w_i = 1/N$. This value can also be viewed as a probability of the return occurrence.

N = total number of returns

Table 9.3 presents an example of the calculation of the downside deviation for a sample of returns given a target of zero.

TABLE 9.3

Russell Top 50 Index Quarterly Downside Semivariance

Quarterly Analysis with Tau = 0.0%			
Quarter	Return (%)	$d(i)$	Deviation
200109	−13.39	1	−13.39
200112	8.98	0	0.00
200203	−1.69	1	−1.69
200206	−16.40	1	−16.40
200209	−15.93	1	−15.93
200212	10.55	0	0.00
200303	−2.52	1	−2.52
200306	13.95	0	0.00
200309	1.16	0	0.00
200312	10.17	0	0.00
200403	−0.57	1	−0.57
200406	1.04	0	0.00
Mean squared deviation = target semivariance:			59.2957
Target semideviation or downside risk:			7.70

Source: Russell research database.

Note in Table 9.3 that the only returns that enter into the final calculations are the quarters with a 1 in column 3, the $d(i)$ column. Notice also that we are using equal weights in computing the statistic. The square root of the lower partial moment of degree 2 is the target semideviation.

Downside semivariance is a special case of LPM with the power $p = 2$ and τ set equal to the mean.

If $R_i = R_p - R_f$ (that is, return net of the risk-free rate) is chosen by the analyst, and τ is set to zero, then the downside deviation reflects the variation of negative excess returns.

Downside deviation is a useful statistic when comparing distributions that are not normal and have different means. You can apply the same target τ to each distribution and see how much downside each has.

Upside Semideviation

Upside risk, also referred to as upside semideviation, is the converse of downside semideviation. The only difference is the target τ is used to exclude values below a certain level rather than above it. Since upside variation is presumably good, this statistic can be used to identify those distributions that are desirable. The ratio of upside semivariance to downside semivariance can be used to rank order distributions in terms of desirability relative to a given target.

Positive Skewness in a Return Distribution Is Good

Skewness measures the degree of asymmetry of a distribution. The ratio of upside semivariance to downside semivariance is one measure of asymmetry. Positive skewness in a return distribution is desirable because it means that there is a chance of extremely high returns, but not much chance of extremely low returns. The majority of the observations are below the mean, and the long tail on the upside is the result of outliers on the upside. If the distribution is symmetrically distributed, then the skewness value is zero. In a symmetric distribution, like the normal, the upside and downside risks are the same. For example, the downside semivariance (when the target equals the mean) is half the variance.

Equation (9.4) gives a formula for skewness. Notice that it is the same formula as the standard deviation formula but each deviation is cubed rather than squared. At the end of the calculations, the cube root of the average cubed deviation is taken rather than the square root as in the standard deviation. This yields an average cubed deviation that maintains the notion of an average deviation but adds the direction that most of the big deviations take:

$$\text{Skew} = \sqrt[3]{\frac{1}{N} \sum_{i=1}^{N} (R_i - \bar{R})^3}. \tag{9.4}$$

COVARIANCE

The exploration of the importance of covariance in the construction of efficient portfolios was also contributed by Harry Markowitz. The formula for calculating the sample covariance between two return series is based on comparing the extent to which the deviations of the two series from their respective means tend to reinforce each other or offset each other. These notions are captured in Equation (9.5):

$$C(R_i, R_j) = \frac{1}{T-1} \sum_{t=1}^{T} (R_{it} - \bar{R}_i)(R_{jt} - \bar{R}_j)$$

$$\rho_{i,j} = \frac{C(R_i, R_j)}{\sigma_i \sigma_j}$$

(9.5)

where

$C(R_i, R_j)$ = sample covariance of asset i with asset j returns

$\rho_{i,j}$ = correlation between asset i and asset j returns

σ_i, σ_j = standard deviations of asset i and asset j returns

T = number of returns in the sample

R_{it}, R_{jt} = returns of assets i and j at time t

$\bar{R}_i$, $\bar{R}_j$ = means of returns for assets i and j.

It is possible to find a portfolio of two assets that will have a variance and standard deviation of zero if the correlation between the return patterns of the two assets is negative one, or perfectly negatively correlated.[5] The positive deviation of one asset above its mean is perfectly offset by the negative deviation of the other asset below its mean. So finding the covariance among assets is important in controlling the major measure of risk, the portfolio standard deviation. In fact, the variance of the returns of a portfolio is an average of the covariances among the securities in the portfolio. Standard deviations do not average in portfolios, but covariances do.

---

[5] Zvi Bodie, Alex Kane, and Alan J. Marcus, *Investments*, 2d ed. (Boston, MA: Irwin, 1993), p. 220.

In Table 9.4 we show the calculations for the covariance between General Electric and Exxon Mobil for the 60 months from January 2002 through December of 2006. We show (in abbreviated form) the observed monthly returns, the deviation of the monthly returns from the means, and the product of the two deviations. These are summed up to 9.1509 percent and then divided by 60 observations to arrive at the covariance of 0.1525 percent. We show the means and standard deviations for the monthly returns of each stock as well as the correlation between the two portfolio returns, which works out to be 0.8534.

Substituting the values from Table 9.4 into Equation (9.5) to calculate the correlation coefficient,

$$\rho = 0.8534 = \frac{0.1525\%}{(3.6068\% \times 4.9545\%)/100}.$$

T A B L E 9.4

Equal-Weighted Covariance of GE and XOM

Date	GE Return (%)	XOM Return (%)	GE Deviations (%)	XOM Deviations (%)	Product of Deviations (%)
1-Dec-06	1.05	0.20	0.54	−0.74	−0.0040
1-Nov-06	1.93	2.50	1.42	1.57	0.0223
2-Oct-06	3.54	5.73	3.03	4.79	0.1453
.	.	.	.	.	.
.	.	.	.	.	.
.	.	.	.	.	.
1-Mar-02	4.30	7.91	3.79	6.98	0.2640
4-Feb-02	−2.19	−2.84	−2.70	−3.78	0.1021
2-Jan-02	−1.34	−1.09	−1.85	−2.03	0.0375
Standard deviation (SD):	3.6068%	4.9545%		Sum covariations:	9.1509%
Average:	0.51%	0.93%		Covariance:	0.1525%
Correlation = covariance/SD(GE)*SD(XOM) = :					0.8534

Source: http://finance.yahoo.com/q?s=GE and XOM. Price return only.

TRACKING ERROR AND RESIDUAL RISK

When we compare a portfolio's return against a benchmark, the concept of risk as volatility of return extends to the measurement of the volatility of excess return. Roughly speaking, the extra volatility undertaken for the sake of excess return constitutes the risk of active management.

Regardless of whether excess return is measured arithmetically or geometrically (see Chapter 6), the measures of volatility described in this chapter can be applied to excess return. If the average excess return is regarded as the reward of an active portfolio, then the standard deviation of excess return can be regarded as the corresponding measure of risk. The terms *active risk* and *tracking error* are usually defined simply as the standard deviation of arithmetic excess return.

In the context of the CAPM and factor models of returns, a closely related concept called *residual risk* is relevant. Recall from Chapter 8 that one can estimate various model parameters by regressing portfolio returns on the benchmark returns:

$$R_p - R_f = \alpha + \beta(R_b - R_f) + \varepsilon, \tag{9.6}$$

where

R_p = portfolio return

α = alpha (intercept coefficient) or risk-adjusted excess return

β = portfolio beta (slope coefficient) or sensitivity to the benchmark portfolio

R_b = benchmark return

R_f = risk-free rate of return

ε = error term or residual return

The standard deviation of the residual ε is called *residual risk*. From the form of the regression Equation (9.6), we can see that volatility of the portfolio return can be decomposed into two components. The first, contributed by the benchmark multiplied by beta, is systematic in that it affects all assets with nonzero betas. The second component is residual risk.

When beta equals 1.0, because the regression errors (ε's) must sum to zero, alpha in Equation (9.6) becomes the difference between the average portfolio return and the average benchmark return. That is, it becomes the average arithmetic excess return of the portfolio over the benchmark. The standard deviation of the residual becomes equal to the standard deviation of the excess return. Residual risk and tracking error are equal when beta equals 1.0.

If beta does not equal 1.0, then the alpha estimated in Equation (9.6) is not the same as mean excess return of the fund over the benchmark, and tracking error differs from residual risk. It is very common, however, to simply assume that beta is equal to 1.0, especially if the benchmark is well-suited to the portfolio. In this case, analysts often use the terms tracking error, active risk, and residual risk synonymously.

Another definition of tracking error is based on the average sum of squares of the excess return, instead of the standard deviation of excess return. This version is presented by Schein:[6]

$$\text{RMSTE} = \sqrt{\frac{1}{T}\sum(R_p - R_b)^2}. \tag{9.7}$$

This formula is the root mean square (RMS) excess return, which we call RMS tracking error.

What does statistical theory tell us about the behavior of RMS tracking error? If stock returns are normally distributed or the sample sizes are large enough, we would also expect estimates of beta to be normally distributed. The joint normal distribution produces the elongated "fireman's hat" distribution. For any probability contour line, we obtain an oval. The length and width of the oval around the security market line depends on the standard deviations of the stock distribution and the beta distribution. These ideas are captured in Figure 9.1.

We can see the relationships more clearly in the following by substituting the regression model (9.6) of portfolio return into Equation (9.7):

$$\text{RMSTE} = \sqrt{\frac{1}{T}\sum[\alpha + \beta(R_b - R_f) + \varepsilon - (R_b - R_f)]^2}.$$

[6] Jay L. Schein, "Tracking Error and the Information Ratio," *Journal of Investment Consulting*, vol. 2, no. 2, June 2000, pp. 18–22.

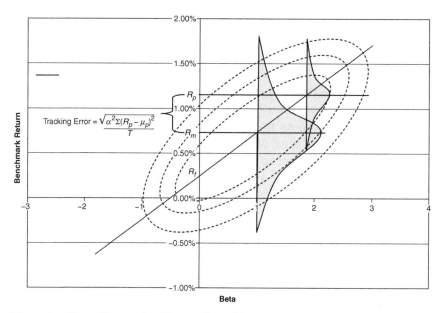

Figure 9.1 Security market line and tracking error

Rearranging the formula we obtain:

$$\text{RMSTE} = \sqrt{\frac{1}{T} \sum [\alpha + \varepsilon + (\beta - 1)(R_b - R_f)]^2}.$$

From this formulation we can see that RMS tracking error is a function of three elements: (1) the size of alpha, (2) the size of portfolio residual risk, and (3) the distance the portfolio beta is away from 1.0. As alpha moves away from zero either positively or negatively, it contributes to RMS tracking error. This makes sense, because by holding the benchmark we have $\alpha = 0$ and $\beta = 1$. To generate alpha you have to depart from holding the benchmark. Of note is the independent role played in RMS tracking error by the differences between the portfolio beta and 1.0. The further away from 1.0 beta becomes, the greater is the tracking error. As the beta moves away from 1.0, RMS tracking error increases independently from the contribution of alpha.

The central point is that the only time alpha equals average arithmetic excess return, and residual risk equals tracking error, is when beta equals 1.0. Be careful when you use the terms *alpha* and *tracking error*.

CHAPTER 10

Risk-Adjusted Return Measures

So far we have presented methods for calculating returns and risk. One of the problems an analyst inevitably encounters is that of figuring out which investment is more attractive than the others. In order to answer this question, the analyst needs to be able to compare different investments in terms of their "desirability." The simplest approach to comparing assets or portfolios of assets is to create a universe (a comprehensive collection) of like assets or portfolios. We will defer the discussion of universes to Chapter 20 on benchmarks. In this chapter, we will focus on statistical measures of asset returns that can be used to rank portfolios in terms of their desirability.

The most commonly used dimension of desirability is the amount of return the investor receives relative to the risk the investor takes to obtain that return. Presuming that more return is preferable to less, and that less risk, however defined, is preferable to more, a variety of measures have been developed that combine return and risk into a single statistic to assess this desirability. This chapter reviews the most well known of those measures. These return-to-risk measures differ according to the way they measure risk and return. As a consequence each of these measures gives slightly different information. By considering several measures, an analyst may gain more insight into a portfolio's desirability than if only a single measure were used.

The measures are defined in terms of a market model regression:

$$R_i - R_f = \alpha_i + \beta_i(R_b - R_f) + \varepsilon_i, \tag{10.1}$$

where

R_i = asset i return

R_f = risk-free rate of return

R_b = benchmark or market return

α_i, β_i = alpha and beta for asset i with respect to the benchmark

ε_i = residual return of asset i.

σ_i denotes the standard deviation of $(R_i - R_f)$, σ_b is the standard deviation of $(R_b - R_f)$, and $\sigma(\varepsilon_i)$ denotes the standard deviation of ε_i. For a portfolio of assets, where the portfolio return is given by $R_p = \Sigma_i w_i R_i$ with portfolio weights w_i, the subscript p will denote the associated portfolio quantities in the regression. Expected values are denoted by $E(\bullet)$. If estimated from averages, the arithmetic average return (not geometric) should be used, as discussed in Chapter 4.

SHARPE RATIO

One of the simplest and most well known measures of risk-adjusted performance is the Sharpe ratio.[1] The measure is highly useful because it is defined simply in terms of the mean and standard deviation of return. In the framework of the CAPM, investors seek to maximize utility defined as $U = E(R_p) - A\sigma_p^2$, where $E(R_p)$ is the portfolio expected return, σ_p^2 is the portfolio variance of return, and A is a coefficient of risk aversion.[2] Maximizing the utility formulated this way is equivalent to maximizing the Sharpe ratio. The Sharpe ratio is

$$SR_p = \frac{E(R_p - R_f)}{\sigma_p}. \tag{10.2}$$

Expressed in terms of expectations, Equation (10.2) is a forward looking, or ex-ante, concept. Replacing the expected returns

[1] William F. Sharpe, "Mutual Fund Peformance," *Journal of Business*, vol. 39, no. 1, January 1966, pp. 119–138; "The Sharpe Ratio," *Journal of Portfolio Management*, Fall 1994.

[2] See Jonathan Berk, "Necessary Condition for CAPM," *Journal of Economic Theory*, vol. 73, 1997, pp. 245–257.

and standard deviation with estimated values gives a historical, or ex-post, measure of risk-adjusted return.

In the hypothetical world of the CAPM, the maximum attainable Sharpe ratio is that of the market portfolio. This result enables each investor to maximize utility by holding a combination of the market portfolio and the risk-free asset. The Sharpe ratio of the market portfolio is the reward for a unit of systematic risk, according to the CAPM.

In the real world, aside from its theoretical foundation, the ratio of reward (average return net of the risk-free rate) to risk (standard deviation of return) provides a meaningful basis to rank the desirability of portfolios. All other characteristics being equal, most investors would prefer a portfolio with a greater Sharpe ratio than one with a lesser ratio.

Note that the ratio is not generally used to evaluate the performance of individual securities, because it does not account for the correlation between one security and another.

Table 10.1 shows examples of the calculations for three common U.S. equity market indexes. These data are based on monthly price changes from September 1987 through December 2006. To facilitate comparisons, Sharpe ratios (and other ratios) are usually annualized—using monthly data, the ratio would be multiplied by $12/\sqrt{12}$, that is, by $\sqrt{12}$.

Over this 232-month period, the broadest index, the Russell 3000, had a slightly higher Sharpe ratio than the large-cap index, the S&P 500, or the small-cap index, the Russell 2000. This result is

T A B L E 10.1

Sharpe Ratios for Three U.S. Equity Indexes

	R3000	S&P 500	R2000
Average excess return (%)	9.00	8.64	9.84
Standard deviation (%)	14.83	14.76	19.19
Sharpe ratio	0.60	0.59	0.51

Source: Yahoo! Finance, http://finance.yahoo.com/q/hp. The data reflect monthly price change only, ignoring dividends and other income, from September 1987 to December 2006. Return is in excess of the risk-free rate. All measures are annualized.

understandable, given that both large-cap and small-cap stocks are included in a broad market index like the Russell 3000.

SORTINO RATIO

The Sortino ratio is an extension of the idea behind the Sharpe ratio, that calls attention to an investor's return target or minimal acceptable return (MAR). Downside risk was defined in Chapter 9 in terms of deviations below a target. The Sortino ratio uses target semideviation in the denominator instead of the standard deviation. This is particularly useful when the return distribution is asymmetric or if a return target is of particular importance to the investor. The formula for the original Sortino ratio[3] is

$$SR_{down} = \frac{E(R_p - \tau)}{\sigma_{down}}, \tag{10.3}$$

where

$E(R_p - \tau)$ = expected portfolio return in excess of a target τ

σ_{down} = target semideviation relative to the target τ.

Various ways of calculating the Sortino ratio from return data have been proposed. The original authors advocate fitting an asymmetric probability distribution (such as a lognormal distribution) to the returns and calculating the ratio from the fitted distribution.[4] More often, the ratio is calculated directly from the sample average (in the numerator) and sample target semideviation (in the denominator). Further, the average return in the numerator is sometimes replaced by the average in excess of the risk-free rate:

$$SR_{down} = \frac{E(R_p - R_f)}{\sigma_{down}}, \tag{10.4}$$

---

[3] Frank Sortino and Lee Price, "Performance Measurement in a Downside Risk Framework," *Journal of Investing*, 1994, pp. 59–65.

[4] For a full discussion, see Frank Sortino and Stephen Satchell, eds., *Managing Downside Risk in Financial Markets*, Oxford: Butterworth-Heinemann, 2001.

TABLE 10.2

Sortino Ratios for Three U.S. Equity Indexes

	R3000	S&P 500	R2000
Average return in excess of the risk-free rate (%)	9.00	8.64	9.84
Downside semideviation, target = 0 (%)	11.57	11.36	14.93
Sortino ratio	0.77	0.76	0.66

Source: Yahoo! Finance, http://finance.yahoo.com/q/hp. The data reflect monthly price change only, ignoring dividends and other income, from September 1987 to December 2006. All measures are annualized.

where

$E(R_p - R_f)$ = expected portfolio return in excess of the risk-free rate R_f

σ_{down} = target semideviation relative to the target τ.

Because the risk-free rate tends to be much less volatile than the portfolio return, the numerators in Equations (10.3) and (10.4) differ approximately by a constant and portfolio rankings based on either version are likely to be the same. The return target is most important for calculating the downside risk in the denominator.

Table 10.2 shows the Sortino ratio calculations for the three indexes using the same data as in Table 10.1. We set the target return at zero. Because market indexes tend to have symmetric return distributions, the relative ranking of these indexes based on the Sortino ratio is the same as that based on the Sharpe ratio over this time period.

MODIGLIANI-MODIGLIANI MEASURE

The Modigliani-Modigliani or M-squared measure[5] was proposed as an alternate way of comparing portfolios with different Sharpe ratios. Instead of a ratio, the measure expresses the risk-adjusted performance as an adjusted return, that of a portfolio with the same risk as

---

[5] Franco Modigliani and Leah Modigliani, "Risk-Adjusted Performance: How to Measure It and Why," *Journal of Portfolio Management*, vol. 23, no. 2, Winter 1997, pp. 45–54.

a market benchmark. Consider a reference portfolio formed by combining the original portfolio return R_p with a position in cash R_f:

$$\left(\frac{\sigma_b}{\sigma_p}\right)R_p + \left(1 - \frac{\sigma_b}{\sigma_p}\right)R_f.$$

The leverage factor σ_b/σ_p is the amount by which the portfolio volatility must be scaled to make the reference portfolio's volatility match that of the benchmark. The expected return of the reference portfolio, after rearranging terms, is the the Modigliani-Modigliani measure (MM):

$$\text{MM}_p = \left[\frac{E(R_p - R_f)}{\sigma_p}\right]\sigma_b + E(R_f) = \text{SR}_p\sigma_b + E(R_f). \qquad (10.5)$$

Therefore, MM is simply the portfolio return adjusted upward or downward to match the benchmark's standard deviation. It is expressed in units of return that can be directly compared to the benchmark return. Subtracting the risk-free rate from Equation (10.5), the MM excess return can be compared to the benchmark's excess return. Table 10.3 shows the MM for the three indexes under the assumption that the Russell 3000 is the benchmark portfolio. Note that the Russell 3000's Modigliani and Modigliani adjusted excess return is exactly the same as its excess return. The S&P 500

T A B L E 10.3

Modigliani-Modigliani Measures for Three U.S. Equity Indexes

	R3000	S&P 500	R2000
Average excess return (%)	9.00	8.64	9.84
Standard deviation (%)	14.83	14.76	19.19
Sharpe ratio (%)	0.60	0.59	0.51
Modigliani-Modigliani excess return (%)	9.00	8.76	7.56

Source: Yahoo! Finance, http://finance.yahoo.com/q/hp. The data reflect monthly price change only, ignoring dividends and other income, from September 1987 to December 2006. Return is in excess of the risk-free rate. All measures are annualized.

standard deviation was below the Russell 3000 standard deviation; hence, its MM is just slightly higher. Meanwhile, the Russell 2000 standard deviation is higher than the Russell 3000 standard deviation; hence, the MM adjusted return is less. Notice, however, that the relative rankings remain the same as with the Sharpe ratio. This will always be the case.

JENSEN'S ALPHA

The expected return of an asset in excess of what the CAPM predicts it to be, was proposed by Jensen as a performance measure.[6] As introduced in Chapter 7, Jensen's alpha is

$$\alpha_i = E(R_i - R_f) - \beta_i E(R_b - R_f). \tag{10.6}$$

Alpha is the expected return adjusted for the return due to taking market risk, or risk-adjusted excess return. We can rewrite Equation (10.6) as

$$\alpha_i = E(R_i) - [\beta_i E(R_b) + (1 - \beta_i)E(R_f)].$$

This formulation shows that alpha is the expected return in excess of a "benchmark," where the benchmark is a combination of the market index and the risk-free asset, held in just the right proportions so as to obtain the same beta risk as the asset or portfolio R_i.

The values for alpha and beta are normally obtained from regression analysis of a return series on a market proxy. Table 10.4 shows examples of alpha using the Russell 3000 as the market proxy.

Over this time period, General Electric and Exxon Mobil both had positive alphas of fairly substantial amounts. Recalling our discussion in Chapter 8 on estimating the CAPM, we note that the R^2 of all three stocks against the Russell 3000 is quite low. Two of the three stocks have a beta greater than 1.0, but Exxon Mobil's beta is quite low with a low R^2 indicating that the benchmark does not fit Exxon Mobil's returns very well. This in turn calls into question how accurate this estimate of alpha really is.

---

[6] Michael Jensen, "The Performance of Mutual Funds in the Period 1945–1964," *Journal of Finance*, vol. 23, no. 2, May 1968, pp. 389–416.

T A B L E 10.4

Regression Statistics for Three Large-Cap Stocks and Three Indexes with the
Russell 3000 as the Market Proxy

	R3000	S&P 500	R2000	GE	GM	XOM
Alpha (%)	0.00	−0.12	0.12	5.52	−1.20	9.36
Beta	1.00	0.99	1.08	1.08	1.08	0.53
R square (%)	100.0	98.2	70.0	50.8	24.6	23.4
Residual standard deviation (%)	0.00	1.94	10.50	15.73	28.16	14.27

Source: Yahoo! Finance, http://finance.yahoo.com/q/hp. The data reflect monthly price change only, ignoring
dividends and other income, from September 1987 to December 2006. Return is in excess of the risk-free rate.
All measures are annualized.

TREYNOR'S MEASURE

One of the drawbacks of the Sharpe ratio is that it's divided by the
standard deviation of the portfolio, which is not a good measure of
risk particularly in a situation where the asset or portfolio can be
combined with other assets or portfolios to diversify away residual
risk. The Sharpe ratio is also problematic when comparing situations
that involve the use of leverage. In situations where residual risk can
be diversified away, the Treynor measure[7] is a better measure for
comparing assets that may be combined into portfolios. The Treynor
measure is calculated according to the following formula:

$$T_p = \frac{E(R_p - R_f)}{\beta_p}, \tag{10.7}$$

where the notation is the same as we have been using previously.
As with other measures, the expected returns can be estimated from
averages and the beta can be estimated from a market model regression, Equation (10.1), using an appropriate benchmark. Treynor
showed that his ratio is invariant to the amount of leverage used in
the portfolio.

---

[7] Jack Treynor, "How to Rate Management of Investment Funds," *Harvard
Business Review*, vol. 43, January–February 1965, pp. 63–75.

APPRAISAL RATIO AND INFORMATION RATIO

The appraisal ratio, more commonly called the information ratio, is the ratio of alpha to residual risk. Residual risk is the standard deviation of the residual return ε_p. Treynor and Black[8] argue that the appraisal ratio is appropriate for evaluating security selection ability. It captures the idea that an active portfolio manager has to depart from the benchmark, that is, take on residual risk, in order to produce alpha. The more alpha the investor produces for a given amount of residual risk, the higher the ratio.

The formula is

$$A_p = \frac{\alpha_p}{\sigma(\varepsilon_p)}. \tag{10.8}$$

As mentioned, the appraisal ratio is also known as the information ratio. In many settings, the portfolio beta with respect to a given benchmark might be close to 1.0, as might be the case if the portfolio strategy is deliberately benchmark-sensitive or if the benchmark is customized for the portfolio. In this case, it may be appropriate to simply assume that beta is 1.0, rather than to estimate it. Doing so simplifies the calculation of the information ratio. The formula for the information ratio IR, assuming beta equals 1.0, is

$$IR_p = \frac{E(R_p - R_b)}{\sigma(R_p - R_b)}, \tag{10.9}$$

where $E(R_p - R_b)$ is the expected return in excess of the benchmark and $\sigma(R_p - R_b)$ is tracking error, the standard deviation of return in excess of the benchmark. Note that information ratios are intimately associated with the chosen benchmark and are best used when comparing return series based on the same benchmark. The information ratio is usually annualized by multiplying it by the square root of the number of observations per year.[9]

---

[8] Jack Treynor and Fischer Black, "How to Use Security Analysis to Improve Portfolio Selection," *Journal of Business*, vol. 46, no. 1, January 1973, pp. 66–86.

[9] Thomas Goodwin, "The Information Ratio," *Financial Analysts Journal*, July/August 1998, pp. 34–43.

COMPARING THE RISK-ADJUSTED MEASURES

Table 10.5 shows the risk-adjusted measures we discussed computed for the example stocks and indexes. All the measures rank the three stocks in the same order in terms of attractiveness. Clearly, with different data we could easily arrive at different rankings.

Because the Sharpe ratio and the Modigliani-Modigliani measure use total risk as the basis for risk-adjusted return, these measures are more appropriate for evaluating entire portfolios, rather than subportfolios or individual stocks. The total risk of an individual asset includes residual risk that might be diversified away, when the asset is held in a well-diversified portfolio.

Jensen's alpha and the Treynor measure, by comparison, use systematic risk as the basis for adjusting the returns. These measures are better suited for evaluating subportfolios or individual

T A B L E 10.5

Comparison of Risk-Adjusted Measures (September 1987 to December 2006)

	R3000	S&P 500	R2000	GE	GM	XOM
Average excess return (%)	9.00	8.64	9.84	15.24	8.52	14.16
Standard deviation (%)	14.83	14.76	19.19	22.38	32.35	16.28
Sharpe ratio	0.60	0.59	0.51	0.68	0.26	0.87
Sortino ratio	0.77	0.76	0.66	NA	NA	NA
Modigliani-Modigliani excess return (%)	9.00	8.76	7.56	10.08	3.84	12.96
Alpha (%)	0.00	−0.12	0.12	5.52	−1.20	9.36
Beta	1.00	0.99	1.08	1.08	1.08	0.53
Treynor measure (%)	9.00	8.76	9.12	14.16	7.80	26.76
Appraisal (Information) ratio	0.00	−0.08	0.01	0.35	−0.04	0.66
R^2 (%)	100.00	98.24	70.00	50.80	24.55	23.38
Residual standard deviation (%)	0.00	1.94	10.50	15.73	28.16	14.27

Source: Yahoo! Finance, http://finance.yahoo.com/q/hp. The data reflect monthly price change only, ignoring dividends and other income, from September 1987 to December 2006. Return is in excess of the risk-free rate. All measures are annualized.

stocks. In our example, GE shows a Sharpe ratio of 0.68, which is only slightly higher than the 0.60 Sharpe ratio of the Russell 3000 benchmark. However, it shows an alpha of more than 5 percent per annum and a Treynor measure of 14, compared with 9 for the benchmark, which suggests that it would be a desirable asset to hold. To mitigate the residual risk of GE, nearly 16 percent per annum, the asset can be held in a diversified portfolio.

The appraisal or information ratio is informative if the focus is on active management relative to a benchmark. The basis for the risk adjustment is residual risk, or tracking error (assuming beta equals 1.0), so the ratio is effectively a measure of active reward to active risk. The benchmark return and risk must be evaluated by other measures.

If you have reasons to believe that the underlying return distributions are asymmetric or skewed, or if the investor has a particular return target with which to define risk, then the Sortino ratio is a good alternative to the Sharpe ratio.

An important caveat should be heeded for all measures based on historical returns data. Estimation error can confound the measurements. Averages, standard deviations, and regressions are notoriously susceptible to outliers. One outlier or one unusual observation can change their values enormously. To see how sensitive your results are, throw out the highest and lowest values in your return series and recalculate your numbers. This will give you some idea of how sensitive your results are to outliers. At the same time remember that extreme observations can also have a lot of information in them, so you should ask why they are extreme. It makes sense to be especially concerned with reliability when the sample sizes are small or when a regression has a low R^2 as discussed earlier.

Lo reports that for hedge funds the Sharpe ratios for portfolios can be inflated by up to 65 percent[10] because the denominators of the Sharpe ratios (the standard deviations) are depressed due to serial correlations in hedge fund returns. Skewness or fat tails can also produce overstated Sharpe ratios, Modigiliani-Modigliani, or

---

[10] Andrew Lo, "The Statistics of Sharpe Ratios," *Financial Analysts Journal,* July/August 2002, pp. 36–50.

Treynor measures. Lower partial moment measures can help in this regard but might make matters worse particularly in the case of heavy skewness.

Finally, the distribution of future returns might not be the same as the distribution of past returns. The principle is that any return distribution abnormalities can easily lead to erroneous results. It is probable that you will consider more than one measure, and that is highly advisable.

CHAPTER 11

Fixed-Income Risk

The issue of risk in fixed income securities is somewhat specialized. A large number of concepts and techniques that have been developed for this asset class have limited applicability elsewhere. Although a full treatment is beyond our scope, in this chapter we review a few essential formulas that should be part of every analyst's toolkit.

A fixed income security can be described by the characteristics of its promised cash flows. A typical bond promises to pay a face value or *par value* at a definite *maturity date*, and periodic interest amounts, or *coupons*, at certain intermediate dates. Typically the coupons are paid semiannually, although by convention the coupon rate is given in annual terms.

Although a typical bond is simple to describe, there are many variations that can quickly lead to complexity. For example, the promised payments might be linked to certain contingencies or indexes. An inflation-linked note has payments linked to a measure of inflation experienced over the term of the note, and an adjustable rate mortgage has payments linked to a market interest rate, for example. Further, the issuer of the security might have the discretion to pay the face value prior to maturity. In the case of a corporate bond, such a bond is *callable*, and, in the case of a mortgage, such a feature is called *prepayment*. Finally, in all cases, there is always a chance that an issuer might default on a promised payment, which could delay or eliminate the payment altogether.

All such variations introduce uncertainty into the timing and amounts of the promised cash flows. Uncertainty in the cash flows leads to differing assessments of the security's value by buyers and sellers in the market, which is a source of risk.

Even if there is no uncertainty in the cash flows, fixed income security prices are set by the market. In equilibrium, securities with similar cash flow characteristics must have similar valuations. Market valuations of certain (that is, definite) cash flows are implied by the term structure of interest rates, which can change over time.

For a bond with cash flows CF_t paid n times per year, with T payments remaining, the bond price P is related to its yield to maturity y by

$$P = \sum_{t=1}^{T} \frac{CF_t}{(1+(y/n))^t}. \tag{11.1}$$

The price is the sum of the present values of the cash flows, all calculated with a single interest rate, the yield to maturity. By convention, bond yields are stated in annual terms; in Equation (11.1), y/n is the yield per period. Similarly, coupon rates are stated in annual terms; for semiannual coupons, the coupon cash flow CF_t is the annual coupon rate times the par value divided by two. The par value paid at maturity is included in the last payment CF_T, along with the last coupon.

With bond prices set by the market, a bond yield defined by Equation (11.1) is essentially an average of the market interest rates for cash flows extending to the bond's maturity. As market interest rates change, bond yields must change. As yields rise, bond prices fall. A change in interest rates is therefore a pervasive factor affecting all fixed income securities. A measure of the sensitivity of bond prices to changes in interest rates is an important measure of systematic risk in fixed income securities.[1]

---

[1] Burton G. Malkiel, "Expectations, Bond Prices, and the Term Structure of Interest Rates," *Quarterly Journal of Economics*, vol. 76, May 1962, pp. 197–218. See also Sidney Homer and Martin L. Liebowitz, *Inside the Yield Book: New Tools for Bond Market Strategy* (Englewood Cliffs, NJ: Prentice Hall, 1972).

DURATION: MACAULAY, MODIFIED, AND EFFECTIVE DURATION

All other characteristics being equal, a bond with a longer maturity is more sensitive to a change in yield than one with a shorter maturity. Duration is a measure of the average time of a bond's promised cash flows. The Macaulay duration is a weighted average of the length of time to each coupon or principal payment. Each payment is weighted by the present value of the cash flow, calculated with the bond's yield, divided by the bond price. The formula for Macaulay duration D is

$$D = \sum_{t=1}^{T} (t/n) \left[\frac{CF_t}{(1+(y/n))^t} \Big/ P \right].$$ (11.2)

Duration is normally measured in years. Given n payments per year, t/n is the time in years to the cash flow indexed by t. The quantity in brackets is the weight given to the cash flow. The weights sum to one by virtue of Equation (11.1).

These ideas are demonstrated in the example shown in Table 11.1, where we have two bonds, each with a face value of $1,000 and a maturity of eight years. One bond is selling for $1,124.20 and carries an 8 percent annual coupon rate, and the other bond is a zero coupon bond selling for $627.41. The yield to maturity of both bonds is 6 percent. The example is simplified by assuming one coupon payment at the end of each year.

In the table, columns 1 and 2 show the year and the cash flows. The third column shows the present value of the cash flows discounted at the yield rate of 6 percent. The fourth column shows the weights, which are the values of the discounted cash flows as a fraction of the price of the bond. The fifth column shows the contribution of each year's cash flow to the overall duration calculation. The sum of these contributions is the duration, which is 6.32 years for the 8 percent coupon bond.

Notice that since there are no coupon payments for the zero coupon bond, they cannot contribute to the overall duration of the bond. In other words, the duration of a zero coupon bond is a constant value equal to the years to maturity. The 8 percent coupon bond has a duration of 6.32 years, while the zero coupon bond has a longer duration of 8 years.

TABLE 11.1

Duration Calculations for an 8-Year, $1,000 Bond with an 8 percent and a Zero Coupon

8 Percent Coupon Bond				
Par value:	$1,000		Bond price:	$1,124.20
Coupon rate:	8.00%		Years to maturity:	8
Yield to maturity:	6.00%		Current yield:	7.12%
Year	Payment	Present Value	Weight	Duration Contribution
1	$80	$75.47	0.067	0.067
2	$80	$71.20	0.063	0.127
3	$80	$67.17	0.060	0.179
4	$80	$63.37	0.056	0.226
5	$80	$59.78	0.053	0.266
6	$80	$56.40	0.050	0.301
7	$80	$53.20	0.047	0.331
8	$1,080	$677.61	0.603	4.822
Sum		**$1,124.20**	**1.000**	**6.319**
		Price		Duration
Zero Coupon Bond				
Par value:	$1,000		Bond price:	$627.41
Coupon rate:	0.00%		Years to maturity:	8
Yield to maturity:	6.00%		Current yield:	0.00%
Year	Payment	Present Value	Weight	Duration Contribution
1	$0	$0.00	0.000	0.000
:	:	:	:	:
7	$0	$0.00	0.000	0.000
8	$1,000	$627.41	1.000	8.000
Sum	**$1,000**	**$627.41**	**1.000**	**8.000**
		Price		Duration

There is a formula for calculating the Macaulay duration of a standard coupon bond that does not require the summation of discounted cash flows. The formula[2] is

---

[2] Zvi Bodie, Alex Kane, and Alan J. Marcus, *Investments*, 5th ed. (New York: McGraw-Hill, 2002) chapter 16, p. 493.

$$D = \left[\frac{1+i}{ni}\right] - \left[\frac{(1+i)+T(c-i)}{nc((1+i)^T - 1)+ni}\right], \tag{11.3}$$

where

n = number of payment periods per year

$i = y/n$ = bond yield per payment period

c = coupon rate per payment period

T = number of payment periods.

Using the example from Table 11.1, $n = 1$, $i = 0.06$, $c = 0.08$, and $T = 8$, we can use the formula to verify that the duration equals 6.32.

Some general observations about the behavior of duration are the following: The duration of a zero coupon bond is equal to its time to maturity. A coupon bond's duration is higher when the coupon rate is lower for a given maturity. For a given coupon rate the duration increases with time to maturity. Holding coupon rate and time to maturity constant, the duration is higher when the yield to maturity is lower.

Modified Duration

Duration measures the sensitivity of the bond price to a change in yield. Taking the derivative of price P in Equation (11.1) with respect to yield y, we can find

$$\frac{dP}{dy} = -\sum_{t=1}^{T} \frac{(t/n)CF_t}{(1+(y/n))^{t+1}} = -\frac{1}{1+(y/n)}\sum_{t=1}^{T} \frac{(t/n)CF_t}{(1+(y/n))^t} = -\frac{1}{1+(y/n)}DP,$$

or $dP/dy = -D_M P$, where

$$D_M = \frac{D}{1+(y/n)}. \tag{11.4}$$

The quantity D_M is called *modified duration* and is equal to Macaulay duration divided by an extra term. Duration's primary use is in calculating the change in price that can be expected for a given change in interest rates or yields. Using modified duration we can estimate the change in price from

$$\frac{\Delta P}{P} \approx -D_M \Delta y \qquad (11.5)$$

where $\Delta P/P$ is the fractional change in price for a small change Δy in yield.

Effective Duration

If a bond has uncertain cash flows, such as in the case of callable bonds or mortgage prepayments, modified duration calculations will not provide good estimates of price changes with changes in interest rates. Consider for example a callable bond that allows the issuer to buy back the bond for $1,000 at any time before the bond matures. The price of this bond will never go above $1,000 no matter how low the market interest rates become. In this case the bond's price sensitivity to interest rates can be quite different from that of a comparable bond without the call option.

To deal with this sort of problem analysts have developed the notion of "effective duration." Effective duration is an attempt to approximate the change in bond value as a function of changing interest rates. The bond's price as a function of yield must be modeled in some way, often using rather data-intensive techniques. Given a model of the bond price at different yields, the effective duration can be calculated from

$$D_E = \frac{P_{-\Delta y} - P_{+\Delta y}}{2P\Delta y}, \qquad (11.6)$$

where

D_E = effective duration
$P_{-\Delta y}$ = price with a small negative change in yield
$P_{+\Delta y}$ = price with a small positive change in yield
P = current price
Δy = small change in yield.

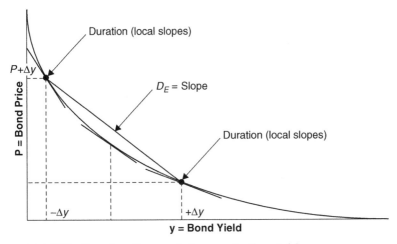

Figure 11.1 Effective duration and changes in the yield

The utility of effective duration is that it measures the sensitivity of a bond price to changes in yield. It is a local sensitivity around the current price of the bond. Figure 11.1 displays the relationship between a plus or minus change in yield and the effective duration.

CONVEXITY

Equation (11.5) suggests that there is a direct one-to-one relationship between changes in interest rates and changes in prices. Assuming a linear relationship between interest rate changes and price changes works well for small changes in interest rates. Unfortunately, as the changes in interest rates become larger, the relationship in Equation (11.5) tends to break down. To obtain more precise estimates of price changes requires the concept of convexity.

The convexity of a bond can be used to adjust the duration estimate of price change in the following way:

$$\frac{\Delta P}{P} \approx -D_M(\Delta y) + 0.5C(\Delta y)^2, \tag{11.7}$$

T A B L E 11.2

Convexity Adjustment to Duration Estimates of Bond Price Changes

Change in Yield from 2% to 8%	$\Delta P/P =$	–30.10%	
Duration forecasted price change $= \Delta P/P = -D^*\Delta y$		Estimated Price Change	Error
Modified duration: 6.4294 Δy: 6.00%		–38.58%	8.48%
Price Change using duration and convexity:			
Modified duration: 6.4294 Convexity: 65.2620			
Formula: $\Delta P/P = -D_M \Delta y + \frac{1}{2}$ * convexity * $(\Delta y)^2$		–26.83%	–3.27%

where

P = bond price

D_M = modified duration

Δy = change in yield

C = convexity.

The formula for the convexity C of a standard coupon bond is[3]

$$C = \frac{1}{P(1+(y/n))^2} \sum_{t=1}^{T} \left[\frac{CF_t}{(1+(y/n))^t} \frac{t^2+t}{n^2} \right]. \qquad (11.8)$$

Table 11.2 shows the calculations for a coupon bond with a par value of $1,000, a 9 percent coupon, 8 years to maturity where the yield changes a great deal from 2 to 8 percent.

The convexity of the bond is a function of yield to maturity and price. When the change in yield is small, the convexity can be ignored, but, as in our example, with large changes the effect of convexity becomes material.

The relation between duration and convexity is shown in Figure 11.2.

Bond investors like convexity because the greater the curvature of the price-yield curve, the less the bond price goes down with a positive change in interest rates and the more the bond price goes up when

---

[3] Ibid., p. 495, footnote 5.

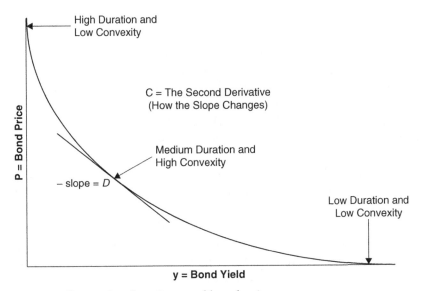

Figure 11.2 Convexity, duration, and bond price

interest rates fall, compared to a bond with the same duration but less convexity. The more spread out the cash flows of a bond, the higher its convexity. For example, a zero coupon bond has no convexity.

PREPAYMENT RISK FOR MORTGAGES AND CALLABLES

Prepayment risk refers to the possibility that the bond or mortgage will be paid off before the full term of the underlying obligation. Prepayment risk applies to callable bonds or bonds that can be redeemed before the full term of the contract. The probability of a callable bond being redeemed is related to interest rates. If the bond issuer issued the bond at a high interest rate and general interest rates fall dramatically, then the issuer is motivated to issue new bonds at a lower interest rate and retire the old bonds at a higher interest rate at a fixed cost because their market values are now higher. This saves the issuer the difference in interest rates.

Issuing new bonds and redeeming issued bonds is not an inexpensive exercise, so bond issuers will not undertake to swap new bonds for old unless the interest rate differences are substantial.

The logic of such trade-offs is multifaceted, so the function relating the probability of prepayment and the difference between the bond interest rate and current interest rate is likely to be nonlinear. The early part of such a curve would be flat where the difference in interest rates is not sufficiently large to cover the cost and effort involved but then would become steeper or accelerate as the interest rate difference grows larger and would become almost vertical (a near certainty) when the difference grows to the range of 5 percent.

There are many factors involved in the shape of these curves such as general market conditions, the quality of the bond, as well as the interest rate differential combined to make the functions unique to each bond.

When a bond is backed by residential mortgages, there is a new twist to prepayment risk. People do refinance their mortgages when interest rates fall, and this leads to early payoff of the previous mortgage, similar to a corporation retiring a callable bond. However, people also pay off their mortgages when they have to move, such as for a new job, even when interest rates may not have fallen. Wall Street firms and academics have put a lot of energy into modeling those prepayment options and the risk they create for the holders of mortgage-backed bonds. We should also mention "walkaway" risk when loan-to-value rises above 110 percent, which happened in 2008 with the large fall in housing prices. Proper modeling going forward will need to incorporate both interest rate driven prepayment risk and interest rate and price driven default risk.

ISSUER-SPECIFIC RISK, DEFAULT RISK, AND CORRELATED DEFAULT RISK

There are other dimensions to the risk of bonds other than their sensitivity to interest rate changes. For corporate bonds the most obvious of these is bond default risk or credit risk. There are various services that rate bonds of corporations such as Standard & Poor's, Moody's Investor Services, Fitch Investor Services, and Duff & Phelps.

The rating of the bonds by these agencies has an enormous impact. In 2007, these agencies' failure to correctly rate the subprime bonds and collateralized debt obligations (CDOs) put them in the spotlight, and they have been partly blamed for the market turmoil of 2007 and 2008. The subprime mortgages were far riskier than the agencies thought. There is some question about the agencies' objectivity in assigning ratings since the agencies earned fees from the CDO marketers for their ratings. This led to "agency" and "moral hazard" problems for the agencies because the fees were high and the CDO-offering organizations could shop around. This may have compromised the rating agencies' objectivity because they knew if they did not offer high ratings, the business would go elsewhere.

The default risk of bonds is not expressed in terms of probabilities of default; rather, bonds are rated in terms of letters with AAA (Aaa) being the highest rating and CCC (Caa) or D (C) being the lowest ratings (see Table 11.3).

Moody's, Standard & Poor's, and Fitch all also assign intermediate ratings at levels between AA and B (e.g., BBB+, BBB, and BBB–) and may also choose to offer guidance (termed a "credit watch") as to whether a bond is likely to be upgraded (positive) or downgraded (negative) or is uncertain (neutral).

The bond rating agencies use a variety of financial ratios to evaluate the quality of the bonds. Among those ratios are the coverage ratios that compare a company's earnings to various fixed costs such as interest expense, sinking fund obligations, or other fixed charges. They also look at leverage ratios such as the debt-to-equity ratio, which measures the extent to which the company relies on borrowing. Liquidity ratios include the current ratio (assets divided by current liabilities) and the quick ratio (current assets divided by liabilities). They also use profitability ratios such as return on assets, operating income to sales, and cash to debt, which relates cash flows to outstanding debt. The agencies also employ analysts who try to understand a company's prospects on more subjective grounds.

T A B L E 11.3

Bond Rating Codes

	Standard & Poor's	Moody	Fitch
Very high quality	AAA AA	Aaa Aa	AAA AA
High quality	A BBB	A Baa	A BBB
Speculative	BB B	Ba B	BB B
Very poor quality	CCC D	Caa C	CCC CC D

Source: Zvi Bodie, Alex Kane, and Alan J. Marcus, *Investments,* 5th ed. (New York: McGraw-Hill, 2002), p. 435.

CHAPTER 12

Conditional Performance Evaluation

Individual investors and institutional investors are always seeking to find active portfolio managers able to deliver abnormal excess performance—expected returns in excess of suitable benchmarks. Yet evidence that a subset of active managers can deliver consistently superior returns remains controversial.[1] Some persistence-in-performance studies have found that the past performance of mutual funds provides some predictive value for future performance.[2]

---

[1] Jon A. Christopherson and Andrew L. Turner, "Volatility and Predictability of Manager Alpha: Learning the Lessons of History," *Journal of Portfolio Management*, Fall 1991, pp. 5–12. Edwin J. Elton, Martin J. Gruber, and Christopher R. Blake, "The Persistence of Risk-Adjusted Mutual Fund Performance," *Journal of Business*, vol. 69, 1996, pp. 133–157.

[2] See Michael C. Jensen, "Risk, the Pricing of Assets and the Evaluation of Investment Portfolios," *Journal of Business*, vol. 42, 1969, pp. 167–247; Robert S. Carlson, "Aggregate Performance of Mutual Funds 1948–1967," *Journal of Financial and Quantitative Analysis*, vol. 5, 1970, pp. 1–32; and Mark Carhart, "On Persistence in Mutual Fund Performance," *Journal of Finance*, vol. 50, 1997, pp. 57–82 for evidence of such persistence in mutual fund performance. Josef Lakonishok, Andrei Shleifer, and Robert Vishny, "The Structure and Performance of the Money Management Industry," *Brookings Papers: Microeconomics* (Washington DC: Brookings Institution, 1992), pp. 339–391, find some persistence of the relative returns of pension fund managers for two- to three-year investment horizons, but not at shorter horizons.

In estimating abnormal excess performance for a sample of pension fund portfolio managers, Christopherson and Turner concluded that the past performance of a manager's portfolio provides little or no useful information about expected future performance. Their study, however, relied upon unconditional performance measures. Their performance measures ignore information about the changing nature of the economy. As we show later, unconditional measures will incorrectly measure expected excess returns when portfolio managers react to market information or engage in dynamic trading strategies. These well-known biases make it difficult to accurately measure alpha and beta.

Ferson and Schadt and Ferson and Warther[3] propose *conditional performance evaluation* (CPE) as a method to more accurately form expectations about excess return and risk. CPE presupposes that portfolio managers can change both their alphas and betas over time based upon the influence of publicly available information about the economy. The methodology implicitly assumes that a portfolio's alphas and betas change dynamically with changing market conditions. To the extent that we are better able to measure beta, we are also better able to measure alpha, and vice versa.[4]

In an actively managed portfolio, time variation in the beta may occur for a variety of reasons. First, the betas of the underlying securities may change over time. Obviously, a portfolio composed

---

T. Daniel Coggin, Frank J. Fabozzi, and Shafiqur Rahman, "The Investment Performance of U.S. Equity Pension Fund Managers," *Journal of Finance*, vol. 48, 1993, pp. 1039–1056 study market timing ability using unconditional models, while Jon A. Christopherson, Wayne E. Ferson, and Debra A. Glassman (CFG), "Conditioning Manager Alphas on Economic Information: Another Look at Persistence in Performance," *Review of Financial Studies*, vol. 11, Spring 1998, pp. 111–142, study persistence of institutional portfolio performance using conditional models. The hot-hands literature shows the same persistence in performance.

[3] Wayne E. Ferson and Rudi Schadt, "Measuring Fund Strategy and Performance in Changing Economic Conditions," *Journal of Finance*, vol. 51, 1996, pp. 425–462, and Wayne E. Ferson and Vincent A. Warther, "Evaluating Fund Performance in a Dynamic Market," *Financial Analysts Journal*, vol. 52, 1996, pp. 20–28.

[4] Recall our earlier discussion in Chapter 8 of Richard Roll's demonstration that trying to measure alpha correctly critically depends on measuring beta correctly.

of stocks with changing betas can experience a change in beta even with no turnover at all. Second, managers may change the beta of their portfolios through their pursuit of alpha. Third, a manager may experience large cash flows into the portfolio, and those cash holdings may cause the beta of the fund to fluctuate. Changing beta may or may not be an active decision by managers.

MODELS FOR PERFORMANCE MEASUREMENT

In Chapter 8 we discussed the mathematics and data issues behind the capital asset pricing model (CAPM). Here we will discuss adapting CAPM performance measurement to CPE performance evaluation and we will provide an example that illustrates the logic of the CPE model.

LOGIC OF CONDITIONAL
PERFORMANCE EVALUATION

How does the conditional approach work? A hypothetical example will illustrate the central idea. In this example, we assume that "bull" and "bear" market conditions serve as a metaphor for commonly understood economic conditions for the class of investors to which the model is being applied. The commonly understood economic conditions include the current levels of interest rates, market prices, and various other measures of economic activity. Let us suppose the equity market can take on two equally likely states that represent widely held expectations based on publicly available information. In a bull state, suppose the expected return for holding the broad equity market is 20 percent. In a bear state, the expected market return is –20 percent; high-quality stocks return –5 percent and have a beta of 0.25.

Suppose further that the expected future return is widely known among skilled professionals. Of course, the actual return is unknown—only the *expected* return given the state of the market is common knowledge. An investment strategy using only this information will not on average yield abnormal returns, and so it should have a measured alpha of zero.

This example assumes, of course, that some classes of investors use the publicly available information and adjust their portfolio beta in bear states while others remain to ride the bear market out. Not everyone can adjust their beta to 0.25 or get out of the market completely. Someone is holding the equities that constitute the market when the expected return is –20 percent.[5]

Consider a portfolio managed to hold the Russell 3000 index in a bull market and quality stocks in a bear market. The portfolio manager's stock-picking ability is zero. In this (admittedly simplistic) world, the only skill required is to read the newspaper, monitor what is widely known, and act upon this information. Conditional on an expected bull market, the beta of the fund is 1.0, the fund's expected return is 20 percent, and the alpha is zero. Conditional on an expected bear market, the fund's equity beta is 0.25, also with an alpha of zero. The conditional approach correctly reports an alpha of zero in each state of the market. By contrast, an unconditional measurement approach that does not adjust beta or take into account the widely known information about expected bull or bear markets incorrectly reports an alpha of 7.5 percent and a beta of 0.625.

The situation is illustrated in Figure 12.1, where the expected returns for the benchmark Russell 3000 index fund plot at –20 percent and +20 percent. The manager acting on common knowledge has expected returns of –5 percent and +20 percent.[6] A line between the two points crosses the vertical axis at 7.5 percent and has a slope of 0.625. Using the conditional approach to evaluation, we have a beta of 1.0 in a bull market and a beta of 0.25 in a bear market—implying that the more precise alpha is zero.

In other words, there are two types of skill: the ability to exploit widely available macroeconomic information and the ability to pick stocks. The unconditional approach confuses the manager's use of models of simple market dynamics with superior security selection ability. The conditional approach tries to separate this naïve market-timing ability from superior stock-picking ability. Using alpha estimates that adjust for common knowledge should provide superior results.

---

[5] The point of this example does not depend on the particular numbers we use. These are chosen to make the calculations easy to comprehend.

[6] These numbers are the expected returns given public information. The actual returns would appear as a random cloud centered at these two points.

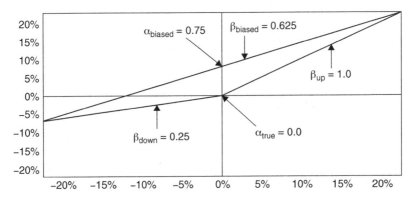

Figure 12.1 Manager with time-varying beta

UNCONDITIONAL ALPHAS AND BETAS

As we reviewed in Chapter 10, Jensen created an unconditional measure of abnormal performance by estimating the following regression using historic data:

$$r_{pt} = \alpha_p + \beta_p r_{bt} + v_{pt},\qquad(12.1)$$

where for portfolio p over time $t = 1, \ldots, T,$

r_{pt} = return of managed portfolio net of the one-month Treasury bill return R_{ft}, or $r_{pt} = R_{pt} - R_{ft}$ with R_{pt} as return of managed portfolio

r_{bt} = return of benchmark portfolio net of one-month Treasury bill return, or $r_{pt} = R_{pt} - R_{ft}$ with R_{bt} as return of benchmark

α_p = unconditional alpha

β_p = unconditional beta

v_{pt} = regression error or residual.

Jensen's alpha is one of the standards for measuring performance. Unconditional alphas, however, are also commonly estimated using various customized benchmark portfolios such as style indexes. They can also be estimated using multiple factor models, in which the betas and explanatory variables are vectors of factor exposures and factor returns. The average value of the excess return,

$a_p = R_{pt} - R_{bt}$, is sometimes used as a simple alternative performance measure, when the beta in Equation (12.1) can reasonably be assumed to equal 1.0.

TIME-VARYING CONDITIONAL BETAS

If expected market returns and managers' betas change over time and are correlated, the regression equation (12.1) is misspecified and alpha and beta will be incorrectly estimated. Ferson and Schadt (1996) propose a modification of Equation (12.1) to address these concerns. They assume that the market prices of securities fully reflect readily available and public information. A vector of market information variables, Z, measures this information. The betas of stocks and managed portfolios are allowed to change with market conditions. Ferson and Schadt assume a linear functional form for the changing conditional beta of a managed portfolio, given the market information variables Z_t:[7]

$$\beta_p(\mathbf{z}_t) = b_{0p} + \mathbf{B}_p' \mathbf{z}_t , \qquad (12.2)$$

where $\mathbf{z}_t = \mathbf{Z}_t - E(\mathbf{Z})$ is a normalized vector of the deviations of $\mathbf{Z}_t$ from the unconditional means, and $\mathbf{B}_p$ is a vector with the same dimension as $\mathbf{Z}_t$.[8] The coefficient b_{0p} can be interpreted as the "average beta" or the beta when all information variables are at their means. The elements of $\mathbf{B}_p$ measure the sensitivity of the conditional beta to the deviations of the $\mathbf{Z}_t$ from their means.

---

[7] In other words, they assume that markets are informationally efficient in a version of the "semistrong form" efficiency of Fama. See Eugene Fama, "Efficient Capital Markets: A Review of Theory and Empirical Work," *Journal of Finance*, vol. 25, 1970, pp. 383–417.

[8] It is important to demean the information variables, using only past data, to avoid biases in the regressions. For an analysis of bias in regressions like Equation (12.3), see Wayne Ferson, Sergei Sarkissian, and Timothy Simin, "Asset Pricing Models with Conditional Alphas and Betas: The Effects of Data Snooping and Spurious Regression," *Journal of Financial and Quantitative Analysis*, vol. 43, no. 2, June 2008, pp. 331–354.

The following modification of the regression equation (12.1) follows from the model of changing betas:

$$r_{pt+1} = \alpha_p + b_{0p} r_{bt+1} + \mathbf{B}_p' \mathbf{z}_t r_{bt+1} + \mu_{pt+1}. \qquad (12.3)$$

Under the null hypothesis of no abnormal performance, the model implies that the *conditional alpha* α_p is zero; however, α_p in Equation (12.3) may differ from Equation (12.1) if the vector $\mathbf{B}_p$ is nonzero.

In the case of a single benchmark return r_{bt+1} and L information variables in $\mathbf{Z}_t$, Equation (12.3) can be viewed as a regression of the manager's return on a constant and $L + 1$ explanatory variables. The products of the future benchmark return and the information variables (i.e., $\mathbf{z}_t r_{bt+1}$) capture the covariance between the conditional beta and the conditional expected market return, given $\mathbf{Z}_t$. Ferson and Schadt (1996) find that this covariance is a major source of measurement error in unconditional alphas of mutual funds. By controlling for this covariance, the model of Equation (12.3) produces more reliable estimates of alpha.

TIME-VARYING CONDITIONAL ALPHAS

In the same way that beta can be dynamic and change with market conditions, alphas may also be dynamic. Using a single coefficient α_p in Equation (12.3) presumes that expected abnormal performance is constant over time. However, if managers' abnormal returns vary over time, a constant alpha may not provide much power to detect abnormal performance.

Christopherson et al.[9] propose modifying regression equation (12.3) to include *time-varying conditional alpha*, allowing the alpha to be a function of $\mathbf{Z}_t$ in the same manner as beta is a function of $\mathbf{Z}_t$:

$$\alpha_{pt} = a_p(\mathbf{z}_t) = a_{0p} + \mathbf{A}_p' \mathbf{z}_t. \qquad (12.4)$$

---

[9] Jon A. Christopherson, Wayne E. Ferson, and Andrew L. Turner, "Performance Evaluation Using Conditional Alphas and Betas," *Journal of Portfolio Management*, vol. 26, no. 1, Fall 1999, pp. 59–72 .

Equation (12.4) approximates the conditional alpha by a linear function.[10] The modified regression is therefore

$$r_{pt+1} = a_{0p} + \mathbf{A}_p' \mathbf{z}_t + b_{0p} r_{bt+1} + \mathbf{B}_p' [\mathbf{z}_t r_{bt+1}] + \mu_{pt+1}. \qquad (12.5)$$

This regression allows us to estimate conditional alphas and track their variation over time as a function of the conditioning information.

Example of Dynamic Alpha and Beta Estimation Equations

To illustrate the model's estimation, let us formulate a simple example. We will choose only two information variables—dividend yield (dividend/price or DP) and the detrended level of short-term Treasury yields (TB). Both variables are readily available at low cost and widely understood to be relevant to future returns. We could choose lagged $\mathbf{z}_t$ to represent whatever level we feel constitutes "common knowledge" or superior knowledge. In the original model in Equation (12.5), the time-varying alpha component is $a_{0p} + \mathbf{A}_p' \mathbf{z}_t$, and the time-varying beta multiplied by the excess return on the market is $(b_{0pb} + \mathbf{B}_{pb}' \mathbf{z}_t) r_{bt+1}$.

In our example, the alpha of the portfolio α_p of the CAPM is replaced with a time-subscripted α_{pt}, which is defined as an average alpha plus an alpha increment/decrement due to the lagged levels of dividend yield (DP) and T-bill yields (TB). These time-varying sensitivities are captured by the terms $b_1 [DP_{t-1}]$ and $b_2 [TB_{t-1}]$, and the complete alpha term becomes

$$a_0 + a_1 DP_{t-1} + a_2 TB_{t-1}. \qquad (12.6)$$

So the risk-adjusted excess return of the portfolio is a conditional linear function of the lagged information variables at the

---

[10] Obviously, the alpha of a portfolio can be dynamic for a variety of reasons besides changes in macroeconomic environment. CFG, 1998 show that alpha generally depends on the covariance between managers' portfolio weights and future asset returns. Conditional on $\mathbf{z}_t$ this covariance and the conditional alpha should be a function of $\mathbf{z}_t$.

beginning of the time period, $a_1 \mathrm{DP}_{t-1}$ and $a_2 \mathrm{TB}_{t-1}$, plus an average risk-adjusted excess return a_0.

The beta component is replaced in a similar way with

$$b_0 r_{bt} + b_1 (r_{bt} \mathrm{DP}_{t-1}) + b_2 (r_{bt} \mathrm{TB}_{t-1}). \qquad (12.7)$$

Therefore, the sensitivity of the portfolio due to the market (or beta of the portfolio) is an average sensitivity to the market excess b_0, plus a conditional sensitivity of the portfolio to predictable market changes. Therefore, the total estimated regression is

$$r_{pt} = a_0 + a_1 \mathrm{DP}_{t-1} + a_2 \mathrm{TB}_{t-1} + b_0 r_{bt} + b_1 (r_{bt} \mathrm{DP}_{t-1}) + b_2 (r_{bt} \mathrm{TB}_{t-1}) + \varepsilon_t.$$

$$(12.8)$$

We can test a variety of different models by constructing them analogously to Equation (12.8).

BENCHMARK PORTFOLIOS

Christopherson, Turner, and Ferson examined managers within four investment styles—growth, value, market-oriented,[11] and small-capitalization, and used four associated Russell-style indexes that constitute appropriate benchmarks for each style. The Russell market-oriented benchmark was the Russell 1000, a value-weighted index of the stocks of large-capitalization firms. The Russell small-capitalization benchmark was the value-weighted Russell 2000 index. These are non-overlapping subsets of the Russell 3000 index universe. The Russell 1000 has been further divided into two groups of stocks forming the Russell Growth and Value indexes. These two indexes are the benchmarks for the Growth and Value styles, respectively.

Christopherson et al. found that using the style indexes as market benchmarks removed some of the explanatory power of the macroeconomic variables, but the ability to discriminate among high- and low-performing managers out of sample was maintained.

---

[11] The classification "market oriented" is often referred to as a blended style or broad market. The style spans the entire market, and over a typical business cycle has marketlike returns.

IMPLICATIONS FOR INVESTORS

The CPE method for evaluating portfolio returns provides alpha estimates that are more effective than traditional CAPM alpha estimates in predicting future returns. The CPE research suggests that the investor should conditionally evaluate the manager's return series using public information variables.[12]

The effect of style on the effectiveness of CPE and CAPM alpha estimates to forecast manager returns is significant. The CAPM with a broad market benchmark produces unstable results, which vary with market conditions and are unreliable in strong markets. When style indexes are used to compute unconditional alphas, the ability to forecast return disappears. The CPE alpha estimates continue to work even when style is included. However, the ability to identify managers likely to be unsuccessful deteriorates slightly when style effects are extracted.

While higher CPE alphas do not guarantee superior returns, they are more likely to successfully predict alphas out of sample than previously available measures.

---

[12] For a more detailed discussion and mutual fund evidence, see Wayne Ferson and Meijun Qian, "Conditional Performance Evaluation Revisited," 2004, in *Research Foundation Monograph* of the CFA Institute, ISBN 0-943205-69-7.

CHAPTER 13

Market Timing

The successful prediction of the direction of the market relative to other asset classes such as cash can produce substantial payoffs for investors. The ability to profitably move from one asset class to another is called *market timing skill*. A long-only equity investor rarely moves from equities to fixed income. However, for situations where managers do have the ability to change their portfolios according to market conditions several different methodologies have been developed for measuring this timing ability. In this chapter we review several of these methodologies.

MERTON-HENRIKSSON
MARKET TIMING MODEL

Merton and Henriksson developed a test based on the idea that an investor who is able to time markets can be modeled as having an option on the difference between the market return and the return on Treasury bills.[1]

The basic idea of the test is to perform a multiple regression in which the dependent variable (portfolio excess return) is regressed against the market return and a second variable that mimics the payoff to an option. This second variable is zero when the market

---

[1] Roy D. Henriksson and Robert C. Merton, "On Market Timing and Investment Performance. II. Statistical Procedures for Evaluating Forecast Skills," *Journal of Business*, vol. 54, October 1981, pp. 513–533.

excess return is at or below zero and is 1 when it is above zero. The model is shown here:

$$R_p - R_f = \alpha + \beta(R_m - R_f) + \gamma D + \varepsilon_p \qquad (13.1)$$

where

α = intercept or alpha

β = market sensitivity

$D = \max(0, R_m - R_f)$ or up-market returns

γ = market timing abilities

In this model, alpha is sometimes (incorrectly) interpreted as risk-adjusted excess return, beta is the linear sensitivity of the portfolio return to the market, while gamma is a measure of the number of free puts the manager's investment strategy generates or their market timing ability.[2]

The application of this model to real-world data in the form of mutual funds data has not been very successful. Merton and Henriksson performed their test on 116 open-ended mutual funds for 1968 to 1980 and found that the gamma estimate was slightly negative but not statistically significantly different from zero.[3] For those managers who did have statistically significant gammas, most of them underperformed, calling into question their true timing ability. Subsequent work by Ferson and Schadt using conditional

---

[2] The intercept may be interpreted as a risk-adjusted excess return only when the variables on the right-hand side of the risk model regressions are themselves excess returns. This is because the intercept is the difference between the average value of the left-hand-side asset and the average value of the right-hand-side variables. While $R_m - R_f$ in Equation (13.1) is an excess return, the problem is that D is not an excess return. Aragon and Ferson (2006) show how to convert the alphas in market timing regressions into valid measures of risk-adjusted excess returns. George O. Aragon and Wayne E. Ferson, "Portfolio Performance Evaluation," *Foundations and Trends in Finance*, vol. 2, no. 2, pp. 83–190, 2006.

[3] See also Stanley J. Kon and Frank C. Jen, "The Investment Performance of Mutual Funds: An Empirical Investigation of Timing, Selectivity, and Market Efficiency," *Journal of Business*, vol. 52, no. 2, 1979, pp. 263–289.

evaluation methods that allowed the parameters to vary over time conditional on public information appeared to work better than the original Merton and Henriksson model.[4] There is some evidence by Liang et al.[5] that hedged funds do have market timing ability using the Merton-Henriksson test. Bollen and Busse found some evidence of timing ability among mutual funds by using daily returns data.[6]

TREYNOR-MAZUY MODEL

Treynor and Mazuy[7] were the first to tackle the problem of managers who time the market or alter their beta with market conditions. The Treynor-Mazuy model is essentially a quadratic extension of the basic CAPM. It is estimated using a multiple regression. The second term in the regression is the value of excess return squared. If the gamma coefficient in the regression is positive, then the estimated equation describes a convex upward-sloping regression "line."

The quadratic regression is

$$R_p - R_f = \alpha + \beta(R_m - R_f) + \gamma(R_m - R_f)^2 + \varepsilon_p \qquad (13.2)$$

where variables are as defined earlier.

As in the Merton-Henriksson model, alpha is often naïvely interpreted (see footnote 2 on previous page) as risk-adjusted excess return and beta is the linear sensitivity of the portfolio return to the market as in the Merton-Henriksson test. Gamma is a measure of the curvature of the regression line. If gamma is positive, this would indicate that the manager's investment strategy demonstrates

---

[4] Wayne Ferson and Rudi Schadt, "Measuring Fund Strategy and Performance in Changing Economic Conditions," *Journal of Finance*, vol. 51, 1996, pp. 425–462.

[5] Bing Liang and Yong Chen, "Do Market Timing Hedge Funds Time the Markets," *The Journal of Financial and Quantitative Analysis*, vol. 42, December 2007, pp. 827–856.

[6] Nicolas P. Bollen and Jeffery. A. Busse, "On the Timing Ability of Mutual Fund Managers," *Journal of Finance*, vol. 56, 2001, pp. 1075–1094.

[7] J. L. Treynor and K. Mazuy, "Can Mutual Funds Outguess the Market?" *Harvard Business Review*, vol. 44, 1966, pp. 131–136.

market timing ability. Investors like market timing for the same reason they like convexity in bonds: you make more money in up markets and lose less money in down markets.

Let us present an artificial example of how these methodologies should work. We will assume a short time series that has both an up and down market within it. We will assume the manager has timing ability and alters beta in anticipation of the changing market. Table 13.1 displays the data; Figure 13.1 shows the relationship between the two portfolios and the market. We have superimposed the estimated regression lines on the graph.

In our example data, we have added specific return around the market return and created hypothetical Merton-Henriksson returns using an alpha of 0.3 and a beta of 1.5 times the market return plus two times the artificial put. The artificial put is the excess return times the indicator function, which takes on a value of 1.0 when the market excess return is above zero and takes on a value of 0.0 when the market is at or below zero. So the series is the excess return when the market is above zero and zero otherwise. To this we add a noise term that has a mean of 0.0 and a standard deviation of 0.65. This produces the data in Table 13.1 labeled the MH portfolio.

T A B L E 13.1

Example of Merton-Henriksson and Teynor-Mazuy Calculations

| | | | Alpha = 0.3 | | |
| | | | Beta = 1.05 | | |
Time	MH Portfolio	TM Portfolio	(Market Return)	MH Gamma = $2\,[(R_m - R_f)^+]$	TM Gamma = 0.5 $[(R_m - R_f)^2]$
1	3.56	3.07	1.3	1.3	1.69
2	7.92	5.46	2.4	2.4	5.76
3	13.31	14.14	4.3	4.3	18.49
4	8.93	6.46	2.7	2.7	7.29
5	−5.11	5.75	−4.3	0	18.49
6	−1.00	−0.42	−2.1	0	4.41
7	−2.08	0.46	−1.6	0	2.56
8	9.94	6.91	2.9	2.9	8.41
9	12.71	13.85	4.2	4.2	17.64
10	11.37	9.78	3.5	3.5	12.25

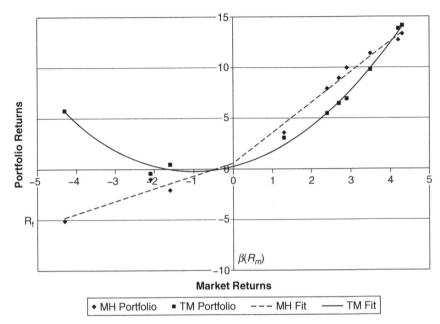

Figure 13.1 Merton-Henriksson and Treynor-Mazuy estimations

The hypothetical Treynor-Mazuy portfolio is created in a similar manner. It also has an alpha of 0.3 and a beta of 1.05, but the gamma is set at 0.5 rather than 2.0. In this model the excess return is squared for all values, so it has no negative values when the market is below zero. The return of this portfolio is shown in column 3, labeled the TM portfolio. The standard deviation of the error term for this model is 0.52.

Ordinary least squares (OLS) regression was applied to each of these portfolios, and the results are shown in Table 13.2. For each model, we estimated a simple market model regression as a baseline for comparison. Notice that the alphas and the betas are wildly misestimated. Both alphas are much higher than the true intercept of 0.3 at 3.02 and 4.93, respectively. The beta associated with trying to pass a straight line through data series that are curved is also doomed to failure. The true beta for both portfolios is 1.05, and the regression estimates them at 2.2 and 1.2. These numbers show that attempting to estimate regressions without taking into account timing ability will yield incorrect alphas and betas.

TABLE 13.2

Regression Statistics for Merton-Henriksson and Treynor-Mazuy Models

	CAPM	Model Fit	True Value
Merton-Henriksson Model			
Alpha	3.02	0.50	0.3
Beta	2.21	1.23	1.1
Gamma		1.79	2.0
R^2	0.97	0.99	
Treynor-Mazuy Model			
Alpha	4.93	0.17	0.3
Beta	1.21	0.98	1.1
Gamma		0.52	0.5
R^2	0.97	0.99	

In Figure 13.1, as mentioned, we plot the data for the Merton-Henriksson and Treynor-Mazuy portfolios. The nonlinear nature of each portfolio is clearly shown in the distribution of the points. We have superimposed on the graph the two estimated regression lines. Note that these lines fit the data quite well.

The statistics in Table 13.2 verify this observation. For the Merton-Henriksson model the estimated intercept is 0.5 compared to the true alpha of 0.3, which is much closer than the CAPM alpha estimate, but not correct.[8]

The beta is estimated at 1.23 compared to the true value of 1.1. The same is true for the Treynor-Mazuy model. The alpha is estimated at 0.17 compared to the true value of 0.3, and the beta is estimated at 0.98 versus the true value of 1.1. The errors in the estimates are due to the specific risk we added to the models.

There are methodological issues in estimating these models such as the skewness in the distribution in the implied option

---

[8] George O. Aragon and Wayne E. Ferson, "Portfolio Performance Evaluation," *Foundations and Trends in Finance*, vol. 2, no. 2, pp. 83–190, 2006.

variable in the Merton-Henriksson model and the skewness in the distribution of the excess return power variable in the Treynor-Mazuy model. However, the methodological issues are overshadowed by the large errors that will be made in model fit by failing to use the correct model.

UP/DOWN MARKET MODEL: UP MARKET
VERSUS DOWN MARKET BETA

An alternative to the Merton-Henriksson test is the up/down regression model where the market returns are divided into two variables. The first variable contains all market values greater than or equal to 0.0. The second variable contains the return data below zero. For each variable, a zero is entered when the value is above or below zero. In this sense we have split the return series into two series of up or down values with zeros filling in the missing values.

This two-variable model is analyzed using standard OLS regression. However, this regression is just a transformation of the first Merton-Henriksson model.

Both models fit the same way, and the estimated regression lines are identical. From a conceptual point of view it may be easier to understand and explain the up-market and down-market betas than it is to explain the beta and gamma in the Merton-Henriksson model.

THE PROBLEM OF NON-TIMING-RELATED
NONLINEARITIES

Models such as we have been discussing are only as effective as our understanding of the underlying data to which they are being applied. To the extent that there are nonlinearities in the data resulting from processes that are not modeled in the explanatory variables then the model will be misspecified and the alpha and beta estimates will be incorrect.

Nonlinearities that can masquerade as timing (or poor timing) ability may arise if the underlying assets in the portfolio are nonlinearly related to the market, such as derivatives. They may also arise if the returns are measured from stale prices, when the extent of the stale pricing is related to market moves.[9] Additional nonlinearities can be created by dynamic trading strategies or by other trading that occurs more frequently than the returns are measured.

Stale and Multiperiod Betas

As we pointed out several times, the models we have been investigating tend to assume a static beta that is invariant over time. The CPE research discussed earlier shows that betas are probably not stable over time. Simple logic would also dictate that betas are not fixed. As a company evolves over time its product lines change, the company grows, and it may change from a small-capitalization company to a larger-capitalization company.

Calculating beta over multiple periods without taking into account the dynamics of company growth and change can easily lead to a misestimation. From a methodological point of view, there is no easy way to deal with this sort of change because the underlying company has changed while there may be limited outward evidence of this. A keen analyst must examine all facets of the business to discover the changing nature of the business. CPE and other time-varying models will be able to detect the changing beta if the correct variables are included in the analysis—but these variables must be related to the relevant company characteristics.

Modeling Illiquid Securities

Illiquid securities such as real estate or art cause problems for all statistical models trying to relate return and risk. Obtaining correct prices and measuring correct price changes, which are fundamental to determining total return, become problematic whenever an asset is illiquid. Stale prices are a particular problem. Modeling the risk characteristics of the illiquid assets is exceedingly difficult.

---

[9] For an analysis of such systemic stale pricing, see Yong Chen, Wayne Ferson, and Helen Peters, "Measuring the Timing Ability of Fixed Income Mutual Funds," October 2006, working paper, University of Southern California, Marshall School of Business.

Sholes-Williams Betas

Sholes and Williams propose a partial solution to estimating betas on a portfolio containing illiquid assets.[10] Asness et al.[11] find that it makes a big difference when estimating the betas for hedge funds.

Consider a model like the following:

$$r_{pt} = \alpha + \beta_0 r_{mt} + \beta_1 r_{mt-1} + \cdots + \varepsilon_t \tag{13.3}$$

where r_{mt} is the excess return of the market and r_{mt-1} is the excess return of the market and the previous time $t - 1$. Alpha (α), beta (β), and specific risk (ε) are as defined as before.

In such a model, the returns on the portfolio are correlated with the lagged market return because of the stale prices in the portfolio's measured return. The number of lags to use depends on how stale the measured returns are. Under the simplifying assumptions that "true" returns are iid[12] and that the market index prices are not stale, Sholes and Williams show that the sum of the coefficient $\beta_0 + \beta1 + \cdots$ in Equation (13.3) is the true beta of the portfolio.

Periodicity of Measurement

One final problem is the periodicity of measurement. Sometimes the analyst has weekly, monthly, and quarterly data. Which of these aggregations of returns should one analyze? Each higher level is a linking of the lower levels. Weekly returns are compounded to obtain monthly returns, and monthly returns are compounded to obtain quarterly returns. Depending on the nature of the nonlinearity the analyst is dealing with, it is possible the analyst would obtain different results using different levels of aggregation. Stock market

---

[10] Myron Scholes and Joesph T. Williams, "Estimating Betas from Nonsynchronous Data," *Journal of Financial Economics*, vol. 5, 1977, pp. 309–327.

[11] Clifford S. Asness, Robert J. Krail, and John M. Liew, "Do Hedge Funds Hedge?" *Journal of Portfolio Management*, Fall 2001, pp. 6–19.

[12] The term *iid* means the random variables are independent and identically distributed if each has the same probability distribution and the variables are mutually independent of each other.

prices move around quite a bit from day to day and certainly within a week. At shorter horizons, "microstructural" aspects of the data, such as bid-ask spreads and nontrading, exert more influence on returns data. At longer horizons, slow-moving trends are more easily detected. Some investor strategies are designed to operate over shorter horizons and some over longer horizons. The choice of the return horizon remains more of an art than a science because many of these factors must be balanced for the problem at hand.

CHAPTER 14

Factor Models

In Chapters 7 to 10 and 12 we discussed the CAPM and the APT as models of asset pricing. We discussed how to estimate the elements of the CAPM using regression analysis and how to use the parameters in risk-adjusted return measures. Here we will begin to delve into "factor models," which are extensions of the earlier ideas. The central idea of factor models is that an asset's return can be described and explained in terms of the asset's characteristics, which determine its sensitivities to various economic and financial risks that are pervasive within the asset class.

THE SINGLE INDEX MODEL

Consider the market model regression often used to estimate elements of the CAPM:

$$r_i = \alpha_i + \beta_i r_b + \varepsilon_i, \tag{14.1}$$

where

r_i = return R_i of asset i minus the risk-free return rate R_f, or $r_i = R_i - R_f$

r_b = return R_b of a benchmark or market portfolio minus the risk-free return rate, or $r_b = R_b - R_f$

α_i = unconditional alpha of asset i

β_i = unconditional beta of asset i

ε_i = specific return of asset i.

If we assume that the specific returns ε_i are uncorrelated between assets, then Equation (14.1) implies a simple model of the covariance between asset i and asset j:

$$\text{Cov}(r_i, r_j) = \begin{cases} \beta_i \beta_j \sigma_b^2, \text{for } i \neq j \\ \beta_i^2 \sigma_b^2 + \delta_i^2, \text{for } i = j \end{cases}$$

where σ_b is the standard deviation of r_b and δ_i is the standard deviation of ε_i, the specific risk of asset i. If there are N assets, the $N \times N$ covariance matrix $\mathbf{V}$ can be written as

$$\mathbf{V} = \boldsymbol{\beta}\boldsymbol{\beta}^T \sigma_b^2 + \Delta$$

where $\boldsymbol{\beta}$ is an $N \times 1$ vector of the asset betas, and Δ is an $N \times N$ diagonal matrix of the specific variances δ_i^2.

This model explains the comovement of assets entirely by a single factor, the market. It is notable for requiring relatively few parameters to estimate. However, the assumption of zero correlation between residual returns is neither a hypothesis nor an implication of the CAPM. Although the market factor is undoubtedly important, we often observe stocks with similar characteristics moving together. Investors and analysts tend to think in terms of characteristics, such as industry membership or size, that might explain the movement of asset prices. Modeling multiple factors allows this intuition to be put to good use.

MULTIPLE FACTOR MODELS

Assuming there are K factors, the multifactor version of Equation (14.1) becomes

$$r_i = b_{i1}f_1 + b_{i2}f_2 + \cdots + b_{ik}f_k + \varepsilon_i, \qquad (14.2)$$

where

b_{ik} = factor exposure (or loading) of asset i to factor k

f_k = return of factor k

ε_i = specific return of asset i.

The asset specific returns ε_i are assumed to be uncorrelated between assets and uncorrelated with the factor returns f_k. If the factor exposures are put into an $N \times K$ matrix $\mathbf{B}$, then the $N \times N$ covariance matrix $\mathbf{V}$ of asset returns can be written as

$$\mathbf{V} = \mathbf{BFB}^T + \Delta, \tag{14.3}$$

where

$\mathbf{B} = N \times K$ matrix of factor exposures

$\mathbf{F} = K \times K$ covariance matrix of factor returns

$\Delta = N \times N$ diagonal matrix of the specific variances δ_i^2, where δ_i is the standard deviation of the specific return ε_i.

There are several types of factor models, depending on how the factors and exposures are defined and estimated. In one type, the factor returns f_k are defined as the returns to particular portfolios, which might be deliberately chosen to emphasize the intended characteristic. For example, the return of a portfolio of stocks in a given industry might be used as a factor return. Or, to represent a characteristic like size, stocks might be sorted by capitalization; the difference between the returns of the smallest and largest quintile portfolios could be used as a factor return. After the time series of factor returns is constructed, the factor exposures b_{ik} can be estimated by a time series regression.

A second type of factor model begins by specifying the exposures b_{ik} in terms of directly observable characteristics. An exposure to a size factor might be defined as the log of the market cap of the stock, for example. Industry factors would be specified as exposures taking values of either 0 or 1. After the exposures are constructed at a given date, the factor returns can then be estimated by a cross-sectional regression. Repeating this process over time produces a time series of factor returns, from which the factor covariance matrix can be calculated.

A third type of factor model, called a statistical factor model (or principal components model), specifies neither the factor exposures nor the factor returns in advance. Instead, the estimation process jointly produces factor exposures and returns. Such factors usually cannot be associated with profile characteristics like size or industry membership, and the nature of the factors can change over time. Nevertheless, there can be information gained from a statistical factor model that might not emerge from predefined factors. Hybrid models exist, which combine features of all three approaches.

FACTOR MODEL ANALYTICS

Once the parameters of a factor model have been estimated, many of the performance measures described in earlier chapters can be calculated in the factor model context. To start, if $\mathbf{w}_p$ is the vector of weights of a portfolio, then the total risk σ_p of the portfolio is given by

$$\sigma_p^2 = \mathbf{w}_p^T \mathbf{V} \mathbf{w}_p.$$

Given weights $\mathbf{w}_b$ of a benchmark portfolio, the betas of all of the assets with respect to the benchmark can be calculated from

$$\beta = \frac{\mathbf{V}\mathbf{w}_b}{\sigma_b^2} = \frac{\mathbf{V}\mathbf{w}_b}{\mathbf{w}_b^T \mathbf{V} \mathbf{w}_b}.$$

The portfolio beta can be calculated from $\beta_p = \mathbf{w}_p^T \beta$ and the total portfolio risk σ_p can be decomposed into a systematic part $\beta_p \sigma_b$ and a residual part ω_p by

$$\sigma_p^2 = \beta_p^2 \sigma_b^2 + \omega_p^2.$$

The betas derived from a factor model are called "predicted betas" to distinguish them from betas estimated directly from a time series regression. Predicted betas depend directly on the given portfolio weights, which allows the effect of changes in portfolio weights to be measured.

In constructing portfolios, it is useful to know the effect of a small change in portfolio weights on the portfolio risk. The marginal contribution to risk MCTR is readily calculated from

$$\mathbf{MCTR} = \frac{d\sigma_p}{d\mathbf{w}_p} = \frac{\mathbf{V}\mathbf{w}_p}{\sigma_p}.$$

The MCTR is an $N \times 1$ vector. Trading a small amount of an asset with a large MCTR for an asset with a small MCTR should decrease the total portfolio risk.

Analogous calculations can be made for active return $r_p - r_b$, that is, portfolio return in excess of the benchmark. By defining active weights as $\mathbf{w}_{pa} = \mathbf{w}_p - \mathbf{w}_b$, the calculation of active risk (also called tracking error), active beta, and marginal contribution to active risk is straightforward, given the covariance matrix of a factor model.[1]

A SIMPLE EXAMPLE

To illustrate these concepts, we give a very simplified numerical example. Let us assume we have a stock market consisting of five securities labeled "A" through "E." Each of these securities has exposures to four factors that we know are priced (rewarded) in the marketplace. The factors that drive returns are a firm "size" measure (the log capitalization of the firm), a "value" factor (whose loadings are the book-to-price ratio of the firm), and the technology sector membership (each stock is either in the tech sector or in the nontech sector). Table 14.1 displays hypothetical values.

TABLE 14.1

Factor Exposures (Raw)

Stock	Market Weight w_i	Size	Book/Price Value	Tech	Nontech
A	0.30	2.90	2.50	0	1
B	0.10	1.10	3.10	1	0
C	0.10	0.70	1.00	0	1
D	0.30	0.40	5.00	1	0
E	0.20	0.10	2.00	0	1
	Weighted mean:	1.19	3.06	0.40	0.60
	Standard deviation:	1.10	1.49		

---

[1] For a full treatment of the analytics of factor models, see Richard C. Grinold and Ronald N. Kahn, *Active Portfolio Management*, 2nd ed., (New York: McGraw-Hill, 2000).

The market cap weights are listed in the table and the weighted means are shown at the bottom, along with the standard deviations of the raw exposures. Factor exposures built from characteristics like book-to-price ratios may have a wide range of units, which can be difficult to interpret. It helps to standardize exposures by measuring deviations from the mean of the universe of stocks used to build the model. In Table 14.2, we show the standardized factor exposures, transformed by subtracting the weighted means and dividing by the standard deviations. With standardized exposures, positive and negative exposures are easily interpreted as being greater than or less than that of the market, respectively.

Returns for the stocks over the period are also listed in Table 14.2. A regression of the stock returns on the standardized exposures gives estimates of the factor returns shown at the bottom of the table. Observe that the weighted mean of the exposures to size and value are zero. The corresponding factor returns, therefore, can be interpreted as the extra return that could be obtained per unit of exposure to the factor. The market as a whole has no exposure to these factors, by definition. The overall market return is absorbed in the 0/1 industry factors, which together play the role of the intercept in an ordinary regression.

Given the factor returns, we can decompose the individual stock returns into a portion contributed by exposure to the factors, and a specific return. For example, stock "A" had an exposure of 1.55 to the size factor, which, multiplied by the factor return of 2.82, contributed 4.37 to the total return. Multiplying the factor exposures by the returns and summing over the factors gives a return of 6.77 explained by the factors. The difference between the total return of 6.87 and that explained by the factors is 0.10, the specific return of stock "A." Calculated values of specific returns are shown in the last column of Table 14.2.

If this procedure, of creating factor exposures and estimating factor returns, were repeated over time, a series of factor returns and specific returns can be created. Suppose that we have done that and have calculated a covariance matrix from the resulting factor return series, in Table 14.3, and the standard deviations of specific returns in Table 14.4.

We now have all of the elements needed to calculate the 5×5 covariance matrix $\mathbf{V}$ from Equation (14.2). Doing so, we can

T A B L E 14.2

Factor Exposures (Standardized) and Estimated Factor Returns

Stock	Market Weight w_i	Size	Book/Price Value	Tech	Nontech	Stock Return	Return Explained by Factors	Specific Return
A	0.30	1.55	-0.38	0	1	6.87	6.77	0.10
B	0.10	-0.08	0.03	1	0	4.75	4.05	0.70
C	0.10	-0.44	-1.38	0	1	0.72	2.00	-1.28
D	0.30	-0.72	1.30	1	0	0.50	1.20	-0.70
E	0.20	-0.99	-0.71	0	1	1.08	-0.10	1.18
Weighted mean exposure:		0.00	0.00	0.40	0.60			
Estimated factor returns:		2.82	-0.84	4.30	2.09			

TABLE 14.3

Factor Covariance Matrix

	Size	Value	Tech	Nontech
Size	196	22	21	14
Value	22	64	36	16
Tech	21	36	225	15
Nontech	14	16	15	100

TABLE 14.4

Stock-Specific Risks

A	B	C	D	E
8	5	18	9	5

calculate the individual stock betas, assuming the benchmark has the market cap weights in Table 14.2. The stock betas and the benchmark total risk is shown in Table 14.5.

Finally, given a vector of portfolio weights, we can analyze the portfolio risk and return in terms of the factors. Suppose we have a portfolio consisting only of assets "A," "B," and "C" held in proportion to their market cap weights. The portfolio weights compared to the benchmark weights are given in Table 14.6.

Multiplying the weights by the factor exposures gives us the exposures of the portfolio, and combining the exposures with the factor returns gives the return decomposition shown in Table 14.7,

TABLE 14.5

Stock Betas and Benchmark Total Risk

A	B	C	D	E	σ_b
1.06	1.04	0.60	1.47	0.39	9.84

T A B L E 14.6

Portfolio, Benchmark, and Active Weights

	Portfolio	Benchmark	Active
A	0.6	0.3	0.3
B	0.2	0.1	0.1
C	0.2	0.1	0.1
D	0.0	0.3	−0.3
E	0.0	0.2	−0.2

T A B L E 14.7

Factor Exposures of the Portfolio and Returns Explained by Factors

	Size	Value	Tech	Nontech	Specific	Total
Exposures						
Portfolio	0.82	−0.50	0.20	0.80		
Benchmark	0.00	0.00	0.40	0.60		
Active	0.82	−0.50	−0.20	0.20		
Returns					*Specific*	*Total*
Portfolio	2.32	0.42	0.86	1.67	−0.06	5.21
Benchmark	0.00	0.00	1.72	1.25	0.00	2.97
Active	2.32	0.42	−0.86	0.42	−0.06	2.24

Evidently, our portfolio benefited from an overweight to the size factor and to the nontech sector, and from an underweight to the value factor. The underweight to the tech sector detracted from performance in this period.

In this chapter, we have only scratched the surface of factor modeling. Factor models can provide a wealth of information that is worth the investment in learning how to use them.

CHAPTER 15

Factors of Equity Returns in the United States

There are many vendors of factor models of the U.S. equity market, and each of them uses a slightly different set of variables to explain stock returns and stock risks. We cannot hope to provide an extensive list of all factors considered, but in Tables 15.1 and 15.2 we show a sampling of the kinds of variables that are used by different vendors. The factors in Table 15.1 are cross-sectional in nature, while those in Table 15.2 are statistical and macroeconomic factors.

VARIOUS FACTOR MODEL FACTORS

Most of these vendors build composite variables, which consist of multiple data items weighted together to form a single exposure variable. A large number of data items are available from data providers such as Compustat and CRSP. Many of these data items are closely related to each other, so to avoid statistical problems in the estimation of factor returns, most vendors try to extract the unique explanatory information within a group of data items. For example, if we wanted to create a variable called "historic growth" for a company, we might create a weighted combination of past growth of sales per share, earnings per share, and cash flow per share. If we wanted to create a "valuation" measure, we might create a weighted combination of price/book, price/sales, price/earnings, and price/ cash flow. These variables have all been used by analysts to measure

TABLE 15.1

Factors Identified for U.S. Equities by Major Vendors of Factor Models

Risk Category	Wilshire Atlas	Barra E3	Vestek	RiskMetrics	Northfield
Market relative	Volatility	Volatility composite	Volatility composite	Volatility	Price volatility
	Price momentum	Momentum	Momentum	Price momentum	Beta
		Trading activity	Beta	Market return	Trading activity
Fundamentals	Log market cap	Size	Log market cap	Small minus big	Market cap
		Size nonlinearity			Revenue/price
	Earnings/price	Earnings yield	Earnings/price		Earnings/price
	Book/price	Book/price	Book/price		Book/price
		Dividend yield	Dividend yield	Dividend yield	Dividend yield
		Earnings variability			Earnings variability
		Leverage		Liquidity	Debt/equity
		Currency sensitivity			
		Growth composite	Long-term growth		EPS growth
			Statistical factors (eigenvalues extracted from residuals)		
Sectors	59	55		10	55

Sources: Wilshire Atlas GR6 Equity Risk Model (Santa Monica, CA: Wilshire Associates, 2006); Barra Aegis System, www.mscibarra.com; Thomson Financial Services, www.vestek.com; The RiskMetrics Group, www.riskmetrics.com; and Northfield Information Services, www.northinfo.com.

T A B L E 15.2

Major Vendors of Macro Economic Factor Models

Statistical Based Factors	Macroeconomic Based Factors
Northfield Information Services	BIRR Portfolio Analysis (Burmeister, Ibbotson, Roll, and Ross)
Short-interval security covariance	Confidence risk: 20-year corporate bond return – 25-year government bond return
	Time horizon risk: 25-year government bond return – 30-day T-bill rate
	Inflation risk: Actual inflation rate (CPI) – expected inflation rate
	Business cycle risk: change in real economic growth (industrial production)
	Market sentiment risk: S&P return not explained by previous four factors, that is, residuals

Sources: BIRR Portfolio Analysis, Inc., www.birr.com, and Northfield Information Services, Inc., www.northinfo.com.

the valuation of a stock relative to others. There is a great deal of research that shows that valuation measures, in particular book-to-market or price-to-book ratios, have been significant risk factors for many years.

There has been research by Burmeister et al.[1] and Chen, Roll, and Ross taking an APT approach[2] to risk control showing that a

---

[1] Edwin Burmeister and M. B. McElroy, "Joint Estimation of Factor Sensitivities and Risk Premia for the Arbitrage Pricing Theory," *Journal of Finance*, vol. 63, no. 3, July 1988, pp. 721–733. Edwin Burmeister and M. B. McElroy, "Arbitrage Pricing Theory as a Restricted Nonlinear Regression Model: NLITSUR Estimates," *Journal of Business and Economic Statistics*, vol. 6, no. 1, January 1988, pp. 28–42. Edwin Burmeister and M. B. McElroy, "Sorting out Risks Using Known APT Factors," *Financial Analysts Journal*, March/April, 1988, pp. 29–42. Edwin Burmeister, Roger Ibbotson, Richard Roll, and Stephen A. Ross, "Using Macroeconomic Factors to Control Portfolio Risk," Unpublished see www.birr.com and www.birr.com/BIRR_Risk_Model.pdf.

[2] Nai-fu Chen, Richard Roll, and Stephen A. Ross, "Economic Forces and the Stock Market," *Journal of Business*, vol. 59, July 1986, pp. 383–403.

considerable amount of stock return variation can be explained by sensitivity to macroeconomic conditions. The macro factors BIRR uses are shown in Table 15.2.

Also in the table we mention Northfield's U.S. Short Term Equity factor model. For this model, Northfield uses what they call a blind-factor model that analyzes short-horizon stock price returns for the stocks in the S&P 500. Using iterated principal components factor analysis, Northfield extracts the first 20 eigenvalues from the correlation matrix of stock returns. The principal components method creates a set of eigenvectors that when multiplied by a vector of eigenvalues is able to reproduce the original matrix closely. In this sense the method distills, summarizes, or reduces a large correlation matrix into 20 different variables, which is a smaller, more manageable set of data that explain the largest portion of the co-movement of these 500 securities.

To normalize the variance of each return series, capture trend, and mean-reversion and to adjust for autocorrelation in returns, an ARIMA[3] process is fitted to each stock's return series. The adjusted residual returns are then analyzed for the 20 factors mentioned. The use of high-frequency data collected over a relatively short sample period helps mitigate the stability problems normally associated with longer-window principal component factor extraction.

Armed with the 20 factor series, loadings are calculated for each security (these are the exposures of the security to each of our common factors) and then Northfield can estimate the variance of any portfolio based on its exposure to the 20 factors.

THE BARRA FACTORS

The composition of risk factors can be as simple as one variable like price-to-book, a weighted combination of many variables, or quite complicated. The number of factors in a factor model is usually empirically derived as determined by the judgment of the model builders.

---

[3] Auto-Regressive Integrated Moving Average (ARIMA) captures the effects of serial correlation and trend in security returns. The residual series from the model are mean-stationary with zero serial correlation. See James D. Hamilton, "Time Series Analysis" (Princeton, NJ: Princeton University Press, 1994).

There is no fixed theoretical number. In the U.S. E3 Model, Barra has distilled a large number of data items, called descriptors, into 13 factors, in addition to 55 industry factors. The 13 factors, called risk indices, and the descriptor variables used to create them are found in Table 15.3. The methods Barra uses to scrub the data and handle outliers, and so forth, are proprietary.[4]

T A B L E 15.3

Risk Factors in the Barra Factor Model with Explanations

Barra Factor	Definition
1. Volatility	This risk index captures relative volatility using measures of both long-term historical volatility (such as historical residual standard deviation) and near-term volatility (such as high-low price ratio, daily standard deviation, and cumulative range over the last 12 months). Other proxies for volatility (log of stock price), corrections for thin trading (serial dependence), and changes in volatility (volume beta) are also included in this descriptor.
	Descriptor variables:
	Beta times sigma, daily standard deviation of prices
	Ratio of high to low stock price last month, log price
	Cumulative range, volume beta
	Serial dependence, option-implied standard deviation
2. Momentum	This risk index captures common variation in returns related to recent stock price behavior. Stocks that had positive excess returns in the recent past are grouped separately from those that displayed negative excess returns.
	Descriptor variables:
	Relative strength
	Historical alpha
3. Size	This risk index captures differences in large vs. small-market capitalization of companies' stock returns.
	Descriptor variable:
	Log of market capitalization
	(Continued)

---

[4] Barra does not discuss exactly how it prepares data in its publicly available information. Its contact is www.mscibarra.com/products/analytics/aegis/.

TABLE 15.3

Risk Factors in the Barra Factor Model with Explanations *(Continued)*

Barra Factor	Definition
4. Size nonlinearity	This risk index captures deviations from linearity in the relationship between returns and log of market capitalization.
	Descriptor variable:
	Cube of log of market capitalization
5. Trading activity	This risk index measures the amount of relative trading in each stock. Stocks that are highly traded are likely to be those with greater institutional interest. Such stocks may display different return behavior than those not widely held by institutions.
	Descriptor variables:
	Share turnover rate monthly
	Share turnover rate quarterly
	Five-year share turnover
	Indicator for forward split volume
	Volume variance
6. Growth	This risk index uses historical growth and profitability measures to predict future earnings growth.
	Descriptor variables:
	Payout ratio over five years
	Variability in capital structure
	Growth rate in total assets
	Earnings growth rate
	Analyst-predicted earnings growth
	Recent earnings change
7. Earnings yield	This risk index combines current and historical earnings-to-price ratios with a measure of analyst-predicted earnings-to-price.
	Descriptor variables:
	Analyst-predicted earnings-to-price
	Trailing annual earnings-to-price
	Historical five-year earnings-to-price
8. Value	This risk index distinguishes between value stocks and growth stocks using the ratio of book value of equity to market capitalization.
	Descriptor variable:
	Book-to-price ratio

T A B L E 15.3

Risk Factors in the Barra Factor Model with Explanations *(Continued)*

Barra Factor	Definition
9. Earnings variation	This risk index measures the variability in earnings and cash flows using both historical measures and analyst predictions. *Descriptor variables:* Variability in earnings Variability in cash flows Extraordinary items in earnings Standard deviation of analyst-predicted earnings-to-price
10. Leverage	This risk index measures the financial leverage of a company. *Descriptor variables:* Market leverage Book leverage Debt to total assets Senior debt rating
11. Currency sensitivity	This risk index measures the sensitivity of a company's stock return to the return on a basket of foreign currencies. *Descriptor variable:* Foreign currencies sensitivity
12. Dividend yield	This risk index computes a measure of predicted dividend yield using the past history of dividends and the market price behavior of the stock. *Descriptor variable:* Predicted dividend yield
13. Nonestimation universe indicator	This risk index flags companies outside the estimation universe. (The factor model coefficient estimation universe has 1,500 securities, so many stocks fall outside this limited universe.) *Descriptor variable:* Binary variable. Firms outside US-E3 estimation universe = 1
14–68. Economic sector membership	Barra's 55 economic sector exposures *Descriptor variables:* Each stock can have exposures of up to five economic sectors derived by Barra based on the sectors in which the company does business. Barra, FTSE, Russell, and others have different economic sector grouping criteria.

Source: Barra Aegis System, www.mscibarra.com, USE3S model descriptors.

The manner in which Barra combines the values for each descriptor variable, that is, the weights it assigns to relative strength and historical alpha when computing the momentum score, for example, is proprietary. The weights are constant over time with occasional adjustments that are not publicized. The variables are z-scored so that the scales of all the variables are comparable.[5]

FACTOR-MIMICKING PORTFOLIOS: HIGH-LOW APPROACH AND FACTOR EXTRACTION APPROACH

It is often useful in portfolio management or performance attribution to be able to understand the behavior of a particular risk factor. We can create portfolios of assets whose characteristics and performance mimic the behavior of that factor in the market. These are called factor-mimicking portfolios. There are several different ways to create these portfolios.

We know from Tables 15.1 and 15.2 that there are a wide variety of factors that we could choose to mimic. The most powerful factors are the "valuation" factors. Fama and French form three basic portfolios that track these factors. One of those factors is the book-to-market factor portfolio. Their approach is the easiest way to create a mimicking portfolio. Take all the stocks in the CRSP database and group the securities into quintiles based upon capitalization-weighted or equally weighted price-to-book ratios. The return to the highest quintile minus the return to the lowest quintile is defined as the return to the high-low book/market factor. To create an investable portfolio that generates the same return, we would have to be long stocks in the top quintile and short stocks in the bottom quintile.

There are other ways to approach this problem. We could, for example, calculate capitalization-weighted z-scores for all the securities in the market and build a portfolio that has a net positive one-standard-deviation z-score exposure to price-to-book.

Another approach is to form portfolios implicitly via the factor return estimation process described in Chapter 14. In this approach

---

[5] For information on Barra factors, see www.mscibarra.com.

we run a regression with stock returns on the left-hand side and factor sensitivities on the right-hand side. Eugene Fama[6] showed that the slope coefficients that are our estimates of the factor returns are actually the excess returns (in excess of cash or a risk-free asset) of factor-mimicking portfolios. These portfolios have positive unit risk exposures to the factor in question while minimizing the variance of their excess return. To have unit exposure, these portfolios are typically long stocks with exposures greater than 1 and short stocks with low or negative exposures. If a multiple regression is used, the mimicking portfolio for a particular factor has zero exposure to all other risk factors whose exposures appear in the regression.

---

[6] Eugene Fama, *Foundations of Finance* (New York: Basic Books, 1976).

CHAPTER 16

Factor Model (Barra) Performance Attribution

In Chapters 14 and 15 we showed how factor models can be constructed and estimated. Factor models usually serve two purposes: (1) risk forecasting and (2) performance attribution. To do risk forecasting you must be able to forecast the risk of each asset and the covariances among the assets. MSCI Barra has extensive models to do this, and we refer you to its website for more information.[1] Performance attribution is our primary focus here. It involves analyzing a historical portfolio using the risk exposures of each asset and the factor returns for each factor. In this chapter we will show how a particular factor model can be used to provide useful information about portfolio performance. We will use the Barra model and Barra terminology to do this. The tables in this chapter can be found in the Barra Aegis System.[2]

---

[1] See the Barra Aegis System, www.mscibarra.com, USE3 model and Richard C. Grinold and Ronald N. Kahn, *Active Portfolio Management*, 2nd ed., (New York: McGraw-Hill, 2000) and earlier Andrew Rudd and Henry. K. Classing, *Modern Portfolio Theory* (Homewood, IL: Irwin, 1987). This book reviews the Barra factor model logic extensively. The current E3 model is not covered, but the internal logic of the older E2 model is very similar.

[2] The data displayed in the tables in this chapter are realistic example data and do not refer to any specific manager or client.

ATTRIBUTION "EXECUTIVE SUMMARY"

The usual point of departure for performance attribution analysis is with the executive summary. It is a high-level summary that provides the overall decomposition of active return over a specific time period. The analysis is based upon quarterly or monthly holdings. The implicit assumption is that there is no portfolio trading during the period. Of course, this is rarely the case, and to the extent that extensive trading has taken place in the portfolio during the period, the analysis can be incomplete and a bit misleading.

The executive summary provides useful risk-adjusted performance statistics like annualized risk (standard deviation), information ratios, and t-stats for each major policy choice. Normally included with this report is the best five and worst five policy decisions that contributed to active return. Active return is the portfolio return minus the benchmark return.

By looking at this report, you can assess the portfolio's overall risk-adjusted performance as well as the manager's strengths and weaknesses. Table 16.1 displays the executive summary in annualized return space.

We will show later on what each of these components means, but for right now let us note the values in row 5 of Table 16.1, "Asset Selection," which are usually of the most interest. These figures estimate asset selection skill. This manager has consistently positive stock selection capability holding other portfolio characteristics constant. The total annualized factor return, that is a return above the benchmark, is 5.75 percent (column 3, row 9) over the full time span. Exposure to the risk indices contributed the most to that return at 3.77 percent with asset selection contributing 1.72 percent. The information coefficient (IC) is strongly positive at 0.88.[3] The t-statistic for asset selection is 1.07, well below 2.0, which normally denotes a significance at the 0.05 level.

---

[3] The IC is the correlation between implied alpha estimated from the portfolio's overweights and underweights and the realized returns. Higher is better.

T A B L E 16.1

Performance Attribution Executive Summary

| | Executive Summary—Annualized Contribution to Active Return | | | | | | | |
| | Trailing Periods (% Return) | | | | Full Time Span | | | |
Source of Return	3 Mon	1 Yr	3 Yrs	5 Yrs	Contribution (%)	Risk (% per Std. Dev.)[4]	IR	T-Stat
1. Expected active	0.69	0.66	0.69	N/A	0.69	N/A	N/A	N/A
2. Market timing	0.18	−0.13	0.36	N/A	0.36	1.41	0.30	0.52
3. Risk indexes	−11.77	−1.20	3.77	N/A	3.77	4.67	0.76	1.32
4. Industries	11.91	1.18	−0.79	N/A	−0.79	2.20	−0.30	−0.53
5. Asset selection	2.09	2.95	1.72	N/A	1.72	2.36	0.62	1.07
6. Trading	N/A	N/A	N/A	N/A	N/A	N/A	N/A	N/A
7. Transaction cost	N/A	N/A	N/A	N/A	N/A	N/A	N/A	N/A
8. Total exceptional active [2 + ⋯ + 7]	2.40	2.80	5.06	N/A	5.06	5.39	0.88	1.53
9. Total active [1 + 8]	3.09	3.46	5.75	N/A	5.75	5.39	0.99	1.72

---

4 "Risk (% per Std. Dev.)" refers to the amount of portfolio risk that is associated with each standard deviation unit. It highlights which source of risk has the greater impact.

TOTAL ANNUALIZED ATTRIBUTION CHART

Figure 16.1 displays the total annualized attribution chart, which is at the heart of Barra's return decomposition system. The figure graphically shows the decomposition of the return into its various components in a hierarchical fashion. Note that the top half of each box has portfolio return components and the bottom half of each box has portfolio risk contribution in terms of standard deviation.

The graph in Figure 16.1 provides an overview of the overall performance attribution, explaining where the active return came from—market timing, risk indices, industries, or stock selection skill, and how the sources of return coincide with the sources of risk. In other words, whether the manager was compensated for the risk he took in a particular bet.

Starting at the top with the *Total* box, we have the total annualized return of the managed portfolio which was 17.86 percent. The bottom half of the box displays the total volatility or standard deviation of the portfolio, which was 16.03 percent (annualized). This indicates that there is a 68 percent chance that the portfolio's return will be within ±16.03 percent deviation from the expected return given the beta.

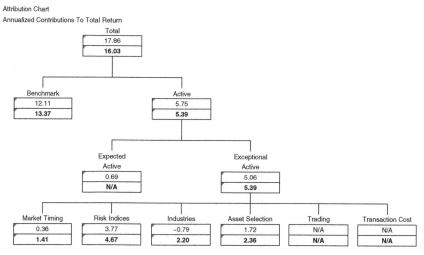

Figure 16.1 Decomposition of Portfolio Return and Risk

The *Benchmark* box displays the total benchmark return (annualized) for the same period, which was 12.11 percent and its volatility was 13.37 percent.

Subtracting the benchmark return from the total return yields the *Active* box. The active return of 5.75 percent is the difference between the portfolio return and the benchmark return. It is often referred to as the excess return. Just below the active return is the active risk, or tracking error, equal to 5.39 percent.[5]

At the next level, active return is decomposed into *Expected Active* return and risk and *Exceptional Active* return and risk. The expected active return is the difference between the expected total return of the portfolio given its beta and the return of the benchmark. The exceptional return is that return above and beyond what is expected given the benchmark. If the portfolio has a beta greater than 1 and the benchmark has a beta of 1, then we would expect the portfolio to have a higher return given our knowledge of the security market line, which shows a relationship between beta and expected return relative to the market.

The exceptional return can be further decomposed into the *Market Timing* box and *Risk Indices* box. The market timing box shows the contribution to active return and risk that is due to the manager's decision to hold cash and to hold assets that have a higher or lower beta, on average, relative to the benchmark's assets. Market timing risk/return answers the questions of whether the decision to hold cash had a positive or negative impact on the performance and whether the decision to hold assets with higher or lower betas had a positive or negative impact on the performance.

The *Risk Indices* box shows the contribution to active return that is due to the managed portfolio's active risk index exposures or style of investing relative to the benchmark. Style factors include such things as size, value, and growth. The risk indices answer the question of whether the portfolio benefited from style deviations away from the benchmark.

---

[5] Note that $5.39 \neq 16.03 - 13.37$; that is, the risks are not additive because of covariances. The active risk is $\sigma_{r_P - r_B} = [\sigma_P^2 + \sigma_B^2 - 2 \operatorname{Cov}(r_B r_P)]^{1/2}$.

The *Industries or Sectors* box is the contribution to active return that is due to the managed portfolio's active industry weights relative to the benchmark. The return and risk due to industries or sectors answers the question of whether the portfolio manager picked the "right" industries to overweight and underweight.

The *Asset Selection* box is the contribution due to the unique choice of assets and not due to any common factor influences in the factor model. This is the sum of the return due to the portfolio manager's overweights and underweights on individual securities rather than factors. This is one of the key elements of the attribution analysis because it answers the question of whether the stocks selected within any industry or style were the best the manager could have selected. It tells analysts how successful the portfolio manager was in overweighting and underweighting assets relative to the benchmark. This is typically the primary source of alpha.

The *Transaction Costs* box and the *Trading* box capture the amount of return and risk that are due to transactions if the user has incorporated transaction costs and trading costs into the analysis. It answers the question of whether the cost of trading detracted too much from return.

ANNUAL ATTRIBUTION REPORT

The annual attribution report, shown in Table 16.2, covers the same information about the sources of return and risk as Figure 16.1 but with some highly useful additional information about the quality of performance, namely, the information ratio and *t*-statistic associated with it. Using these statistics allows the analyst to identify the areas in which the portfolio manager did well on a risk-adjusted basis. It also helps us to determine whether the result is due to the manager's skill or to luck.

The *Contribution (% Return)* and *Risk per Unit of Standard Deviation* columns show the contribution and risk values, respectively, for each source of return, which are the same numbers as in Figure 16.1 from which they were drawn.

The *Information Ratio (Info)* column shows the information ratio measures or the active return achieved per unit of active risk taken for each source of return. It shows risk-adjusted performance, which is useful when comparing portfolios with different levels of risk.

$$\text{Information ratio} = \frac{\text{annualized active return}}{\text{annualized active risk}}.$$

The information ratio for the total active level was 0.99, which is unusually high—an information ratio of 0.7 is considered very good. An information ratio of 0.99 indicates that for each percentage point of active risk taken, 0.99 percent return was earned. Looking at the sources of return, we can see that the manager

TABLE 16.2

Summary Annual Attribution Report

Portfolio Name:
  USVALUE   UB Monthly
Benchmark: SAP500   2002-12 to 2005-11 (36 Months)
Market: SAP500   30-12-2005 (Fri)

ATTRIBUTION REPORT

Annualized Contributions to Total Return

Source of Return	Contribution (% Return)	Risk (% per Std. Dev.)	Info Ratio	T-Stat
1. Risk free	1.75	N/A	N/A	N/A
2. Total benchmark	12.11	13.37		
3. Expected active	0.69	N/A	N/A	N/A
4. Market timing	0.36		0.3	0.52
5. Risk indexes	3.77	4.67	0.76	1.32
6. Industries	−0.79	2.2	−0.3	−0.53
7. Asset selection	1.72	2.36	0.62	1.07
8. Trading	N/A	N/A	N/A	N/A
9. Transaction cost	N/A	N/A	N/A	N/A
10. Total exceptional active [4 + ⋯ + 9]	5.06	5.39	0.88	1.53
11. Total active [3 + 10]	5.75	5.39	0.99	1.72
12. Total managed [2 + 11]	17.86	16.03		

achieved the highest information ratio in risk indices, which indicates that the manager was successful in selecting styles or factors
and did so even on a risk-adjusted basis.

The *T-Statistic* column allows us to determine whether the
manager's information ratio is based on skill rather than luck. In
general, a *t*-statistic larger than 2 indicates that the performance is
significantly different from zero, with a 95 percent confidence
level.

In this example, the *t*-statistic for the active risk was 1.72. It
indicates the performance has a 93 percent confidence level, which,
as mentioned, means that there's a 7 percent chance of this result
being misleading.

ANNUALIZED CONTRIBUTIONS
TO RISK INDEXES

In Figure 16.1 we noted that the total return due to exposure to risk
indices was 3.77 percent. The next logical step in our analysis is to
decompose the total risk index return into the 13 risk index factors.
The object of this analysis is to show how much average active
exposure the portfolio had to each risk index (or style) and whether
or not the bets on risk indices were rewarded with return. Table 16.3
displays the average risk exposure and the contributions to both
risk and performance.

The largest positive contribution to the overall return of
3.55 percent came from the risk index exposure bet on the size factor.
The portfolio is significantly underexposed to this factor with an
average active exposure equal to –1.80. This means that the portfolio
consisted of assets with significantly smaller market capitalization
than the benchmark. Since the size factor was not positively rewarded
during this time period, the result of this bet was a positive contribution of 3.55 percent to overall active return. On the other hand, the
portfolio took a positive active bet on the yield factor, which turned
out to be negatively rewarded (–1.43 percent) and contributed negatively to the overall return with a *t*-statistic of –2.95.

The information ratio indicates that the negative bet on the
growth factor was the most successful policy on a risk-adjusted
basis. It provided an information ratio of 1.23, which is high with a
t-statistic of 2.13.

T A B L E 16.3

Annualized Contributions to Risk Index Return

Portfolio Name: USVALUE
Benchmark: SAP500
Market: SAP500

UB Monthly
2002-12 to 2005-11 (36 Months)
30-12-2005 (Fri)

Total Annualized Attribution

Source of Return	Average Active Exposure	Contribution (% Return)			Total Risk (% per Std. Dev.)	Info Ratio	T-Stat
		Average [1]	Variation [2]	Total [1 + 2]			
Size	-1.7958	-3.8808	-0.3268	3.554	3.6814	0.8763	1.5178
Value	1.6258	1.3624	0.1721	1.5345	2.042	0.6612	1.1453
Growth	-0.2298	0.3725	0.0332	0.4056	0.2822	1.2327	2.1351
Earnings variation	0.3061	0.4458	-0.1607	0.2851	0.4105	0.6263	1.0847
Leverage	0.2652	0.2303	-0.0441	0.1862	0.3167	0.5158	0.8934
Momentum	-0.0492	-0.0502	0.1293	0.0791	0.4088	0.2017	0.3493
Currency sensitivity	-0.1527	-0.0584	0.0469	-0.0115	0.2228	-0.0267	-0.0462
Earning yield	-0.0113	-0.0393	-0.0082	-0.0475	0.0782	-0.499	-0.8643
Trading activity	0.1779	-0.0882	0.0115	-0.0767	0.2828	-0.2717	-0.4705
Not in-estimation universe	0.0287	0.0492	-0.136	-0.0869	0.1451	-0.5199	-0.9005
Size nonlinearity	-0.575	-0.1764	-0.1032	-0.2796	1.3652	-0.1814	-0.3143
Volatility	0.3252	-0.3036	-0.0383	-0.3419	1.4794	-0.1715	-0.2971
Yield	0.5448	-1.4379	0.01	-1.4279	0.6908	-1.7054	-2.9538
Total		-1.4379	0.01	3.7726	4.6656	0.761	1.318

165

The *Average Active Exposure* column displays the average difference between the portfolio and benchmark exposures over the analysis period. Active exposures of a 0.2 or more standard deviation should be considered significant active bets because 58 percent of the distribution falls below this value. In this portfolio the size and value average risk exposures were the two largest average active bets. The portfolio has the highest negative active exposure to the size factor and the highest positive active exposure to the value factor. The *Average Contribution* column displays the average contribution of each risk factor that results from the average active exposure held over the analysis period. The *Variation Contribution* column displays the return due to variation or timing which comes from deviations in the average active exposure that are presumably made by the portfolio manager to time market movements.

The *Total Contribution (1 + 2)* column shows the sum of the first two columns and reflects whether the bets on each factor worked or not. At the bottom of this column is the *Total-Total Contribution (%Return)* sum of 3.77 percent, which matches the risk index contribution in Figure 16.1.

INDUSTRIES: TOP-10 AND BOTTOM-10 CONTRIBUTORS TO ACTIVE RETURN

Table 16.4 shows which industries the manager overweighted or underweighted and whether or not those bets paid off. As we can see in the upper left-hand corner of the table, in this portfolio, the average bet on the securities and asset management industry was most successful. The manager overweighted the industry by 8.89 percent relative to the benchmark on an average basis. Because the industry did well, the bet worked, contributing 0.56 percent to the overall return.

On the other hand, the policy to underweight the energy reserves industry at –3.50 percent was not positively rewarded, yielding a –0.93 percent loss. This result implies that the industry performed well and, in retrospect, the manager should have overweighted this industry but did not.

The *Average Active Exposure (%)* column shows the average weight difference between the portfolio and the benchmark for each industry. The *Total Contribution (% Return)* column shows the result

T A B L E 16.4

Top-10 and Bottom-10 Industry Bets

Portfolio Name: USVALUE
Benchmark: SAP500
Market: SAP500

UB Monthly 2002-12 to 2005-11
(36 Months) 30-12-2005

Annualized Contributions to Industry Return

Sources of Return	Average Active Exposure (%)	Contribution Return			Total Risk (% per Std. Dev.)	Info Ratio	T-Stat
		Average [1]	Variation [2]	Total [1 + 2]			
Top-10 Industries							
Securities and asset management	8.89	0.36	0.21	0.56	0.83	0.58	1.01
Life/health insurance	10.13	0.36	0.12	0.48	0.98	0.42	0.72
Gas utilities	7.53	0.27	0.02	0.3	0.66	0.38	0.66
Computer hardware	−3.75	0.21	0.02	0.24	0.48	0.4	0.7
Mining and metals	1.09	0.17	−0.01	0.16	0.18	0.77	1.34
Internet	1.3	0.16	−0.01	0.15	0.33	0.41	0.71
Drugs	−4.03	0.03	0.12	0.15	0.45	0.29	0.5
Electric utility	0.59	0.04	0.07	0.11	0.16	0.62	1.08
Telephone	−0.81	0.07	0.03	0.11	0.15	0.6	1.04
Semiconductors	−0.82	0.1	0	0.1	0.2	0.45	0.78

(Continued)

TABLE 16.4

Top-10 and Bottom-10 Industry Bets *(Continued)*

Sources of Return	Average Active Exposure (%)	Contribution Return			Total Risk (% per Std. Dev.)	Info Ratio	T-Stat
		Average [1]	Variation [2]	Total [1 + 2]			
Bottom-10 Industries							
Energy reserves	-3.5	-0.96	0.03	-0.93	0.54	-1.46	-2.52
Airlines	2.18	-0.55	-0.02	-0.57	0.45	-1.09	-1.88
Medical products	-3.25	-0.41	0.05	-0.36	0.24	-1.29	-2.23
Oil refining	-1.5	-0.29	0.03	-0.27	0.13	-1.66	-2.88
Medical services	-1.53	-0.25	0.02	-0.23	0.21	-0.94	-1.62
Oil services	-0.9	-0.2	-0.01	-0.21	0.21	-0.86	-1.49
Media	1.57	-0.24	0.03	-0.21	0.2	-0.94	-1.62
Consumer durables	1.7	-0.15	0	-0.15	0.14	-0.92	-1.59
Defense and aerospace	-1.52	-0.14	0.01	-0.12	0.19	-0.55	-0.96
Motor vehicles and parts	0.42	-0.04	-0.05	-0.09	0.1	-0.73	-1.26

of the industry bet. For the top-10 industries the total return contribution is positive ranging from 0.56 to 0.10, while in the bottom-10 industries the total returns range from –0.93 to –0.09. Overall the industry bets contributed negatively to the portfolio return at –0.79.

ASSET SELECTION: ANNUALIZED ATTRIBUTION

In Table 16.5 we explore the asset selection capability of this manager. The table shows the breakdown of the asset selection return, that is, the return from stock selection after removing common factor influences. We first break down total asset selection into "assets held in portfolio" and "benchmark assets not held." Then we decompose the assets held into overweighted assets and underweighted assets.

In this portfolio, total asset selection return was 1.72 percent, meaning the overall stock selection ability of the manager is good—the portfolio performed relatively well even though the t-ratios are not statistically significant. When we look at the decomposition, we find that most of the asset selection return came from the manager's decision to include certain assets in the portfolio (1.24 percent). This return was composed of the returns to assets overweighted relative to the selected benchmark and the returns to assets underweighted

T A B L E   16.5

Contributions to Asset Selection Return

Annualized Contributions to Asset Selection Return				
Source of Return	Contribution (% Return)	Risk (% Std. Dev.)	Info Ratio	*T*-Stat
1. Overweighted assets	1.09			
2. Underweighted assets	0.15			
3. Assets held in portfolio [1 + 2]	1.24			
4. Benchmark assets not held	0.48			
5. Total asset selection [3 + 4]	1.72	2.36	0.62	1.07

relative to the benchmark. Most of the asset selection return is explained by overweighted assets. In conclusion, the manager was proficient in overweighting high-performing assets and underweighting or not holding poor performing assets.

The third row of the table "Assets held in the portfolio" is the sum of the overweights and underweights. This number is the total return due to selected assets that were overweighted and underweighted relative to the benchmark. This value shows the total return for assets in the benchmark portfolio that were not held in the managed portfolio. These are stocks the portfolio manager could have purchased but did not and the value shows us the returns that could have been obtained, but were not, and in that sense it is a measure of opportunity cost.

The fourth row value of 0.48 percent is a return achieved by assets that are in the benchmark but are not held in the portfolio, that is, assets not chosen for the portfolio. In row 5, "Total asset selection," we see the total asset selection return, 1.72 percent, which comes from stock selection rather than styles, industries, or beta.

CHAPTER 17

Contributions to Return

Performance calculated at the total portfolio level summarizes a lot of data within a single return number. Dissecting the total portfolio return into components allows an analyst to uncover the sources of the return. In this chapter, we build a framework for decomposing total return into components, by computing portfolio weights and returns. The resulting decomposition is called *contributions to return*.

A portfolio consists of a collection of assets that may be grouped into *segments*. Usually, a natural grouping of the assets is available for a particular analysis. A large institutional fund, for example, may have divided its market value among several investment managers. Or a fund may be invested in several asset classes, resulting in a natural segmentation of assets. Within a single asset class, assets can be grouped by means of a sector or industry classification scheme, often provided by an index vendor for the constituents of an index.

A grouping scheme or segmentation can consist of a hierarchy of segments that extends all the way down to the individual security level. More segments certainly enable a more detailed analysis, but too many segments can make the overall picture difficult to grasp. A finer segmentation also requires more data to be collected than for a higher-level analysis. The choice of segmentation depends on the purpose of the analysis and on the availability of data.

Given a segmentation scheme, each segment can be regarded as a subportfolio and the return of each segment can be calculated. Returns alone, however, do not reflect the relationship between the segments and the total. That relationship is captured by the segment *weights*, which are the fractions of total fund value invested in the given segments.

For example, suppose we have assembled the beginning and ending market values of a portfolio consisting of equities and bonds as in Table 17.1. Using the two asset classes as segments, the beginning market values BV_1 and BV_2 of the segments sum up to the total beginning value $BV_1 + BV_2 = BV$. Dividing by BV converts the beginning market values into weights $w_1 = BV_1/BV$ and $w_2 = BV_2/BV$. Because the beginning values sum up to the total, the weights therefore sum to 1, or $w_1 + w_2 = 1$. Weights may be expressed in percentages as shown in the table.

We can calculate the return R of a segment or of the total portfolio using the formula

$$R = \frac{EV}{BV} - 1, \tag{17.1}$$

where EV and BV are the ending and beginning market values of the segment or of the total. Using subscripts to denote the segments, Equation (17.1) for the total portfolio can be expanded to

$$
\begin{aligned}
R &= \frac{EV_1 + EV_2}{BV} - 1 \\
&= \frac{BV_1}{BV}\frac{EV_1}{BV_1} + \frac{BV_2}{BV}\frac{EV_2}{BV_2} - 1 \\
&= w_1(1 + R_1) + w_2(1 + R_2) - 1 \\
&= w_1 R_1 + w_2 R_2.
\end{aligned}
\tag{17.2}
$$

T A B L E 17.1

Example Contributions to Return

Segment	Beginning Value	Ending Value	Weight	Return	Contribution
Equities	705	726	59.5%	2.98%	1.77%
Bonds	480	488	40.5	1.67	0.68
Total	1,185	1,214	100.0	2.45	2.45

The product of a segment weight and a segment return is the segment *contribution to return*. Equation (17.2) shows that the contributions to return sum to the total portfolio return.

If weights and returns are all calculated from underlying market values as in Table 17.1, the returns will satisfy the *portfolio property*:

$$\sum_i w_i R_i = R$$

$$\sum_i w_i = 1. \tag{17.3}$$

This condition means that the segment returns are consistent with the total portfolio return. The internal consistency of weights and returns is critical to many analyses.

Consistency should not be considered a trivial matter in practice. The data available for an analysis may consist of weights and returns that have been previously calculated for a variety of uses. Sometimes weights and returns obtained from different data sources or systems might not be consistent with the return calculated at the total portfolio level.

One example of inconsistency arises if some assets of the portfolio are deliberately left out of the analysis. Short-term cash assets, for example, are sometimes ignored. Of course, the weights of assets that are included can be normalized to sum to 1, but obviously the total portfolio return might not equal the sum of segment contributions if some segments are missing.

Another more common example of inconsistency arises from cash flows between segments. In Table 17.1, we assumed that there were no transactions within the period. If cash flows occurred within the period, then return should be calculated using the methods of Chapter 5 that adjust for cash flows. In general, with intraperiod cash flows, beginning weights calculated as fractions of beginning market value will not be internally consistent with time-weighted returns as in Equation (17.3). If the returns are calculated using the modified Dietz method, then weights should be calculated from the adjusted beginning market values. The adjusted beginning market values and returns of the Dietz method *are* internally consistent.

However, returns from various segments may be calculated by different systems or supplied from different sources and the data to calculate internally consistent weights may be unavailable. In this case, using beginning market values to calculate segment weights can still be useful, but it is important to understand that the weighted returns might not sum to the true total portfolio return. Using beginning market value weights is a type of buy-and-hold approximation. One approach used in some systems is to calculate the difference between the actual total portfolio return (if it is available) and the weighted sum of the segment returns and to report the difference as a separate line item. This item might be suggestively labeled "trading activity," for example. Another approach is simply to ignore the discrepancy and to define the total portfolio return as the weighted sum of the segment returns.

Clearly, how one handles the discrepancy should depend on the goals of the analysis and the availability of data. If there are few intraperiod transactions and the cash flows between segments are relatively small, then the buy-and-hold assumption is likely to be reasonable. Some examples of contribution analysis using this assumption are

- In a multi-asset plan, a policy asset allocation is typically set and the asset class weights are held within tight limits through a rebalancing strategy. The beginning weights or even the policy weights might give reasonable contributions to return from the asset classes.

- In a multimanager portfolio, a monthly report may be created showing the performance of each manager and of the total fund. Deposits and withdrawals to and from the fund might be routinely handled through a liquidity reserve account primarily invested in short-term cash assets, with occasional transfers of funds to the managers. If the transfers are relatively small, a contribution to return report based on beginning market value weights might reasonably depict the relative contributions of each manager.

- In an equity portfolio, returns for individual stocks may be obtained from common data sources, while beginning market values may be obtained from an account statement. A portfolio manager might calculate contributions to return from this data to get the top and bottom contributing stocks, for example.

In situations where one wishes to account for all sources of return, no matter how small, it may be worthwhile to assemble the data for internally consistent weights and returns. If the residual from using inconsistent weights and returns is large relative to the calculated return contributions, the accuracy of the contributions to return might be questionable.

Inconsistent weights and returns can lead to discrepancies in calculations with that data. Understanding how segment weights and returns are calculated is the key to avoiding such discrepancies.

CHAPTER 18

Performance Attribution

Portfolio performance measured relative to a benchmark gives an indication of the value-added by the portfolio. Equipped with weights and returns of portfolio segments, we can dissect the value-added into useful components. Various decompositions have been devised that attempt to associate components of return with portfolio decisions or market factors or both. Such decompositions comprise the topic of *performance attribution*.

At a most basic level, the only way that the performance of a portfolio can differ from that of a benchmark is if the security weights of the portfolio differ from those of the benchmark. There are many ways in which weights at the security level can differ, however, and the introduction of portfolio segments leads to natural questions. Some classic settings for attribution analysis are the following:

- In a multi-asset class fund, each asset class might be managed as a separate portfolio, each with an appropriate asset class benchmark. The top-level asset allocation decision is clearly distinct from the portfolio decisions made within asset classes. This distinction leads to the attribution of performance to asset allocation decisions apart from security selection decisions within asset classes.
- In a multicountry portfolio, selection of securities within countries can lead to the overall country weights differing from those of the benchmark. How much of the return can be attributed to allocation to countries as opposed to security selection within countries?

- In an equity portfolio, segmenting the securities by sector or industry is common. Sometimes the sector or industry weights are considered to be a side effect of the security selection decisions by portfolio managers. Although in this case it is debatable whether or not sector allocation is a separate "decision," it is useful to know how much value was added or subtracted by straying from the benchmark's sector or industry weights. A portfolio manager might place explicit sector or industry deviation constraints on the portfolio as a risk control measure and might therefore be interested in the effectiveness of these constraints.

An attribution approach based on portfolio segmentation is perfectly suited for these settings. The most common approach is attributed to Brinson and Fachler (1985) and Brinson, Hood, and Beebower (1986) and is called *sector-based attribution* or *Brinson attribution*. Another approach to attribution is called *factor-based attribution*, for which a factor model is a prerequisite. A decomposition of return by factors enables the return to be attributed to active exposures to the factors. Factor-based attribution, discussed in Chapters 14–16, derives from Fama (1972).

SECTOR-BASED ATTRIBUTION FRAMEWORK

The basic idea of sector-based attribution is to compare the portfolio segment returns to their respective benchmarks in order to measure the value-added from security selection within segments. To account for all the pieces, two other portfolios are constructed with which to compare performance. The portfolios are commonly identified[1] as

> I *Benchmark portfolio,* using benchmark weights and benchmark returns
>
> II *Segment-allocated portfolio,* using the actual portfolio weights and benchmark returns
>
> III *Security-selected portfolio,* using benchmark weights and actual portfolio returns

---

[1] Brinson, Hood, and Beebower (1986) use these Roman numerals as quadrant identifiers. Although the names given to these portfolios vary by author, these names are descriptive of the concepts.

IV Actual portfolio, using the actual portfolio weights and actual portfolio returns

In the preceding, weights and returns refer to the *segment* weights and returns. The four portfolios are depicted in Figure 18.1.

In effect, portfolios II and III are intermediate or *notional* portfolios that reflect different types of decisions. The segment-allocated portfolio differs from the benchmark only in its segment weights, while the security-selected portfolio has the same segment weights as the benchmark but differs in its segment returns. Comparing these two portfolios with the benchmark leads to a measurement of the effect of the two types of decisions. The comparisons are summarized in Table 18.1.

To account fully for the actual portfolio return, Brinson et al. (1985, 1986) suggest the decomposition:

Allocation effect (II − I)
+ Selection effect (III − I)
+ Interaction effect (IV − III − II + I)
= Active management effect (IV − I)

Note an additional effect called "interaction" in the decomposition; the allocation and selection effects as defined do not combine to explain the active management effect completely. We explain the motivation for using the word *interaction* subsequently.[2]

		Returns	
		Actual	Benchmark
Weights	Actual	IV Actual Portfolio	II Segment- Allocated Portfolio
	Benchmark	III Security- Selected Portfolio	I Benchmark Portfolio

Figure 18.1 Four portfolios constructed from segment weights and returns

---

[2] Brinson and Fachler (1985) call this effect "cross product" and Brinson, Hood, and Beebower (1986) call this effect "other." The term *interaction* is now in common use.

TABLE 18.1

Portfolios Compared to Measure Effects of Decisions

Portfolios Compared		Effect Measured
Actual	Benchmark	Active management effect
Segment-allocated	Benchmark	Allocation effect
Security-selected	Benchmark	Selection effect

The preceding conceptual framework is straightforward. To calculate the effects, however, several important topic areas must be noted. Choices made within each of these areas lead to variants of the basic approach.

Time Periods   The easiest way to understand the decomposition is to look at it in a single-period setting, with beginning-of-period weights and single-period returns. We use this setting later in describing the decomposition further. But in reality, market value weights are constantly changing and in principle the length of a period is a user's choice. The results will depend on period length. Most often, a "period" is dictated by data availability. Monthly or quarterly periods are commonly used, although daily attribution is possible with some systems.

Cash Flows   The framework by itself does not address cash flows between segments. It is natural, therefore, to use time-weighted returns in the analysis, which adjust for cash flows (see Chapter 5 for useful approximations). If there are intraperiod cash flows, then care must be taken to use internally consistent weights as discussed in Chapter 17. For example, if the Dietz method is used, then weights should be calculated from the adjusted beginning market values. Alternatively, another approach is to use shorter periods (even daily) with a buy-and-hold assumption. In this case, one should acknowledge and understand the possible discrepancy between actual return and the weighted return as discussed in Chapter 17. Also, if there are relatively large intraperiod cash flows, one should carefully consider whether the period length is short enough to capture reasonably the relative performance of the portfolio.

Linking Multiple Time Periods   Given a choice of period length, most analyses examine performance over multiple time periods. Algorithms to link attribution effects over time are discussed in Chapter 19.

Arithmetic versus Geometric Effects   In the general description earlier, we were deliberately vague in suggesting how to "compare" two portfolio returns. The easiest way to explain the detailed decomposition is to consider the difference between two returns, the *arithmetic excess return*. However, analogous decompositions have been proposed for *geometric excess returns*. Chapter 6 describes some key differences between these two types of excess return. One advantage of geometric effects is that the linking method is completely straightforward, requiring little explanation. The key disadvantage of geometric effects is that the formulas to calculate them are more difficult to grasp. Geometric effects are discussed in Chapter 19.

Bottom-Up versus Top-Down   Depending on the goals of the analysis and the nature of the investment approach, one might give more priority to one or the other of the effects of allocation or selection. If priority is given to security selection, with sector allocation thought of as a side effect, then the decomposition can be simplified by combining the interaction effect with allocation. This approach is called a *bottom-up attribution*. Conversely, if sector allocation (or asset allocation in a multi-asset portfolio) is considered of high priority, one may combine the interaction effect with the selection effect, resulting in a *top-down attribution*. These two variants are summarized in Table 18.2. Specific formulas are discussed in the next section.

Currency Effects   If the portfolio consists of assets in multiple currencies—a multicountry portfolio, for example—then it might be of interest to separate the effects of currency movements from the local components of return. Sector-based attribution can be augmented to include currency effects (see Chapter 19).

Futures and Options   If futures, options, or other derivative assets are in the portfolio, then extra care must be taken in measuring weights and returns (see Chapter 19).

TABLE 18.2

Portfolios Compared to Measure Effects in Top-Down and Bottom-Up Attribution

Portfolios Compared		Effect Measured
Top-Down Attribution		
Segment-allocated	Benchmark	Allocation effect
Actual	Segment-allocated	Selection effect
Bottom-Up Attribution		
Actual	Security-selected	Allocation effect
Security-selected	Benchmark	Selection effect

SINGLE-PERIOD ARITHMETIC SECTOR-BASED ATTRIBUTION

Setting aside all the preceding choices, the easiest way to grasp the sector-based attribution formulas is to consider arithmetic excess returns in a single-period setting, with a given segmentation and given internally consistent weights and returns. The *active management effect* is the arithmetic excess return

$$R - \bar{R},$$

where R is the actual portfolio return and $\bar{R}$ is the benchmark return for the period. This quantity is often simply called the *active return*.

For segments indexed by i, we assume that the portfolio weights w_i and returns R_i together with the total portfolio return R satisfy the portfolio property $R = \sum_i w_i R_i$. Using overbars to denote benchmark quantities, the benchmark return is given by $\bar{R} = \sum_i \bar{w}_i \bar{R}_i$.

Allocation Effect

The *segment-allocated portfolio return*, denoted $\hat{R}$, is defined by actual weights and benchmark returns,

$$\hat{R} = \sum_i w_i \bar{R}_i.$$

The *allocation effect* A is measured by $\hat{R} - \bar{R}$. Substituting the portfolio formulas into this expression and simplifying leaves

$$\hat{R} - \bar{R} = \sum_i (w_i - \bar{w}_i)\bar{R}_i. \tag{18.1}$$

The difference in weights $w_i - \bar{w}_i$ is called the *active weight*. Because the formula does not depend on the actual portfolio segment returns, the allocation effect measures the excess return due to active weights, that is, segment weights that differ from those of the benchmark.

Although this intuition is correct at the total level, Equation (18.1) is not so intuitive at the segment level. It is more informative to measure the allocation effect for segment i as

$$A_i = (w_i - \bar{w}_i)(\bar{R}_i - \bar{R}), \tag{18.2}$$

in which the segment return is calculated in excess of the total benchmark return. Including the "minus $\bar{R}$" in the formula does not affect the sum over all segments, because the active weights sum to zero. But this form of the formula offers a clear interpretation: It is beneficial to overweight segments that perform better than the overall benchmark. Similarly, it is also beneficial to underweight segments that perform relatively more poorly than the overall benchmark. It is detrimental either to overweight underperforming segments or to underweight overperforming segments. These relations are depicted in Figure 18.2.

Because Equation (18.2) for the allocation effect was presented in Brinson and Fachler (1985), while Brinson, Hood, and Beebower (1986) used Equation (18.1), Equation (18.2) is sometimes called the *Brinson-Fachler allocation effect*.

		Benchmark Return	
		Segment > Total	Segment < Total
Segment Weight	Actual > Benchmark	+	−
	Actual < Benchmark	−	+

Figure 18.2 Allocation effect. Boxes with + are beneficial; those with − are detrimental.

Selection Effect

The selection effect is measured by comparing two portfolios that differ only in their segment returns, presumably as the result of different security weights *within* segments. The *security-selected portfolio return*, denoted $\tilde{R}$, is defined by benchmark weights and actual returns,

$$\tilde{R} = \sum_i \bar{w}_i R_i.$$

The *selection effect S* is measured by $\tilde{R} - \bar{R}$. Substituting the portfolio formulas into this expression and simplifying leaves

$$\tilde{R} - \bar{R} = \sum_i \bar{w}_i (R_i - \bar{R}_i).$$

For segment i, the selection effect is simply

$$S_i = \bar{w}_i (R_i - \bar{R}_i),$$

which is the excess return of the segment weighted by the benchmark segment weight. By using benchmark weights, this formula measures the effects of "pure" security selection without introducing the additional impact of the active allocation decision on that particular segment.

Interaction Effect

As defined earlier, the sum of the allocation effect $\hat{R} - \bar{R}$ and the selection effect $\tilde{R} - \bar{R}$ does not equal the total active management effect $R - \bar{R}$. The remainder, $R - \hat{R} - \tilde{R} + \bar{R}$, is called the *interaction effect I*. The name is justified by expanding the total by segment through the relation

$$R - \hat{R} - \tilde{R} + \bar{R} = \sum_i (w_i - \bar{w}_i)(R_i - \bar{R}_i),$$

which can be verified by multiplying out the right-hand side and identifying the respective portfolios. For segment i, the interaction effect is

$$I_i = (w_i - \bar{w}_i)(R_i - \bar{R}_i),$$

which is the difference in weights times the difference in returns for the segment, between the actual portfolio and the benchmark. Because the difference in weights reflects allocation and the difference in returns is the result of selection, this effect measures interaction between the two. Intuitively, it is beneficial to overweight segments of the fund that outperform the corresponding segments of the benchmark.[3] This relation and similar ones for other combinations are depicted in Figure 18.3.

Constructed as earlier, the allocation, selection, and interaction effects sum to the total active management effect. The top-down and bottom-up variants mentioned earlier (see Table 18.2) simplify things by adding the interaction effect with the selection or allocation effect, respectively. Table 18.3 summarizes the segment-level formulas for the original method and for the top-down and bottom-up variants.

Example

For an example of these calculations, consider the weights and returns for three monthly periods given in Table 18.4. The cumulative returns for the portfolio and benchmark are also shown for reference. Comparing the portfolio weights to the benchmark, the fixed-income asset class has been underweight throughout the three months, while the equity assets have been overweight.

		Segment Return	
		Actual > Benchmark	Actual < Benchmark
Segment Weight	Actual > Benchmark	+	−
	Actual < Benchmark	−	+

Figure 18.3 Interaction effect. Boxes with + are beneficial; those with − are detrimental.

---

[3] Laker (2000), Spaulding (2003/2004), Campisi (2004), and Laker (2006) contain thoughtful discussions of the interaction effect.

T A B L E 18.3

Formulas for Arithmetic Sector-Based Attribution Effects

Effect	Original	Top-Down	Bottom-Up
Allocation A_i	$(w_i - \bar{w}_i)(\bar{R}_i - \bar{R})$	$(w_i - \bar{w}_i)(\bar{R}_i - \bar{R})$	$(w_i - \bar{w}_i)(R_i - \bar{R})$
Selection S_i	$\bar{w}_i(R_i - \bar{R}_i)$	$w_i(R_i - \bar{R}_i)$	$\bar{w}_i(R_i - \bar{R}_i)$
Interaction I_i	$(w_i - \bar{w}_i)(R_i - \bar{R}_i)$	N/A	N/A

Note: Segments are indexed by i; overbars denote benchmark quantities. The active management effect is decomposed into $R - \bar{R} = \sum_i (A_i + S_i + I_i)$.

T A B L E 18.4

Example Weights and Returns for Sector-Based Attribution

Asset Class	Weights (%)		Returns (%)	
	Portfolio	Benchmark	Portfolio	Benchmark
Month 1				
Large-cap equity	60	55	−3.70	−1.90
Small-cap equity	10	5	−3.50	−5.30
Fixed income	30	40	−0.10	−0.90
Total	100	100	−2.60	−1.67
Cumulative			−2.60	−1.67
Month 2				
Large-cap equity	60	55	4.10	2.10
Small-cap equity	10	5	3.70	4.30
Fixed income	30	40	2.90	2.40
Total	100	100	3.70	2.33
Cumulative			1.00	0.62
Month 3				
Large-cap equity	60	55	3.50	2.10
Small-cap equity	10	5	1.20	1.40
Fixed income	30	40	1.00	0.40
Total	100	100	2.52	1.39
Cumulative			3.55	2.01

Using sector-based attribution, we can determine the extent to which this asset allocation contributed to relative performance, in addition to the contribution from security selection within the asset classes. Arithmetic attribution results are given in Table 18.5.

We can observe that a large portion of the relative performance in months 2 and 3 came from security selection in large-cap equity. In month 1, however, large-cap equity underperformed its benchmark, detracting from performance. The fixed-income asset outperformed its benchmark in all three periods, contributing positively to the selection effect. The underweight to the fixed-income asset class produced mixed results, as indicated by the allocation effect.

The small-cap equity segment outperformed its benchmark in month 1 and underperformed in month 2. Given the overweight in that asset, the interaction effect has the same sign as the selection effect for that asset. Because the magnitude of the interaction effect in the small-cap equity segment happens to be comparable to that

T A B L E 18.5

Arithmetic Sector-Based Attribution for the Example

Asset Class	Arithmetic Effects (%)			
	Allocation	Selection	Interaction	Total
Month 1				
Large-cap equity	−0.01	−0.99	−0.09	−1.09
Small-cap equity	−0.18	0.09	0.09	0.00
Fixed income	−0.08	0.32	−0.08	0.16
Total	−0.27	−0.58	−0.08	−0.93
Month 2				
Large-cap equity	−0.01	1.10	0.10	1.19
Small-cap equity	0.10	−0.03	−0.03	0.04
Fixed income	−0.01	0.20	−0.05	0.14
Total	0.08	1.27	0.02	1.37
Month 3				
Large-cap equity	0.04	0.77	0.07	0.88
Small-cap equity	0.00	−0.01	−0.01	−0.02
Fixed income	0.10	0.24	−0.06	0.28
Total	0.14	1.00	0.00	1.14

T A B L E 18.6

Top-Down and Bottom-Up Attribution for the Example

Asset Class	Top-Down Effects (%)			Bottom-Up Effects (%)		
	Allocation	Selection	Total	Allocation	Selection	Total
Month 1						
Large-cap equity	−0.01	−1.08	−1.09	−0.10	−0.99	−1.09
Small-cap equity	−0.18	0.18	0.00	−0.09	0.09	0.00
Fixed income	−0.08	0.24	0.16	−0.16	0.32	0.16
Total	−0.27	−0.66	−0.93	−0.35	−0.58	−0.93
Month 2						
Large-cap equity	−0.01	1.20	1.19	0.09	1.10	1.19
Small-cap equity	0.10	−0.06	0.04	0.07	−0.03	0.04
Fixed income	−0.01	0.15	0.14	−0.06	0.20	0.14
Total	0.08	1.29	1.37	0.10	1.27	1.37
Month 3						
Large-cap equity	0.04	0.84	0.88	0.11	0.77	0.88
Small-cap equity	0.00	−0.02	−0.02	−0.01	−0.01	−0.02
Fixed income	0.10	0.18	0.28	0.04	0.24	0.28
Total	0.14	1.00	1.14	0.14	1.00	1.14

of selection, we would expect to see distinctly different results in a top-down versus a bottom-up view. Top-down and bottom-up attribution results are shown in Table 18.6.

Depending on the perspective, the selection effect in month 1 for small-cap equity is either 18 bps (top-down) or 9 bps (bottom-up). To enable an analyst or a client to correctly interpret an attribution result, it is important to disclose the calculation method if the interaction effect is not shown separately.

References

Gary P. Brinson and Nimrod Fachler, "Measuring Non-U.S. Equity Portfolio Performance," *Journal of Portfolio Management*, vol. 11, no. 3, Spring 1985, pp. 73–76.

Gary P. Brinson, L. Randolph Hood, and Gilbert L. Beebower, "Determinants of Portfolio Performance," *Financial Analysts Journal*, vol. 42, no. 4, July/August 1986, pp. 39–44.

Stephen Campisi, "Debunking the Interaction Myth," *The Journal of Performance Measurement*, vol. 8, no. 4, Summer 2004, pp. 63–70.

Eugene F. Fama, "Components of Investment Performance," *Journal of Finance*, vol. 27, no. 3, June 1972, pp. 551–567.

Damien Laker, "What Is This Thing Called Interaction?" *The Journal of Performance Measurement*, vol. 5, no. 1, Fall 2000, pp. 43–57.

Damien Laker, "Performance Attribution with Zero-Weighted Sectors," *The Journal of Performance Measurement*, vol. 10, no. 4, Summer 2006, pp. 33–46.

David Spaulding, "Demystifying the Interaction Effect," *The Journal of Performance Measurement*, vol. 8, no. 2, Winter 2003/2004, pp. 49–54.

CHAPTER 19

Linking Attribution Effects

Calculating attribution effects period by period yields a great amount of information about the portfolio over time. How can these effects be aggregated over time to produce a useful multiperiod summary? This chapter addresses this question.

As shown in Chapter 3, the return R over T periods can be calculated from the individual period returns R_t, $t = 1, \ldots, T$, by the *linking formula*

$$R = (1 + R_1)(1 + R_2) \cdots (1 + R_T) - 1. \tag{19.1}$$

Using overbars for the benchmark, the multiperiod benchmark return is

$$\bar{R} = (1 + \bar{R}_1)(1 + \bar{R}_2) \cdots (1 + \bar{R}_T) - 1.$$

In arithmetic attribution, the single-period return difference $R_t - \bar{R}_t$ is decomposed into the sum of a number of effects. It is natural to look for a similar decomposition of the multiperiod return difference $R - \bar{R}$. One approach would be to simply add the effects over time. However, doing so leaves a residual, because the sum of return differences does not equal the difference between compounded returns:

$$R - \bar{R} \neq (R_1 - \bar{R}_1) + (R_2 - \bar{R}_2) + \cdots + (R_T - \bar{R}_T). \tag{19.2}$$

Leaving an unexplained residual is not appealing when the goal is to explain the source of returns. Linking the single-period return differences does not equal the difference in compounded returns either:

$$R - \bar{R} \neq (1 + R_1 - \bar{R}_1)(1 + R_2 - \bar{R}_2) \cdots (1 + R_T - \bar{R}_T) - 1.$$

Another approach would be to change the perspective from arithmetic excess return $R - \bar{R}$ to geometric excess return $(1 + R)/(1 + \bar{R}) - 1$. As discussed in Chapter 6, the geometric excess return does link naturally through time:

$$\frac{1 + R}{1 + \bar{R}} = \left(\frac{1 + R_1}{1 + \bar{R}_1} \right)\left(\frac{1 + R_2}{1 + \bar{R}_2} \right) \cdots \left(\frac{1 + R_T}{1 + \bar{R}_T} \right).$$

Although linking is straightforward in this approach, there remains a problem in that the single-period geometric attribution effects are not as easily formulated as the arithmetic effects are.

The challenge of linking attribution effects over time arises because market values—and therefore weights, weighted returns, and effects—are naturally additive *within* periods, while returns are naturally multiplicative *across* periods. Attempting to add returns over time leaves a residual. In this chapter, we approach this problem by first deriving the linking formula for arithmetic excess return at the total portfolio level. The formula reveals cross products between periods that are key to understanding the residual in Equation (19.2). Different ways of handling the cross products lead to different formulas for linking attribution effects. We then derive the logarithmic linking coefficient method and show that it is nearly equivalent to a particular way of handling the cross products.

MULTIPERIOD CONTRIBUTIONS TO RETURN

Consider first a simpler problem, in which we want to calculate contributions to return from the portfolio segments over time. This problem is a special case of attribution, in which the benchmark is always zero and the return is attributed to the segments. As discussed in Chapter 17, for a single period t, given the weights w_{it} and returns R_{it} (for segments indexed by i and periods indexed by t), the formula $R_t = \sum_i w_{it} R_{it}$ provides a sensible decomposition. The weighted return $w_{it} R_{it}$ can be clearly understood as the amount of return contributed by asset i.

To be more concrete, consider the two-asset, two-period example shown in Table 19.1. What would we consider a sensible "contribution to return" for asset i over multiple periods? The problem, of course, is that returns compound over time, and a sensible answer depends on how one views the reinvested gains.

For the example, assuming an initial market value of 1,000.00, Table 19.2 accounts for the gains in market value by source. The gains are calculated using the mutual fund principle in which all units of market value are invested into segments in proportion to the overall segment weights.

In period 1, the 40 percent return from stocks on a beginning value of 500.00 resulted in a market value gain of 200.00. This market value, when split in proportion to the 55/45 percent weights at the start of period 2, earned an additional 11.00 market value units from stocks and 18.00 from bonds in the second period. A similar accounting is done for the market value gain of 50.00 from bonds in the first period. Finally, the original principal value of 1,000.00 yielded a gain of 55.00 from stocks and 90.00 from bonds in period 2. All these gains add up to the total market value gain of 431.25—so all the gains have been accounted for.

T A B L E 19.1

Example Weights, Returns, and Contributions to Return by Segment

Period	Segment	Weight (%)	Return (%)	Contribution (%)
1	Stocks	50	40.00	20.00
	Bonds	50	10.00	5.00
	Total	100	25.00	25.00
2	Stocks	55	10.00	5.50
	Bonds	45	20.00	9.00
	Total	100	14.50	14.50
Two periods	Total		43.13	

T A B L E 19.2

Example Gains in Market Value by Source, Given an Initial Value of 1,000.00

Period 1		Period 2		
Source	Gain	Source	Gain	Total Gain
Stocks	200.00	Stocks-stocks	11.00	
		Stocks-bonds	18.00	
Bonds	50.00	Bonds-stocks	2.75	
		Bonds-bonds	4.50	
		Stocks	55.00	
		Bonds	90.00	
Total	250.00		181.25	431.25

Now, it is clearly sensible to assign the gains from stocks of 200.00 in the first period and 55.00 in the second period to stocks. Further, it is also clear that the 11.00 unit gain, representing "interest on interest" from reinvested gains from stocks into stocks, should be attributed to stocks. But beyond that, an assignment of gains to stocks is not as clear-cut. There are two pieces, 18.00 and 2.75, that can be identified as having been gained from stocks in one period and from bonds in the other period. To which segment should these gains be attributed?

One natural view flows from the principle that all gains are reinvested into segments in proportion to the overall segment weights. Thus a contribution from any segment in a given period grows in subsequent periods at the rate of return of the total fund—in effect, as new shares of a mutual fund would. In light of this principle, it may be sensible to assign contributions to the asset segments from which they originate and to grow the contributions at the subsequent total portfolio rate. The gains attributed to segments in this view would be

Stocks: $200.00 + 11.00 + 18.00 + 55.00 = 284.00$
Bonds: $50.00 + 2.75 + 4.50 + 90.00 = 147.25$,

which added together equals the total gain of 431.25.

Expressed as a formula, the contribution from asset i over three periods, for example, would be

$$w_{i1}R_{i1}(1+R_2)(1+R_3)+w_{i2}R_{i2}(1+R_3)+w_{i3}R_{i3}. \qquad (19.3)$$

An alternative view, however, would ignore where the accumulated market value came from and focus on the generation of return in the current period. In the example, the gains attributed to segments in this view would be

$$\text{Stocks: } 200.00 + 11.00 + 2.75 + 55.00 = 268.75$$
$$\text{Bonds: } 50.00 + 18.00 + 4.50 + 90.00 = 162.50,$$

which, again, added together equals the total gain of 431.25. The general formula for three periods would be

$$w_{i1}R_{i1}+(1+R_1)w_{i2}R_{i2}+(1+R_1)(1+R_2)w_{i3}R_{i3}. \qquad (19.4)$$

By summing over i, both of these formulas add up to the cumulative return $(1+R_1)(1+R_2)(1+R_3)-1$. But both of these formulas create cross products between asset segments and assign the result to segment i. Wherever the total return R_t appears, the influences of all asset classes are represented—in Equation (18.3) subsequent to the attributed period, and in Equation (18.4) prior to the attributed period.

Which formula is a "correct" calculation of the contribution of segment i to return? The methods are distinguished by where they choose to assign the "interest on interest" that arises when gains from one segment are reinvested in another segment. A sensible third method splits the cross-reinvested gains between segments. In this view, the gains attributed to segments would be

$$\text{Stocks: } 200.00 + 11.00 + \frac{18.00}{2} + \frac{2.75}{2} + 55.00 = 276.375$$

$$\text{Bonds: } 50.00 + \frac{18.00}{2} + \frac{2.75}{2} + 4.50 + 90.00 = 154.875,$$

which, again, added together equals the total gain of 431.25. We now derive a generalization of the third method.

Begin by writing the linking Equation (18.1) in a recursive form. Let CR_t be the cumulative return to period t, so that

$$1 + CR_t = (1 + R_1)(1 + R_2) \cdots (1 + R_t).$$

The cumulative return can be calculated recursively by

$$1 + CR_t = (1 + CR_{t-1})(1 + R_t), \quad \text{starting from} \quad CR_0 = 0. \qquad (19.5)$$

Multiplying out the right-hand side and subtracting 1 leaves

$$CR_t = CR_{t-1} + CR_{t-1} R_t + R_t.$$

The cumulative return is *almost* the sum of the previous period cumulative return plus the current period return. The middle term $CR_{t-1} R_t$ reflects the compounding effect, "interest on interest." With single-period R_t decomposed into the sum of single-period contributions, the middle term creates the cross products identified in the preceding example. Now, by combining the middle term with the first term, we have

$$CR_t = CR_{t-1}(1 + R_t) + R_t.$$

This recursive formula is analogous to Equation (19.3). The prior period cumulative return is carried forward at the rate of return of the total portfolio, and then the current return is added. Similarly, combining the middle term with the last term leaves

$$CR_t = CR_{t-1} + (1 + CR_{t-1})R_t,$$

which is analogous to Equation (19.4). In both of these forms, if R_t is decomposed into the sum of contributions to return, then the cumulative contributions can be calculated recursively. But these formulas produce a bias in how the periods are weighted. If the returns are all positive, for example, then Equation (19.3) weights the earlier period contributions more heavily than later periods, while Equation (19.4) weights later periods more heavily than earlier periods. We see this in the preceding example, in which the contribution from stocks is 284.00 using the first method and 268.75

using the second. The third method divides the middle term in half and, after combining terms, leaves

$$CR_t = CR_{t-1}\left(1+\frac{R_t}{2}\right)+\left(1+\frac{CR_{t-1}}{2}\right)R_t.$$

In the preceding example, the contribution from stocks is 276.375 by this method, in between the other two results. We now extend these methods to excess returns.

EXCESS RETURN RECURSION

Consider the analogous recursion for arithmetic excess return. Let $E_t = R_t - \bar{R}_t$ be the return difference for period t, and let $CE_t = CR_t - \overline{CR}_t$ be the difference in cumulative returns through period t.

Substituting $CR_{t-1} = \overline{CR}_{t-1} + CE_{t-1}$ and $R_t = \bar{R}_t + E_t$ into the return recursion equation (19.5) and multiplying out leaves

$$1+CR_t = (1+\overline{CR}_{t-1})(1+\bar{R}_t)+CE_{t-1}(1+\bar{R}_t)+CE_{t-1}E_t+(1+\overline{CR}_{t-1})E_t.$$

Because $1+\overline{CR}_t = (1+\overline{CR}_{t-1})(1+\bar{R}_t)$, by subtracting this equation from the preceding one, we obtain a recursion for CE_t, namely,

$$CE_t = CE_{t-1}(1+\bar{R}_t)+CE_{t-1}E_t+(1+\overline{CR}_{t-1})E_t, \quad \text{starting from} \quad CE_0 = 0.$$
$$(19.6)$$

Looking at the first term in the formula, it might appear that the cumulative excess return fundamentally grows at the benchmark rate of return. However, an equivalent recursion can be derived, by rearranging and substituting terms:

$$CE_t = CE_{t-1}(1+R_t)-CE_{t-1}E_t+(1+CR_{t-1})E_t.$$

In this version, the first term suggests that the excess return grows at the actual portfolio rate of return. We give a third version later, in which the excess return grows at a rate in between the portfolio and the benchmark rates of return.

If the single-period excess return is decomposed into arithmetic attribution effects as described in Chapter 18,

$$E_t = A_t + S_t + I_t, \qquad (19.7)$$

then, if it were not for the middle term in Equation (19.6), the cumulative effects could be cleanly accumulated with the recursion. But the middle term $CE_{t-1}E_t$ introduces cross products—allocation effects in one period compounded with selection effects in another period, for example. Combining the middle term in Equation (19.6) with the first term leaves

$$CE_t = CE_{t-1}(1 + R_t) + (1 + \overline{CR_{t-1}})E_t. \qquad (19.8)$$

Given the decomposition (19.7), multiperiod effects can be defined by applying the recursion (19.8). For example, we can define multiperiod effects CA_t, CS_t, and CI_t by the recursion $CA_t = CA_{t-1}(1 + R_t) + (1 + \overline{CR_{t-1}})A_t$ and similarly for CS_t and CI_t. By virtue of Equations (19.7) and (19.8), the multiperiod effects defined this way add up to the total, or $CE_t = CA_t + CS_t + CI_t$. The procedure is a generalization of Equation (19.3), in which attributed effects grow over time at the total portfolio rate of return.[1]

Equation (19.6), however, permits an alternate formula, by adding together the last two terms on the right-hand side, leaving

$$CE_t = CE_{t-1}(1 + \overline{R_t}) + (1 + CR_{t-1})E_t. \qquad (19.9)$$

Again, multiperiod effects can be defined by applying this recursion; for example, $CA_t = CA_{t-1}(1 + \overline{R_t}) + (1 + CR_{t-1})A_t$. This procedure is a generalization of Equation (19.4), in which the attributed effects are compounded on top of the cumulative portfolio return prior to that point.[2]

---

[1] Valtonen (2002) calls this method "1-cumulative linkage." The method is equivalent to what Frongello (2002/2003) calls the "reversed Frongello linking algorithm."

[2] This method is equivalent to those described by Frongello (2002) and Bonafede, Foresti, and Matheos (2002) and, as noted by Laker (2002), is called "dollar" attribution by some practitioners. Valtonen (2002) calls this method "0-cumulative linkage."

As mentioned earlier regarding Equations (19.3) and (19.4), Equation (19.8) tends to weight earlier periods more heavily, while Equation (19.9) tends to weight later periods more heavily, if excess returns are positive. Recognizing this fact suggests a middle ground: *divide the cross product in half*. By adding half of the middle term to the first and the last terms, the recursion can be written as[3]

$$CE_t = CE_{t-1}\left(1 + \frac{\bar{R}_t + R_t}{2}\right) + \left(1 + \frac{\overline{CR}_{t-1} + CR_{t-1}}{2}\right)E_t. \quad (19.10)$$

Again, multiperiod attribution effects can be defined by, for example,

$$CA_t = CA_{t-1}\left(1 + \frac{\bar{R}_t + R_t}{2}\right) + \left(1 + \frac{\overline{CR}_{t-1} + CR_{t-1}}{2}\right)A_t,$$

and similarly for CS_t and CI_t. This formula tends to weight the periods more evenly. To illustrate, consider an example using weights and returns deliberately exaggerated to make the point, in Table 19.3 (from Laker 2005).

The active return was gained entirely from selection in the first period and from allocation in the second. Calculating the effects for the combined period using the three recursions gives the results in Table 19.4.

Note that Equation (19.8) gives a larger selection effect than allocation, because it occurred first. Conversely, Equation (19.9) gives a larger allocation effect, because it occurred last. Equation (19.10) treats the periods more evenly.

AN IDEALIZED ATTRIBUTION SYSTEM

We have identified the cross product $CE_{t-1}E_t$ as the stumbling block standing in the way of a simple additive recursion for accumulating excess returns. The cross product reflects the compounding of returns from past periods with returns in the current period. As mentioned in Chapter 18, a *period* is defined by the time interval between points

---

[3] Valtonen (2002) calls this method "0.5-cumulative linkage."

TABLE 19.3

Exaggerated Weights, Returns, and Single-Period Effects

Asset	Weights (%)		Returns (%)		Single-Period Effects (%)			
	Portfolio	Benchmark	Portfolio	Benchmark	Allocation	Selection	Interaction	Total
Period 1								
Equities	50	50	10	0	0	5	0	5
Bonds	50	50	10	0	0	5	0	5
Total	100	100	10	0	0	10	0	10
Period 2								
Equities	100	50	10	10	5	0	0	5
Bonds	0	50	−10	−10	5	0	0	5
Total	100	100	10	0	10	0	0	10

Source: From Laker 2005.

TABLE 19.4

Combined Two-Period Effects for the Example Inputs in Table 19.3

Method	Allocation (%)	Selection (%)	Interaction (%)	Total (%)
1-Cumulative formula (19.8)	10.0	11.0	0.0	21.0
0-Cumulative formula (19.9)	11.0	10.0	0.0	21.0
0.5-Cumulative formula (19.10)	10.5	10.5	0.0	21.0

at which the portfolio valuations are measured. In reality, market values (and therefore weights) are constantly changing. For another perspective on this problem, consider an idealized setting where market values change continuously and smoothly. In this setting, suppose that market value data could be recorded very frequently and that the period of measurement is very short. With such instantaneous data, the returns over time actually would be continuously compounding, or additive, instead of multiplicative. The formula relating instantaneous returns r_t to the return over a discrete period is

$$1 + R = e^{\int r_t dt} \quad \text{or} \quad \ln(1+R) = \int r_t dt. \tag{19.11}$$

Think of the integration in Equation (19.11) as a summation over time of a large number of returns over very short time periods. With this in mind, imagine an ideal attribution system decomposing these instantaneous returns into instantaneous effects. The internal consistency relation $r_t = \sum_i w_{it} r_{it}$ also applies to instantaneous returns. Therefore, a decomposition as in Chapter 18 could be applied to instantaneous weights and returns to obtain instantaneous effects a_t, s_t, and i_t:

$$r_t - \bar{r}_t = a_t + s_t + i_t.$$

Now, the instantaneous effects naturally sum over time:

$$\int (r_t - \bar{r}_t)\, dt = \int a_t\, dt + \int s_t\, dt + \int i_t\, dt. \tag{19.12}$$

We view practical attribution systems as approximations of an ideal system such as Equation (19.12). In this light, we may think of effects A_t over short periods as approximations to instantaneous effects a_t. As a simple approximation, using sums instead of integrals, we might write

$$\int (r_t - \bar{r}_t)\,dt \approx \sum_t (A_t + S_t + I_t). \qquad (19.13)$$

And, because of the relation (19.11) between instantaneous and discrete returns,

$$\frac{1+R_t}{1+\bar{R}_t} \approx e^{A_t + S_t + I_t} \quad \text{or} \quad \ln(1+R_t) - \ln(1+\bar{R}_t) \approx A_t + S_t + I_t.$$

Given the approximation (19.13), we could simply define approximate geometric effects by

$$1 + \tilde{A}_t \approx e^{A_t} \quad \text{and} \quad 1 + \tilde{A} \approx e^{\sum_t A_t}.$$

However, doing so would leave an unexplained residual.

LOGARITHMIC LINKING COEFFICIENTS

Recognizing that discrete returns and effects already constitute an approximation, it is fair to distribute the residual proportionately. Define the coefficient

$$k_t = \frac{\ln(1+R_t) - \ln(1+\bar{R}_t)}{R_t - \bar{R}_t}, \qquad (19.14)$$

where, if $R_t = \bar{R}_t$, then let $k_t = 1/(1 + R_t)$. With this coefficient, the equation

$$\ln(1+R_t) - \ln(1+\bar{R}_t) = k_t(R_t - \bar{R}_t)$$

ensures that any arithmetic decomposition of $R_t - \bar{R}_t$ on the right adds up to the total on the left. Because the quantity on the left can be further summed over time, no cross products arise. Given the coefficient (19.14), the geometric form of the effects

$$\tilde{A}_t = e^{k_t A_t} - 1, \quad \tilde{S}_t = e^{k_t S_t} - 1, \quad \text{and} \quad \tilde{I}_t = e^{k_t I_t} - 1$$

can be linked within a period to recover the geometric excess return

$$\frac{1+R_t}{1+\bar{R}_t} = (1+\tilde{A}_t)(1+\tilde{S}_t)(1+\tilde{I}_t).$$

Geometric effects can be linked naturally over time, so the geometric effect $\tilde{A}$ for multiple periods is

$$\tilde{A} = (1+\tilde{A}_1)(1+\tilde{A}_2)\ldots(1+\tilde{A}_T)-1$$

and similarly for $\tilde{S}$ and $\tilde{I}$. Together, the geometric excess return over the combined periods decomposes into

$$\frac{1+R}{1+\bar{R}} = (1+\tilde{A})(1+\tilde{S})(1+\tilde{I}). \tag{19.15}$$

Finally, to transform back to a multiperiod arithmetic decomposition, calculate a k for the combined period as

$$k = \frac{\ln(1+R) - \ln(1+\bar{R})}{R-\bar{R}}, \tag{19.16}$$

where, if $R = \bar{R}$, then $k = 1/(1 + R)$. Dividing the logarithm of Equation (19.15) by k leaves an additive decomposition of excess return. Pulling it all together, define the multiperiod arithmetic effects by

$$A = \sum_t \frac{k_t}{k} A_t, \quad S = \sum_t \frac{k_t}{k} S_t, \quad \text{and} \quad I = \sum_t \frac{k_t}{k} I_t. \tag{19.17}$$

Because $R - \bar{R} = \sum_t (k_t/k)(R_t - \bar{R}_t)$ and $R_t - \bar{R}_t = A_t + S_t + I_t$, we have the desired additive decomposition $R - \bar{R} = A + S + I$. The coefficients k_t/k are called *linking coefficients*, and the method is called the *logarithmic linking coefficient* method of combining arithmetic attribution effects over time.

A LINK TO RECURSIVE METHODS

At first glance, it appears that the coefficients k_t/k can only be calculated after the entire time series of returns are available, because the k in the denominator depends on all the returns. Valtonen (2002) notes that the effects can be calculated recursively. Interestingly, the recursive version of the method is very similar to Equation (19.10) and reveals a connection between the methods.

Using the notation CR_t of Equation (19.5) to denote cumulative return to period t, let ck_t be the cumulative coefficient

$$ck_t = \frac{\ln(1+CR_t) - \ln(1+\overline{CR}_t)}{CR_t - \overline{CR}_t}. \tag{19.18}$$

In particular, note that at the final period $ck_t = k$. Then, consider the recursion

$$CE_t = CE_{t-1} \frac{ck_{t-1}}{ck_t} + \frac{k_t}{ck_t} E_t, \quad \text{starting from} \quad CE_0 = 0. \tag{19.19}$$

At each period, the coefficient k_t/ck_t multiplies the current period effects, while the coefficient ck_{t-1}/ck_t updates the denominator of the cumulative coefficient multiplying previous periods. Recalling that $E_t = R_t - \overline{R}_t$, this recursion leads to the same final results as Equation (19.17). The calculations can be done "on the fly," however, without waiting for the end of the return series.

The resemblance between Equations (19.19) and (19.10) is striking. In fact, the coefficients in these two recursions are virtually the same. To see this, recall that the slope of the natural logarithm function at x is $1/x$. Equation (19.14) is a centered approximation to the slope evaluated at $1+(\overline{R}_t + R_t)/2$. That is,

$$k_t = \frac{\ln(1+R_t) - \ln(1+\overline{R}_t)}{R_t - \overline{R}_t} \approx \frac{1}{1+(\overline{R}_t + R_t)/2}.$$

Further, because to a very good approximation (by multiplying out the right-hand side and dropping higher-order terms),

$$1+\frac{\overline{CR}_t+CR_t}{2} \approx \left(1+\frac{\overline{CR}_{t-1}+CR_{t-1}}{2}\right)\left(1+\frac{\overline{R}_t+R_t}{2}\right),$$

it follows that

$$\frac{k_t}{ck_t} \approx 1+\frac{\overline{CR}_{t-1}+CR_{t-1}}{2}$$

and

$$\frac{ck_{t-1}}{ck_t} \approx 1+\frac{\overline{R}_t+R_t}{2}.$$

Consequently, recursions (19.19) and (19.10) are virtually the same. Any intuition that a reader might gain from studying the derivation of one should apply to the other. In particular, note that although it appears that Equation (19.14) is distributing the difference between $\ln(1+R_t)-\ln(1+\overline{R}_t)$ and $R_t-\overline{R}_t$ among the attribution effects, the excess return recursion (19.6) shows that a substantial portion is naturally apportioned, with only $CE_{t-1}E_t$ in question. Dividing that term in half leads to the even-handed result that the natural growth of excess return is midway between the portfolio and the benchmark returns.

OTHER METHODS

An approach that calculates multiperiod effects directly from multiperiod returns is the *notional portfolio* method described by Davies and Laker (2001). Instead of linking single-period effects, this method compares the *cumulative* returns of the segment-allocated and security-selected portfolios (of Figure 18.1) to define multiperiod effects. The total effects are easy to calculate and enable a clear interpretation by simply comparing two portfolios. The example from Laker (2005) illustrates a key difference between this method and others. Using the weights and returns in Table 19.3, the returns of the four notional portfolios are shown in Table 19.5.

Comparing the cumulative returns gives the attribution effects over the two periods shown in Table 19.6. Compare these effects to those in Table 19.4 calculated using the three cumulative methods.

TABLE 19.5

Returns for Notional Portfolios of the Example

Asset	I Benchmark	II Segment-Allocated	III Security-Selected	IV Portfolio
Period 1	0	0	10	10
Period 2	0	10	0	10
Cumulative	0	10	10	21

Interestingly, the notional portfolio method produces an interaction effect for the combined period, while there is no interaction effect shown within either of the two single periods in Table 19.3. This is because the allocated and selected portfolios, when compared to the benchmark, measure a type of *pure* allocation effect and *pure* selection effect, respectively. The cross-product terms—allocation in one period compounded with selection in another period—that are divided between periods by the cumulative methods are all assigned to the interaction effect.[4] Laker (2002) also notes that the method only defines effects at the total portfolio level and must be supplemented by other methods to define segment-level effects. Although these features might be seen as flaws by some, the simple calculation of pure effects gives additional information about the sources of returns when used in combination with other approaches.

In the approaches presented earlier, we deliberately pushed equalities as far as possible to understand where the various residuals come from and what they represent. Other approaches abandon

TABLE 19.6

Attribution Effects for the Example

Method	Allocation II − I	Selection III − I	Interaction IV − III − II + I	Total IV − I
Notional	10.0	10.0	1.0	21.0

---

[4] Valtonen (2002), Menchero (2004), Banchik (2004/2005), and Laker (2005) note this fact.

the notion of an idealized model and simply consider ways of distributing the accumulated residual in Equation (19.2), or in

$$R - \bar{R} \approx \sum_t (R_t - \bar{R}_t).$$
(19.20)

One approach[5] divides this residual proportionately among all terms in the sum on the right-hand side, by calculating the coefficient

$$Q = \frac{R - \bar{R}}{\sum_t (R_t - \bar{R}_t)}$$
(19.21)

so that $R - \bar{R} = \sum_t Q(R_t - \bar{R}_t)$. Another approach, offered by Menchero (2000), distributes the residual in Equation (19.20) so that certain instabilities that arise with Equation (19.21) are avoided. By transporting the residual across periods, instead of confining residuals to the periods in which they arise, smoothing of the cumulative effects may be achieved.

For most series of typical returns, calculations using any of these methods produce very similar results. Returns must be relatively large and volatile for differences to be apparent. Large and volatile returns might indicate that the period length should be reduced in order to capture more detail.

EXAMPLE

Using the data from the example in Table 18.5 of Chapter 18, we calculate here the attribution effects over time using the logarithmic linking coefficient method. The sum of the arithmetic excess returns over the three months is 1.58 percent, while the difference between the cumulative portfolio and benchmark returns is 1.53 percent. The residual, 0.05 percent, is small, as is typically the case with monthly returns over a few periods. Using Equation (19.14) to calculate k_t for each of the three months and multiplying by the arithmetic effects in Table 18.5 gives the continuously compounding effects in Table 19.7. The geometric effects calculated using Equation (19.15) are also shown for comparison.

---

[5] Attributed to Campisi (2002/2003) in Spaulding (2002).

Continuously Compounding Effects and Geometric Effects for the Example in Table 18.5

Asset Class	Continuously Compounding Effects (%)				Geometric Effects (%)			
	Allocation	Selection	Interaction	Total	Allocation	Selection	Interaction	Total
Month 1	$k =$	1.0218	ck =	1.0218				
Large-cap equity	−0.012	−1.012	−0.092	−1.115	−0.012	−1.007	−0.092	−1.109
Small-cap equity	−0.185	0.092	0.092	−0.002	−0.185	0.092	0.092	−0.002
Fixed income	−0.079	0.327	−0.082	0.167	−0.079	0.328	−0.082	0.167
Total	−0.276	−0.593	−0.082	−0.950	−0.276	−0.591	−0.082	−0.946
Month 2	$k =$	0.9707	ck =	0.9919				
Large-cap equity	−0.011	1.068	0.097	1.154	−0.011	1.074	0.097	1.160
Small-cap equity	0.096	−0.029	−0.029	0.037	0.096	−0.029	−0.029	0.037
Fixed income	−0.007	0.194	−0.049	0.139	−0.007	0.194	−0.049	0.139
Total	0.078	1.233	0.019	1.330	0.078	1.240	0.019	1.339
Month 3	$k =$	0.9809	ck =	0.9730				
Large-cap equity	0.035	0.755	0.069	0.859	0.035	0.758	0.069	0.863
Small-cap equity	0.001	−0.010	−0.010	−0.019	0.001	−0.010	−0.010	−0.019
Fixed income	0.097	0.235	−0.059	0.273	0.097	0.236	−0.059	0.274
Total	0.132	0.981	0.000	1.113	0.133	0.986	0.000	1.119

Because the magnitudes of the original returns in Table 18.4 are rather ordinary for monthly returns (a few percent), the transformed effects in Table 19.7 are very close to the arithmetic effects in Table 18.5. Nevertheless, the continuously compounding effects can be summed over time and the geometric effects can be linked over time. The cumulative arithmetic effects, calculated by dividing the accumulated continuously compounding effects by the respective coefficients ck_t from Equation (19.18), are shown in Table 19.8.

Based on the cumulative effects after three months, we see that security selection in the large-cap equity and fixed-income asset classes were the major contributors to excess return, while the asset allocation overweight on equities detracted from performance.

T A B L E 19.8

Cumulative Arithmetic Attribution Effects for the Example

Asset Class	Cumulative Arithmetic Effects (%)			
	Allocation	Selection	Interaction	Total
Month 1				
Large-cap equity	−0.01	−0.99	−0.09	−1.09
Small-cap equity	−0.18	0.09	0.09	0.00
Fixed income	−0.08	0.32	−0.08	0.16
Total	−0.27	−0.58	−0.08	−0.93
Month 2				
Large-cap equity	−0.02	0.06	0.01	0.04
Small-cap equity	−0.09	0.06	0.06	0.04
Fixed income	−0.09	0.53	−0.13	0.31
Total	−0.20	0.65	−0.06	0.39
Month 3				
Large-cap equity	0.01	0.83	0.08	0.92
Small-cap equity	−0.09	0.05	0.05	0.02
Fixed income	0.01	0.78	−0.19	0.59
Total	−0.07	1.66	−0.06	1.53

OTHER TOPICS

Geometric Attribution

Although the attribution formulas in Chapter 18 are easily derived from the arithmetic excess return $R - \bar{R}$, linking the effects over time presents challenges. Because the geometric excess return $(1+R)/(1+\bar{R})-1$ links naturally over time, the question arises: can attribution formulas be derived that decompose the geometric excess return?

We described one possible scheme earlier, in which the coefficient k_t is multiplied by arithmetic effects to transform them to continuously compounding form. The geometric form of the effects

$$\tilde{A}_t = e^{k_t A_t} - 1, \quad \tilde{S}_t = e^{k_t S_t} - 1, \quad \text{and} \quad \tilde{I}_t = e^{k_t I_t} - 1 \quad (19.22)$$

link together to the geometric excess return

$$\frac{1+R_t}{1+\bar{R}_t} = (1+\tilde{A}_t)(1+\tilde{S}_t)(1+\tilde{I}_t).$$

A similar construction is described in Burnie, Knowles, and Teder (1998) and Bacon (2004). Observe that the geometric excess return can be written as

$$\frac{1+R}{1+\bar{R}} - 1 = \frac{R - \bar{R}}{1+\bar{R}}. \quad (19.23)$$

This formula makes clear the meaning of geometric excess return. The arithmetic excess return is the difference in wealth at the end of a period as a fraction of *beginning* wealth. The geometric excess return is the difference in ending wealth as a fraction of *ending wealth produced by the benchmark.*

In this light, an additive decomposition of $R - \bar{R}$ can therefore be scaled by $1/(1+\bar{R})$ to express the effects as a fraction of ending benchmark wealth. The effects constructed this way are very close to those given by Equation (19.22). A drawback of the approach, however, is that only the total effects can be linked; the sector-level effects cannot be linked. Nevertheless, the single-period decomposition is easy to understand, because it is just a scaling of the original arithmetic effects.

Other approaches to geometric attribution are described by Allen (1991), McLaren (2001), Wong (2003/2004), Menchero (2000/2001), and Menchero (2005).

Currency

One setting where geometric attribution is particularly compelling is with multicurrency portfolios. Asset values translate to other currencies by multiplying by exchange rates. Hence, the currency component R_C of return naturally compounds with the return R_L of an asset in local currency to produce the return R in base currency:

$$R = (1 + R_L)(1 + R_C) - 1.$$

The geometric attribution approach described by Allen (1991) uses compounded notional portfolios with multicurrency assets. The geometric multicurrency attribution approach is most fully developed in Bacon (2004).

Ankrim and Hensel (1994) apply the arithmetic attribution approach to multicurrency portfolios by defining approximate country returns as $K = R_L + R_L R_C$ so that

$$R = K + R_C.$$

The usual sector-based attribution is then applied to the return K. The currency return R_C is further decomposed into a forward premium and a currency surprise term. The decomposition enables the effect of currency management to be measured.

Karnosky and Singer (1994) avoid the problem with the cross product $R_L R_C$ by using continuously compounding returns in a multicurrency model.

Futures and Options

Portfolios that include derivative assets like futures and options require special care. Although a futures contract has a "price," which is the basis for determining gains/losses on the futures position, the investor is not required to "pay" this price on opening the contract.

Instead, futures have a net realizable value that represents the profit or loss arising from changes in price each day. Since all gains and losses are generally realized at the end of each trading day (through adjustments to the variation margin), the net realizable value of the contract will always be zero at the start of the day.

For futures, therefore, we cannot measure return as simply the change in market value. Instead, we use the *notional market value* of the futures position as the basis for return calculations. The notional market value is the equivalent amount of physical security that would cause the same change in net realizable value for given change in the price of the underlying security.

The concept of notional value derives from the fact that a basket of cash and futures simulates the price behavior of the security or basket that the future represents. A basket of cash and stock futures, for example, represents a notional stock position. The rate of change in this notional market value provides us with a meaningful assessment of the return arising from futures investment.

With options, notional value can also be derived from the effective economic exposure of the options positions. Unlike futures, option prices do not move in a symmetrical manner in response to movements in the underlying security or index. The exposure is determined by the hedge ratio (or delta) of the option, which depends on the stock price, the option strike price, the term to maturity of the option, the expected variance of the stock price, and the risk-free rate. Given the hedge ratio, the option position can be replaced by effective positions in the underlying stock and cash. Stannard (1996, 1997) describes this approach in detail.

We note that the notional positions created in this approach can be highly levered, implying both long and short asset positions. With short positions in a portfolio, care should be taken to segregate the long positions from the short positions, so as to avoid cancellation of market values that may occur in the denominators of weight and return calculations. A full treatment of performance measurement and attribution with short positions is given in Menchero (2002/2003).

NOTES

This chapter combines Cariño (1992, 1999, 2002) with additional perspective. In the 1980s, numerous Russell associates debated formulas along these lines. One method advocated by Jeannette Kirschman was affectionately known as the "Kirschman algorithm." The debate led to the suggestion by John Gillies of the transformation to continuous time. Many articles on attribution linking have appeared since 1998, and we are unable to be comprehensive in this exposition. In addition to the papers cited in the text, valuable insight is given in Singer, Gonzalo, and Lederman (1998); Mirabelli (2000/2001); Spaulding (2002); and the entire issue of *The Journal of Performance Measurement*, vol. 7, no. 1, Fall 2002, which was devoted to attribution linking.

REFERENCES

Gregory C. Allen, "Performance Attribution for Global Equity Portfolios," *Journal of Portfolio Management*, Fall 1991, pp. 59–65.

Ernest M. Ankrim and Chris R. Hensel, "Multicurrency Performance Attribution," *Financial Analysts Journal*, March/April 1994, pp. 29–35.

Carl R. Bacon, *Practical Performance Measurement and Attribution* (New York: John Wiley and Sons, 2004).

Sean Banchik, "Pure and Inter-Period Interaction Effects in Multi-Period Attribution," *The Journal of Performance Measurement*, vol. 9, no. 2, Winter 2004/2005, pp. 53–63.

Julia K. Bonafede, Steven J. Foresti, and Peter Matheos, "A Multi-Period Linking Algorithm That Has Stood the Test of Time," *The Journal of Performance Measurement*, vol. 7, no. 1, Fall 2002, pp. 15–26.

J. Stephen Burnie, James A. Knowles, and Toomas J. Teder, "Arithmetic and Geometric Attribution," *The Journal of Performance Measurement*, vol. 3, no. 1, Fall 1998, pp. 59–68.

S. Campisi, "While We Expound on Theory, Have We Forgotten Practice?" in "Reader's Reflections," *The Journal of Performance Measurement*, vol. 7, no. 2, Winter 2002/2003, pp. 7–8.

David Cariño, "Performance Calculations," *Russell Research Commentary* (Tacoma, WA: Russell Investments, June 1992).

David Cariño, "Combining Attribution Effects Over Time," *The Journal of Performance Measurement*, vol. 3, no. 4, Summer 1999, pp. 5–14. Also appeared as *Russell Research Commentary*, August 1999.

David Cariño, "Refinements in Multi-Period Attribution," *The Journal of Performance Measurement*, vol. 7, no. 1 , Fall 2002, pp. 45–53.

Owen Davies and Damien Laker, "Multiple-Period Performance Attribution Using the Brinson Model," *The Journal of Performance Measurement*, vol. 6, no. 1, Fall 2001, pp. 12–22.

Andrew Scott Bay Frongello, "Linking Single Period Attribution Results," *The Journal of Performance Measurement*, vol. 6, no. 3, Spring 2002, pp. 10–22.

Andrew Scott Bay Frongello, "Attribution Linking: Proofed and Clarified," *The Journal of Performance Measurement*, vol. 7, no. 1, Fall 2002, pp. 54–67.

Andrew Scott Bay Frongello, "The Recursive Family Dilemma," in "Reader's Reflections," *The Journal of Performance Measurement*, vol. 7, no. 2, Winter 2002/2003, pp. 8–11.

Denis Karnosky and Brian Singer, *Global Asset Management and Performance Attribution* (Charlottesville, VA: The Research Foundation of the Institute of Chartered Financial Analysts, 1994).

Damien Laker, "A View from Down-Under," *The Journal of Performance Measurement*, vol. 6, no. 4, Summer 2002, pp. 5–13.

Damien Laker, "Toward a Consensus on Multiple-Period Arithmetic Attribution," *The Journal of Performance Measurement*, vol. 9, no. 3, Spring 2005, pp. 26–37.

Andrew McLaren, "A Geometric Methodology for Performance Attribution," *The Journal of Performance Measurement*, vol. 5, no. 4, Summer 2001, pp. 45–57.

Jose Menchero, "An Optimized Approach to Linking Attribution Effects Over Time," *The Journal of Performance Measurement*, vol. 5, no. 1, Fall 2000, pp. 36–42.

Jose Menchero, "A Fully Geometric Approach to Performance Attribution," *The Journal of Performance Measurement*, vol. 5, no. 2, Winter 2000/2001, pp. 22–30.

Jose Menchero, "Performance Attribution with Short Positions," *The Journal of Performance Measurement*, vol. 7, no. 2, Winter 2002/2003, pp. 39–50.

Jose Menchero, "Multiperiod Arithmetic Attribution," *Financial Analysts Journal*, vol. 60, no. 4, July/August 2004, pp. 76–91.

Jose Menchero, "Optimized Geometric Attribution," *Financial Analysts Journal*, vol. 61, no. 4, July/August 2005, pp. 60–69.

Andre Mirabelli, "The Structure and Visualization of Performance Attribution," *The Journal of Performance Measurement*, vol. 5, no. 2, Winter 2000/2001, pp. 55–80.

Brian D. Singer, Miguel Gonzalo, and Marc Lederman, "Multiple-Period Attribution: Residuals and Compounding," *The Journal of Performance Measurement*, vol. 3, no. 1, Fall 1998, pp. 22–27.

David Spaulding, "Is Linking Attribution Effects as Hard as it Looks?" *The Journal of Performance Measurement*, vol. 6, no. 3, Spring 2002, pp. 32–39.

John C. Stannard, "Measuring Investment Returns of Portfolios Containing Futures and Options." *The Journal of Performance Measurement*, vol. 1, no. 1, Fall 1996, pp. 27–33. Reprinted in vol. 10, no. 2, Winter 2005/2006, pp. 64–70.

John C. Stannard, "Measuring Investment Returns of Portfolios Containing Derivatives: Part II—Performance Attribution," *The Journal of Performance Measurement*, vol. 1, no. 3, Spring 1997, pp. 5–9.

Erik Valtonen, "Incremental Attribution With and Without Notional Portfolios," *The Journal of Performance Measurement*, vol. 7, no. 1, Fall 2002, pp. 68–83.

Cecilia Wong, "Attribution—Arithmetic or Geometric? The Best of Both Worlds," *The Journal of Performance Measurement*, vol. 8, no. 2, Winter 2003/2004, pp. 10–18.

CHAPTER 20

Benchmarks and Knowledge

Investors want to know how well their investments performed. However, performance is relative and cumulative. The base level is zero—did wealth grow or shrink? At the next level, the performance of the portfolio is compared with various alternatives that the investor could have pursued but did not. One of the first comparisons is how well the investments performed compared to what other investors obtained from their investments. *Universes* of other funds have a long established history in the investment industry and are used for precisely this purpose. The next level is to compare investment performance with naïve passive investments. A range of investment products can be used for this purpose starting with the lowest-risk investment such as 90-day T-bills. However, if you are an equity investor, the comparison with fixed-income instruments is not an appropriate comparison. A better comparison would be with an equity *broad market index*. A still finer comparison might be to compare your equity portfolio with an equity *style index* within the broad market index with a style similar to your portfolio.

The object at each level is to determine how much return the investor could have obtained compared with what the investor did attain. Implicit in this sort of analysis is a breakdown or decomposition of the utility of the decisions the investor (or the portfolio decision maker) makes while managing the investment portfolio.

Note also that there are several levels here. We start with gross overall return, and then we account for what can be earned with the risk-free rate. Next we use broad market indexes and then we account for still more return with a style index. Finally, we can match the portfolio risk dynamics with a conditional performance evaluation (CPE) benchmark, a substyle portfolio, or a normal portfolio. At each level, we can also take out what can be explained by others with a similar investment approach, that is, a universe, style universe, or substyle universe. At each level we are using a naïve benchmark/portfolio that we could have invested in instead of the portfolio under investigation. *We are raising the bar at each level and making the hurdles more difficult to pass for portfolio managers.* We are making it more difficult to achieve positive risk-adjusted excess return or alpha.

PEER UNIVERSES

In the early 1980s, before the advent of style indexes, the main benchmarks for the comparison of U.S. equity portfolios were the Dow Jones Industrial Average and the S&P 500 stock index. However, many investment management strategies are not well measured by these indexes. To deal with this mismatch, universes were created to provide meaningful comparisons. A *peer universe* is a collection of investment funds or portfolios managed by professional portfolio managers that follow a similar investment strategy. These investment funds are chosen on the basis of an asset class and an approach to investing within the asset class. The collecting and allocating of funds to universes is undertaken by the purveyor of the universe, which itself is usually an investment services company like Lipper, Morningstar, Nelson Information, or Russell. Access to the data on membership, performance, and characteristics of members of the universe typically is available for a fee.

Membership Issues

There are a variety of issues with universes. The first is the quality of the classification process. Some peer universes rely on self-identification on the part of the funds that are placed in the universe. The problem with this approach is that some professional investment managers "game" the system. They attempt to be placed in the universe in which they will look good and hence attract investors.

Herding Behavior

Investment managers, like all human beings, live under the dictates of social norms and human behavior. Although one might find few investment managers who would admit it, Wermers (1999) and other researchers have documented what is called "herding behavior."[1] Anyone who has watched a flock of birds fly through the air or a group of sheep moving across a field, or who recalls from a Western movie the buffalo stampede, has seen this sort of behavior. Driving down the freeway shows you some everyday aspects of herding behavior. If you speed up, the car next to you also tends to speed up. If two lanes merge, there is always someone who speeds up to get in front of the other people. Much of this behavior is unconscious or not really thought out.

In the investment world the same sort of thing happens. However, herding behavior is most frequently found in the apparently unjustified (in terms of fundamentals or significant economic information) movement of investors into and out of securities and groups of securities in sectors. One of the classic cases of this behavior was in 1984 when managers who call themselves "value managers" systematically avoided oil stocks. As a group they underweighted oil companies and services.

Managers believed these securities were subject to political risk because investors were unhappy with the behavior of the oil companies during the political and military crisis of 1979. There was genuine fear that these companies might be subjected to governmental sanctions or penalties. Their profits might have been confiscated because they were excessive. For these reasons professional money managers chose not to buy these securities even though the rest of the market had a different opinion as reflected in the stock prices.

The dot-com bubble of the late nineties appears similar. Many managers underweighted the dot-com stocks because they felt the securities as a group were wildly overpriced. The rest of the market disagreed, and during this period many managers and their universes underperformed their style indexes.

---

[1] Russ Wermers, "Mutual Fund Herding and the Impact on Stock Prices," *Journal of Finance*, vol. 54, no. 2, 1999, pp. 581–622.

While peer universes have their difficulties, the group sentiment aspect of peer universes is precisely the aspect that keeps them
a major part of performance evaluation. In addition to knowing
how an objective index performed, it is reasonable that a fund
manager would want to know how his or her fund performed compared to the rest of the universe.

Survivorship Problems

One of the major problems with peer universes is that they tend to
suffer from *survivorship bias*. This bias occurs for several reasons.
A manager or fund that has poor performance either loses investors
and may be forced to close or the fund manager may reposition the
assets into a new fund, effectively closing the old fund. In either
case, when a fund closes, its data no longer contribute to the universe statistics. This generates a culling out of "losers."

Managers also drop out for purely business reasons. Providing
data to universe creators takes time and energy and costs money.
Managers take this time and make this effort because they hope or
expect that it is in their interest to have their names included in the
universe list. It is a form of advertising. However, if they get no
business from having their names in the universe list, or if their
performance shows up as being very poor compared to their peers,
they may decide to stop providing the information because it is not
helping their business.

For whatever reason, the dropouts from universes tend to be
those managers or funds with poor performance, thereby biasing
subsequent returns of the universe upward toward the performance of successful managers. Ankrim (1998)[2] documented the
extent of this bias within Russell universes. Ideally, the dynamics
of why managers are involved in the universe or drop out of the
universe should be understood when the user is interpreting the
information.

---

[2] Ernie Ankrim, "Peer-Relative Active Portfolio Performance: It's Even Worse
Than We Thought," *The Journal of Performance Measurement*, vol. 2, Summer
1998, pp. 6–11.

The Standard: Peer Universe Box Charts

One of the standard tools used in displaying peer universe information is the box plot like the one shown in Figure 20.1. Charts such as
these show the distribution of universe returns. In this example the
return is for managers in the Russell U.S. equity value universe over
the fourth quarter of 2008; the last year; and the last two, three, four,
and five years annualized. The top and bottom of the boxes refer to
the maximum and minimum manager return, respectively. The line
across the middle of each box refers to the median manager return,
which is the line where 50 percent of the universe is above and
50 percent is below. The dashed lines identify the return of the
manager at the first quartile (below which 75 percent of the universe
lies) and the third quartile (below which 25 percent of the universe
lies). The return of the relevant benchmarks also will be displayed
somewhere in the box by easily identifiable symbols. Symbols are
usually shown representing the return of a broad market index such
as the S&P 500, the Wiltshire 5000, or the Russell 3000.

For a specific portfolio, the return of the manager within the
distribution of the universe is often identified, usually with an
asterisk. In this way the analyst is able to interpret the return of the

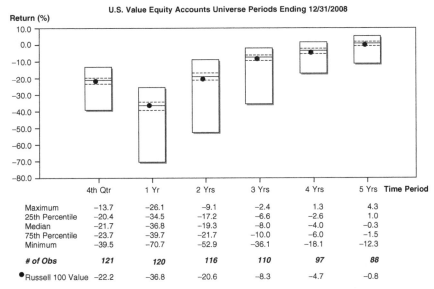

Figure 20.1 Russell U.S. equity value universe box chart. *Source:* Russell
Investments.

portfolio relative to the universe and other benchmarks. Note how the boxes move up and down with different time windows indicating the changing cumulative return over time. Note also that the box sizes grow and shrink indicating the expansion and contraction of the distribution of the underlying universe returns.

Graphs such as this are highly useful for understanding the performance of a manager relative to other managers in the universe and to passive indexes that the investor could have purchased. They are widely used in the industry because they pack in a lot of useful information.

Investability

One of the problems with peer universes is that of investability. After the fact, one can create a mean for a universe or a median. However, if an investor were to buy shares of the portfolios of all the managers in the universe, the investor would not obtain the universe median return in practice. Unfortunately, because of the statistical properties of the median, one cannot purchase the median return of the universe before the fact. If sufficient information is available about all the universe members, one could buy a representative sample of portfolios from the universe, but, for the most part, this is not a realistic option because of transaction costs and administrative overhead. Hence, one cannot realistically expect to obtain the mean or median return of a universe. That is one of the reasons why broad market indexes and style indexes were created.

Linking Universe Medians versus Linking Universe Means

Universes provide a useful framework for evaluating a money manager in terms of what you could have achieved had you held every other portfolio in the universe. It is a natural desire to be able to compare a manager on a month-by-month or quarter-by-quarter basis with a universe containing the manager over the same time periods. Since the distribution of returns in the universes is often skewed positively or negatively (e.g., the two- and three-year graphs in Figure 20.1), analysts often use the median return. To compare a manager over time, some analysts may attempt to link universe medians over time.

Median returns might be linked using the linking formula in Equation 3.2, because they are returns and any set of returns can be linked mathematically. However, linking medians is unrealistic in terms of investment strategies. One cannot buy the median manager portfolio beforehand. The median manager above which 50 percent of the universe falls and below which 50 percent of the universe falls emerges only after the fact. If you bought all the portfolios in the universe on an equal-weighted basis, the return you would receive would be the mean return, or the average return of all those portfolios. If the distribution is not normally distributed, the mean and median will be different. Therefore, linking medians over time is not really appropriate.

PASSIVE MARKET INDEXES

The next higher hurdle for managers to beat is a *broad market index*. As mentioned, the Dow Jones Industrial Average and the S&P 500, followed by the Wilshire 5000 and the Russell 3000, are indexes that have long been used to evaluate equity portfolios in the United States. With the evolution of modern portfolio theory (MPT) and the CAPM with its notions of broad market indexes representing "the market," plan sponsors and fund managers had a framework for building more effective portfolios and evaluating their performance.

The creation of an S&P 500 index fund by Vanguard in 1976 was symptomatic of this revolution in fund management. From that point forward, plan sponsors did not have to buy or contract with active money managers to manage their equities; they could simply buy the index funds and receive the "market" return for much lower fees. Research quickly revealed, and has confirmed over and over again, that most active mutual funds and most active money managers have a difficult time providing performance superior to the S&P 500 index fund after fees.

Also, from that point forward, fund managers and plan sponsors were not meeting their fiduciary obligations if they did not ask themselves whether their investment strategy and plan was outperforming a low-cost passive alternative such as the S&P 500 index fund.

Passive Style Indexes

A still higher hurdle for managers is an equity style index. In the late eighties and early nineties, Russell Investments (known then as the Frank Russell Company) created a series of indexes that provided "market segment" proxies called *style indexes*. S&P and other index providers quickly followed suit providing a wide variety of equity style indexes that could be used as benchmarks for equity funds, and passive index funds followed.

We delve into the philosophy of creating indexes and examine in detail how to build indexes in Chapters 21–26. For now, we just want to show how these indexes fit into the overall picture.

The simple idea behind most existing indexes is to create a basket or list of securities that represent the market or market segment that the analyst wants to measure. For example, if you wanted a utilities index, you would devise a set of rules that allowed you to identify utility stocks. You would then apply a weighting scheme to this list of securities. This weighted list of securities then becomes the index, and by keeping track of its price changes and other capitalization changes one can generate a return series that will closely match what would have happened had you bought all the securities. An index fund does buy the securities and is judged by how closely it tracks the underlying theoretical index return (i.e., returns without transaction costs or fees). Normally index funds track the underlying index within 50 to 100 basis points and charge a management fee of 25 to 75 basis points.[3] This provides a very realistic and low-cost alternative to hiring active investment managers. In this sense index funds raise the performance bar for active fund managers enormously.

The Virtues of Indexes versus Peer Groups

We have already mentioned one of the virtues of using indexes to evaluate manager performance. Indexes do not exhibit herding

---

[3] Leonard Kostovetsky, "Index Mutual Funds and Exchange-Traded Funds," *The Journal of Portfolio Management*, vol. 29, no. 4, Summer 2003, pp. 80–92. Kostovetsky quantifies the differences and examines the explicit and implicit costs inherent in both ETFs and index funds.

behavior like the oil bias of value managers in 1984. Nor do they suffer from survivorship bias or the investability problems of universes. They represent the entire market sentiment.

Unfortunately, no matter how many indexes are created, they never seem to be a perfect match with the manager the investor wants to hire or the manager the investor has in his or her portfolio. While broad market benchmarks like the Russell 3000, the Wilshire 5000, and the S&P 500 let you see how well the equity portfolio behaved compared with the general market, style indexes bring you closer to what the typical manager actually invests in. To come still closer to passively measuring what a money manager does, the concept of normal portfolios was created. It is to this subject we now turn.

MANAGER-SPECIFIC STOCK-MATCHING BENCHMARK: NORMAL PORTFOLIOS

The most difficult benchmark for a managed portfolio to outperform is a specialized index called a *normal portfolio*. It is the most difficult because it matches the stock selection process of a manager as closely as possible using simple selection rules.

The notion of a normal portfolio was first introduced by the Barra organization.[4] The choice of the word *normal* to describe a portfolio is intended to capture the idea that for each money manager there exists a habitat of securities whose composition is very similar to the manager's average portfolio over time. In this sense the normal portfolio is long-term "typical" or "average." But average or typical what? *It is not clear that there should be a unique or single normal portfolio for a manager.* There is more than one reasonable average in which we might be interested; hence, there might be

---

[4] See Mark Kritzman, "How to Build a Normal Portfolio in Three Easy Steps," *Journal of Portfolio Management,* Summer 1987, pp. 21–23. Factor model normal portfolio methodology is discussed in *The Normbook* (Berkeley, CA: Barra, September 1988). For a discussion of more philosophical issues see Arjun Divecha and Richard Grinold, *Normal Portfolios: Issues for Sponsors, Managers, and Consultants* (Berkeley, CA: Barra, February 1989).

more than one normal portfolio we could construct. One useful definition of *normal portfolio* is as follows:

> A normal portfolio is a set of securities that contains all of the securities from which a manager normally chooses, weighted as the manager would normally weight them in a portfolio. As such, a normal portfolio is a specialized index.[5]

The object of using a normal portfolio as a benchmark is to improve one's understanding of a manager's investment activities by comparing the manager's performance against a passive investment alternative that approximately matches the manager's investment activity. The aggregate of the normal portfolios for a group of managers can be used to manage the total risk exposure of a fund. It is simple to identify overexposed or underexposed sectors or risks by comparing such a combination of normal portfolios to a target asset class benchmark. Thus, a properly constructed normal portfolio may be used as a performance measurement benchmark and as a tool for constructing manager mixes.

Managers tend to specialize in different segments of the market, and broad market indexes become inadequate as benchmarks for managers because they contain many stocks managers would normally not even consider, much less choose. They also contain stocks in proportions managers would normally not hold. As a result, the average equity characteristics of many managers' portfolios can be quite different from those of a broad market index.

Inappropriate use of broad market indexes can cause us to make incorrect judgments regarding a manager's riskiness and skill. For example, a manager who specializes in defensive stocks will often outperform a broad market index during bear markets and underperform it during bull markets. In other words, when a manager's style is in favor, the manager appears to be skillful, and when the style is out of favor, the portfolio returns indicate a lack

---

[5] Jon A. Christopherson, "Normal Portfolios and Their Construction," in Frank J. Fabozzi (ed.), *Portfolio and Investment Management* (Chicago: Probus Publishing, 1989) pp. 389–97. Also see "Selecting an Appropriate Benchmark: Problems With Normal Portfolios and Their Uses," *Russell Research Commentary*, (Tacoma, WA: Russell Investments, April 1993).

of skill. Without an adequate normal, it is difficult to determine if the manager has skill.

Therefore, to produce a useful performance benchmark, we must create a portfolio whose characteristics can be used to determine a manager's stock selection capability and, if appropriate, sector allocation skill. Presumably, the manager adds value by selecting the better performing stocks and/or the better performing sectors within his normal universe. If his portfolio return is worse than his normal universe return, then the manager made mistakes in choosing stocks, in departing from his normal weighting scheme, in choosing sectors, or all three.

The following subsections describe the creation of a normal portfolio in more detail.

The Beginning Universe of Securities

The goal in the first step is to capture stocks from which the manager normally chooses and on which one can obtain information reliably and readily. There are a number of ways of isolating the beginning universe. Choosing subsets on the basis of capitalization is an easy first cut. Whichever stock list is used should include all the stocks a manager normally considers and for which you can obtain reliable information. Narrow stock lists can exclude important stocks the manager may hold.

Choosing Securities for the Normal Portfolio

Assuming the chosen universe contains all or most all of the stocks from which the manager is likely to select, the next step is to reduce the list of stocks to those that more closely match the list from which the manager actually does select. This is usually accomplished by using screening criteria consistent with the manager's stock-selection habit patterns. Decision rules are required for this process; that is, it is necessary to have a numerical basis for deciding whether or not a stock belongs in the normal. Table 20.1, panel A, is an example of the kind of information one needs to know in order to build a normal portfolio. This example is typical of a well-known money management firm with a growth orientation.

T A B L E 20.1

Example of Normal Portfolio Specification

<table>
<tr><td colspan="2" align="center">A. Screening Procedure</td></tr>
<tr><td colspan="2">Using the Russell 1000 as the beginning universe, choose all stocks that meet the following criteria:</td></tr>
<tr><td>1   Capitalization</td><td>> $2.5 billion (i.e., medium and large cap)</td></tr>
<tr><td>2   Yield</td><td>< 2% (less than Russell 1000 level of 2.08%)</td></tr>
<tr><td>3   Price/book</td><td>< 2 (less than Russell 1000 level of 2.47)</td></tr>
<tr><td>4   EPS 5-year growth</td><td>< 9% (less than the mean of the distribution)</td></tr>
<tr><td>5   Historical beta</td><td>> 0.85</td></tr>
<tr><td>6   Earnings variability</td><td>> −0.5 std. deviation (below the mean of the distribution)</td></tr>
<tr><td colspan="2" align="center">B. Weighting Scheme</td></tr>
<tr><td colspan="2">Equal weight within the following parameters:</td></tr>
<tr><td>   Capitalizations segment</td><td>   % of portfolio</td></tr>
<tr><td> $2.5 billion–$65.4 billion</td><td>   50% equal weighted</td></tr>
<tr><td> $65.5 billion and up</td><td>   50% cap weighted</td></tr>
<tr><td>   IBM (a specific company)</td><td>   No more than 5%</td></tr>
<tr><td colspan="2" align="center">C. Rebalancing Scheme</td></tr>
<tr><td colspan="2">Usually normal portfolios are rebalanced quarterly or semiannually.</td></tr>
</table>

The screening process should accurately capture the subuniverse of stocks and is usually determined through communication with the manager or developed independently based on the analyst's assessment of the manager's key selection criteria. In either case, the content of the screens is critical. Since, in our example, the manager chooses among large- rather than small-capitalization stocks, we would choose a broad, large-capitalization subset as the beginning universe, for example, the Russell 1000. We would then subdivide or screen the universe further on such criteria as those listed in Table 20.1, panel A.

There are no unambiguous rules about setting screening values. The only good check is the reasonableness of the resulting subuniverse given the manager's style of investing.

Two ways to judge the reasonableness of a subuniverse are (1) by evaluating how well the manager's return patterns fit the normal and (2) by evaluating how well the normal fits the manager's portfolio characteristics. If we had to choose between the two criteria, we should be more concerned with the portfolio characteristics than with similarity of performance because of the role of specific return or noise in stock returns. However, we would expect to find, on average, significantly higher correlations between the manager's performance and the normal than with the broad market. We would also expect a lower residual variance relative to the normal than relative to the broad market.

Weighting the Securities

Once the normal subuniverse of stocks has been specified, the critical problem of how to combine them into an index remains—that is, what weights should be applied to each stock. In Chapter 22 we discuss the virtues of different weighting schemes in more detail. Most broad market indexes such as the Russell indexes and the S&P 500 are capitalization- or float-weighted. Most active managers, on the other hand, would rather not capitalization-weight their portfolios. The reason for this lies in the way managers select stocks for their portfolios. Their research generates a list of stocks to buy. They may argue that their confidence in their choices is about equal and does not rise with the capitalization of the stock. Hence, they may tend toward equal weighting. Using the correct weighting scheme does matter enormously.

Limitations

There are certain implicit assumptions about normal portfolios that one should bear in mind when creating and using normal portfolios. An assumption inherent in the methodology is that the universe of securities from which a manager chooses can be determined by the fundamental stock characteristics used in screens. "Catalysts for an earnings turnaround" or "the stock has a franchise" are things not found in stock characteristic databases and they cannot be captured in a normal portfolio using screens.

Furthermore, some styles of management such as market-timing behavior would represent bets against a normal portfolio. If the manager has the discretion to time the equity market by moving funds out of equities and into cash or other assets, this dynamic behavior cannot be captured in a normal portfolio of equities only. A normal portfolio for market timers must also have a "normal" or typical weight in the type of securities that the manager uses in market timing (e.g., cash). The screening methodology has limits in terms of its ability to capture an investment strategy.

FOR WHAT SHOULD A MANAGER BE GIVEN CREDIT?

This question is related to the whole purpose of performance evaluation. If, for example, a manager, through intuition or research, arrives at a low price/earnings (P/E) investment strategy that buys only out-of-favor or undervalued stocks, then how much value added over a broad market benchmark should the manager be granted—all the low-P/E style performance above or below the broad benchmark or only that portion not explained by a low-P/E normal portfolio?

This question, of course, recalls the question of why we hire active managers in the first place. Presumably we do so because we think managers can add value over a passive alternative. But normal portfolios or other specialized indexes muddy the waters. To the extent that active managers do not add excess return above their normal portfolios, the fund manager (as a fiduciary) "should" create a passive portfolio of the securities in the normal portfolio and save a portion of the active management fees for the benefit of the fund participants.

Managers, naturally, want the credit for the outcomes of their style of investing. If we capture most of the manager's performance by creating a passive portfolio, or investing in a normal portfolio with the manager's cooperation, are we "stealing" his alpha? We certainly are raising the bar represented by the benchmark portfolios higher and higher. Eventually, we reach a point where few managers can add value. Ultimately, the process of closely matching a manager's investment strategy might push a manager toward taking specific risk against the benchmark; these incentive effects of the benchmarking process are an important part of the problem.

How Close to the Manager's Ideal Portfolio Do We Wish to Come?

Does the fund manager want a customized normal portfolio that matches the manager's style as closely as possible or a more generic normal that captures the manager's general style of management? The virtue of a close match is that it allows us to know more precisely where the manager added value—that is, how well he chose securities. The virtue of the more generic normal is that we can judge how well the manager does as a variation on a theme. Did the manager's skill in security weighting, sector allocation, and security selection add value?

However, a more generic normal portfolio makes it possible to judge the skill of other managers of a similar style. The broader the normal portfolio, the more useful it is for answering the question of how much better off the fund would be with manager A rather than manager B (given that the generic normal portfolio fairly accurately captures the investment style of both).

As mentioned earlier, a different benchmark implies different incentives for a fund manager who strives to outperform the benchmark. If the benchmark is narrowly targeted, the incentives are tighter, while, if it is more general, there is more management flexibility.

CHAPTER 21

Elements of a Desirable Benchmark

The future of performance measurement and benchmark philosophy is uncertain. What is clear is that the number and complexity of investment opportunities continue to multiply. Our central focus has been, What happens to a unit of market value invested (performance measurement)? We have viewed the answers to that question in terms of what the investor could reasonably have achieved with limited special knowledge (index investing). This approach has the virtue of being simple and is an extension of traditional approaches. However, the changing nature of the opportunity set and the complexity of its components make answering these simple questions continuously more difficult. At the same time, new innovations in performance measurement and benchmarking should strive to answer these fundamental questions. Acknowledging the limitations of the current state-of-the-art should not prevent our specification of the fundamental elements of a desirable benchmark.

ORIGINS OF U.S. EQUITY BENCHMARKS

Charles Dow created the first widely followed index in 1884 when he published an average of the prices of eleven stocks—nine railroads and two industrials. This index, the ancestor of today's Dow Jones Transportation Average, was the precursor of the Dow Jones Industrial Average (DJIA), launched in 1896.[1] The DJIA is widely

---

[1] See "Dow Jones History" at www.dowjones.com/TheCompany/History/History.htm.

quoted around the world to this day and reflects the average price of 30 industrial stocks, carefully chosen, to reflect the U.S. equity market. This index has shortcomings for portfolio evaluation because it covers only a few stocks and their prices are averaged. The index does not tell the investor very much about the behavior of the prices of other large-cap, midcap, or small-cap companies. Even so, the DJIA captures most of the movement of the U.S. market on a daily basis.

The limitations of the Dow Jones Averages led to the next major innovation in index construction. In 1923, the Standard Statistics Company created the first widely published capitalization-weighted index, covering 233 stocks. Standard Statistics merged with Poor's Publishing in 1941, forming Standard & Poor's Corp. In 1957, the company began publishing the S&P 500, which was and is viewed as a standard index for the U.S. equity market and is widely used as a broad benchmark for U.S. equities.[2]

At the time, the Standard Statistics index was a major innovation because it both significantly broadened the capture of the market from the 30 Dow stocks and it applied a more representative stock-weighting methodology in which each stock was weighted according to what the market thought the stock was worth, that is, capitalization weighting. However, as equity market investors became more sophisticated, the S&P 500's limitations (it is a sampling of 500 stocks from over 7,000 available and represents about 75 percent of the U.S. market capitalization) led to the creation of two broad-based capitalization-weighted indexes for the U.S. equity market.

The Wilshire 5000 Total Market Index took breadth to an extreme when it was created in 1974 by the founder of Wilshire Associates.[3] The index, now called the Dow Jones Wilshire 5000, was also a capitalization-weighted index covering everything trading on any exchange of the U.S. equity market. Unfortunately, neither this index nor its constituents could be purchased or sold on a reliable basis since many of the microcap stocks from stock number

---

[2] See "A History of Standard & Poor's" at www2.standardandpoors.com/spf/html/media/SP_TimeLine_2006.html.

[3] See the Wilshire Associates website, www.wilshire.com/Indexes/Broad/.

3,000 down to 5,000 were thinly traded and extremely small (below $10 million in total market cap).

These shortcomings led to the launch in 1984 of the next major index, the Russell 3000, which was the first index to balance broad market representation with investor accessibility and weight the index according to float (one of several innovations that we discuss later). Russell used active manager portfolio holdings to analyze the investment habitat and concluded that the largest 3,000 securities represented a comprehensive capture of the market accessible to investment managers. As a broad market index, the Russell 3000 consistently captures 98 percent of the U.S. market capitalization and is segmented into relevant market capitalization tiers including the first small-cap index, the Russell 2000.

The world of indexing can be confusing because there are so many indexes, and there are so many different baskets of securities that are called indexes that an analyst can become overwhelmed. So let us turn to the question, What does the word *index* mean in the investment context?

THE FUNDAMENTAL MEANING AND PURPOSES OF A FINANCIAL INDEX

An economic price index is a statistic designed to measure how the prices of a given class of goods or services, taken as a whole, differ between time periods or geographic locations.[4] In investments, the focus is on a given class of securities—equities or bonds of a given country or a group of countries, for example—and on changes in wealth over time. A financial market index is a statistic designed to measure the *return* of a class of securities.

There are essentially four modern uses of financial market indexes, as outlined by Schoenfeld (2002)[5]:

---

[4] The first price index may have been created in the eighteenth century, according to Wikipedia, The Free Encyclopedia, http://en.wikipedia.org/w/index. php?title=Price_index&oldid=225774700 (accessed July 24, 2008).

[5] Stephen A. Schoenfeld, "Perfection Impossible," *Journal of Indexes*, 2nd quarter, 2002. Also in *Active Index Investing* (Hoboken, NJ: Wiley, 2004), Chapter 5.

Gauge of Public or Market Sentiment   Each of the indexes described earlier attempts to accomplish a relatively simple task, which is to tell the investing public what happened in the equity markets during the day. The behavior of indexes is influenced by a wide variety of factors such as the prospects for economic recession or expansion, war and rumors of war, as well as the general feeling of confidence among the people who make up the market. In this sense an index is a sentiment indicator for an asset class.

Performance Measurement   Indexes act as benchmarks for evaluating actively managed portfolios. As discussed in Chapter 20, indexes provide a standard of performance or hurdle against which to measure a managed portfolio. They are tools for identifying a manager's skill and can be used to dissect the portfolio return and identify sources of outperformance.

Asset Allocation   Indexes have come to occupy a central place in the management of multi-asset class funds such as pension funds, endowments, and foundations. In such a fund, creating a grand portfolio of individual securities is a nearly intractable task, given the hundreds of thousands of securities available to invest in. Most often, the task is approached in a hierarchical manner, with decisions made at the highest level between broad asset classes. The exact details of the particular investments within asset classes can generally be addressed separately from the asset allocation decision. Indexes can be used to form expectations of the return and risk characteristics of entire asset classes, thereby serving as proxies for the actual investments.

Basis for Investment Vehicles   Index funds operate as investment portfolios for people who want the return available in a market without having to buy the individual securities. Numerous derivative securities—futures, options, and so forth—on indexes have been created that serve many uses in hedging, trading, asset allocation, and so on. Particular features of indexes, such as replicability and turnover, may make them more or less desirable as a basis for investment vehicles.

WHERE YOU STAND ON THE "BEST" INDEXES DEPENDS ON WHERE YOU SIT

There is one thing that seems to always be true in the index business, and that is "where you stand depends on where you sit."[6] The "best" index yields the most precise measurement of what it sets out to measure as determined by the users of the index. However, *best* is subjective. There are different opinions about how to build the best index. Much of the debate about which is best centers around the viewpoint of the index user.

Different index users have different agendas. When we hear criticisms of indexes or promotions of alternative index methodologies, we should bear in mind the interests of the advocates. Different users have different interests at stake, so they are not unbiased observers in these discussions.[7]

The Index User Community and Their Interests

Stock Traders, Arbitrageurs, Prop Desks   Traders are typically liquidity providers for index funds and active managers during index transitions and rebalances. As liquidity providers, traders prefer indexes with components that have high degrees of liquidity and are easily bought and sold. Traders employ a wide variety of strategies to accomplish their stock-level trading on their client's or own (prop desk) behalf. They tend not to like indexes with securities that are thinly traded and whose prices are not easily determined, as they incur higher risk given that they may not be able to reverse their positions quickly or without market impact.

---

[6] Rufus E. Miles, Jr., "The Origin and Meaning of Miles' Law," *Public Administration Review,* vol. 38, no. 5, September/October, 1978, pp. 399–403. Miles coined several laws of organizational behavior such as *Miles' law*: "Where you stand depends on where you sit," which points out that the sort of stand you take on issues depends on your position in an organization.

[7] In the interests of full disclosure, two of the authors of this book have been very involved in the creation of Russell indexes and tend to view the problems from that perspective. Hence, what follows reflects their experience and opinions as participants in the index provision business. They are not completely unbiased observers.

Index Funds and Passive Managers   Most index fund providers benefit from indexes that have a small turnover over time. Every time there is a change in the underlying list of components, the index fund must buy and sell securities to match the updated index. It takes time, money, and people to execute these trades. From an organizational point of view, this is burdensome. From a performance point of view, if an index fund fails to get prices used by the index provider for purchases and sales, their index fund performance might not track the underlying index well. The standard deviation of the return difference between the index and the index fund is called *tracking error*. Tracking error is a measure by which index fund managers are evaluated for their ability to replicate an index. Higher tracking errors tend to discourage potential investors from using their funds and can hurt their business.

Individual Investors   Individual investors are concerned with their wealth. They tend to be more concerned with the growth of each unit of wealth of their personal portfolios. With regard to index funds, individuals are most concerned with the overall return of index funds after fees, which are influenced by turnover costs, capitalization changes, dividend income, and associated tax implications. Individuals also care about how different index funds round out their asset allocation decisions, and the degree to which they offer diversification benefits and do not overlap with other investments. For this reason, the methods used to build and maintain indexes are of interest to individuals.

Long-Term Investors   Most long-term investors (individual or organizational) desire an index that tracks the underlying list of securities prices, capitalization changes, and total returns as closely as possible. They buy and hold securities for long periods and are thus not particularly concerned with liquidity but are very interested in total returns.

Institutions   While institutions have a fiduciary responsibility to a constituency they serve, they are generally tax exempt and hence are not concerned with tax implications. They are, however, very concerned with being able to explain to their boards or those to whom they report exactly what happened to the list of assets and why.

Active Money Managers   Many professional active money managers are very interested in the construction and maintenance of indexes. They are judged against indexes, and their livelihoods depend on beating these indexes. Consequently, the cynical observer may see that some active managers prefer indexes that are easy for them to outperform. Take managers who specialize in buying and selling small-cap securities, for example. There are times when they would like to be judged against a large-cap equity index rather than a small-cap equity index, given that these segments typically run at different times. There are other times when they would complain if they were compared to a large-cap index. Clearly, it doesn't make sense to evaluate a small-cap manager against a large-cap index at any time, and most professional active managers want to be evaluated fairly. Thus, active managers generally prefer indexes that represent the investment pond from which they fish. Many large-cap managers tend to like indexes that are equal weighted rather than capitalization weighted, because managers resist taking bets in the largest stocks and systematically underweight them.[8] Depending on how skillfully they trade, managers may like or dislike the liquidity of constituents underlying an index.

Index Providers   Those groups or organizations that collect royalties for building and providing indexes to the marketplace are also interested parties. With the rise of exchange traded funds (ETFs) and futures and options based on the indexes they produce, royalties provide an increasingly large amount of income to index providers. Hence, the purveyors of indexes have a vested interest in their indexes being widely used and popular because these investment vehicles (index funds, futures, options, and ETFs) contribute to their profitability. They try to balance the concerns and interests of all the players mentioned.

---

[8] See Dennis J. Trittin, "Assessing the bias against the largest cap stocks by institutional managers," *Russell Indexes White Paper* (Tacoma, WA: Russell Investments, March 2005).

THE BEST INDEX IS BASED ON FOUR
PRINCIPLES OF USEFUL INDEXES

The characteristics of a good benchmark are, like beauty, in the eye of the beholder. However, we present reasons why we believe each of the criteria we advocate are the best choices. *Best* is defined here in terms of what gives benefit to individual investors and institutional investors who represent groups of individual investors—not necessarily banks and insurance companies or investment management companies. In this sense, we choose sides.

As a point of departure, we return to the central question that individual and institutional investors always have: What happened to my invested wealth today? We believe this question is the basis for all index and benchmark construction. This consideration leads us to those principles that the authors think are most important in the construction and maintenance of indexes.[9]

Principle I: A "Naïve" Alternative

Benchmarks should yield the return and risk an investor could obtain without any extraordinary knowledge of the investment opportunity set—a naïve return series.

Regardless of how you approach performance measurement, one of your first concerns will be the baseline against which to compare all other evaluations. As mentioned in Chapter 20, the first baseline is whether the investment returns more than zero or less than zero. The second baseline is whether the investment exceeded the risk-free rate. The third baseline is a relevant asset class index, which provides returns on average above the risk-free rate over time.[10] A desirable property of an equity index is that its rules do not require proprietary or unusual knowledge. This characteristic can be called *naïve investor* or *rules based*.

---

[9] The authors would like to emphasize that the principles we espouse here are from an institutional or individual or passive investor viewpoint and are not necessarily the Russell index group's point of view.

[10] If an asset class benchmark cannot outperform the risk-free rate on average over time, no investor would invest in the asset class the benchmark measures. It has to outperform the risk-free rate in the long run to even be considered for investment.

The average investor must be able to follow the construction rules without any special skill or analytical capabilities. Capitalization-weighted indexes and equal-weighted indexes using published weights or combinations thereof meet these criteria. Other asset-weighting strategies might not meet this requirement.

Principle II: Completeness

Given the purposes of a benchmark, a benchmark should include all the assets available for investment.

The index should cover all the practical opportunities in the asset class.[11] If an index fails to include expected securities, it may lead to unintended consequences for investors. An investor might want to know what return could have been achieved had the missing assets been included. If a manager is evaluated with an index that does not contain securities that it should, this may lead to charges of unfairness in the evaluation. This characteristic can be called *completeness*. Though completeness may not always be achievable in practice for a variety of practical reasons, it is a goal to strive for. The practical drawback of full inclusion is the cost of acquiring the information and dealing with the timing of information. Several features of a good index follow as corollaries of the completeness principle.

The index should reflect the ability of an investor to purchase the asset and should adjust capitalization for restricted shares, cross-owned shares, and shares that are not available to the public. It should reflect the free float or amount of capitalization readily available for purchase. This characteristic can be called *investability*. The virtues of investability are part of the virtues of completeness.

The index should be built according to rules widely accepted in the investment community. This characteristic can be called *intuitive believability*. We will discuss investment style in Chapter 24 where we will see the importance of an index being based on what groups of investors intuitively feel is representative of how they invest.

---

[11] Information, data, and investment limitations make investing in some "opportunities" impractical, so "practical opportunities" means those assets one could reasonably be able to purchase or sell without extraordinary effort.

The index should be built to minimize as much as possible the advantage of any one class of investors over another. Front running or other manipulations by large-market players should not be possible or be as minimized as possible. This characteristic can be called *fairness*.[12]

Principle III: Simplicity

Benchmarks should be constructed in a transparent method that can be replicated by users.

There should be no obscure or proprietary methods used in the index. If exceptional knowledge or tools are required to calculate the factor exposure of a stock in order to assign its proper weight in the index, this makes it a less desirable index. It is less desirable because the average investor cannot replicate the investment strategy easily.

The index should be built to minimize administrative and transaction costs. A better index is one that minimizes turnover and list management. The index should start with the simplest and easiest weighting scheme to begin with. In this sense anything but capitalization weighting or equal weighting is inconsistent with Occam's razor—when in doubt, keep it simple. This characteristic can be called *simplicity*.

The data should not be proprietary or otherwise secret; otherwise, the average investor cannot re-create it and thereby will be unable to understand or anticipate changes in the indexes. This characteristic can be called *no propriety methods or data*.

The index should have clear unambiguous published rules for construction that can be replicated by a competent analyst. This characteristic can be called *openness and clarity*.

The index should include assets for which complete and reliable data can be obtained repetitively in a timely manner. The users of the index should have confidence that the index number is accurate each time they use it. This characteristic can be called *reliability*.

---

[12] This section benefits from Laurence B. Siegel, *Benchmarks and Investment Management* (Charlottesville, VA: The Research Foundation of AIMR, 2003).

Principle IV: Representative Weighting

We believe that most benchmarks should be capitalization weighted and then float adjusted when possible. A good index should be *float weighted*, if possible, because restricted shares, shares that are never traded, or shares otherwise not available for purchase do not reflect the true opportunity set. The capitalization should be adjusted downward. This is called *float adjusted*.

The resulting market price or value of a security in the index reflects market sentiment and market opportunity in proportions that can be purchased by the average investor. Rather than imposing the index constructor's estimate of what a stock is worth or relying on some algorithm that produces stock weights, the index should not try to outguess the value that market participants assign each asset. The number of shares being traded and the price that participants are willing to pay for those shares is an unambiguous measure of what a stock or asset is truly worth. This characteristic accepts market participants' weights implicit in capitalization.

Another advantage of capitalization weighting, as opposed to equal weighting, for example, is that a capitalization-weighted index does not require as much rebalancing. If you buy a capitalization-weighted index portfolio and there are no changes in the list of firms, then in theory your portfolio automatically rebalances the same as the index, with no trading. To track an equal-weighted index, in contrast, you must rebalance to equal weights by buying stocks that have fallen in value and selling stocks that have risen.

DESIRABILITY TRADE-OFFS

In Chapters 27 and beyond, we review a variety of indexes. We try to evaluate each of these indexes in terms of their desirability characteristics as outlined earlier. At this point, you should understand that there are some trade-offs when using these criteria.

For example, there is an inherent conflict between completeness, having all securities within an asset class in the index, and investability. Some of the securities are not available for trading. A classic example of this is the Wilshire 5000. When index funds were first created to match the index, it turned out that the smallest 2,000 securities in the Wilshire 5000 were essentially untradable because they were either pink sheet stocks, which required trading by appointment, or they were traded so infrequently that accurate prices could not be obtained. Furthermore, most institutional investors employed by retirement funds and other institutional investors avoided these securities. In other words, these stocks were not investable because they could not be bought and sold by fund managers in sufficient volume that a full replication of the Wilshire 5000 index could have been constructed without incurring exceptionally high transaction costs or unusual delays in buying and selling the illiquid securities. About 2 percent of listed stocks fall into this small illiquid group.

Because of the illiquidity of very small cap stocks, when Russell set out to create a broad market index in 1983, the Russell 3000 was created rather than a Russell 6000. Today it is much easier to obtain reliable prices on the securities and to trade them, but it is still difficult to go above 4,000 securities and obtain reliable data. That is why in the 1980s and 1990s, most index funds that claimed to be Wilshire 5000 indexes were in fact Russell 3000 index funds. The correlation between the two indexes is 0.99.

There is also an inherent conflict between making the indexes representative of an investment strategy while at the same time keeping those indexes simple and inexpensive to maintain. The Russell 3000, for example, is reconstituted once a year near the end of June. Reconstitution refers to the adding and deleting of securities to/from the indexes and the adjustments of the weights among the securities in the indexes. The stock market is dynamic. Successful companies grow and their stock prices rise, and, as a consequence, they rise in capitalization. Other companies are less successful and their prices decline. During index reconstitution, new securities enter and existing securities fall out of the Russell 3000. Whenever this happens, transaction costs are incurred by those seeking to maintain investment funds or index funds that track the index. The more frequent the reconstitution, the greater are the transaction costs inherent in tracking the index and the less those who track the index.

There also is a trade-off between transaction costs and representation. As we shall see, when style indexes are created to capture the behavior of segments of the overall market, there are movements in the characteristics of the securities and the market as a whole that cause stocks to move between the styles over time. Consequently, the reconstitution of style indexes produces substantial levels of transaction costs. However, these transaction costs are necessary to enable the index to accurately represent the intended style as market conditions change.

ISSUES WITH INDEX CONSTRUCTION

Passive index investing does not occur in a vacuum. Investors tracking indexes must buy and sell the securities that make up the index. The S&P 500 index inclusion or exclusion effect is well documented.[13] It has been shown that, on average, when a stock goes into the S&P 500, its price rises, and when a stock is dropped from the S&P 500, the price falls. Among the reasons for this price change is a supply-and-demand effect. Generally one would expect that when a stock enters a popular index, demand for the stock may increase, possibly due to increased liquidity, lower informational costs, information signals, and so on. Furthermore, there may be temporary imbalances in buy and sell orders around the effective date of the inclusion. These imbalances can arise because investors who wish to replicate the index, such as index funds, may feel compelled to buy the stock on the effective date in order to minimize tracking error. Active investors might anticipate these trades, buying the stock in advance expecting to sell it around the date of inclusion, supplying liquidity to the indexers.

Concern with Russell 2000 index rebalancing has also been well publicized as it occurs every year in June, and there have been a variety of academic studies published about historical Russell rebalances prior to 2002. For example, Madhavan writes "a portfolio long additions and short deletions to the Russell 3000 index

---

[13] See Mark Garry and William Goetzmann, "Does De-listing from the S&P500 Affect Stock Price?" *Financial Analysts Journal*, vol. 42, no. 2, March/April, 1986, pp. 64–69. However, Schleifer found that it does affect prices. Andrei Schleifer, "Do Demand Curves for Stocks Slope Down?" *Journal of Finance*, vol. 41, no. 3, 1986, pp. 579–590. More recent work includes Messod Beneish and Robert Whaley, "S&P 500 Index Replacements, A New Game in Town," *Journal of Portfolio Management*, Fall 2002, pp. 1–10; P. Jain, "The Effect on Stock Price of Inclusion or Exclusion from the S&P 500," *Financial Analysts Journal*, vol. 43, no. 1, January/February 1987, pp. 58–65; Ananth Madhaven and Kewei Ming, "The Hidden Costs of Index Rebalancing: A Case Study of the S&P 500 Composition Changes of July 19, 2002," working paper (September 3, 2002, posted on the website for ITG, Inc.).

(constructed after the termination of the new index weights at the end of May) yielded a mean return over the period 1996–2001 of 15% in the month of June. From March–June, the cumulative return exceeds 35%." Since 2003, the opposite result has occurred. Deletions from the Russell 2000 outperformed the additions each reconstitution from 2003–2008 according to Lehman Brothers.

There are a few reasons for this sea change in which deletions from the Russell 2000 have been outperforming additions: (1) the exchange environment is more controlled primarily on NASDAQ-listed stocks, (2) index fund investors aren't passive and employ a variety of trading strategies to transition their portfolios over time, (3) opportunistic trading outpaces index funds driven in large part by hedge funds, and (4) the increased use of Russell 2000 futures and exchange traded funds. Russell has implemented changes to mitigate the impact of reconstitution: adding IPOs more frequently; using the NASDAQ Closing Cross prices, which eliminated much of the reconstitution "gaming" behavior observed in the nineties; publishing provisional and legacy indexes, which enable portfolio managers to track indexes that rebalance on different dates than the official reconstitution; and, since 2007, using a banding methodology to reduce unnecessary turnover between the Russell 2000 and Russell 1000, whereby stocks near the breakpoints remain in their respective index if they have not materially changed in size. In a study using data from the reconstitutions of 2000 through 2006, Cariño and Pritamani (2007)[14] found evidence that the Russell reconstitution effect is temporary and continues to diminish over time.

Free-Float Mismatch—The Yahoo! Effect

An extraordinary S&P 500 inclusion effect occurred on December 7, 1999, the day before Yahoo! Inc. was added to the S&P 500 index.[15]

---

[14] David R. Cariño and Mahesh Pritamani, "Price Pressure at Russell Index Reconstitution," *Russell Research Commentary* (Tacoma, WA: Russell Investments, April 2007). Eric J. Weigel and Katie B. Weigel reported price pressure in the early Russell 2000 reconstitutions, in "Membership Effects in the Russell 2000 Index," *Russell Research Commentary*, (Tacoma, WA: Russell Investments, October 1992).

[15] Steven A. Schoenfeld, "The Importance of Float Adjustment: the Yahoo! Example," *Active Index Investing* (Hoboken, NJ: Wiley, 2004), p. 77.

On that day Yahoo!'s price rose by $67.25 per share or 24 percent. Why? The reason had to do with the way the S&P 500 was weighted. Yahoo! was included at its full capitalization weight in the S&P 500 even though large numbers of the shareholders of Yahoo! stock were not at liberty to sell that stock. Most of the shares were held by employees, venture capitalists, and other investors who were restricted in their ability to sell the shares. In reality only about 10 percent of the shares were truly available for purchase—in other words, *the float did not match the capitalization.* At the time, the S&P 500 was the index with the most associated passive index assets in the world. Since so many index funds had to buy the stock in order to track the index weight, an obvious mismatch between supply and demand occurred and a huge price spike resulted. This event is the quintessential example of the importance of float adjustment to index construction and is likely to have influenced S&P to subsequently implement float-adjusted weights in their index family.

THE PARADOX OF ASSET MANAGEMENT

The exact amount of funds invested in asset management vehicles like index funds is difficult to measure since it changes on a daily basis, but there are estimates that as much as 35 percent of all U.S. equities are indexed. As William Sharpe pointed out about active management,[16] "after costs, the return on the average actively managed dollar will be less than the return on the average passively managed dollar." Just as Sharpe suggests, only around 40 percent of actively managed funds outperformed benchmarks, according to some studies.[17] Most consultants and investment advisers are very much aware of how difficult it is for actively managed portfolios to outperform a comparable passive index. It is sometimes very difficult for consultants and advisers to advocate to their clients anything other than passive management.

---

[16] William F. Sharpe, "The Arithmetic of Active Management," *The Financial Analyst Journal*, vol. 47, no. 1, January/February 1991, pp. 7–9.

[17] See Mark M. Carhart, "On Persistence in Mutual Fund Performance," *Journal of Finance* , vol. 52, 1997, pp. 57–82, and Burton Malkiel, "Returns from Investing in Mutual Funds 1971 to 1991," *Journal of Finance*, vol. 50, 1995, pp. 549–572.

Indeed, often individual investors are advised to index most if not all of their investments.

This leads to the "student's proof of market inefficiency," which says basically "if every investor believes that markets are efficient, the market could not be efficient because no one would analyze securities."[18] If everyone believed in market efficiency, very few would be motivated to do the necessary research and evaluation to discover deficiencies in current prices. In such a world, price changes would slow to a crawl or cease because there would be no one who would believe that it is wise or prudent to pay anything other than the market price. This, in turn, leads to the paradox that in order for passive management to be a viable investment strategy, it critically depends upon a large number of individuals who do not believe that current market prices are efficient.

As more and more money is invested in index vehicles, the markets tend to become less efficient. Yet inefficiency should make active investment more attractive and hence lead to a fall in the percentage of market capitalization invested in passive vehicles. The interplay of these tendencies determines the degree of market efficiency.

Active management is not essentially a zero-sum game in which there are as many investors who win as who lose because the economy grows and assets become more valuable. Those who can see which direction values are going can make above-average returns even as the whole stock market rises. To the extent that active investors get the prices right, prices change and the movement of passive investors toward the new prices provides profits for active investors.

---

[18] Roger G. Ibbotson and Gary P. Brinson, *Global Investing: The Professional's Guide to the World Capital Markets* (New York: McGraw-Hill, 1993), p. 39.

CHAPTER 22

Index Weighting

Indexes vary in many details of construction. One key detail is the method by which the constituents of the index are weighted. In very general terms, there are three categories of weighting schemes used by index providers: (1) *price weighting*, whereby the constituents are held in proportion to their prices; (2) *capitalization weighting*, also called *market value weighting*, whereby the constituents are held in proportion to a measure of their market capitalizations; and (3) *alternative weighting*, a category for methods other than the first two.[1] We discuss these methods in this chapter.

The weights of the holdings in a portfolio, of course, are directly related to the return. In a managed portfolio, the weights are under the control of the portfolio manager and have a direct impact on the portfolio return. In an index, the weights must be specified by a rule of some sort, which, in turn, directly affects the index return. The *difference* in weights between a managed portfolio and an index directly affects the *difference* in returns. Portfolio managers, therefore, have a need to know how an index is weighted.

---

[1] Weighting schemes for stock indexes have been discussed ever since the earliest indexes were constructed. Frederick Macaulay, in *Theoretical Problems Suggested by the Movements of Interest Rates, Bond Yields and Stock Prices in the United States since 1856* (New York: National Bureau of Economic Research, 1938), p. 145, groups the weighting schemes that existed at that time into essentially these three categories.

In a *price-weighted* index, the number of shares equals 1 for all included stocks and the weights of the stocks are proportional to the prices—hence the term *price weighted*. The impact on the index value of a change in price of a stock is proportional to the stock's price. Although the index value might be viewed as an average price, and therefore easy to understand, the price-weights may bear no relationship to the relative sizes or importance of the companies in the market. Nevertheless, the most widely quoted indicator of the U.S. equity market is the Dow Jones Industrial Average, which is a price-weighted index.

Most other common indexes are *capitalization weighted*. In pure capitalization weighting, the number of shares held by the index is equal to the number of outstanding shares of stock. Hence, the price times the number of shares outstanding is the market cap of a stock, and its weight in the index is proportional to its market cap.

Many indexes are constructed using an adjustment to the number of outstanding shares, where shares that are illiquid or are not available to the public are removed. Such an adjusted number of shares is called *free-float shares*, and the corresponding market cap is called *float-adjusted market cap* or simply *float*. A *float-weighted* index is a capitalization-weighted index that uses free-float shares.

Other weighting schemes include equal weighting, volume weighting, or weighting by other characteristics. In these schemes, the number of shares must be calculated and adjusted periodically to produce the desired weights.

ADVANTAGES AND DISADVANTAGES
OF CAPITALIZATION WEIGHTING

Capitalization weighting is used in most broad market indexes for several compelling reasons. The most basic reason is that weighting by market value is an objective way of measuring the relative economic importance of index constituents. Shares of firms offered in the market comprise the opportunity set for investors. Valuing available shares at market prices clearly measures the market's assessment of the relative values of the firms.

Another reason, of significant practical importance, is the fact that a cap-weighted index requires less rebalancing than other types. Index adjustments due to corporate actions, that is, mergers, spin-offs, and so forth, and dividends can result in weight changes for any type of weighting scheme. But changes in prices alone do not result in adding or removing shares in a cap-weighted index—the index remains cap-weighted after a change in prices. Other weighting schemes require periodic rebalancing trades to bring the weights back to those required by the scheme. For an investor attempting to replicate the index, these trades incur transaction costs, which are not required by the essentially buy-and-hold strategy of a cap-weighted index.

Further reasons for capitalization weighting are of a more theoretical nature, yet are also strongly compelling. Capitalization weighting has the property called *macroconsistency*[2]: If all investors held cap-weighted index funds, and if there were no active investors, then all shares would be held with none left over. With other weighting methods, not all investors could hold the index. A cap-weighted index is therefore a better representation of a typical investor's opportunity set than other methods.

Macroconsistency is one step away from one of the central results of the original capital asset pricing model (CAPM): a cap-weighted portfolio of all stocks in a market is efficient—all investors in the CAPM world would hold the market portfolio, combined with a position in cash to reflect each investor's risk tolerance. Despite the flaws of the CAPM, and challenges to the efficiency of the market portfolio, there is no other simple, objective portfolio that is demonstrably more efficient. This is not to say that other portfolios might not outperform a cap-weighted index from time to time—there is opportunity for active management, after all. But an alternative weighting scheme that requires complex rules or data can hardly be regarded as a consensus view of the market. The role of the market portfolio in the CAPM establishes capitalization weighting as an important baseline methodology.

---

[2] Laurence B. Siegel, *Benchmarks and Investment Management* (Charlottesville, VA: The Research Foundation of AIMR, 2003), p. 5.

Laurence Siegel calls capitalization weighting "by far the most important innovation in equity index construction" and "the central organizing principle of good index construction."[3] We fully agree with this view. As an objective, practical, and theoretically grounded method, capitalization weighting is widely regarded as the standard weighting method for indexes.

The disadvantages of capitalization weighting are not inconsequential. As mentioned earlier, some managers, particularly large-cap managers, tend to not capitalization-weight their portfolios for a variety of reasons. The most often cited reason is related to the manager's aversion to putting too much money in any one stock (such as IBM or XOM)—managers typically want stock name diversification. When compared against a capitalization-weighted portfolio, this aversion can be seen as a bet against certain sectors and stocks.

Capitalization weighting tends to weight some sectors of the market more than would the average institutional money manager. In our experience, capitalization weighting will cause differences between the average characteristics of the manager's portfolio as well as differences in performance.

Finally, during market bubbles such as the dot-com bubble, or other periods of "market irrationality" or "exuberance," where herding behavior drives the prices of some securities far above traditional Graham Dodd fundamental values, capitalization weighting takes the investor along for the ride. However, the prices do reflect what people were willing to pay for stocks—someone did buy Amazon.com at $356 per share on January 4, 1999.

Note, however, that weighting other than by capitalization has theoretical difficulties also. As mentioned earlier, not every investor can purchase equal-weighted portfolios, and non-cap-weighted benchmarks make passive management difficult. Furthermore, if one were to create a non-cap-weighted portfolio, a cap-weighted portfolio would also have to be created to be able to understand the performance effect of underweighting large-capitalization stocks. This is not a moot point. For example, in the latter part of 1996 and early 1997, large-cap stocks performed much better than did the

---

[3] Ibid., p. 1.

overall market. Managers who did not cap-weight their portfolios were negatively affected by their capitalization bets. It seems reasonable that the fund manager would want to know the extent of this bet against large-cap stocks. The key point is that a cap-weighted index has neutral weighting and that all non-cap-weighted indexes should be benchmarked against them.

PORTFOLIO EQUITY CHARACTERISTICS: CAPITALIZATION WEIGHTING VERSUS EQUAL WEIGHTING

In an equity market, the question naturally arises as to what is the price-to-earnings ratio, the price-to-book ratio, or any other equity characteristic statistic that might be computed for the market as a whole.

The simplest answer would be to compute the average statistic, say price-to-book, with each stock contributing equally to the overall statistic. After all, the mean or average is the center of the distribution. Recalling basic statistics, we know that for a distribution such as the height of males, if we were to choose a male randomly from the distribution of males and guess his height, the guess that would minimize our errors in guessing heights would be the mean or average.

Unfortunately, equal-weighted statistics for equity markets leads to confusion. Given the equal-weighted price-to-book ratio, it is difficult to answer the question, What is the ratio of total market value divided by total book value of the market?

A statistic like price-to-book ratio refers to price *per share* divided by book value *per share*. For a given firm, the statistic is equal to the ratio of the total market capitalization (price times number of shares outstanding) divided by total book value. For a portfolio, averages of per-share values are less meaningful than total values. The ratio for a portfolio can be calculated from the per-share ratios, but only by way of capitalization weighting.

For ratios of price per share to another characteristic (price-to-book, price-to-earnings, etc.), it simplifies matters if we invert the ratio, putting the price in the denominator (book-to-price, for example). If $BV = \sum_{n=1}^{N} BV_n$ is the total book value of N firms, and if

$MV = \sum_{n=1}^{N} MV_n$ is the total market value, then the ratio BV/MV for the entire portfolio can be written as

$$\frac{BV}{MV} = \frac{\sum_{n=1}^{N} BV_n}{MV}$$

$$= \sum_{n=1}^{N} \frac{MV_n}{MV} \frac{BV_n}{MV_n}$$

$$= \sum_{n=1}^{N} w_n \left(\frac{BV_n}{MV_n} \right),$$

where $w_n = MV_n/MV$ is the market cap weight and BV_n/MV_n is the book-to-market (or book-to-price) ratio of firm n. Hence, the ratio for the portfolio as a whole is the cap-weighted average of the ratios for the individual constituents.

A numerical example helps to clarify this point. Imagine a highly simplified market that has only two securities with a total capitalization of 100. One of the securities has a capitalization of 80 and the other has a capitalization of 20. Let's say that the price-to-book ratios of the two stocks are 4 and 10, respectively, as shown in Table 22.1.

On an equal-weighted basis the price-to-book of the market is 7. But if we asked what the market-to-book of the overall market is, the answer would be 100/22 or about 4.5. The same result can be

T A B L E 22.1

Market Values and Price-to-Book Ratios for the Example

Stock	MV	Price-to-Book (P/B)	BV = MV/(P/B)	B/P = 1/(P/B)
A	80	4	20	0.25
B	20	10	2	0.10
Total	100	MV/BV = 100/22 = 4.5	22	BV/MV = 22/100 = 0.22
Average		7		
Weighted average				0.22

calculated by taking the cap-weighted average book-to-price, which equals 0.22, and inverting it.

One of the departure points for answering questions about how to calculate index characteristics begins with this question: Do you analyze the problem and compute the statistics on an equal-weighted basis or on a market value-weighted basis? It is really a question of whether you're viewing the securities as essentially equal in importance (equal weighting) or from a market value view-point (value weighting). Some money managers like to look at mar-kets from an equal opportunity perspective, while others who focus on wealth accumulation tend to look at markets from a value-weighted perspective. Much of the debate about whether an index is "good" or not stems from such differences in perspective.

CHALLENGES TO CAPITALIZATION WEIGHTING

Alternative Weighting Methods

Some contend that capitalization-weighted indexes are inefficient and suboptimal. Robert Arnott argues that capitalization-weighted indexes assign higher weight to higher-priced securities and, because the average investor makes mistakes in assessing stock prices, capitalization-weighted indexes systematically overweight expensive stocks and underweight inexpensive stocks.[4] This pro-duces inefficiency in identifying the "true value" of securities. He argues we can obtain a better index by taking "price" out of the valuation measure and focusing on fundamental measures that are economically important.

Arnott's firm Research Affiliates advocates using other mea-sures of company size to weight stocks in a portfolio such as: sales (five-year trailing average), cash flow (five-year trailing average), book value, dividends (five-year trailing average), revenue (five-year trailing average), and employment. The Research Affiliates Fundamental Index (RAFI) uses a composite measure of size based on the four metrics of sales, cash flow, book value, and dividends.

---

[4] Robert D. Arnott, Jason Hsu, and Philip Moore, "Fundamental Indexation," *Financial Analysts Journal*, March/April, 2005.

The RAFI 1000 index is constructed using the following approach: (1) rank all stocks by each of the four metrics, (2) select 1,000 largest by each metric, (3) weight the selected stocks by each metric, (4) average the weights by the four metrics and then (5) select the 1,000 largest by the composite weight. The indexes are rebalanced once a year.

The proof offered that capitalization-weighted indexes are inefficient lies in the fact that fundamental-weighted portfolios often outperformed capitalization-weighted indexes with the same or less risk over historical periods. Arnott therefore concludes that fundamental indexes are better indexes.

Jeremy Siegel[5] of Wisdom Tree Investments, Inc., argues that we are now on the verge of a great new revolution because recent research demonstrates that it is possible to capture higher returns and lower volatility than capitalization-weighted indexes through the construction of new "broad-based indexes." These indexes weight securities on the basis of fundamental measures of firm worth such as dividends or earnings rather than market price.

Siegel argues that the efficient market hypothesis is the philosophical foundation for capitalization-weighted indexes and that it implies that the price for each security "represents the best, unbiased estimate of the true underlying value of the firm." However, he then cites the work of Banz, Keim, Basu, Dreman, as well as Fama and French showing that small-cap stocks and value stocks received higher returns than one would expect based on CAPM. He says, "prices can be influenced by speculators and momentum traders as well as by insiders and institutions that often buy and sell stocks for reasons unrelated to fundamental value such as for diversification, liquidity and taxes." The prices of securities are subject to noise that temporarily shocks stocks away from their true values. Because the shocks can last for long periods of time the unpredictability caused by this noise makes it difficult to design a trading strategy that consistently produces superior returns. He calls this new paradigm the "noisy market hypothesis."[6]

---

[5] Jeremy J. Siegel, "The 'Noisy Market' Hypothesis," as quoted in *The Wall Street Journal* (14 June 2006) p. A-9. Dr. Siegel is the Russell E. Palmer Professor of Finance at Wharton and is senior investment strategy adviser to Wisdom Tree Investments, Inc.

[6] Ibid., p. A-10.

Siegel goes on to point out that when noise drives the price of a stock lower than its fundamental value, "then it is likely—but not certain—that overweighting such stock will yield better than normal returns."[7] Conversely, when noise drives a stock price higher than its fundamental value, there is a high probability that its price will subsequently fall yielding inferior returns. These same sorts of arguments are used by value investors on a daily basis. "Mean reversion" and "regression to the mean" have been shown to be factors in stock prices. Alternative index weights rather than capitalization weights are supposed to capture these mispricings.

Seigel then goes on to point out that value-oriented portfolios outperformed capitalization-weighted indexes during and after the dot-com bubble. He particularly likes a dividend-weighted portfolio in a bear market environment. He also points out that Fama and French's research has shown that value portfolios outperformed growth portfolios historically.

Criticisms of Alternative-Weighted Indexes

We have discussed what we and most people, we believe, think are elements of good indexes. We described many desirable properties of indexes—but high performance of the indexes is not one of the criteria. Arnott argues that the capitalization-weighted indexes are inefficient and hence inferior to fundamentally weighted indexes. As we have mentioned, information ratios are not one of the criteria for judging a good index.

Students of investment style may notice from the criteria used to calculate the RAFI weights that they have a value bias. Growth expectations are not reflected in the weighting, and fast-growing companies are underweighted and underrepresented. A bias toward value stocks is built into the weights. It is also clear that the largest companies by market capitalization will tend to be weighted less. Average market capitalization will be smaller than in a capitalization-weighted index. The reason the strategy works is because it takes advantage of two well-known phenomena that have historically been priced in the market—a bet on value stocks and a bet on small-cap stocks. Will these bets always pay off? There is considerable debate about this. While these anomalies appear to be consistently

---

[7] Ibid., p. A-11.

rewarded over time, there are substantial periods of time in which they are not rewarded.

From an interview with Eugene Fama and Kenneth French, Fama said, ". . . it's just value versus growth. It's nothing more than that. The argument that they've invented the notion that these measures capture mispricing is ludicrous. It's been in the academic literature for a long time." So is it just another way of capturing the value premium? French: "It's not even another way. It's the same way." Fama: "It's a triumph of marketing and not a new idea. It's a repackaging of old ideas."[8]

Clifford Asness has pointed out that any and all investors can buy a capitalization-weighted index, but it is not possible for all investors to buy a fundamentally weighted index.[9] This is the same argument we mentioned earlier about equal-weighted portfolios. The reason lies in the amount of capitalization available for very small companies that have large weights in the fundamentally weighted indexes. There simply may not be enough free float available for index fund managers to purchase a fundamental index weight.

Alternative-weighted indexes are ambiguous on the objective and clear rules criteria because the indexes require proprietary algorithms and information. The problems associated with turnover when the indexes are rebalanced are unknown. It may be difficult for market makers to anticipate exactly how much the weighting of the securities is going to change due to the proprietary nature of an alternative-weighted index methodology.[10]

---

[8] From an interview with Eugene F. Fama and Kenneth R. French, *Journal of Indexes*, March/April 2007. Straight Talk: Fama and French, "Numeral Indexes, Noise and the Nonsense of Active Management" (see www.indexuniverse .com/JOI/).

[9] Clifford Asness, "The Value of Fundamentally Weighted Indices" (New York: AQR Capital Management, LLC, 2005), p. 2.

[10] Two papers on the subject of fundamental weights for indexes are André Perold, "Fundamentally Flawed Indexing," *Financial Analysts Journal*, vol. 61, no. 6, November/December 2007, pp. 31–37, and Jason C. Hsu, "Why Fundamental Indexation Might—or Might Not—Work: A Comment," *Financial Analysts Journal*, vol. 64, no. 2, March/April, 2008, pp. 17–18.

Our conclusion is that alternative-weighted indexing represents an active quant strategy that uses proprietary methodology to produce a value tilt. As such it does not provide the revolution in index methodology its proponents claim, but it is interesting as an active strategy. As Fama said, alternative-weighted indexes are ". . . a triumph of marketing, and not of new ideas."[11]

Confusion on the Meaning of *Index*

As we pointed out earlier, superior performance is not one of the characteristics that we normally associate with a benchmark or an index. Rather, it is a characteristic we seek when we pay for active portfolio management. Index performance is an outcome, not a design objective or characteristic.[12] Claiming superior performance as a basis for superiority of an index confuses the purpose of an index with the purpose of active management. The argument is like saying a pollster has created a better sample of citizens than another pollster because the new sample has a higher average height. As if increased tallness makes for a more representative sample. The index seeks to tell us what return a dollar invested passively in the market earned, while the active manager seeks at a minimum to beat the market alternative and more broadly to maximize the return on a dollar invested. Proponents of alternative-weighted indexes invite confusion between performance achievement and performance measurement.

Periodically, it seems that someone discovers that a capitalization-weighted and float-adjusted index is inefficient because an analyst finds, for a past time period, a set of weights that can be applied to an index list of stocks, that provided greater return with less risk than the commonly used broad market indexes. Robert Haugen did it in the late 1980s with his "efficient index"[13] and now new alternative-weighted indexers are making a similar argument.

---

[11] Eugene Fama, "Straight Talk: Fama and French," *Journal of Indexes*, March/April 2007, p. 11.

[12] These comments benefit from the insights of Don Ezra in 2005.

[13] Robert A. Haugen and Nardin L. Baker, "The Efficient Market Inefficiency of Capitalization-Weighted Stock Portfolios," *Journal of Portfolio Management*, vol. 17, no. 3, 1991, pp. 35–40.

In both cases old traditional indexing methods were to be replaced with a new weighting scheme.

However, using the prices investors are willing to pay for the available equity ownership likely will remain the primary basis for weighting stocks in an index. Benchmarks tell investors what they could have obtained if they had invested their money like everybody else, that is, in the market.

Having said this, we recognize that Arnott, Siegel, and many ETF providers have created portfolios that fall into the gray area between classic indexes and traditional active management. They are not passive, because they utilize active proprietary weighting strategies that are marketed to outperform the cap-weighted alternatives. They are not fully active either because they are portfolios that passively track an active strategy risk/return profile or isolate a particular beta. Alpha may or may not be an objective, but marketing literature implies that alpha above cap-weighted indexes is a goal. This new category of strategy "indexes" has many members, and it is likely to garner more attention given its application in the ETF arena. Many current portfolios underlying ETFs fall into this category, as ETFs currently require an index to underlie the fund. We believe there is a role for these products in investors' portfolios, but exactly how they can be most effectively used has yet to be fully explored. For now, the most important thing to consider is that portfolio strategies, including this category of strategy indexes, should be evaluated against comparable strategies and passive market alternatives.

CHAPTER 23

Practical Issues with Building Indexes

In this chapter we investigate the intricacies associated with building an index by delving into the index construction methodology and rules used by the Index group at Russell Investments. The reason for taking this approach lies in the complexity of building indexes. At each step in the index construction process the builders must make a series of decisions about construction and handling of data. There is more than one "right way" to make these decisions, and different index providers make different decisions on some of these issues. As the old adage says, "There's more than one way to skin a cat," and our objective here is to show you one way to "skin the cat." In Chapters 27 and 28 we will provide some comparisons and contrasts with indexes provided by other vendors.

INDEX CALCULATIONS

Although key details of construction vary by index provider—such as which securities to include and how to weight them—the essential calculation of index values is fairly standard. A stock index is a portfolio in the sense that it represents shares of stocks held over time. An *index value*, however, is not simply the aggregate market value of the shares held. An index value is, by design, a tool to measure the return from holding the underlying shares of the constituent stocks. Changes in holdings, such as occur when stocks are added to or deleted from the index, usually result in a change in the total market value represented by the index. The index value, however, must not change at such an occurrence, because the index value is supposed to measure the changes in prices of stocks *held*, not the change in market value due to the change in holdings. The return that an index value is designed to measure, therefore, is manifestly the *time-weighted* return of the index holdings.

As described in Chapter 5, the time-weighted return of a portfolio can be calculated from portfolio market values at the times of cash flows. When an index provider changes the index holdings, whether as a result of corporate actions such as mergers, or as a result of constituent changes, the changes are normally done after the close of trading on the applicable day. The net change in market value resulting from index changes, valued at the closing prices, is effectively a cash flow as defined in Chapter 5. If EV_{t-1} is the ending market value (number of shares multiplied by price per share, summed over all stocks held) of the index holdings on day $t-1$, then the market value *after* adjusting for any changes in holdings becomes the beginning market value BV_t for the next day. That is,

$$BV_t = EV_{t-1} + P_{t-1} - S_{t-1}, \qquad (23.1)$$

where P_{t-1} and S_{t-1} are the market values of added shares (purchases) and deleted shares (sales), respectively, valued at the closing prices on day $t-1$.[1]

Index values can be calculated both without dividends and with dividends. An index value without dividends is called a *price-return index*; an index value assuming reinvested dividends is called a *total return index*.

The return relative of a price-return index for day t is therefore

$$1 + r_t = \frac{EV_t}{BV_t}, \qquad (23.2)$$

where BV_t is the adjusted beginning market value [Equation (23.1)] and EV_t is the ending market value of the index holdings on day t (before adjusting for changes).

To account for dividend income in an ordinary portfolio, the dividend amount appears as a receivable on the ex-dividend date

---

[1] Note that this beginning value is not necessarily equal to the value of the holdings at the opening prices on day t, but instead is the value at the close of day $t-1$ adjusted for changes in holdings. Despite the risk of confusion, this beginning value is sometimes called the *beginning adjusted market value*.

and normally is considered a cash flow into the liquidity reserve segment of the portfolio. In an index, there is no liquidity reserve—the dividend income is not represented in the ending market value and must be directly accounted for. The return relative of a total return index for day t therefore is calculated as

$$1 + r_t = \frac{EV_t + DIV_t}{BV_t},\qquad(23.3)$$

where DIV_t is the market value of the dividends of stocks that trade ex-dividend on day t, and EV_t are BV_t are as defined before. The dividend market values are ordinarily based on holdings at day $t - 1$ (number of shares multiplied by dividend amount per share). Although a stock's price typically drops on the ex-dividend date by the amount of the per-share dividend, a total return index does not drop accordingly. Conceptually, dividend income is effectively reinvested at the total portfolio level. The holdings (numbers of shares), however, are typically not adjusted for dividend income because an index that "holds" all the shares in the market cannot "buy" more shares with the dividend, for example.

Given the index value IV_{t-1} at the end of day $t - 1$, the new index value at the end of day t is

$$IV_t = IV_{t-1}(1 + r_t),\qquad(23.4)$$

where $1 + r_t$ is the return relative [Equation (23.2)] for a price-return index or [Equation (23.3)] for a total return index. At the inception date of an index, an index *base value* must be assigned to start the process off.[2]

---

[2] According to Alfred Cowles III, in *Common Stock Indexes 1871–1937* (Bloomington: Principia Press, 1938, p. 26), the Standard Statistics Co. (which merged with Poor's Publishing to form S&P) described this method as a *base-weighted aggregative* method. This term was used by Irving Fisher in *The Making of Index Numbers*, 3d ed. (Cambridge: Riverside Press, 1927, p. 59), to describe *Laspeyres' method*, in which base period quantities are valued at the base and current periods. In contrast, *Paasche's method* uses current period quantities. In the context of time-weighted returns, the Laspeyres and Paasche methods are equivalent, because quantities—numbers of shares held—are constant over the relevant holding period.

A slight reordering of the preceding calculations gives a convenient formula for the real-time calculation of a price-return index. Substituting Equation (23.2) into Equation (23.4) gives $IV_t = IV_{t-1}(EV_t/BV_t)$. By calculating a quantity, called *the divisor*,

$$U_t = \frac{BV_t}{IV_{t-1}}, \qquad (23.5)$$

a price index value IV can be calculated throughout trading day t from the formula

$$IV = \frac{V}{U_t}, \qquad (23.6)$$

where V is the market value of the index holdings (number of shares times price per share, summed over all stocks held). The divisor remains unchanged throughout a trading day, while the market value moves as prices change. Substituting the index value $IV_{t-1} = EV_{t-1}/U_{t-1}$ at the close of day $t-1$ into Equation (23.5) gives a convenient formula for updating the divisor after the close of trading:

$$U_t = U_{t-1}\frac{BV_t}{EV_{t-1}}, \text{ (for a price-return index)}, \qquad (23.7)$$

where BV_t and EV_{t-1} are as in Equation (23.1). A similar derivation for updating the divisor of a total return index gives

$$U_t = U_{t-1}\frac{BV_t}{EV_{t-1}+DIV_{t-1}}, \text{ (for a total return index)}, \qquad (23.8)$$

where BV_t and EV_{t-1} are as in Equation (23.1) and DIV_{t-1} is the market value of the dividends of stocks that trade ex-dividend on day $t-1$.

This method, in which the index value is calculated from the market value of holdings divided by the divisor, is known as the *divisor method.*[3] The divisor is analogous to the number of units of a

---

[3] Minor details may vary among index providers.

mutual fund, while the index value is analogous to the mutual fund's net asset value. As described in Chapter 5, a return calculated from the index value (or net asset value) is the true time-weighted return of the index holdings.

Now consider the weighting of the index holdings. If there are N stocks in an index, the total market value V represented by the index is $V = \sum_{n=1}^{N} p_n q_n$, where p_n is the price per share of stock n and q_n is the number of shares. The index value is therefore

$$IV = \frac{\sum_{n=1}^{N} p_n q_n}{U},$$

and the return relative of the index on day t can be written as

$$1 + r_t = \sum_{n=1}^{N} w_{nt}(1 + r_{nt}),$$

where $w_{nt} = p_{nt-1} q_{nt} / \sum_{n=1}^{N} p_{nt-1} q_{nt}$ is the weight and $1 + r_{nt} = p_{nt}/p_{nt-1}$ is the return relative of stock n (in a total return index, weights and returns would be adjusted for dividends). The weights at the beginning of the day are the *adjusted* beginning values, being adjusted for changes in holdings after the previous close.

In a *price-weighted* index, the number of shares q_n equals 1 for all included stocks and, at inception, the divisor U is set equal to N. The index value at inception is the arithmetic average of the prices of the stocks. The weights of the stocks in a price-weighted index are $w_n = p_n / \sum_{n=1}^{N} p_n$, which are proportional to the prices—hence, the term *price-weighted*. The impact on the index value of a change in price of a stock is proportional to the price of the stock. The most well-known examples of price-weighted indexes are the Dow Jones Averages. Over time, the divisor is adjusted for corporate actions such as spin-offs and stock splits by way of Equation (23.7), and therefore the divisor does not remain equal to N for long. The current divisors for the Dow Jones Averages are available at the Web site www.djindexes.com.

In a *capitalization-weighted* index, the number of shares q_n is equal to the number of outstanding shares of stock n. Hence, $p_n q_n$ is the market cap of stock n and its weight in the index is proportional to its market cap. Capitalization weighting is used in most common indexes.[4]

Many capitalization-weighted indexes adjust the number of outstanding shares for illiquid or closely held shares that are not generally available for purchase in the market. Such an adjusted number of shares is called *free float* or *available shares,* and the corresponding market cap is called *float-adjusted market cap* or simply *float.* A *float-weighted* index is a capitalization-weighted index using free-float shares. The Russell indexes have been float-weighted since their inception in 1979.

Other weighting schemes include equal-weighting, volume-weighting, or weighting by other characteristics. In these schemes, the number of shares q_n must be calculated to produce the desired weights.

DECISIONS THAT HAVE TO BE MADE BY THE INDEX CREATOR

The index builder needs to make a series of basic decisions. The list of decision issues includes the following:

- Rules-based transparent construction method or committee-based selection method
- Degree of market representation, defining the eligible universe of assets
- From the eligible universe, whether or not to select a representative sample or to broadly represent the opportunity set
- A fixed number or variable number of securities to be included in the index
- Index membership rules and geographic restriction rules (What is a U.S. company? How do you deal with multinationals?)

---

[4] The first published stock index to use capitalization weighting was introduced in 1923 by the Standard Statistics Company, the predecessor of S&P.

- The total number of securities or market capitalization to be included
- The minimum price, minimum liquidity, float, and the exclusion criteria (if any)
- Rules for determining small-, mid-, and large-capitalization stocks from the broad market
- How often to reconstitute the indexes and how to go about doing it
- The security-weighting method
- The source of asset prices to use, when they are set to avoid stale prices
- The style or habitat rules that identify styles
- The methods used to categorize stocks into styles such as breakpoint versus nonlinear methods versus weighted combinations
- The treatment of corporate actions like exchange delisting, mergers, acquisitions, tender offers, spin-offs, share buybacks, or splits
- Choosing the methods, prices, and communication of changes that seek to either be replicable by investment managers or methods that represent the overall changes but are not necessarily achievable by managers
- The handling of dividends and cash flows
- The handling of data problems and adjustments such as book value write-downs, missing values, and so forth
- For international or global indexes, the special handling of very large securities (like News Corp in Australia, Unilever in the Netherlands, NTT in Japan, or gold stocks in Canada) and of cross-holdings (in Korea, Japan, and other countries).

As you can see, the preceding list is long and the details are complex since a decision made in one place can affect the character and behavior of the indexes in another place. Much of the index methodology Russell pioneered has been adopted by other leading indexes and has become industry standard. So let us begin our discussion of equity indexes with the construction of the Russell 3000E, which is a very broad-market U.S. equity index, and see how Russell handles these issues. [5]

RUSSELL U.S. EQUITY INDEX CONSTRUCTION

The Russell indexes are transparent and rules based. All the rules regarding construction and maintenance of the Russell indexes are published and available publicly—see www.russell.com/indexes. This openness allows anyone who wants to use the indexes to track and replicate any of the Russell indexes.

All Russell U.S. equity indexes are subsets of the Russell 3000E Index. The "E" stands for extended market. The index extends index membership beyond the original 3,000 stocks of the Russell 3000 by adding the next smallest 1,000 very small capitalization stocks. Each Russell index is a subset of the Russell 3000E Index as broken down by market capitalization and style.

The construction rules fall into the following broad categories:

- Defining eligible securities
- Defining index membership by size (market capitalization)
- Adjustments to shares outstanding (float adjustments)
- Determining style
- Maintenance—corporate action–driven changes, initial public offerings, reconstitution, and so forth

The following overview is a summary of the construction rules. For the complete rules, see the Russell Investments Web site, www.russell.com/indexes.

---

[5] The following discussion is based on the current construction methods paper, *Russell U.S. Equity Indexes Construction and Methodology.* Some portions are verbatim extractions from the paper, available at www.russell.com/indexes/ about. The Russell index effort has been the product of many people including two of the authors, but one of the primary champions of Russell indexes has been Kelly Haughton.

Defining Eligible Securities

The Russell 3000E and its subindexes reflect approximately 99 percent of the U.S. equity market capitalization and 100 percent of the investable U.S. market. To be eligible for inclusion, a security must be an equity security and pass several criteria.

- *U.S. Incorporated Companies and U.S. Benefit-Driven Incorporated Companies:* U.S. incorporated companies are eligible for inclusion in the Russell U.S. indexes. Beginning during the reconstitution of 2007, companies incorporated in certain other countries or regions, such as Antigua, the Bahamas, or the Cayman Islands, are also reviewed for eligibility in the U.S. indexes. Companies incorporated in these regions are considered benefit-driven incorporation (BDI) companies, because they typically incorporate in BDI regions for operations, tax, political, or other financial market benefits.
- *Trading Requirements:* Eligible securities must trade on a major U.S. exchange. Bulletin board, pink-sheets, or over-the-counter (OTC) traded securities are not eligible for inclusion.
- *Minimum Trading Price:* Stocks must trade at or above $1.00 on their primary exchange on the last trading day in May to be eligible for inclusion in the Russell U.S. indexes during annual reconstitution or during the IPO eligibility periods. However, if a stock falls below $1.00 intrayear, it will not be removed from the indexes until the next reconstitution.
- *Minimum Available Shares/Float Requirement*: Companies with only a small portion of their shares available in the marketplace are not eligible for inclusion.
- *Company Structure:* Companies structured in the following ways are excluded: royalty trusts, limited liability companies, closed-end investment companies (however, business development companies are eligible), blank check companies, special-purpose acquisition companies, and limited partnerships.

- *Shares Excluded:* The following share types are not eligible for inclusion: preferred and convertible preferred stock, redeemable shares, participating preferred stock, warrants and rights, and trust receipts.
- *Deadline for Inclusion:* Stocks must be listed on the last trading day in May and Russell must have access to documentation verifying the company's eligibility for inclusion.

Defining Membership by Size (Market Capitalization)

The total market capitalization of each eligible security is calculated by multiplying total outstanding shares by the market price as of the last trading day in May.

- *Determining Total Shares Outstanding:* Only common stock is used to determine market capitalization for a company.
- *Determining Price:* The last traded price on the last trading day in May on the primary exchange is used to determine market capitalization. In the case where multiple share classes exist, a primary trading vehicle is determined and the price of the primary trading vehicle (usually the most liquid) is used in the calculations.
- *Primary Trading Vehicle:* The common share class with the highest trading volume, price, and float-adjusted shares outstanding (or highest combination of the three) will be considered the primary trading vehicle. In certain cases, further rules apply to gauge the materiality of the differences between variables.
- *Initial Public Offerings:* IPOs are added quarterly to Russell's U.S. index family based on total market capitalization ranking within the market-adjusted capitalization breaks established during the most recent reconstitution. IPOs must meet all Russell U.S. index eligibility requirements and additional criteria relating to the timing of the initial offering period.
- *Determining Index Membership:* Once the market capitalization for each security is determined using total shares and price, each security is placed in the appropriate Russell market

T A B L E 23.1

Size Index Breakpoints Based on Descending Total Market Capitalization

Index	Companies Included
Russell 3000E	1–4,000
Russell 3000	1–3,000
Russell Top 200	1–200
Russell 1000	1–1,000
Russell Midcap	201–1,000
Russell 2000	1,001–3,000
Russell 2500	501–3,000
Russell Microcap	2,001–4,000

capitalization-based index. The largest 4,000 securities become members of the Russell 3000E Index. All remaining indexes are a subset of this index. Table 23.1 lists the breakpoints for dividing companies into each capitalization-based index.

- *Banding:* After the initial market capitalization breakpoints are determined by the ranges listed in Table 23.1, new members are assigned based on the breakpoints, while existing members are reviewed to determine if they fall within a cumulative 5 percent market cap range around these new market capitalization breakpoints.[6] If an existing member's market cap falls within this cumulative 5 percent of the market capitalization breakpoint, it will remain in its current index rather than be moved to a different market capitalization-based Russell index.

---

[6] "Banding" or setting a range of values rather than using a single breakpoint is a method that comes out of the money management community. Managers who use breakpoints to select stocks such as the top 100 stocks rank-ordered on alpha estimates use banding to reduce portfolio turnover due to stocks at the edge moving back and forth into and out of the portfolio based on minor data changes like price changes. If the stock has been in the portfolio but has moved across the line but not far enough, the stock is retained until the next evaluation point.

Adjustments to Shares Outstanding (Float Adjustments)

After size segment membership has been determined, a security's shares are adjusted to include only those shares available to the public, called *free float*. The purpose of this adjustment is to exclude from market calculations the capitalization that is not available for purchase and therefore is not part of the investable opportunity set. Stocks are weighted in the Russell U.S. indexes by their available, or float-adjusted, market capitalization, which is calculated by multiplying the primary closing price by the available shares. Adjustments are based on information recorded in SEC corporate filings or other reliable sources in cases of missing or questionable data. The following types of shares are removed from total market capitalization to arrive at free float or available market capitalization.

- *Cross Ownership: by another Russell 3000E or Russell Global Index member.* Shares held by another member of a Russell index (including Russell global indexes) are considered cross owned, and all shares will be adjusted regardless of percentage held.
- *Large Corporate and Private Holdings:* Shares held by another listed company (nonmember) or private individuals will be adjusted if greater than 10 percent of shares outstanding. However, not included in this class are institutional holdings including investment companies, partnerships, insurance companies, mutual funds, banks, or venture capital firms.
- *ESOP or LESOP Shares:* These shares are adjusted if they comprise 10 percent or more of the shares outstanding.
- *Unlisted share classes:* Classes of common stock that are not traded on a U.S. exchange are adjusted.
- *IPO Lock-ups:* Shares locked up during an initial public offering are not available to the public and will be excluded from the market value at the time the IPO enters the index.
- *Government Holdings:* Holdings listed as "government of" are considered unavailable. Shares held by government investment boards and/or investment arms will be treated similarly to large private holdings and removed if the holding is greater than 10 percent. Any holding by a government pension plan is considered an institutional holding and will not be removed from available shares.

Determining Style

Russell uses a "nonlinear probability" method, described in detail in Chapter 26, to assign stocks to the growth and value style indexes. The term *probability* is used to indicate the degree of certainty that a stock is value or growth based on its relative book-to-price ratio and I/B/E/S forecast long-term growth mean. This method allows stocks to be represented as having both growth and value characteristics, while preserving the additive nature of the indexes.

The method is applied separately to the stocks in the Russell 1000, Russell 2000, and the smallest 1,000 stocks in the Russell Microcap indexes. Research indicates that valuations of small stocks on average differ from those of large stocks. Treating the Russell 1000, Russell 2000, and smallest microcap stocks separately prevents possible distortion to relative valuations that may occur if the Russell 3000E was used as the base index.

Index Maintenance

The Russell indexes are regularly maintained to reflect changes in the equity market. In broad terms, changes are driven by corporate actions, initial public offerings, and annual reconstitution.

Corporate Action–Driven Changes

- *Timing of Corporate Actions:* Changes to the Russell U.S. indexes are made when an action is final. To determine if an action is complete, a variety of reliable public sources are used, including company press releases, SEC filings, exchange notifications, Bloomberg, or other sources determined to be reliable.
- *"No Replacement" Rule*: Securities that leave the index for any reason (e.g., mergers, acquisitions, or other similar corporate activity) are not replaced. Thus, the number of securities in the indexes over the year will fluctuate according to corporate activity.
- *Mergers and Acquisitions:* Mergers and acquisitions result in changes to the membership and to the weighting of members within the Russell indexes. Merger and acquisition activity is applied to the index after the action is determined

to be final. Specific rules apply, depending on whether the affected companies are existing members of Russell indexes.

- *Reincorporations:* Members of the index who are reincorporated to another country are deleted from the index when the reincorporation is final. Members of the Russell Global Index reincorporating to the United States (territory or BDI) will be added to the Russell 3000E when the reincorporation is final.
- *Reclassifications of Shares (Primary Vehicle):* The primary vehicle share class is typically reexamined at reconstitution, at the time of a major corporate action event, or with the issuance of a new share class.
- *Rights Offerings:* Rights offered to shareholders are reflected in the index on the date the offer expires for nontransferable rights, and on the ex-date for transferable rights. In both cases, the price is adjusted to account for the value of the right and shares are increased according to the terms of the offering on that day. The value of the right is determined using the market value of the right, if available.
- *Changes to Shares Outstanding:* Changes in shares outstanding due to buyback (including Dutch auctions), secondary offerings, merger activity with a nonindex member, and other potential changes are updated at the end of the month in which the change shows up in vendor-supplied updates and is verified by Russell using an SEC filing. For a change in shares to occur, the cumulative change to shares outstanding must be greater than 5 percent. The float factor determined at reconstitution is applied to the new shares issued or bought back.
- *Spin-offs:* The only additions between reconstitution dates result from spin-offs, reincorporations, and initial public offerings. Spin-off companies are added to the parent company's index and capitalization tier of membership if the spin-off company is large enough. To be eligible, the spun-off company's total market capitalization must be greater than the market-adjusted total market capitalization of the smallest security in the Russell 3000E Index at the latest reconstitution. The spin-off company's style index is determined by the style index membership of the parent entity.

- *Tender Offers:* A company acquired as the result of a tender offer is removed when the tender offer has fully expired and it is determined the company will finalize the process with a short-form merger. Shares of the acquiring company, if a member of the Russell 3000E, will be increased simultaneously at $t + 1$, if applicable.

- *Delisting:* Only companies listed on U.S. exchanges are included in the Russell U.S. indexes. Therefore, when a company is delisted from a U.S. exchange and moved to OTC, the company is removed from the Russell indexes.

- *Bankruptcy and Voluntary Liquidations:* Companies who file for a Chapter 7 liquidation bankruptcy will be removed from the Russell U.S. indexes at the time of the bankruptcy filing. Companies filing for a Chapter 11 reorganization bankruptcy will remain members of the index, unless the companies are delisted from the primary exchange. In that case, normal delisting rules will apply.

- *Stock Distributions:* Stock distributions can take two forms: (1) a stated amount of stock distributed on the ex-date or (2) an undetermined amount of stock based on earnings and profits on a future date. In both cases, a price adjustment is done on the ex-date of the distribution. Shares are increased on the ex-date for category (1) and on the pay-date for category (2).

- *Dividends:* Gross dividends are included in the daily total return calculation of the indexes based on their ex-dates. The ex-date is used rather than the pay-date because the marketplace price adjustment for the dividend occurs on the ex-date. Monthly, quarterly, and annual total returns are calculated by compounding the reinvestment of dividends daily. The reinvestment and compounding is at the total index level, not at the security level.

- *Halted Securities:* Halted securities are not removed from the Russell indexes until they are actually delisted from the exchange. If a security is halted, it remains in the index at the last traded price from the primary exchange until the security resumes trading or is officially delisted.

Initial Public Offerings

Since September 2004, eligible IPOs have been added to Russell U.S. indexes at the end of each calendar quarter. IPOs are added each quarter to make sure new additions to the investing opportunity set are reflected in the representative indexes. IPOs are defined as any security newly available to the public for investing, one that is truly being made available for general investment for the first time. If a security had traded publicly previously, even on a restricted basis, it is not eligible for inclusion as an IPO. Such a stock may, however, be eligible during the next reconstitution period along with all other eligible securities.

Annual Reconstitution

Annual reconstitution is the process by which the Russell indexes are completely rebuilt. As Russell indexes have grown in popularity, more and more attention has been focused on the consequences of reconstitution. Several large brokerage houses publish studies each year on the probable impact of reconstitution, and academics have written several papers on the price impact of Russell reconstitution. However, Cariño and Pritamani (2007) show that after adjusting for sector and factor returns, the price impact of Russell reconstitution has been relatively small.[7] In addition, there has been an explosion of short interest in the Russell 2000 vehicles (e.g., ETFs, options, and futures).

The process starts on May 31 of each year. All eligible securities are ranked by their total market capitalization. The largest 4,000 become the Russell 3000E Index, and the remainder of the Russell indexes is determined from that set of securities. In 2004 Russell adopted the NASDAQ Closing Cross as the source of closing prices for NASDAQ-listed stocks on reconstitution day.

Since 2004, reconstitution has occurred on the last Friday in June. At times this date falls before a long U.S. holiday weekend and liquidity is low, so to ensure liquidity in the markets, reconstitution will continue to be effective the last Friday in June with the following exceptions: if the last Friday in June is the 28, 29, or 30, reconstitution occurs the Friday prior.

---

[7] David R. Cariño and Mahesh Pritamani, "Price Pressure at Russell Index Reconstitution," *Russell Research Commentary* (Tacoma, WA: Russell Investments, April 2007).

CHAPTER 24

Styles, Factors, and Equity Benchmarks

DEFINING EQUITY STYLE[1]

To constitute a style of investment, an investment philosophy must be held in common by a group of investors. While the exact implementation of the philosophy may differ, the group shares a generally similar view about which factors determine stock prices and how best to outperform market averages. If a philosophy were unique to a single manager, it would more appropriately be called an investment "insight" that belonged to that firm alone.

The concept of equity styles emerged in the 1970s as analysts noted clusters of portfolios with similar characteristics and performance patterns. Groups of managers seemed to share certain ideas about the best way to succeed in investing. The data being observed were a manifestation of philosophical views about the drivers of stock price movements.

---

[1] This chapter is based on Jon A. Christopherson and Paul R. Greenwood, "Equity Styles and Why They Matter," *The Journal of Investment Consulting*, vol. 7, no. 1, Summer 2004, pp. 21–36. Earlier version of this paper can be found in the chapter "Equity Style: What It Is and Why It Matters." With C. Nola Williams in Frank J. Fabozzi, ed., *Selected Topics in Equity Portfolio Management* (New Hope, PA: FJF Publishing, 1998), pp. 143–162. An earlier version was the opening chapter in T. Daniel Coggin and Frank J. Fabozzi, eds., *The Handbook of Equity Style Management* (Philadelphia, PA: Fabozzi and Associates Publishing, 1995).

To see this point, consider Figure 24.1 in which two investors are evaluating the same statistic from two opposing investment perspectives. They are assessing a stock's prospects using the price/earnings ratio, a ratio commonly applied in the industry. The "growth" investor is concerned primarily with the earnings component of the ratio. If the investor believes the company will deliver a future earnings growth rate and if the price/earnings ratio remains constant, then the stock price is likely to increase as earnings materialize.

The key risk for a growth investor, the "growth trap," occurs when the investor believes the recent growth in earnings will continue indefinitely and then holds onto the stock as growth falls short of expectations. Growth investors are also particularly vulnerable to the P/E multiple declining during market corrections when they fall for some unanticipated reason. This can occur at a market top or at the peak of an earnings cycle. It can also occur near the peak of the life cycle of a company as it reaches maturity and its growth slows. The growth investors need to thoroughly understand the sources and sustainability of the company's growth and have a sound prediction of its continued growth; otherwise they will simply pay a high price for a stock that will not appreciate.

Figure 24.1 Value and growth perspective on price/earnings ratio

The "value" investor, on the other hand, is primarily concerned with the price component of the ratio and generally cares less about the future earnings growth of the company. For this stock to be of interest, the value investor must deem the P/E ratio "cheap" by some comparison. The value investor's assumption is that the ratio is too low (perhaps due to an overly pessimistic assessment of the company's future) and that the P/E multiple will revert to normal or market levels when other investors realize the prospects are not as bad as thought. In this analysis, the investor anticipates that the P/E multiple will rise without necessarily having to rely on stellar earnings growth.

The value investor's primary risk is frequently referred to as the "value trap." It occurs when the investor has not correctly assessed the stock's cheapness and other investors' concerns about the company prove to be correct. The "trap" is holding onto a stock because it appears to be getting "cheaper" only to find that the low price of the security is well deserved, such as just before a company goes bankrupt. When the price of a security is falling, the value investor needs to thoroughly understand why it is falling and not buy the stock simply because the price is low.

Both of these types of investors view the other perspective with skepticism. The value investor questions whether the growth investors get the earnings estimates right often enough to add superior return. The growth investor questions why the value investor wastes time buying junk stocks with poor appreciation potential.

These two types of investors may assess the same stock at different points in its price and earnings pattern and from these two opposing valuation perspectives as shown in Figure 24.2. Often the value investor is the earlier buyer of a stock. If investor predictions are right, the price increases. This may be accompanied by earnings increases although that was not the primary motivation for the value investor to buy the stock. As the price increases, the value investor becomes uncomfortable with what seems to be expensive multiple levels and sells.

By now the growth investor has noticed the improving fundamentals of the company, which prompt interest in its future growth potential. The growth investor will purchase the same stock the value investor viewed as too expensive and retain it for as long as the growth pattern emerges as anticipated.

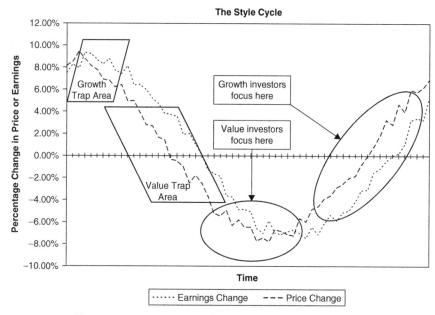

Figure 24.2 Change in price versus change in earnings

Both investors are following logical courses, and empirical evidence can be found to support the profitability of both approaches. They buy and sell the same stock at different points along the price and earnings curves, both of which offer investment potential so long as the stock follows its typical pattern.

Note that in Figure 24.2 there is a period of overlap when both the value and growth investor may hold the same stock. An analysis of industry group performance also shows that stock groups often migrate from one group of investors to others as equities experience a full business cycle.

TYPES OF EQUITY STYLES

While industry terminology for U.S. equity styles varies somewhat, style definitions have converged to the point where they typically include descriptors of both the capitalization orientation and the general location on the growth/value continuum.

<== Growth/Value ==>

Large-Cap Value	Large-Cap Market Oriented	Large-Cap Growth
Midcap Value	Mid-Cap Market Oriented	Midcap Growth
Small-Cap Value	Small-Cap Market Oriented	Small-Cap Growth

<== Company Size ==>

Figure 24.3 Overview of styles within the broad market

Figure 24.3 depicts how these styles relate to different segments of the equity market. The market is frequently broken down into a 3×3 matrix based on capitalization and investment style. For example, segments may be referred to as small-cap value, midcap market-oriented (or midcap core), or large-cap growth.[2] Manager universes are created to measure how investors following these styles perform in practice.

Value Style and Substyles

As seen in Figure 24.3, value managers (as well as growth- and market-oriented managers) may focus on different capitalization tiers of the market. While these managers differ in how they define *value*, they consider the stock's current price critical. Some organizations focus on companies with low absolute or relative P/E ratios (price is in the numerator), while others stress issues with above-market yields (price is in the denominator). Additional valuation

---

[2] Large-cap value, large-cap market-oriented, large-cap growth, midcap value, midcap market-oriented, midcap growth, small-cap value, small-cap market-oriented, and small-cap growth. Russell, S&P and other firms have indexes for all these segments.

measures these investors often consider are price/book value and price/sales ratios. Value managers' portfolios frequently have historical growth and profitability characteristics well below market averages, contrasting sharply with the characteristics of growth managers. Grinblatt, Titman, and Wermers found that value-style mutual funds are likely to have exposure to stocks with negative price momentum, and Ferson and Khang find a similar pattern for pension fund managers.[3]

There are many ways to segment value-oriented managers into substyles in order to facilitate even more robust comparisons. Analysts have identified three such distinct substyles as low P/E, contrarian, and yield.

Low-P/E managers focus on companies selling at low prices relative to current, normalized, or discounted future earnings. These companies typically fall into defensive, cyclical, or out-of-favor industries.

Contrarian managers emphasize companies selling at low valuations relative to their tangible book value and having a history of poor price performance. They often favor stocks that have fallen sharply, such as depressed cyclicals, financially distressed companies, and/or firms with virtually no current earnings or dividend yield. Contrarian investors purchase stocks in hopes that a cyclical rebound or company-specific earnings turnaround will result in a substantial price appreciation. The quality of companies owned is frequently below average, largely because corporate earnings are depressed and financial leverage is relatively high.

High-yield managers are the most conservative value managers, focusing on companies with above-average yields that are able to maintain or increase their dividend payments. They are more common among investors focusing on large-cap stocks than they are among midcap and small-cap managers.

---

[3] Mark Grinblatt, Sheridan Titman, and Russ Wermers, "Momentum Investment Strategies, Portfolio Performance, and Herding: A Study of Mutual Fund Behavior," *American Economic Review*, vol. 85, no. 5, 1995, pp. 1088–1105. Wayne Ferson and Kenneth Khang, "Conditional Performance Measurement Using Portfolio Weights: Evidence for Pension Funds," *Journal of Financial Economics*, vol. 65, August 2002, pp. 249–282.

Growth Style and Substyles

Growth managers attempt to identify companies with above-average growth prospects. Regardless of the source of expected future growth or the current valuation, growth not reflected in the current price is the key focus. They pay higher valuations for the superior growth rates and profitability they anticipate. Other typical characteristics of growth managers include the selection of higher-quality companies, with an emphasis on consumer, service, health care, and technology stocks, and lighter weightings in deep cyclicals and defensive stocks.

Like all styles, growth managers can be further segmented into different categories. The growth style tends to have two substyles of managers: consistent growth and earnings momentum.

Consistent-growth managers emphasize high-quality, consistently growing companies. Such companies are more prevalent in the large-cap arena than they are among small-cap stocks, though there are some managers who focus on consistent growth in all capitalization ranges.

Because such businesses have very predictable earnings and extensive records of superior profitability, valuation multiples are frequently well above the market averages. Consistent-growth managers typically underweight cyclicals, and they tend to purchase market leaders in consumer-oriented industries.

Earnings momentum managers, by contrast, prefer companies with more volatile, above-average growth. They attempt to purchase companies in anticipation of earnings acceleration. They are usually willing to purchase companies in any economic sector, as long as they offer the best potential earnings growth. Sometimes, but by no means always, such managers will also seek companies that are demonstrating relatively strong price momentum.

Market-Oriented Style and Substyles

Market-oriented managers, or what many people refer to as "core" managers, do not have a strong or persistent preference for the types of stocks emphasized in either value or growth portfolios; consequently, their performance and portfolio characteristics are closer to broad market averages over a business cycle than they are to particular style indexes. A wide variety of managers with different philosophies fall into this category. For example, a market-oriented manager may find a "pure" growth or value orientation overly restrictive and prefer selecting stocks wherever they might fall on the growth-to-value spectrum. Others may purchase securities embodying both growth and value characteristics. The managers in this group tend to fall into the following substyles: value bias, growth bias, market normal, and growth at a reasonable price.

Value-biased managers or *growth-biased* managers have portfolios with a tilt toward value or growth. The tilts are not sufficiently distinct to put them in either the value or growth styles.

Many *market normal* managers construct portfolios with growth and valuation characteristics that are similar to the broad market over time. Also included are those willing to make meaningful bets in growth or value stocks across time but with no continued preference toward either.

Growth at a reasonable price managers seek companies with above-average growth prospects selling at moderate valuation multiples. Unlike managers in other market-oriented substyles, growth at a price managers generally do not offer wide diversification in portfolio structure or capitalization breadth.

Large-Capitalization Styles

Managers that focus on larger capitalization issues have always represented a very large portion of the active management universe. Large-cap stocks tend to be less volatile than midcap and small-cap stocks, and their greater liquidity makes them much less expensive to trade. Because they are widely followed by institutional and individual investors, they tend to be more efficiently priced, and thus the active management opportunity is comparatively small.

In the pre-ERISA days (before 1974) most large-cap investment products fell into the market-oriented camp; however, in the investment management boom that followed ERISA, investment specialization flourished and products with pronounced growth/value orientations became commonplace, as did products focused on different capitalization sizes.

Midcapitalization Styles

In the mid-1990s, a new "style" emerged in the marketplace called "midcap" investing. Investors in this area focus on the bottom 20 to 30 percent of stocks within the large-cap universe, outside of the "mega-cap" stocks composing about 70 percent of the marketplace. Midcap stocks are considerably smaller than those held by most large-cap investment managers, and larger than those held by small-cap investment managers. Indeed most midcap managers focus on stocks that are between the 200th and 1,000th largest stock in the U.S. market, which consistently captures approximately 20 to 30 percent of the U.S. market's capitalization. The argument for this style is that midcap stocks make an attractive investment because (1) their earnings are not as volatile as small-cap stock's earnings and their balance sheets are stronger, hence they are easier to correctly evaluate, and (2) they receive far less investor scrutiny than large-cap stocks and thus offer greater opportunities for accurately finding mispricings. The U.S. midcap market has performed very well over time as illustrated by the following example: If one would have invested $1 in each of the Russell Midcap, Russell Top 200 (mega cap), and Russell 2000 (small cap) indexes in January 1979, the Midcap investment would be the most valuable of the three on July 31, 2008, with $51.37.

The variety of midcap managers is similar to that of large-cap or small-cap managers. While midcap investment products have yet to meet with the widespread acceptance of large-cap and small-cap products, the number of product offerings in this segment has increased dramatically.

Small-Capitalization Styles

The major distinguishing feature of small-cap managers is a focus on small companies. These investors are drawn to this market segment because they find more opportunities to add value through research since the companies are less widely followed by institutional investors. Indeed, much of the academic research on market return anomalies had demonstrated that market inefficiencies tend to be much larger among smaller-capitalization issues. As with large-cap and midcap managers, small-cap managers employ a myriad of approaches but for the most part can be readily classified as being growth-, value-, or market-oriented.

EVIDENCE OF STYLES

Portfolio Characteristics

Different management styles produce different portfolio character-istics and performance patterns. Figure 24.4 illustrates how much portfolios can vary across a few key portfolio characteristics. It com-pares average portfolio attributes for large-cap growth, large-cap value, and large-cap market-oriented managers as of March 31, 2008. The same patterns can be seen when reviewing midcap and small-cap managers.

Styles divide on valuation characteristics as expected accord-ing to our descriptions of investment philosophy. Thus, value man-agers' portfolios have lower price/book ratios and higher dividend yields. The growth managers' characteristics are the opposite of value managers, while market-oriented managers are firmly in the middle. When it comes to a "growth" characteristic like forecasted earnings growth, the statistics conform to expectations with growth

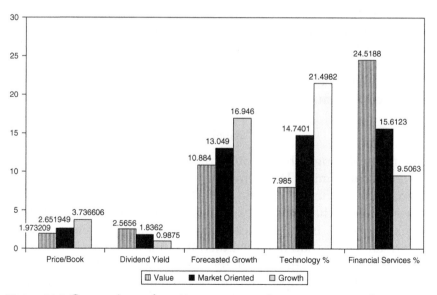

Figure 24.4 Comparison of equity manager universe average style characteristics as of March 31, 2008. *Source:* Russell Investments.

managers owning companies with relatively high expectations for future earnings growth.

Figure 24.4 also provides an example of how economic sector exposures vary across equity styles with growth managers demonstrating a preference for technology examples and value managers a bias toward financial services issues.

Performance Patterns

As we have said, a style should have differing portfolio characteristics and these characteristics should (to the extent different equity characteristics are rewarded in the market) result in different performance patterns, particularly over short time horizons. Figure 24.5 shows performance for the average manager in six different styles. For ease of viewing reasons we have omitted midcap on this graph. In this example, the focus is on style variation around the whole market.

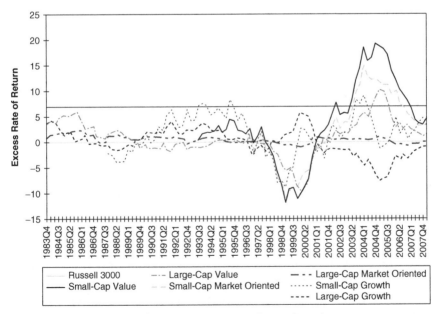

Figure 24.5 Five-year rolling excess returns for style universe means versus Russell 3000 Index period ending March 31, 2008. *Source:* Russell Investments.

We have plotted excess returns net of the Russell 3000 Index for rolling five-year periods that shift quarterly; the Russell 3000 Index is represented by the horizontal line.

Note the style rotation of performance over time and the difference style can make in shorter-term results. Growth was the lagging large-cap style throughout the early 1980s but rebounded to become the most dominant style in the early 1990s, ebbing somewhat in the mid-1990s and crashing with the dot-com bubble. Value managers behaved inversely to growth managers.

Throughout all periods, the market-oriented group tracked market returns most closely, which would be expected given their tighter factor bets relative to the market. The most prominent cycle is that of the small-cap value style, which lagged significantly relative to large-cap styles in the 1980s, outperformed during the early 1990s, fared poorly from 1995 to 1998, and then relatively strongly through the end of 2003.

HISTORICAL PERSPECTIVE ON STYLES

Interestingly, while the preceding style definitions are commonly used today, the relative popularity of any style varies across time largely as a function of how successful managers of any given style have been at surpassing index returns. Since 1990, small-cap managers have had a great deal of success outperforming their benchmarks, and it is also the area that has witnessed the greatest growth in number of product offerings. In fact, the Russell Small Cap Universe grew substantially from 1990 to 2003.

The reasons for the significant growth in investment products have a lot to do with the business of money management. When a style is hot, doing well, the demand for new firms and new products grows. Money managers are business people who have an interest in making a profit. They will frequently adapt their business strategy to meet the demands of the marketplace. Large organizations can open and shut down funds, hire and fire portfolio managers, and adapt quickly to these business opportunities. As a consequence, the number of managers in each style is likely to continue to move in a lagged fashion with the market excess returns of any given style.

CAPM, FACTOR MODELS, AND THE BEHAVIOR OF STYLES

One might sensibly ask how styles and style indexes behave in light of the capital asset pricing model (CAPM) theory and the assumption of efficient markets. If the equity market is efficient, then all stocks are correctly priced given all information. By extension, any choice of a market subset will yield a market return subject to variation due to sample size and the random character of specific risk. If all stocks are driven by the same single factor, the market, all stocks will move up or down depending on their beta and all other return will be specific return. In such a world, no stock characteristic would lead to differential expected return. Multiple priced factors arise in the world of Merton's (1973) asset pricing model and Ross' (1976) APT model.[4] Subsets of stocks with focused exposure to different risks could have different expected returns. Empirical work by Chen, Roll, and Ross (1986) and others support this view.[5] The work of Fama-French gave academic credence to the style anomalies.[6] Multifactor models of Barra and others have also shown stock sensitivity to forces that can change stock prices above and beyond the effect of the market.

A few points emerge from this discussion. If styles exist, then certain other things must also exist. First, the returns to style portfolios/indexes must be significantly different than the return for the broad market.[7] Second, the style portfolios/indexes returns must be

---

[4] Robert C. Merton, "An Intertemporal Capital Asset Pricing Model," *Econometrica*, vol. 41, 1973, pp. 867–887, and Stephen A. Ross, "The Arbitrage Theory of Capital Asset Pricing," *Journal of Economic Theory*, vol. 13, 1976, pp. 341–360.

[5] Nai-Fu Chen, Richard Roll, and Stephen A. Ross, "Economic Forces and the Stock Market," *Journal of Business*, vol. 56, 1986, pp. 383–403.

[6] Eugene F. Fama and Kenneth R. French, "The Cross-Section of Expected Stock Returns," *Journal of Finance*, vol. 47, 1992, pp. 427–465.

[7] Using the "law of large numbers," we know that the mean to samples of stocks drawn from the market randomly will have means that differ in relation to the square root of the sample size. The larger the portfolio size, the smaller the differences. The style indexes have well over 200 stocks in them each, so the differences in returns are not likely to be due to specific risk but rather to differences in priced factor exposures.

significantly different from each other. Third, style portfolios/ indexes should have on average different factor exposure patterns from the market as a whole and from each other.

A large number of indexes have been created over the years since Russell first introduced its style indexes in 1988–1989. The variety and diversity of style index definitions are beyond the scope of this chapter.[8] We do use the Russell 1000 Growth and Value Indexes to demonstrate the presence of style cycles that are somewhat independent from manager portfolios.

Briefly, the Russell Growth and Value indexes are created by rank ordering all stocks in the Russell 1000 by price/book and their long-term earnings per share growth forecasts. The capitalization-weighted median is computed. All stocks above the median breakpoint have greater weights in the Russell 1000 Growth Index, and all stocks below the median have greater weights in the Russell 1000 Value Index. The choice of price/book was the result of extensive research.[9] While it is a simple rule, it is not simplistic and has been supported by subsequent academic research.[10]

WHICH EQUITY STYLE IS BEST?

The returns of the Russell style indexes begin in 1979. As shown in Figure 24.6, the spread in quarterly returns between the Russell 1000 Growth and Value indexes and the spread between the Russell 1000 and 2000 is almost always substantially different from zero. Over the period, large-cap stocks outperformed small-cap stocks

---

[8] For a review of the differences among style indexes see Melissa R. Brown and Claudia E. Mott "Understanding the Differences and Similarities of Equity Style Indexes," in T. Daniel Coggin and Frank J. Fabozzi, eds., *The Handbook of Equity Style Management*, 2d ed. (New Hope, PA: Frank J. Fabozzi Associates, 1997), Chapter 2, pp. 23–50.

[9] For a discussion of the research paths explored see Kelly Haughton and Jon A. Christopherson, "Equity Style Indexes: Tools for Better Performance Evaluation and Plan Management," *Russell Research Commentary* (Tacoma, WA: Russell Investments, September 1989), reprinted in Chapter 25 of this book. See Chapter 26 for the current nonlinear weighting scheme.

[10] Eugene F. Fama and Kenneth R. French, "Common Risk Factors in Returns of Stocks and Bonds," *Journal of Financial Economics*, February 1993, pp. 3–56.

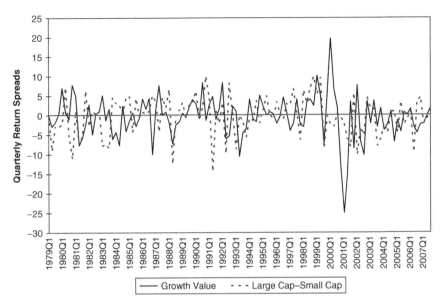

Figure 24.6 Growth-value and large cap–small cap return spreads

much of the time. The same can be said for value stocks, which out-performed growth stocks about twice as often.

Figure 24.7 shows the cumulative return differences from 1979 through the first quarter of 2008. Returns will look different depending on the beginning date, but over this period the advantage of value over growth has been about 40 percent and small over large has been over 25 percent. However, at the end of the fourth quarter of 1991, the cumulative return differential since first quarter 1979 was essentially zero. From second quarter 1989 through fourth quarter 1991, growth recovered all the return differential it had lost from 1983 through 1989. If analysts had stopped watching the returns in early 2000, they would have concluded growth investing and large-cap investing were the superior market segments.

This raises the issue of whether we can expect any one style to underperform consistently for a long period of time. While there is evidence small-cap stocks and value stocks perform better over time than larger capitalization issues and growth stocks, there have been very long periods where this return advantage has not been evi-dent. Moreover, when one examines the returns of active managers,

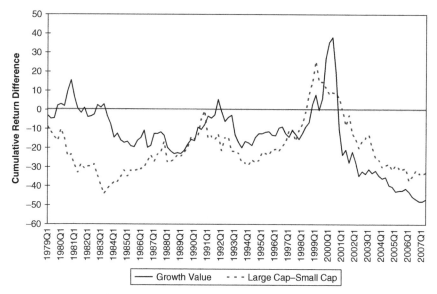

Figure 24.7 Cumulative growth-value and large cap–small cap returns

the story is somewhat different. Growth managers across the capitalization spectrum have generally met with more benchmark relative success than their value counterparts. Thus, investors inclined to bet on a particular style need to have a very long time horizon and a solid understanding as to how the use of active management will impact the likelihood of benefiting from a strategic style tilt. In any case, the index returns demonstrate that the style segments of the market behave differently from the market as a whole and do so for long periods of time.

Finally, from a purely theoretical point of view, we would not expect any one style to outperform any other over the long term on a risk-adjusted basis (although it could *before* risk adjustments). The reasons for this lie in the valuations of the securities. For example, after a period of above-market performance of value stocks, the valuation measures such as P/E begin to approach the P/E of growth stocks. At this point investors begin to ask themselves why they are paying such a high price for mediocre growth prospects when for just a little more money they can buy stocks with much better growth prospects. So, they tend to sell the value stocks and buy the growth stocks. At a cyclical top or a period of above-market performance for growth stocks, investors begin to ask themselves if these earnings growth rates are sustainable and whether or not they are paying too much for this uncertain continued growth. So, they tend to sell growth stocks and buy value stocks. Analogous logic can be found in the comparative valuations of large- and small-cap stocks.[11]

---

[11] For a discussion of these style valuations patterns, see Jon A. Christopherson, Dennis J. Trittin, and Natalie LaBerge, "Has Growth Become Value?" *Russell Research Commentary* (Tacoma, WA: Russell Investments, November 1989), and Dennis J. Trittin, "Has Growth Become Value? (Reprise)," *Russell Research Commentary* (Tacoma, WA: Russell Investments, May 2007).

CHAPTER 25

Equity Style Indexes: Tools for Better Performance Evaluation and Plan Management

By Kelly Haughton and Jon Christopherson

Soon after the launch of the Russell style indexes in 1987, Kelly Haughton and Jon Christopherson wrote the following paper to explain the ideas and research underlying the indexes and their intended uses. The paper was distributed to Russell clients in September 1989 but was never published externally. Although certain details of index construction have evolved since this paper was written—the current Russell style methodology is described in Chapter 26—the essential ideas are as applicable today as they were then. The paper is reproduced here, excluding historical data tables and appendixes.

Note: The Russell Earnings Growth Index was renamed as the Russell 1000 Growth Index and the Russell Price-Driven Index was renamed as the Russell 1000 Value Index in 1991.

INTRODUCTION

Money managers who invest exclusively in the U.S. equity market often specialize in subsets of the market. For years we have observed differences among managers' portfolio characteristics and described them in terms of investment styles. These styles most commonly reflect differences in the universes of securities from which the managers select. This paper focuses on the development of a set of equity indexes to assist the plan sponsor with performance attribution and aggregate equity portfolio management.

We will discuss two style indexes: the Russell Earnings Growth Index and Russell Price-Driven Index. These benchmarks complement the Russell 1000 Index and Russell 2000 Small Stock Index to yield four common equity style benchmarks: Earnings Growth, Price-Driven, Market-Oriented, and Small Capitalization. Until development of these indexes, a plan sponsor had only other active managers of a similar style against which to compare a specialized manager. The new style indexes provide a passive comparison tool for evaluating sets of managers in the same style as well. The availability of the Russell indexes also allows plan sponsors to make the active/passive decision by style in a systematic way.

STYLE DEFINITIONS

The Russell 1000 is the benchmark we recommend for most Market-Oriented style managers, and the Russell 2000 is the benchmark for the Small Capitalization style. The Price-Driven and Earnings Growth styles are new specialized indexes and require some definition.

Price-Driven

Price-Driven managers focus on the price and value characteristics of a security in the selection process. These managers buy stocks from the low price portion of the market, and are sometimes called *value* or *defensive/yield* managers.

While differences exist in how Price-Driven managers define *value*, a stock's current market price is generally the critical variable. For example, some organizations focus on companies having low absolute or relative P/E ratios (price is in the numerator), while others stress issues with above-market yields (price is in the denominator). Additional measures that are often used include price/book ratios and price/sales ratios (price is in the numerator). A stock whose price has declined because of adverse investor sentiment may also attract some of these managers. Historical growth and profitability characteristics of value stocks are frequently well below market averages, and overall characteristics are in sharp contrast to the stocks of Earnings Growth managers.

The typical manager in the Price-Driven style has portfolio characteristics similar to those in Table 25.1. In general, these managers focus on securities with low valuations relative to the broad market.

T A B L E 25.1

Representative Portfolio Characteristics Versus Russell 1000 Index

Portfolio Characteristics	Price-Driven Universe	Earnings Growth Universe
P/E ratio	Less	Greater
Dividend yield	Greater	Less
Price/book ratio	Less	Greater
Beta	Less	Greater
ROE	Less	Greater
Dividend growth	Less	Greater
Forecasted growth	Less	Greater

Earnings Growth

Earnings Growth managers focus predominantly on earnings and revenue growth and attempt to identify companies with above-average growth prospects. In general, two basic categories of securities are owned by Earnings Growth managers:

- Companies with consistent above-average (historical and prospective) profitability and growth
- Companies expected to generate above-average near-term earnings momentum based upon company, industry, or economic factors

In the latter case, desirable securities may not have exhibited above-average historical growth but are expected to have above-average growth over the near future. Growth managers are willing to pay above-market multiples for the superior growth rate/profitability they anticipate. Typical characteristics of growth portfolios include the following:

- Selection of higher-quality companies
- Emphasis on consumer, service, health care, and technology stocks
- Light weightings in deep cyclicals and defensive stocks

As shown in Table 25.1, Earnings Growth managers focus their investments in securities with above-market growth history and prospects. We will return to the actual portfolio characteristics of the style indexes later.

PERFORMANCE EVALUATION AND STYLES

In the past, most plan sponsors compared *all* their U.S. equity manager returns against the S&P 500 regardless of the manager's investment style. This method of analysis leads to entire styles of management rising and falling in favor based on differences between the performance of their universes and the broad market. Unfortunately, a broad market index is of minimal use when the plan sponsor needs to know how much a specialized manager's performance is due to general style considerations and how much is due to factors such as stock selection or sector allocation.

A finer set of performance measurement tools that more closely matches the investment styles of individual managers is needed to ensure identification of elements attributable to investment style. There are three alternative performance attribution solutions to the problem of management style: universe medians, normal portfolios, and style indexes.

Universe Medians

To evaluate managers in specialized equity styles, Russell maintains universes classified by basic investment style. The performance of managers in these universes is used to compare and contrast managers of a given style.

The medians of these universes are reported as part of quartile charts and show how managers of various styles have fared during a given period. These medians provide an active comparison for manager returns, but they do not reveal whether the aggregate group of managers is doing well relative to their normal universe of equities. Using style indexes augments the evaluation of active manager returns by providing a passive comparison free of manager group trends.

Normal Portfolios

Another tool for manager performance evaluation and plan management is the portfolio-specific or manager-specific normal portfolio. This concept is widely discussed and increasingly being used. In an article by Christopherson[1] the following definition of normal portfolios is made:

> A normal portfolio is a set of securities that contains all the securities from which a manager normally chooses, weighted as the manager would weight them in a portfolio. As such, a normal portfolio is a specialized index.

Normal portfolios give the manager evaluator a customized benchmark that is ideally suited for a particular manager. It can be constructed to take advantage of all the nuances of a specific manager's process. For example, in creating a normal for a manager who utilizes only original security research in portfolio construction and who does not have a utility analyst, utilities can be eliminated from the normal portfolio because such stocks would not be in the universe from which the manager normally chooses.

Note that normal portfolios are inconsistent with the use of style universes as active comparisons. Style universes assume there is a collection of managers sufficiently similar that a comparison of their performance is meaningful. Customized normal portfolios assert that the differences between manager universes are sufficiently larger to make comparisons inappropriate. We believe it is useful to be able to compare an active manager's performance against *both* a passive benchmark and other active managers.

Christopherson also points out that normal portfolios can be difficult to create and maintain. They require databases and computer expertise to create. In addition, the databases and normal portfolio criteria must be kept current; otherwise, the normal loses its applicability as a benchmark. A limited number of normal portfolios are available from consulting services, but these are not cheap

---

[1] Jon A. Christopherson, "Normal Portfolios and Their Construction," Russell White Paper (Tacoma, WA, 1988), also included in Frank J. Fabozzi, ed., *Portfolio and Investment Management* (Chicago, IL: Probus, 1989), pp. 381–397.

and plan sponsors must ensure that the supplied normal portfolio represents the same product they receive from the manager.

Another difficulty with using normal portfolios is that plan management using normal portfolios can be complex and cumbersome. For example, how should managers be mixed in order to achieve a composite equal to the policy portfolio?

This process is so complex that, despite its theoretical attractiveness, there are few plans using normals and a completeness fund.[2]

Style Indexes

Given the grossness of broad market indexes, the cost (in terms of time, complexity, and expense) of managing normal portfolios, and the insufficiency of information provided by universe medians, a better tool is needed for evaluating manager skill.

Style indexes meet the need in several ways. Style indexes are more precise than broad market indexes; the performance evaluation they provide is based on subdividing the market into the sets of stocks from which managers of each style usually select. This allows plan sponsors to better control and understand managers' short- and long-term bets.

Style indexes are less costly to a plan sponsor than normal portfolios because Russell maintains the indexes for the user. They are also simpler to manage than a collection of normals, and they can be easily combined to achieve a target equity exposure—no completeness fund required. Furthermore, as discussed below, style indexes usually account for most of the behavior captured in a normal portfolio, with much less cost and effort.

Since style indexes can be used as the normal for a broader group of managers, they can also be used in combination with the style universes to show the opportunity cost of not choosing other managers in a particular style.

---

[2] A completeness fund is a portfolio created to ensure exposure to segments and/or factors in the market that the aggregate of normal portfolios systematically ignores. It is different from a compensating core in that it focuses on consistent, long-term bets taken by the aggregate of managers rather than on offsetting shorter-term bets managers might take for tactical reasons.

STYLE INDEX CONSTRUCTION

The primary purpose of style indexes is to provide a broad picture of the differences in performance and fundamental characteristics between the broad market and the Earnings Growth and Price-Driven segments. Thus, when the Earnings Growth Index outperforms the Price-Driven Index, we would expect that most Earnings Growth managers will outperform most Price-Driven managers. Our task is to create a portfolio of stocks that will yield desirable fundamental characteristics (such as those outlined in Table 25.1) and produce performance patterns that track the Earnings Growth and Price-Driven universes. To accomplish this, we need decision rules to decide which stocks belong in the universes and stock position rules to determine the weights of the stocks in the indexes.

Decision Rule

The decision rule on how to divide the Market-Oriented universe (Russell 1000 Index) is largely empirical. We currently divide the universe based on a capitalization-weighted median book-to-price ratio. From our observations of multiple trial portfolio sets, this decision rule results in indexes that are more representative of the Earnings Growth and Price-Driven styles than other, more complex decision criteria.

Such a decision rule has the strength of being quite simple, and a simple decision is easy to explain. Nevertheless, our primary basis for evaluating the rule is its effectiveness in creating appropriate indexes. Table 25.2 lists some of the factors we explored in

T A B L E 25.2

Factors Considered for Style Indexes

Valuation Factors	Fundamental Factors
Dividend yield	Dividend growth (five-year average)
Price/earnings ratio	Return on equity (five-year average)
Price/book ratio	EPS growth (five-year average)
Dividend payout ratio	

constructing various test indexes. We will not review those test results but will mention that a variety of valuation factors and fundamental factors were considered. These factors failed to provide satisfactory portfolios essentially because of two problems—the timeliness and the reliability of data. In terms of timeliness, substantial problems would be encountered if one tried to use a factor that required a five-year history, such as dividend growth or ROE. What would be done with new companies, companies that merge, or companies that are acquired? Valuation factors cause problems as well; fluctuating earnings and soon-to-be-omitted dividends can cause difficulties in using several of the ratios listed in Table 25.2. Price to book proved to be a solid, effective, and reliable discriminatory variable.

Capitalization Weighting of the Indexes

Capitalization weighting (or market weighting) means the securities in the style indexes are weighted according to their availability for investment or their availability in the market. Without any information about a manager's decision-making process, we would normally choose to capitalization weight the benchmark. Capitalization weighting a benchmark index means that, in effect, managers are being held responsible for their weighting decisions. Further, to make use of an index in a passive fund it is desirable, if not necessary, for the index to be capitalization weighted.

While there are drawbacks to capitalization weighting the style indexes, we believe a compelling case for this scheme is the ability to passively replicate the indexes and the desirability of holding managers responsible for their security weightings.

The primary criticism of capitalization weighting is that managers generally do not capitalization weight their portfolios; therefore, a capitalization-weighting scheme will cause securities in the indexes to have, on average, a larger capitalization size than will the managers' portfolios. Since utility and energy stocks are of larger capitalization than the average stock, capitalization weighting will result in the indexes having higher weights in these sectors than money managers normally will have. However, when managers equal weight their portfolios, they are making an inherent bet against large stocks. Style indexes hold managers accountable for these inherent bets.

On the other hand, our equity style indexes have been constructed such that most portfolio characteristics other than capitalization are representative of the typical portfolios of managers within each style. Capitalization weighting may result in significant performance differences, but in the past these differences have been insufficient to change the sign of the Earnings Growth Index or Price-Driven Index return versus the Russell 1000. Hence, capitalization weighting the style indexes may not create as much distortion as some might believe.

Membership

Choosing a capitalization-weighting scheme requires putting stocks into an index at market weight. If the stock is questionable as to its membership, we do not include it in both style indexes at reduced weights.[3] We developed a decision rule for inclusion that strictly results in a yes or no decision. The decision rule is based on prices and fundamental characteristics and ultimately establishes an arbitrary dividing line between membership and nonmembership. No matter what rule is chosen, there will be stocks near the borderline. Movement of these stocks into or out of an index by crossing the deciding line could cause significant changes in an index, but this has not occurred.

Russell has already divided the broad market into large capitalization (Russell 1000) and small capitalization (Russell 2000) stocks via an arbitrary numeric count dividing line. Having the broad universe (Russell 3000 Index) divided into two segments has proven a useful investment strategy tool for designing aggregate equity portfolios for plan sponsors. Hence, we decided to maintain the additivity of the two style indexes to equal the Russell 1000. This decision makes style diversification and investment strategy easy to implement and simple to discuss. Figure 25.1 shows how the Russell indexes can be combined to achieve a broad market portfolio such as the Russell 3000. This will make passive management relative to

---

[3] Although this option was seriously considered, it was decided that maintaining the capitalization additivity of the two style indexes to the Russell 1000 was more desirable than scaling into a stock based on its purity as a member of each style.

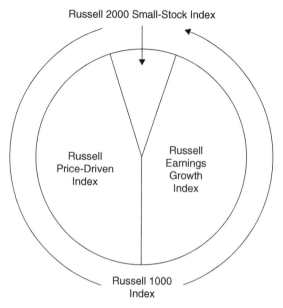

Figure 25.1 Composition of the Russell 3000 Index

these benchmarks easy and provide a large degree of flexibility in designing aggregate equity portfolios.

Since we have chosen to capitalization weight and to use the Market-Oriented Russell 1000 stock list as our universe, stocks in the Russell 1000 must be in one of the two segments (Earnings Growth Index or Price-Driven Index). Just as with the Russell 1000 and Russell 2000, there should be no orphans and no overlap.

VALIDATION OF STYLE INDEXES

The index portfolios produced by our methodology should look like the portfolios of managers we classify as Earnings Growth or Price-Driven. In this section we present several sets of data that demonstrate the index portfolios are consistent with the manager universes; they look like the average portfolio or the average normal portfolios of managers most analysts would classify as Price-Driven or Earnings Growth. These benchmarks are much more representative of these specialized managers' selection universes than the broad market and hence are better performance evaluation tools.

Fundamental Characteristics of Style Indexes

Table 25.3 displays some of the portfolio characteristics of the style indexes as of December 1988. The table shows that the Price-Driven Index has below-market valuation statistics (e.g., price/earnings ratio, price/book ratio) and high dividend yield, whereas the Earnings Growth Index is on the opposite side of the market. Also, the Earnings Growth Index has above-market growth statistics (e.g., historical EPS growth, I/B/E/S forecasted growth, and historical dividend growth), while the Price-Driven Index has below-market growth statistics.

Figures 25.2 and 25.3 show line charts of selected portfolio characteristics from December 1987 to December 1988. Again, characteristics such as beta, dividend yield, price to book, ROE, and earnings-per-share growth all bracket the Russell 1000 as style portfolios would be expected to do. Historical charts reveal the same patterns.

In terms of economic sectors, Price-Driven manager portfolios typically have large holdings in defensive stocks such as utilities and financial services and small holdings in sectors such as technology, health care, and consumer discretionary—important growth sectors of the 1980s. Furthermore, since the collapse of OPEC's power and falling energy prices, oil stocks (until recently) would be expected to be at a low price relative to their assets; hence, we would expect larger holdings in this sector than the market average.

T A B L E 25.3

Equity Profile Characteristics of Indexes (December 1988)

Portfolio Characteristics	Russell Price-Driven Index	Russell Earnings Growth Index	Russell 1000 Index
Price/earnings ratio	10.6	14.8	12.4
Dividend yield	4.7	2.5	3.6
Price/book ratio	1.2	3.0	1.8
Beta (relative Russell 3000)	0.9	1.0	0.9
ROE	12.6	19.9	16.4
Dividend/share growth	5.0	11.1	8.2
Forecasted growth	15.3	22.1	18.8

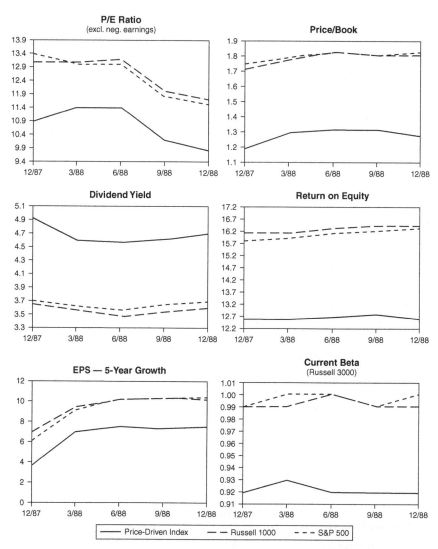

Figure 25.2 Quarterly fundamental statistics of the Russell Price-Driven Index

On the other hand, Earnings Growth managers have comparatively large holdings in growth sectors such as technology and health care and small holdings in sectors such as utilities, oil, and autos and transportation. Profiles of the style indexes show that the indexes have all the economic sector characteristics of the managers.

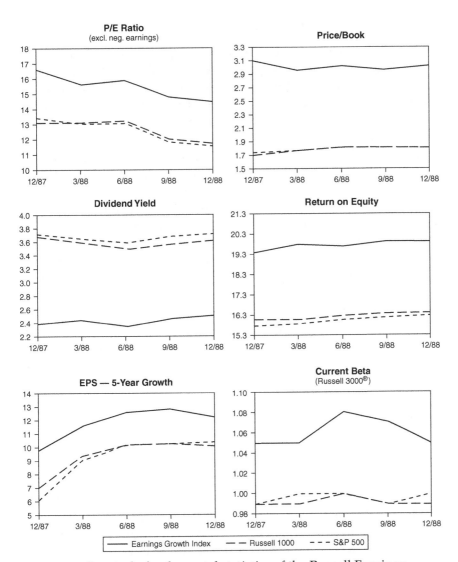

Figure 25.3 Quarterly fundamental statistics of the Russell Earnings Growth Index

Thus, we can conclude that key fundamental characteristics of each style index are similar to the equity profile of a typical manager of that style. This indicates that the subuniverses of stocks that comprise our style indexes contain the type of stocks from which each style of manager would normally choose, that is, they constitute rough normal portfolios.

Performance of Style Indexes

The performance of the style indexes compared to the Russell market indexes is the most appropriate test. Table 25.4 displays the yearly returns for all the Russell indexes. As clearly shown, the Price-Driven Index and Earnings Growth Index bracket the Russell 1000 for every time period, but neither always outperforms or underperforms the Russell 1000. Over the 10 years covered here, the Price-Driven Index has outperformed all other indexes, as we would expect, given the history of value and large capitalization stocks in the 1980s.

An important question is how well the style indexes account for the manager's returns. Figure 25.4 illustrates the problem. We know that the broad market will explain over 90 percent of the performance of most managers, and we would expect a normal portfolio to explain nearly 100 percent of a manager's return. Consequently, we would expect the style indexes to explain more variance than broad market indexes but probably less than a good normal portfolio. One way to attack this problem is to regress the quarterly return series of the average return of the managers in each of our style universes against the style indexes and the broad market.

T A B L E 25.4

Annual Rate of Return in Percent, Calendar Years

Period	Russell 3000 Index	Russell Price-Driven Index	Russell 1000 Index	Russell Earnings Growth Index	Russell 2000 Index
1988	17.82	23.16	17.23	11.27	24.89
1987	1.94	0.50	2.94	5.31	(8.77)
1986	16.71	19.98	17.87	15.36	5.68
1985	32.16	31.51	32.27	32.85	31.05
1984	3.39	10.10	4.75	(0.95)	(7.30)
1983	22.74	28.29	22.13	15.98	29.13
1982	20.74	20.04	20.30	20.46	24.95
1981	(4.43)	1.26	(5.10)	(11.31)	2.03
1980	32.51	24.41	31.88	39.57	38.58
1979	24.11	20.55	22.31	23.91	43.09

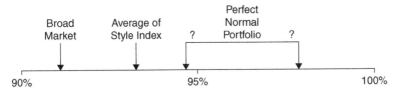

Note: Market-oriented manager R^2 of 0.95 is not unusual.

Figure 25.4 Percentage of specialized style manager performance explained by index

If the style indexes are better proxies than the broad market for the style universes, then we would expect the beta of the average manager characteristic line regression relative to the style index to be closer to 1.0, the standard error closer to zero, and the R-squared closer to 1.00.

Table 25.5 shows the characteristic line regression statistics of the style universe average portfolios for the Price-Driven and the Earnings Growth universes compared to the Price-Driven, the Earnings Growth, and the Russell 1000 indexes. Our performance expectations are confirmed.

The beta for the Price-Driven universe average versus the Price-Driven Index approaches 1.0; it climbs from 0.860 versus the Russell 1000 to 0.974 when compared to the Price-Driven Index.

T A B L E 25.5

Quarterly Manager Average Returns Regressed on Benchmark (December 31, 1988)

Average Price-Driven	Russell 1000 Index	Russell Price-Driven Index
Beta	0.860	0.974
Standard error	2.011	1.567
R-squared	0.933	0.961
% residual variance explained by style index = 41.8%		

Average Earnings Growth	Russell 1000 Index	Russell Earnings Growth Index
Beta	1.074	0.951
Standard error	2.007	1.340
R-squared	0.955	0.980
% residual variance explained by style index = 55.6%		

This means the universe average varies more like the Price-Driven Index than like the Russell 1000—its risk characteristics more closely resemble the Price-Driven Index.

The correlation for each universe average should be higher with the style index than with the broad market indicators because, if the style index is a better normal, we would expect (over time) Price-Driven managers to correlate more highly with the Price-Driven Index than with the Russell 1000. This expectation is confirmed. This event must also be judged in terms of what a better benchmark is able to accomplish. Since there is so little of the unexplained variance to explain, the slight improvement from 93 to 96 percent (i.e., 3 percent) accounts for 42 percent of the variance unaccounted for by the market as a whole.

The same analysis and results should be expected for Earnings Growth managers. Here the results are not as clear. As expected, the beta of the managers is closer to 1.0 by about 2 percent when compared to the Earnings Growth Index than when compared to the Russell 1000. Also, the R-squared is higher when compared with the Earnings Growth Index than when compared to the Russell 1000. The Earnings Growth Index accounts for 55 percent of the variance unexplained by the market. All these results are as expected and further support the argument that style indexes are good proxies for management styles.

USES OF THE STYLE INDEXES

An additional test of the appropriateness of a benchmark for a group of managers is whether the benchmark is (on average, over time) closer to the median manager than a broad market index. If an index consistently appears in either the first or fourth quartile, it is likely to indicate a problem with the benchmark, not with the managers.

The following quartile charts (Figures 25.5 to 25.8) show the Russell style universe quartile distributions from 1979 through 1988 marked with the style indexes. We can clearly see why the style indexes are superior to broad market indexes (the Russell 1000 and the S&P 500). For example, in 1987 most Price-Driven managers looked like losers compared to the broad benchmark (the Russell 1000) and even worse when compared to the S&P 500. However, when evaluated against their style index, the median

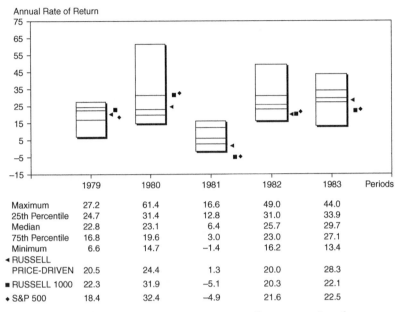

	1979	1980	1981	1982	1983
Maximum	27.2	61.4	16.6	49.0	44.0
25th Percentile	24.7	31.4	12.8	31.0	33.9
Median	22.8	23.1	6.4	25.7	29.7
75th Percentile	16.8	19.6	3.0	23.0	27.1
Minimum	6.6	14.7	−1.4	16.2	13.4
◄ RUSSELL PRICE-DRIVEN	20.5	24.4	1.3	20.0	28.3
■ RUSSELL 1000	22.3	31.9	−5.1	20.3	22.1
♦ S&P 500	18.4	32.4	−4.9	21.6	22.5

Figure 25.5 Price-driven accounts, return quartiles as previously published, calendar years: 1979–1983

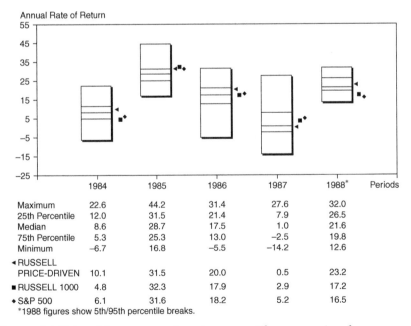

	1984	1985	1986	1987	1988*
Maximum	22.6	44.2	31.4	27.6	32.0
25th Percentile	12.0	31.5	21.4	7.9	26.5
Median	8.6	28.7	17.5	1.0	21.6
75th Percentile	5.3	25.3	13.0	−2.5	19.8
Minimum	−6.7	16.8	−5.5	−14.2	12.6
◄ RUSSELL PRICE-DRIVEN	10.1	31.5	20.0	0.5	23.2
■ RUSSELL 1000	4.8	32.3	17.9	2.9	17.2
♦ S&P 500	6.1	31.6	18.2	5.2	16.5

*1988 figures show 5th/95th percentile breaks.

Figure 25.6 Price-driven accounts, return quartiles as previously published, calendar years: 1984–1988

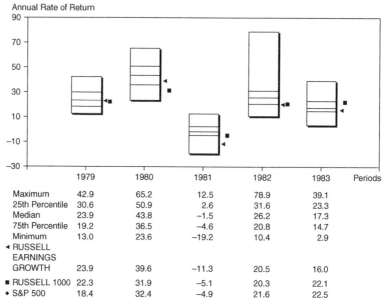

	1979	1980	1981	1982	1983
Maximum	42.9	65.2	12.5	78.9	39.1
25th Percentile	30.6	50.9	2.6	31.6	23.3
Median	23.9	43.8	-1.5	26.2	17.3
75th Percentile	19.2	36.5	-4.6	20.8	14.7
Minimum	13.0	23.6	-19.2	10.4	2.9
◄ RUSSELL EARNINGS GROWTH	23.9	39.6	-11.3	20.5	16.0
■ RUSSELL 1000	22.3	31.9	-5.1	20.3	22.1
♦ S&P 500	18.4	32.4	-4.9	21.6	22.5

Figure 25.7 Earnings growth accounts, return quartiles as previously published, calendar years: 1979–1983

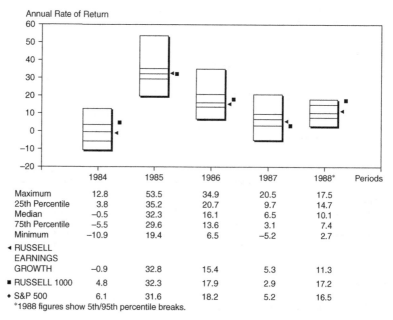

	1984	1985	1986	1987	1988*
Maximum	12.8	53.5	34.9	20.5	17.5
25th Percentile	3.8	35.2	20.7	9.7	14.7
Median	-0.5	32.3	16.1	6.5	10.1
75th Percentile	-5.5	29.6	13.6	3.1	7.4
Minimum	-10.9	19.4	6.5	-5.2	2.7
◄ RUSSELL EARNINGS GROWTH	-0.9	32.8	15.4	5.3	11.3
■ RUSSELL 1000	4.8	32.3	17.9	2.9	17.2
♦ S&P 500	6.1	31.6	18.2	5.2	16.5

*1988 figures show 5th/95th percentile breaks.

Figure 25.8 Earnings growth accounts, return quartiles as previously published, calendar years: 1984–1988

manager outperformed the benchmark. Conversely, most Earnings Growth managers in 1987 looked like outstanding winners when compared to the Russell 1000, and yet they barely exceeded the more appropriate Earnings Growth Index. This example reinforces the point made earlier that broad market benchmarks are inappropriate for judging managers in a given style because styles move in and out of favor.

The one historical oddity is 1981. Oil stocks performed dramatically different from the rest of the market. Price-Driven managers avoided oil stocks as they entered the managers' index and, thus, collectively outperformed both the broad market and their style index. Earnings Growth managers collectively underweighted oil stocks relative to the broad market in this period as well. At the beginning of 1981, the Earnings Growth index contained most of the oil stocks. In making this collective bet, they outperformed both their style index and the broad market.

Since many plan sponsors tend to receive such quartile charts with the position only of their managers superimposed, the use of style indexes can provide a better insight into the manager's performance. Noting the positions of the style indexes helps determine how much of relative performance is due to the manager's style being in or out of favor and how much is due to skill. The same comparison logic is true of performance attribution analytics, such as Russell's Analysis of Management Effect.

CONCLUSION

The style indexes presented in this paper fill a gap in the types of benchmark tools needed to more accurately evaluate the performance and behavior of money managers. They represent a generic normal portfolio for managers who focus on value—the Price-Driven Index—and for managers who focus on the growth potential of companies—the Earnings Growth Index.

The resulting style index portfolios represent the kind of aggregate portfolio we would expect typical Price-Driven and Earnings Growth managers to own. They also have all the portfolio characteristics we would expect of the average manager's portfolio within each style. The performance data shows that style groups of managers (universes) have a higher correlation with their respective style indexes than with the broad market.

These indexes can be used to achieve a better understanding of the kind of bets managers take and the risks with which they feel comfortable. Moreover, the indexes provide an idea of how much of a manager's results are attributable to his general style of investing and how much represents his value added (or opportunity cost) versus his universe. These style benchmarks are an improvement over broad market indexes and should provide better tools for performance evaluation and aggregate equity portfolio management.

At the same time, the Price-Driven Index and Earnings Growth Index fit well into a passive management strategy. Their capitalization weighting allows for easy passive management, and their complementary nature allows plan sponsors to balance active managers with passive funds within styles of investment. The style indexes offer a simple way to balance the active and passive components of the total mix to approximate the overall policy portfolio.

CHAPTER 26

Russell Style Index Methodology

The Russell style index methodology has undergone a process of evaluation and improvement since 1987, when the first U.S. style indexes were launched. As described in Chapter 25, the methodology was initially based on ordering the index constituents on book-to-price ratio, a characteristic commonly viewed as a measure of value. The original methodology divided an overall index into two equal market capitalization components, with the lower half (by book-to-price) constituting the growth index and the upper half constituting the value index.

The methodology was significantly enhanced in the 1990s by adding a second variable, a long-term growth forecast, to capture the growth expectations that exist among market analysts. Also introduced was a method for allowing a blend of value and growth, whereby certain index constituents likely to be held by both value and growth managers are given weight in both the value and the growth indexes.

In this chapter, we outline the steps of the Russell style index algorithm.[1] We then describe the rationale for certain features of the methodology.

---

[1] This description is based on the methodology as it existed in 2009.

STYLE INDEX ALGORITHM

The basic idea underlying any style index methodology is that investment styles, as expressed in the portfolios held by investment managers, can be distinguished by portfolio characteristics such as book-to-price ratio, dividend yield, and long-term growth. Consequently, of the universe of stocks in a given market, a subset generally held by managers of a given style should be identifiable by values of security characteristics. Given a characteristic believed to be relevant, sorting stocks by the value of that characteristic allows an overall index to be partitioned into subindexes representing the respective styles.

The Russell algorithm implements this basic idea by using a nonlinear function to standardize, or normalize, the values of security characteristics on a scale ranging from zero to one. The standardized scores from multiple characteristics are combined to form a composite value score. The final assignment of stocks to style indexes is also based on a nonlinear function that allows stocks near the middle of the range to be blended, or split, between both the value and the growth indexes. After sorting the constituents by their composite scores, the function assigns style probabilities resulting in about 35 percent of the total market cap assigned to pure value, about 35 percent to pure growth, and about 30 percent split between value and growth.

Style probabilities are assigned to each index constituent. A value style probability is a number between zero and one indicating the degree of the stock's membership in the value index. The stock's growth style probability is one minus its value probability. The value index consists of the shares of the underlying index multiplied by the respective value probabilities; similarly, the growth index consists of the shares multiplied by the respective growth probabilities. Because the value and growth probabilities sum to one, the market cap of the value and growth indexes sum to the market cap of the underlying index.

Security Characteristics and Market Relativity

The style probabilities are calculated annually at reconstitution based on two security characteristics as of the last trading day in May:

- Book-to-price ratio (BP)
- I/B/E/S long-term growth forecast, mean (LTG)

The book-to-price ratio is an indicator of value, while the long-term growth forecast is an indicator of growth.[2] Stocks in the global index are grouped into market segments and the security characteristics are used to measure the degree of value or growth relative to a given segment. As of the 2009 reconstitution, the market segments for calculating style probabilities were: U.S. large cap, U.S. small cap, global ex-U.S. large cap, and global ex-U.S. small cap. The style algorithm is run separately on each market segment.

Although it is not part of the global index, the style algorithm is also run separately on the smallest 1,000 stocks of the U.S. Microcap Index.

Within each market segment, the input characteristics data are first normalized to form a value score and a growth score. Then, the value and growth scores are combined to form a composite value score (CVS). Finally, the value probabilities are assigned based on the composite value scores. Stocks with missing data are treated by substituting averages at various stages of the process. A diagram of the overall algorithm is shown in Figure 26.1.

Nonlinear Probability Algorithm—Steps 1, 2, and 6

The nonlinear probability algorithm used at Steps 1, 2, and 6 employs the function

$$Y = \begin{cases} \dfrac{1}{1+\exp\left(\dfrac{5(X_M - X)}{X_M - X_L}\right)}, & X \le X_M \\[4ex] \dfrac{1}{1+\exp\left(\dfrac{5(X_M - X)}{X_U - X_M}\right)}, & X > X_M \end{cases}$$

---

[2] Currently, LTG is not used to determine style probabilities in the Russell/Nomura indexes for reasons unique to Japan. The reasons are reviewed in Jon A. Christopherson, Yasuyuki Kato, and Jeffrey A. Hansen, "Russell/NRI Japan Equity Style Indexes: Rulebook for Index Construction," *Russell Research Commentary* (Tacoma, WA: Russell Investments, April 1996).

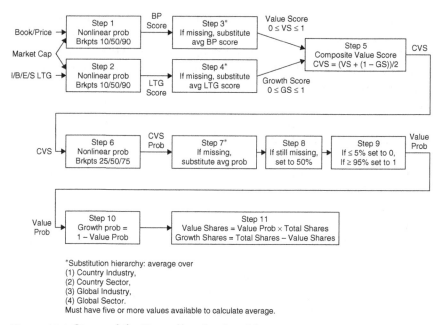

Figure 26.1 Steps of the Russell style algorithm

where X is the input variable (BP, LTG, or CVS) and Y is the output score or probability. The parameters X_L, X_M, and X_U are the lower, middle, and upper breakpoints. The breakpoints for the BP and LTG scores (Steps 1 and 2) are the 10th, 50th, and 90th cap-weighted percentiles. The breakpoints for the CVS probability (Step 6) are the 25th, 50th, and 75th cap-weighted percentiles. The 10th cap-weighted percentile, for example, is the value X_L such that at least 10 percent of the market cap has a value of X less than or equal to X_L and at least 90 percent of the market cap has a value of X greater than or equal to X_L. The other percentiles are defined similarly.

Figure 26.2 is a graph of this function using BP inputs for global ex-U.S. ex-Japan large cap as of the end of May 2007. The function effectively normalizes the BP inputs to scores between zero and one. Because the calibration breakpoints depend on percentiles, the shape of the curve is resistant to outliers.

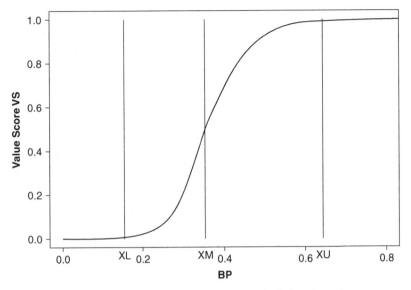

Figure 26.2 Example graph of the nonlinear probability function

Missing Data—Steps 3, 4, 7, and 8

The missing data rule used at Steps 3, 4, and 7 assigns scores/ probabilities based on averages of nearest neighbors of the stock with missing characteristics. A hierarchy of groupings is used for computing the averages; a group must have at least five available scores/ probabilities from which to calculate an average. If there are less then five available, then the next level of the hierarchy is used. The substitution hierarchy is: country industry, country subsector, country sector, global industry, global subsector, and global sector. If a probability is still missing after Step 7, then the probability is set to 0.5 in Step 8.

Composite Value Score—Step 5

The composite value score is calculated by

$$CVS = 0.5 + \frac{VS - GS}{2},$$

where VS is the value score and GS is the growth score. This formula is equivalent to the average of VS and $(1 - GS)$. A diagram of the transformation from value and growth scores into the composite value score is shown in Figure 26.3.

Small Probability Cutoff Rule—Step 9

The 5%/95% rule (Step 9) at the end of the algorithm eliminates small probabilities and the resulting small positions. It also has the effect of setting the market cap in pure value or pure growth to roughly 35 percent each. The remaining 30 percent market cap is smoothly blended between growth and value based on the CVS, as shown in Figure 26.4.

Combining Figure 26.3 with Figure 26.4, the contours of value probabilities plotted against VS and GS are shown in Figure 26.5.

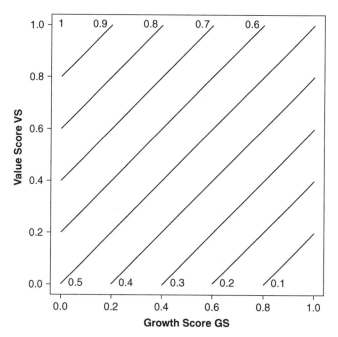

Figure 26.3 CVS contours plotted against value score VS and growth score GS

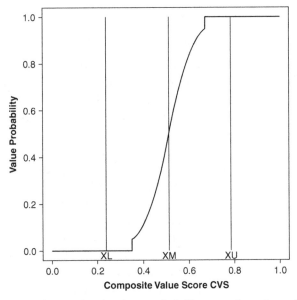

Figure 26.4 Example graph of value probability as a function of CVS after the small probability rule is applied

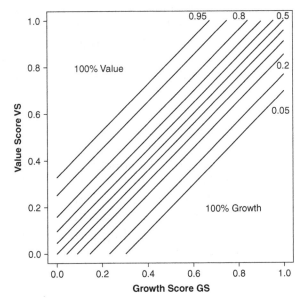

Figure 26.5 Example contours of value probabilities plotted against VS and GS

RATIONALE FOR KEY FEATURES

Nonlinear Probability Algorithm

Russell uses a "nonlinear probability" method to assign stocks to the growth and value style indexes. The term *probability* is used to indicate the degree of certainty that a stock is value or growth based on its security characteristics. This method allows stocks to be represented as having both growth and value characteristics, while preserving the additive nature of the indexes.

The nonlinear nature of the methodology emerged from an empirical examination of the price/book values of growth and value managers in the late 1980s. While studying investment manager styles, Christopherson created two portfolios from the aggregate of the manager portfolios in the Russell growth manager universe and value manager universe. Cumulative frequency distributions, or ogives, were calculated showing how the price/book values cumulated from low to high. For value managers, as the price/book value increased, the number of managers owning the stock dropped in a nonlinear fashion. For growth managers, just the opposite occurred. As the price/book of a stock began to rise, more and more growth managers began to own the stock.

At the time, the Russell methodology used a breakpoint method, as described in Chapter 25, whereby all stocks below the cap-weighted median price/book were assigned to the value index and stocks above the median were assigned to the growth index. This method led to the problem, called the "whale in the bathtub,"[3] in which large numbers of securities changed from growth to value at reconstitution time when a single large stock like Kodak moved across the capitalization-weighted median value.

These observations lead to the conclusion that stocks close to the median should be 50%/50% in both indexes. The nonlinear approach acknowledged the empirical observation and solved the "whale" problem. The original function was hand fitted and subsequently reformulated into the preceding formula[4] and was introduced into the style indexes in 1993.

---

[3] This phrase was coined by John Stannard in Russell's London office.

[4] The formula was suggested by Ernie Ankrim.

The 5 Percent Rule

The methodology includes a small position cutoff rule. If a stock's probability is less than or equal to 5 percent in one style index, then the probability is set to zero. This rule eliminates many small positions in a large number of stocks that contribute little to the growth/value performance. Eliminating small positions reduces turnover and makes the indexes easier to replicate passively.

Characteristics Used to Indicate Value and Growth

The book-to-price ratio was initially chosen as the variable used to discriminate between value and growth because of its reliability as an indicator (see Chapter 25). It has been widely used in academic studies such as Fama and French[5] and subsequently by most other style index creators. In a series of studies of other markets,[6] we found that book-to-price is a reliable indicator of style in those markets as well. A second variable, a long-term growth forecast based on analyst estimates, was added to the

---

[5] Eugene F. Fama and Kenneth R. French, "The Cross-Section of Expected Stock Returns," *Journal of Finance,* vol. 47, June 1992, pp. 427–465, and "Common Risk Factors in the Returns on Stocks and Bonds," *Journal of Financial Economics,* vol. 33, February 1993, pp. 3–56.

[6] Jon A. Christopherson, Timothy J. Hicks, and Amy T. Barton, "Canadian Equity Style Indexes," *Russell Technical Note* (Tacoma, WA: Russell Investments, July 1995). The condensed version, of the same name, appeared in *Risks and Reward,* August 1995, pp. 7–9. Jon A. Christopherson, John Douglas, and Peter Gunning, "Australian Equity Style Indices: Tools for Performance Evaluation and Plan Management in the Australian Market," *Russell Research Commentary* (Tacoma, WA: Russell Investments, January 1996). Jon A. Christopherson, Yasuyuki Kato, and Jeffrey A. Hansen, "Japanese Equity Style Indices: Tools for Performance Evaluation and Plan Management," *Russell Research Commentary* (Tacoma, WA: Russell Investments, September 1996). Robert Collie, Jon A. Christopherson, and John Stannard, "UK Style Indices: Use and Calculation," *Russell Research Commentary* (Tacoma, WA: Russell Investments, May 1997).

U.S. style methodology in 1994 to reflect growth expectations of market analysts.[7]

Haughton and Pritamani reexamined the two-factor methodology in 2005.[8] They evaluated the effect of adding supplementary characteristics to distinguish value from growth. Indexes constructed with alternative variables were compared to style universes, that is, peer groups of actual manager portfolios classified by style. Turnover of the candidate indexes was also measured. The U.S. study concluded that none of the alternative combinations of variables was clearly superior in representativeness and turnover to the existing methodology.

The introduction of the global indexes in 2007 presented another opportunity to revisit the methodology, this time from a global perspective. Using U.S. manager style universes, Cariño[9] again found that style indexes using the two legacy factors are very representative of U.S. style-oriented portfolios. Further, compared with global manager style universes, we found that the two-variable methodology produces global style indexes that are nearly as representative as any combination of more variables tested.

The use of book-to-price and long-term growth to allocate stocks into value and growth categories does not suggest that these are the only variables used by investment managers. While not all value managers might use book-to-price to select securities and not all growth managers might use long-term growth, the correlations of these variables to other indicators is strong. Overengineering style indexes by adding variables and creatively weighting them very quickly becomes a complicated methodology that is less representative of style manager processes broadly. The role of indexes

[7] Jon A. Christopherson and Amy Barton, "Comparing Style Index Performance: How Can the Russell and S&P Indexes Behave So Differently?" *Journal of Performance Measurement*, vol. 5, no. 3 (September), 1999, pp. 33–45, show that style characteristics, weighting, membership criteria, and other design choices can lead to significant return differences among indexes.

[8] Kelly Haughton and Mahesh Pritamani, "U.S. Equity Style Methodology," *Russell Research Commentary* (Tacoma, WA: Russell Investments, August 2005).

[9] David R. Cariño, "Global Style Indexes: Validating the Russell Methodology," *Russell Research* (Tacoma, WA: Russell Investments, July 2008).

in the market is better served by a clear, well-understood approach. Investors, money managers, and other users of the indexes all benefit from the robust, familiar two-variable approach.

Market Relativity

The overall approach of the Russell global indexes is based on a view of global equity markets as essentially one large investment opportunity, rather than a collection of individual country markets. This viewpoint is reflected in the definition of cap size tiers, for example. The dividing line between large-cap and small-cap indexes is a band between the 85th and 90th capitalization percentiles. One implication of this global cap break is that individual country segments of the index are not all split at 90%/10% large/small cap. Countries will vary in their split between large and small cap in the index. Thus, size is defined on a *global-relative* basis rather than a *country-relative* basis.

This view is based on observations of how global managers are forming portfolios. Feldman and Haughton[10] document the increasingly global view of the markets by investors.

We approached the split between value and growth styles in a similar way. Instead of defining style on a country-relative basis, we took a global view of style. In a country-relative approach, the value-growth weights of each country in an index would be roughly 50–50; put another way, the country weights of the style indexes would be roughly the same as the country weights of the total index. By contrast, in a global-relative approach, the value-growth split of the total index is roughly 50–50, but individual country segments may have value-growth weights something other than 50–50. Cariño[11] gives strong evidence that a global ex-U.S. ex-Japan approach provides a superior fit to global manager style universes.

---

[10] Barry Feldman and Kelly Haughton, "Indexes Brief: Defining Global Small Cap" (Tacoma, WA: Russell Investments, May 2008).

[11] Cariño, "Global Style Indexes: Validating the Russell Methodology."

CHAPTER 27

U.S. Equity Benchmarks

In Chapter 21 we presented a series of criteria that we believe are fundamental to good indexes. In this chapter we present lists of most of the indexes that are currently available for U.S. equities. We present the index names, selected index characteristics, and our assessment of whether these indexes have the desired characteristics. These evaluations, of course, are our assessments, and it is likely that others doing the same evaluation might arrive at different conclusions.

The organizations offering families of indexes have various backgrounds. For example, Morgan Stanley Capital International (MSCI) began its organizational life offering international equity indexes and has recently expanded to offer a family of U.S. indexes. The U.S. indexes and the international indexes added together constitute a global index so that each stock is in only one index. Russell Investments, which began as a consulting company offering indexes for its U.S. clients, has recently expanded its offerings to include a global family of indexes. The Russell 3000E is the broadest Russell index for the United States, while the Russell/Nomura Total Market Index covers Japan and the recent Russell Global Index covers the rest of the world. Dow Jones, creator of the famous Dow Jones Industrial Average, collaborated with Wilshire Associates, author of the Wilshire 5000, to create the family of indexes known as the Dow Jones U.S. Total Stock Market Indexes. Dow Jones also has a separate set of indexes known as the Dow Jones Global Total Stock

Market Indexes. Finally, Standard & Poor's has joined forces with Citigroup (who acquired the Salomon Smith Barney indexes) to create a family of global equity indexes.

This is all very confusing to the average investor. Moreover, index providers are continuously changing their offerings. So, let us start by outlining the families of indexes provided by the major vendors. Each of the families has U.S. and global components. In this chapter we focus on the U.S. components, and in Chapter 28 we focus on the global/international indexes.

S&P AND S&P/CITIGROUP
FAMILY OF INDEXES

The S&P 500 is the oldest capitalization-weighted index in the world. The index has been the standard index against which most professional money managers have been evaluated since the 1960s when CAPM and MPT emerged to dominate "in the know" performance evaluation and plan management. The index is widely used and followed. It is also the basis for many of the original equity derivative products. Futures, options, and lately ETFs based on the S&P 500 have a long history of use.[1]

The list of 500 securities is created and maintained by a committee that carefully selects securities for the index based on their liquidity, their sector and industry, and their capitalization tier. The objective is to create an index that fairly represents the entire market—and they have been very successful at doing this. It is a stratified sample but is not random and does have a liquidity and success bias. Unfortunately, to keep the list at 500, the committee has to pick and choose stocks in each industry without having all stocks in the industry—this means, for example, that GM might have been in the index at a time when Ford might not. This choosing of representative stocks is not a problem unless your portfolio has one and not the other and the stock happens to perform well or poorly. From a money manager point of view, at one point you look like a great investor and at another you look not so great depending on whether you have Ford in your portfolio and it does/does not do well.

---

[1] See the S&P Web site, www.standardandpoors.com/indices, for more information about the S&P indexes.

The underlying problem is the narrowness of 500 stocks when there are 3,000 or so that most managers choose from. On the other hand, 500 stocks are much easier and less expensive to trade than 3,000.

With the advent of the Wilshire 5000 and the Russell 3000, Standard & Poor's expanded their stock list beyond the 500, creating the S&P Composite 1500. The original 500 plus 1,000 other securities are included—400 of which are in the S&P MidCap 400 index and 600 of which are in the S&P SmallCap 600 index.

In 2004 Standard & Poor's acquired the Citigroup Global Equity indexes, which had evolved from the Salomon Smith Barney indexes, which, in turn, had evolved from the original Salomon-Russell International indexes.

The S&P Composite 1500/Citigroup Growth and Value indexes use seven stock characteristics to determine growth and value weights. The characteristics used to generate growth weights are five-year earnings-per-share growth, the five-year sales-per-share growth, and the five-year internal growth defined as five-year ROE times 1 minus the payout ratio. The characteristics used to generate value weights start with book/price ratio and add the cash-flow/price ratio, the sales/price ratio, and dividend yield.

Each of these variables is standardized across the stocks in each time period. The three growth and value z-scores are equally weighted in computing the average style z-score. The stocks are arranged on the continuum between the highest growth score and the highest value score. The stocks are broken into three equal capitalization groups: one-third pure growth, one-third mixed, and one-third pure value. The stocks in the middle that are neither pure growth nor pure value have their market cap distributed between the style indexes based on their distances from the midpoint of the pure-value group of stocks and the midpoint of the pure-growth group of stocks.[2]

The S&P SmallCap 600/Citigroup Growth and Value, S&P MidCap 400/Citigroup Growth and Value, and S&P 500/Citigroup

---

[2] The formula is described in detail on the S&P Web site in 2005 in a paper called, "Introducing a Comprehensive Style Index Solution: Methodology of Standard & Poor's U.S. Style Indexes." See www2.standardandpoors.com/spf/pdf/index/style_nextgeneration_whiteppr.pdf.

Growth and Value style indexes are all created using the same methodology.

DOW JONES INDEXES

The Dow Jones family of indexes has grown far beyond the Dow Jones Industrial Average of 30 stocks. For many years Dow Jones has also published the Dow Jones Transportation Average and the Dow Jones Utility Average. Dow Jones publishes many indexes, and the reader should consult their Web site, www.djindexes.com, for the complete family of indexes. Dow Jones joined with Wilshire Associates in 2004 to offer the Dow Jones Wilshire set of U.S. and Global indexes, which became the Dow Jones Total Stock Market Indexes in April 2009.[3]

The current benchmark indexes we focus on are the Dow Jones Global Total Stock Market Index, the Dow Jones U.S. Total Stock Market Index, and the associated style indexes. The indexes are capitalization weighted and float adjusted.

The major indexes are the Dow Jones U.S. Total Stock Market (DJ U.S. TSM) Index and the Dow Jones U.S. Completion Total Stock Market Index (which is the DJ U.S. TSM minus the S&P 500 securities). The Dow Jones style indexes use the DJ U.S. TSM and decompose it by capitalization tier into the DJ U.S. Large-Cap TSM Index (top 750 names), the DJ U.S. Small-Cap TSM Index (the next 1,750 names), the DJ U.S. Mid-Cap TSM Index (the 501st to 1000th names), and the DJ U.S. Micro-Cap TSM Index (the 2,501st and smaller names).

The Dow Jones U.S. Growth and Value TSM Indexes are based on these capitalization breakdowns. To create the growth and value indexes, each stock's z-scores on selected characteristics are Winsorized.[4] The characteristic z-scores are subjected to cluster analysis, and the distances of each characteristic from the cluster

---

[3] See the Dow Jones Web site, www.djindexes.com, and the Wilshire Associates Web site, www.wilshire.com/indexes, for more information about Dow Jones and Wilshire indexes.

[4] "Winsorization" refers to a data recoding procedure where outliers (values beyond chosen points on the distribution of values) are set to the value at the chosen points. The procedure affects the mean and standard deviation statistics, but it prevents extreme values from dominating the evaluation.

centers is used to compute a growth distance and a value distance. These are calculated separately and combined to obtain a final style score. The stocks are rank ordered on the style score, and 50 percent are placed in one index and 50 percent in the other.

The variables used to determine growth/value scores and weights include price/book, projected earnings growth, projected price/earnings, dividend yield, trailing revenue growth, and trailing earnings growth.

The style indexes use buffer zones and other rules to reduce turnover. The style indexes are rebalanced twice a year in March and September.

RUSSELL INDEXES

The Russell index family is offered by Russell Investments.[5] The U.S. index methodology is summarized in Chapter 23. The indexes originated with the creation of the Russell 3000 in 1983 at the request of large Russell consulting clients who were using the S&P 500 at the time to evaluate managers and build plans. The Russell consultants and clients had noticed that managers were hard to evaluate because they had stocks in their portfolios that were not in the S&P 500. The Wilshire 5000 was supposed to be the answer, but information on the smallest stocks in the index was unreliable. Getting timely prices was a particular problem. Russell clients wanted something better.

To address these issues, Russell research led by Kelly Haughton took the holdings of the managers in their clients' portfolios and rank ordered them by capitalization. They found that very few managers bought any stocks smaller than the 3,000th largest security because the managers quickly ran up against the SEC 5 percent rule. This rule requires that anyone owning more than 5 percent of the capital of a company must declare who they are and file a great deal of paperwork. Information and prices for these small companies were unreliable. So, money managers ignored the very smallest companies for these reasons. Russell's objective in creating the index was to create an index that measured what the clients' managers were buying.

---

[5] See the Russell Investments Web site, www.russell.com/indexes, for more information about Russell indexes.

The clients also complained about not having a good index to measure managers who specialized in small-capitalization stocks. No well-built index existed. Russell extracted the smallest 2,000 out of the 3,000 to create the Russell 2000 Index, which today is the most widely followed and used small-cap index in the world. The Russell 1000 became the medium- to large-capitalization index.

Russell was the first to build a comprehensive broad market index and then decompose it into capitalization styles. Russell was also the first to create a family of float-weighted indexes for the reasons we discussed in Chapter 23.

The list of stocks from which all current Russell U.S. indexes flow is the Russell 3000E master list, which contains the 4,000 largest securities, representing over 99 percent of the U.S. equity market capitalization. All Russell U.S. indexes are subsets of this list. The original Russell 3000 contains the largest 3,000 stocks. The largest 1,000 stocks, comprising the Russell 1000, are further segmented into the Russell Top 200 and the Russell Midcap Index, which contains the 800 smallest stocks in the Russell 1000. The Russell 2000, comprising the 2,000 smallest stocks in the Russell 3000, represents approximately 10 percent of the market cap of the Russell 3000. To measure the performance of the small- to mid-cap segment, commonly referred to as *smid* cap, the Russell 2500 was created, which contains the 2,500 smallest stocks in the Russell 3000. To represent the very smallest segment of the market, the Russell Microcap Index was created, which contains the 1,000 smallest stocks in the Russell 2000 plus the next 1,000 stocks.[6] The Russell Microcap Index makes up less than 3 percent of the U.S. equity market.

In 1985 Christopherson, Haughton, and the Russell team[7] began work on the Russell growth and value style indexes. They were released to the public in 1987. They used the capitalization-weighted median price/book as the breakpoint between value and growth. Any stock above the median was in the growth index, and anything below the median was in the value index. These were the first

---

[6] See Steve Swartley, "The Russell Microcap Index," *Russell White Paper* (Tacoma, WA: Russell Investments, June 2005).

[7] The Russell team included Monica Butler, Dennis Trittin, Duncan Smith, and Madelyn Smith.

float-weighted growth and value indexes in the world.[8] These indexes were derived from observations of Russell clients' money manager portfolios. The indexes were found to track the average return of the managers in the growth and value universes quite well.

Initially, the quarterly reconstitution of the style indexes produced a great deal of turnover for the indexes, which index fund providers and clients seeking to manage an index fund as part of their core portfolios did not like. To address this problem and to create a more intuitively appealing methodology, Russell introduced the nonlinear method of determining growth and value scores described in Chapter 26. The methodology also tended to prevent massive movements of stock capitalization at reconstitution when a large company moved across the capitalization-weighted median line in either direction. Other capitalization tier indexes were created such as the midcap and microcap indexes. The style methodology is applied separately to the Russell 1000, Russell 2000, and the smallest 1,000 stocks in the Russell Microcap, thereby covering all cap tier indexes of the family.

The Russell growth and value indexes are created by sorting the universe of companies by book/price ratio and separately by the I/B/E/S long-term forecast growth rate. The information is equal weighted to arrive at a composite value score for each company. The composite score is used to generate the probability that a stock is either a growth or a value style stock, as detailed in Chapter 26. About 30 percent of the market cap of the underlying index is split between the growth and value indexes in different proportions based on the probability calculated. The remaining 70 percent of the market cap is completely in either one index or the other. Russell rebalances its family of indexes annually near the end of June using market values and characteristics on the last trading day in May.

MSCI FAMILY OF INDEXES

In 2003 MSCI launched its U.S. equity indexes. They offer a broad market index as well as value and growth indexes using a proprietary value and growth scoring methodology. The indexes

---

[8] See Chapter 25 for an explanation of how the indexes were created, how they compared with manager universes, and how they could be used for evaluation.

are rebalanced twice a year, and minor adjustments are made at the end of each quarter. The indexes use buffer zones to reduce the level of turnover at reconstitution. They use buffer zones for both the size and the style index reconstitutions. The indexes are capitalization weighted and float adjusted. A minimum float screen and a liquidity screen are applied to the securities to exclude small and limited availability securities.[9]

The master list of securities for the MSCI family of indexes for U.S. equities covers over 99 percent of the stocks in the U.S. market by capitalization. The master list is decomposed into a broad market index that has about 3,000 securities, and the investable market index that contains the top 2,500 securities and covers about 98 percent of the investable universe. From this list of 2,500 securities, they carve out a small-cap index that contains the bottom 1,750 of 2,500 securities, and a prime market index that contains the other 750 securities. The prime market index of 750 securities is decomposed into a large-cap index that contains the largest 300 securities and a midcap index that has the next 450 securities (i.e., stock number 301 to stock number 750). A microcap index is created out of all those securities falling below the 2,500th stock. There is no set number of securities in the microcap index; however, each security must have at least $20 million in capitalization.

Each of these capitalization segments is decomposed into growth and value indexes. Three variables are used to calculate the value weight for each security: book-to-price, price-earnings ratio based on one-year forecasted earnings, and dividend yield. Five variables are used for the growth weight: long-term forecasted earnings per share (EPS), short-term forecasted EPS, current internal growth, five-year EPS growth rate, and five-year sales per share growth rate.

These variables are manipulated to produce a growth and value score that places the stock somewhere in two-dimensional growth and value space. These values are further reduced into a score on a value/growth spectrum and then transformed into weights in the growth index and the value index.

---

[9] See the MSCI Barra Web site, www.mscibarra.com, for more information about MSCI indexes.

Major Market Index

The Major Market Index (MMI) is an index composed of the prices of 20 major companies and is used primarily by traders. Prior to 1997, the Dow Jones Company would not allow derivatives to be created based on the Dow Jones Industrial Average of 30 securities. This led to the creation of the MMI. The 20 stocks chosen are members of the Dow Jones 30 stock industrial average. The Major Market Index is calculated by summing the current prices of the 20 stocks. There is no capitalization weighting or float adjustments to this index. It does, however, track the Dow Jones industrial average very closely. This index is also not used to evaluate professional investment managers or plans.

CRSP COMPOSITE AND DECILE INDEXES

The favorite set of indexes for academic research is the decile indexes offered by the Center for Research in Security Prices (CRSP) at the University of Chicago. The CRSP database has daily prices for over 26,000 stocks that are listed on the NASDAQ, NYSE, and AMEX exchanges. The database does not include OTC bulletin board stocks. The historical database covers both active and inactive securities. The database has extensive historical records with data going back to 1925 for the NYSE, 1962 for the AMEX, and 1972 for the NASDAQ. The data from the ARCA exchange was added in 2006. The data covers dividends and corporate actions and other company information.

The decile portfolios are formed based on the decile breakpoints that come from a rank order of the NYSE securities on the basis of capitalization. Each decile is approximately the same number of NYSE names. Once the decile capitalization breakpoints have been determined, the stocks from the AMEX and NASDAQ are sorted into the NYSE-based deciles. All the stock names and their capitalization in each decile form each decile portfolio. These deciles are grouped into convenient indexes such as CRSP 1–2 (largest securities by capitalization), CRSP 3–5, CRSP 6–8, CRSP 9–10, CRSP 6–10 (the small securities by capitalization), and CRSP 1–10 index. The return for each decile is an equal-weighted return. The decile portfolios are rebalanced annually.[10]

---

[10] Information on the CRSP databases and indexes can be found at the CRSP Web site, www.crsp.com/products/indices.htm.

The academic community has lower-cost access to these indexes, while practitioners pay list price for the holdings and return series. The indexes are equal weighted, but most academic research capitalization weights the securities. However, none of these indexes is float adjusted. The work of Fama and French has made these indexes famous and has furthered their use as benchmarks for comparison in capital market studies, but they are not generally used by the investment community to evaluate professional money managers.

OTHER INDEXES: NYSE AND NASDAQ INDEXES

There are other indexes that are reported in the news quite frequently. For reasons of space we cannot go into extensive detail on how each of these is created. We present brief introductions.

NYSE Composite Index

The NYSE Composite Index is based on the prices of all securities traded on the NYSE. The composite index contains over 2,000 securities with 64 percent of them being U.S. securities, 23.5 percent being European, 3.9 percent being Canadian, and the other 8.6 percent from other regions. There are 360 non-U.S. companies. The types of stocks include all common stocks, ADRs, REITS, tracking stocks, and foreign companies. The stocks are capitalization weighted and float adjusted. The indexes are calculated on both a price return basis and a total return basis.[11]

The NYSE Composite Index tends to lean toward large-cap securities, and since it does not cover all the stocks in the U.S. equity market, it is not used as a benchmark by fiduciaries and plan sponsors.

NASDAQ Composite Index

The NASDAQ Composite includes all domestic and international common stocks traded on the NASDAQ exchange. There are

---

[11] See the NYSE Web site, www.nyse.com/about/listed/mkt_indexes_nyse. shtml, for more information about NYSE indexes.

approximately 3,000 securities including foreign and domestic common stocks, ADRs, limited partnerships tracking stocks, and ordinary shares. Stocks not included include closed-end funds, convertible debentures, ETFs, preferred stocks, rights, warrants, and derivative securities.[12]

The composite index is capitalization weighted using total outstanding shares and current prices. There is no float adjustment. Corporate actions are accounted for on the ex-dates, and there is no need for rebalancing.

COMPARING INDEX CONSTRUCTION ISSUES

The complexity of all the indexes being offered can be quite confusing. There are a few ideas that will help clarify some of these issues. The different index family groups take slightly different approaches to each of these issues. Let us examine the commonalities and differences.

Master List Issues

All index families begin with a master list of securities that is then broken down into subindexes based on size characteristics and growth/value characteristics. In the multimanager, multistyle approach to fund construction, it is useful for these components to sum to the overall master list. The families of indexes differ on the number of securities that are included in their master lists and the amount of market capitalization covered by the list. In Figure 27.1 we attempt to graphically display the different approaches taken.

In the United States there are approximately 7,000 securities that are publicly traded. As we mentioned, many of the smaller securities trade very infrequently, sometimes by appointment, and are called *pink-sheet* stocks. Each family of indexes has to make choices between the number of stocks covered, the reliability of attaining timely data, and the objectives of creating indexes. This results in different master lists of securities.

---

[12] See the NASDAQ Web site, www.nasdaq.com/indexes, for more information about NASDAQ indexes.

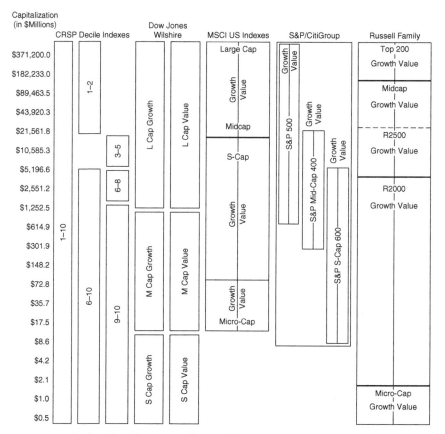

Figure 27.1 Index family master list and approximate capitalization breakpoints

In Figure 27.1 the size of the boxes refers to the number of securities covered by the index master list. However, the number of securities is not synonymous with the amount of money invested in each security. There are other dimensions not covered in the numbers in the figure: the amount of capitalization covered by the indexes, and the capitalization that is available for trading, which is the float.

It is clear from the chart that the Russell and Dow Jones indexes cover the most names and capitalization as do the CRSP indexes. Note however that the S&P/Citigroup equity indexes have less coverage. The figure also shows the capitalization breaks for large-cap, midcap, small-cap, and microcap indexes as well as the growth and value representations within each of those capitalization groups.

Capitalization Breaks for Size Styles

It is clear from the figure that index families differ on what they mean by large-cap or small-cap, much less midcap. There are no crystal-clear definitive rules that divide small-cap stocks from other stocks. The basis for the Russell 2000 breakpoint was empirically derived from the portfolios of managers that called themselves small-cap. However, the small-cap breakpoints for other families of indexes are in the same neighborhood, and the precise location of the breakpoint is a matter of choice. Other capitalization breakpoints have emerged over time such as very large cap (sometimes known as mega cap), but again the precise breakpoint is not clear.

The CRSP indexes combine the capitalization tiers in various ways and make no distinction between growth and value. The S&P groups overlap because they are outgrowths of the S&P 500, which spans the spectrum from the very largest stocks to fairly small stocks. The 1,000 securities that complement the S&P 500 make up the S&P 1500, so there must be some overlap. The MSCI and Russell indexes use more clearly delineated sets of capitalization breaks before they create the growth and value divisions. Russell has provided a large number of different capitalization breaks to meet client demands. Hence the large-cap Russell 1000 index has been decomposed into the top 200 very large cap index and the next 800 midcap index. The most widely known small-cap index is the Russell 2000, but many small-cap managers have securities in their portfolios slightly larger than the top end of the Russell 2000. The Russell 2500 was created to evaluate these sorts of portfolios.

Methodologies for Determining Degree of Growth and Value Orientation

As discussed in Chapter 25, the first commercially available style indexes were created by Russell in the late 1980s. Their choice of characteristics for determining growth and value initially was capitalization-weighted price-to-book. Over the years their methodology has evolved to include IBES forecasted long-term growth and a nonlinear methodology that places some weight of each stock into both the growth and value indexes when that stock's price-to-book and forecasted growth values fall in the middle of the range of values.

The various families of indexes have created similar measures for style indexes. In Table 27.1 we show the variables that each provider uses to determine style. There are many redundancies in these lists, but no two lists are exactly the same. At the bottom of the table we have noted the methods used to combine these different elements of growth and value measures into a single value on the growth/value dimension. The reason for this reduction to a single value lies in the need to be able to assign each stock to a growth or value index (or proportion them in each index).

T A B L E 27.1

Variables Used to Define Style by Index Provider

Style Variable Used	Russell Family	MSCI Family	Dow Jones TSM Family	S&P/ Citigroup Family
Book to price	X	X	X	X
Forecasted earnings to price		X	X	
Sales to price				X
Dividend yield		X	X	X
Cash flow to price				X
Long-term forecasted EPS growth rate	X	X	X	
Short-term forecasted EPS growth rate		X	X	
Historical EPS growth rate		X	X	X
Historical sales per share growth rate		X	X	X
Sustainable growth rate		X		X
Methodology	Weighted probabilities	Weighted z-score	Weighted z-score	Weighted z-score

For a variety of reasons, the index providers have sought to differentiate themselves from each other using different combinations of variables and degree of "style purity." Some are more complex than others, and complexity has conceptual merit given that style managers generally employ complex procedures to buy and sell securities. However, some important impacts of complexity within a benchmark should be considered: it consistently increases turnover when more variables are utilized to classify stocks, and indexes created with complex methodologies are less able to represent a broad range of style manager behavior.

At first blush it is tempting for the user to believe that the more variables one uses to determine style the better. While it is certainly true that most growth and value investors examine a large number of variables when selecting securities, unfortunately, it does not follow that a large number of variables are necessary to be able to create a better index that closely tracks the managers' portfolios and returns.

Christopherson and Haughton's 1989 paper in Chapter 25 demonstrated that using a single variable, price-to-book, and a simple breakpoint methodology one can create portfolios that track the average growth and value manager returns quite closely—assuming you have all the securities from which the managers normally choose and each security is weighted by its float.

However, this raises the question: what makes one style index better than another? The goal in building style indexes is to create a reasonable benchmark for managers within each style. To make style indexes more practical, it is useful to evaluate the ease with which products—such as index funds and ETFs—can be created using the indexes as bases.

Christopherson and Haughton used the closeness of fit, R^2, with manager universe returns as the criterion for good fit in addition to similarities of equity characteristics between the index and the manager universe. Haughton and Pritamani[13] revisited the question of

---

[13] Kelly Haughton and Mahesh Pritamani, "U.S. Equity Style Methodology," *Russell Research Commentary* (Tacoma, WA: Russell Investments, August 2005).

what makes a good style index and used these criteria to evaluate alternative methodologies:

- *Representativeness:* A fundamental characteristic of a good benchmark is that it should represent the investment opportunity set from which active managers pick stocks.
- *Turnover:* An index is a practical benchmark if its returns can be achieved by a passive investor. The higher the turnover, the less likely it is that a passive investor can achieve the benchmark return due to trading costs associated with higher turnover.

If a style index is based on a more complex methodology than another less complex style index, then we would prefer the less complex methodology unless the more complex methodology provides a substantial marginal improvement in either representativeness or turnover.

Based on these criteria, Haughton and Pritamani evaluate Russell's style indexes over the period July 1994 to June 2004, compared against the style universe returns from two vendors: Lipper and Russell. They also evaluated the recently introduced MSCI U.S. style index methodology using the preceding criteria. They found that using a large number of variables to determine growth and value style does not improve the performance of the style indexes in terms of these criteria.

Using Russell style universes, Cariño[14] again found that style indexes using the two legacy factors are very representative of U.S. style-oriented portfolios. Further, compared with global manager style universes, we found that the two-variable methodology produces global style indexes that are nearly as representative as any combination of more variables tested.

INDEX COMPARISONS

There are many different indexes to consider. Each family group has a wide variety of indexes, all of which fit within one framework. To make sense out of this collection we have grouped them into

---

[14] David R. Cariño, "Global Style Indexes: Validating the Russell Methodology," *Russell Research* (Tacoma, WA: Russell Investments, July 2008).

general categories by capitalization and style. In this section, we present tables containing our assessments given the principles of useful indexes described in Chapter 21. Table 27.2 covers the broad market indexes. Table 27.3 covers large-cap indexes. Table 27.4 covers midcap and Table 27.5 covers small-capitalization indexes. Table 27.6 covers microcap indexes. Within each capitalization group there are also associated equity style indexes.

Broad Market Indexes

Broad market indexes, listed in Table 27.2, are the indexes usually based on the style family master list of stocks. These indexes can be viewed as the "market portfolio" of the CAPM. As mentioned in Chapter 23, each index provider faces a series of practical problems in creating indexes, so these broad market indexes will vary depending on the choices that the index creator made. The number of securities in a master list ranges from about 5,000 in the Dow Jones U.S. Total Stock Market indexes to 1,500 in the S&P Composite 1500.

T A B L E   27.2

Broad Market U.S. Equity Indexes

Index Name	Naïve Based-Fairness	Completeness-Investable	Nonproprietary-Simplicity	Capitalization Weighted	Float Adjusted
CRSP 1–10	Yes	Yes	Yes	Yes	No
Dow Jones Industrials (30)	Yes	No	Yes	No	No
Dow Jones U.S. Total Stock Market Index	Yes	Yes	Yes	Yes	Yes
MSCI US Broad Market	Yes	Yes	Yes	Yes	Yes
Russell 3000 Index	Yes	Yes	Yes	Yes	Yes
Russell 3000E Extended Market Index	Yes	Yes	Yes	Yes	Yes
S&P Composite 1500	No	No	No	Yes	Yes

This is a considerable range. Since all these indexes are broad market indexes, one would hope that the price-to-book ratios of all the indexes would be nearly identical as would be their dividend yields. This clearly need not be the case, given the differences in master lists.

Large-Cap Indexes

Large-cap indexes can be defined in various ways as Figure 27.1 shows. The Russell large-cap index is the Russell 1000, but that index can be broken down into the Top 200 and the Midcap 800. The problem has to do with the definition of "large." In Table 27.3 our definition of large-cap is rather broad. We include very large capitalization indexes such as the Russell Top 200 and also the Russell 1000. The S&P 500 spans a large portion of the spectrum but is often viewed as a large-cap index. The NYSE Composite has been included even though the smallest-capitalization stock in the composite can be viewed as a small security. We have also included the RAFI Index

T A B L E 27.3

Large-Capitalization U.S. Equity Indexes

Index Name	Naïve Based-Fairness	Completeness-Investable	Nonproprietary-Simplicity	Capitalization Weighted	Float Adjusted
CRSP 1–2	Yes	Yes	Yes	Yes	No
DJ Large Cap TSM Index	Yes	Yes	Yes	Yes	Yes
MSCI US Large Cap	Yes	Yes	Yes	Yes	Yes
NASDAQ 100	Yes	No	Yes	Yes	No
NYSE Composite	Yes	No	Yes	Yes	No
Research Affiliates Fundamental Index	No	No	No	No	No
Russell 1000 Index	Yes	Yes	Yes	Yes	Yes
Russell Top 200 Index	Yes	Yes	Yes	Yes	Yes
S&P 500	No	No	No	Yes	Yes

and the NASDAQ 100 even though these indexes have their own unique characteristics that cause them to be different from the other indexes. What is particularly notable is that the smallest securities in each of these large-cap indexes is considerably different.

Midcap Indexes

Again, there is no clear definition of what constitutes a midcapitalization index or what does not. In Table 27.4 we include a large number of midcapitalization indexes that have quite different definitions of what constitutes midcapitalization securities. All these indexes are capitalization weighted but not all are float adjusted. In our opinion the MSCI indexes and the S&P indexes do not fully cover the midcap investable universe. The indexes have quite a wide range of largest values and smallest values. These differences in the range of values lead to different portfolios of securities and hence different portfolio characteristics. These differences in the portfolio characteristics should cause the user to be careful in choosing among these benchmarks to evaluate a given portfolio.

T A B L E 27.4

Midcapitalization U.S. Equity Indexes

Index Name	Naïve Based-Fairness	Completeness-Investable	Nonproprietary-Simplicity	Capitalization Weighted	Float Adjusted
NASDAQ Composite	Yes	No	Yes	Yes	No
NASDAQ Industrial	Yes	No	Yes	Yes	No
CRSP 3–5	Yes	Yes	Yes	Yes	No
DJ Mid-Cap TSM Index	Yes	Yes	Yes	Yes	Yes
MSCI US Mid Cap 450	Yes	Mostly	Yes	Yes	Yes
Russell Midcap Index	Yes	Yes	Yes	Yes	Yes
S&P Mid-Cap 400	No	No	No	Yes	Yes

Small-Cap Indexes

Rolf Banz[15] and others have shown that small stocks tend to perform quite differently than large stocks and are generally considered a major risk factor. Although this factor is not always positively rewarded—indeed there have been long periods of time when small stocks did not perform particularly well—small-capitalization exposure is nevertheless a risk factor that the investor needs to understand and measure. Table 27.5 lists all the small-capitalization indexes. The observations and caveats we made earlier about the large-cap indexes hold true for the small-cap indexes for each of the families covered.

In the small-cap area it is much more important for an index to be float-weight adjusted because many small-capitalization securities have large private holdings or shares that are not available in the marketplace. For example, IPO lockups, which are shares of

T A B L E 27.5

Small-Capitalization U.S. Equity Indexes

Index Name	Naïve Based-Fairness	Completeness-Investable	Nonproprietary-Simplicity	Capitalization Weighted	Float Adjusted
CRSP 6–10	Yes	Yes	Yes	Yes	No
CRSP 6–8	Yes	Yes	Yes	Yes	No
DJ Small-Cap TSM Index	Yes	Yes	Yes	Yes	Yes
MSCI US Small Cap	Yes	Mostly	Yes	Yes	Yes
Russell 2000 Index	Yes	Yes	Yes	Yes	Yes
Russell 2500 Index	Yes	Yes	Yes	Yes	Yes
Russell Small Cap Completeness Index	Yes	Yes	Yes	Yes	Yes
S&P Small-Cap 600	No	No	No	Yes	Yes

[15] Rolf W. Banz, "The Relationship Between Market Value and Return of Common Stocks," *Journal of Financial Economics*, March 1981, pp. 3–18.

recently floated companies owned by the company principals who cannot trade the shares for a specified period of time, dramatically affect the available float for those companies. Failure to float adjust such companies will cause the index to measure the opportunity set poorly.

Microcap Indexes

Microcap indexes are a relatively new development in the index world. As mentioned earlier when talking about the history of capitalization-weighted indexes, we pointed out that the Wilshire 5000 had many securities in the bottom capitalization tiers for which index fund managers could not obtain current prices nor had sufficient liquidity to be able to trade securities. Over the years the trading of the smallest securities has grown with the computerization of trading, which has also led to more accurate pricing. The net effect is that microcapitalization stocks can now be traded effectively. This led Russell and others to create microcap indexes, which are reviewed in Table 27.6. The Russell indexes are the only ones to offer growth and value style indexes. It should also be noted that

T A B L E 27.6

Microcapitalization U.S. Equity Indexes

Index Name	Naïve Based-Fairness	Completeness-Investable	Nonproprietary-Simplicity	Capitalization Weighted	Float Adjusted
Russell Microcap Growth Index	Yes	Yes	Yes	Yes	Yes
Russell Microcap Value Index	Yes	Yes	Yes	Yes	Yes
CRSP 9–10	Yes	Yes	Yes	Yes	No
MSCI US Micro Cap	Yes	Mostly	Yes	Yes	Yes
Russell Microcap Index	Yes	Yes	Yes	Yes	Yes
DJ Micro-Cap TSM Index	Yes	Yes	Yes	Yes	Yes

the top in terms of capitalization of the Russell microcap indexes reaches into the range of the Russell 2000 index. It is important to note that the various indexes cover different capitalization ranges. These differences predictably lead to differences in portfolio characteristics. Again, the user should bear these differences and capitalization ranges in mind when choosing a benchmark to evaluate a portfolio.

CONCLUSION

The preceding review establishes that a large number of U.S. equity indexes can be used as benchmarks for the market as a whole. Index family components exist for just about any subset of securities that behave differently from the market as a whole. The choice of benchmark does make a large difference in the quality and accuracy of the user's analysis. Construction issues also make a difference, so the user should be familiar with the different choices made by index providers. The key differences start with the master list of securities. Indexes also differ in how the stocks are weighted and how they are assigned to various subgroups of the master list.

CHAPTER 28

Global and International Equity Benchmarks

When it comes to international and global equity benchmarks, there are major families like the U.S. benchmarks. The oldest and most well-known of these families is the Morgan Stanley Capital International (MSCI) family. There are issues in international and global indexes that make them unique. The chapter title and statement "global and international equity benchmarks" itself points to one of these issues. However, there are many others as well that we will try to alert the reader to.

GLOBAL VERSUS INTERNATIONAL

Since World War II, the world has undergone a massive economic transformation. In 1965 about 5 percent of the gross national product of the United States was involved in international trade. In 2000 that number had grown to over 50 percent. The same is true for nearly every country in the world.

Economic globalization refers to the increasing interdependence of world economies that has emerged from the global flow of capital and technology. This can also be described as the integration of markets and economies. This global integration has largely grown from the mix of rapid developments in science and technology along with the growth of a free market/free trade economic environment. The result has been an increasing cross-border division of labor. Science and technology have greatly reduced the cost of transportation and communication, making economic globalization possible. Ocean shipping costs have dropped to half what they were in 1930; the airfreight and telecommunication costs have declined by similar amounts. The price levels of computers since 1960 have been reduced by over 95 percent. This kind of technological advancement has greatly reduced the cost of international trade and investment, thus making it possible to organize and coordinate global production. Products for large global corporations are routinely designed in one country, the product parts are produced in another country, and the products are sold in a third country. The development of the networking-based economy has given rise to a large group of support companies that make the concept of national boundaries for economic activities meaningless.

The growth of global financial transactions is even more dramatic.

> In 1980, the total volume of cross-border transactions of stocks and bonds of major developed countries was still less than 10% of their GDP. However, this figure had far surpassed 100% in 1995. The value of the average daily transactions of foreign exchanges have grown from US$ 200 billion in the middle of 1980's to the present US$ 1,200 billion, which is 85% of the foreign exchange reserves of all the countries in the world and 70 times as large as the value of the daily export of commodities and services.[1]

The result of globalization is to change the focus of some companies within an economy away from solely domestic markets to global markets. This change of focus should not be lost on any index provider. A much larger proportion of the corporations in the United States earned substantial portions of their earnings outside the United States. Ford, General Motors, Microsoft, and others (the list is nearly endless) all earned substantial portions of their revenue outside the United States—some even more than they did inside the United States. This has long been true of some oil companies.

When it comes to creating equity benchmarks for measuring the performance of stocks and groups of stocks, globalization presents a problem. Are Exxon, GM, Ford, Microsoft, Caterpillar, and so forth, U.S. corporations or global corporations? The answer is that they are global corporations, whose headquarters may be in the

---

[1] Gao Shangquan, "Economic Globalization: Trends, Risks and Risk Prevention" (*United Nations*, CDP Background Paper No. 1, 2000), pp. 1–3.

United States, and the sentiments of its executives may be with the U.S. government as people, but they do business all over the world. The term *international index* suggests that the world can be broken into a group of nation states and that corporations reside in one of those nation states. Global corporations clearly present a problem for this paradigm.

One way to view this problem is to think of these corporations conceptually as residing in a fictional country or continent called "Pangaea."[2] Unfortunately, the available data that index providers use are collected and reported in terms of nations. General Motors is incorporated in the United States and has subsidiaries around the world. The stock for General Motors is traded in the United States and other countries as is Toyota and other Pangaea companies, so the country of origin, into which a stock should be placed, becomes murky at best. Each index provider has to deal with this particular problem, and, predictably, they take different approaches.

Another problem that is of primary importance is the problem of free-float. The float adjustments that were discussed in terms of U.S. indexes become doubly important in international and global indexes because the problem is much more acute. *Chaebols* (conglomerates) in Korea and *keiretsus* (loose coalitions of business groups) in Japan are symptomatic of a cross-ownership problem as mentioned earlier only more so. The cross-ownership patterns in these two countries are so complex that only a local analyst who understands the subtleties of business in these countries has a chance of correctly making adjustments. Objective data sources that provide this service are hard to find.

There is also the problem of keeping track of currencies and the effect of currencies on benchmark performance and characteristics. And finally, the convention within the investment community has been to divide countries (and the companies headquartered in those countries) into developed and emerging market categories, which have become increasingly difficult to defend as the global economy matures—witness Mittal Steel.

---

[2] "Pangaea" is a name that scientists gave to a supercontinent in which all Earth's current continents were joined together before plate tectonics moved the continents to their current positions.

There are so many decisions that each family of index providers have to make that we cannot possibly cover all the similarities and differences between these index families. Our approach will review some of the decisions made by the Russell family of indexes in creating their global equity indexes and in the process review the major decision categories that each index family must address. We will point out obvious and important differences as we go along.

MSCI INDEX FAMILY

The oldest and best-known family of international indexes is the Morgan Stanley Capital International (MSCI) indexes. The indexes were initially created by Capital International, a joint U.S. and Swiss venture, which was eventually merged with Morgan Stanley to form MSCI. MSCI recently acquired Barra to create the current organization, MSCI Barra. The methods for constructing the indexes have evolved considerably over time.

The original MSCI indexes were composed of securities selected by a group of analysts in Europe. The choice of securities was driven by a desire to capture the behavior of stocks in different countries. Their original target was to sample securities in a country in such a way as to capture 65 percent of the capitalization of each country (not float adjusted) and to sample each of the major economic categories within the country. Recently MSCI has completely revamped their indexes.

The current set of MSCI International Equity indexes consists of several index families that cover 69 markets. They seek to capture 85 percent of the capitalization in each of the countries in which they have an index. All the indexes are now free float–adjusted market capitalization weighted to deal with the cross-ownership and restricted share problems that have plagued all international indexes.[3] To construct a country index, all listed securities in the market are identified. Securities are classified in accordance with the Global Industry Classification Standard (GICS), and screened

---

[3] The following discussion of MSCI Barra indexes uses information that can be found at the MSCI Barra Web site, www.mscibarra.com/products/indices/equity/definitions.jsp. There are references to more detailed material also listed on this Web site.

by size, liquidity, and minimum free float until 85 percent of the capitalization is obtained. MSCI uses the same policy in both the developed and emerging markets. The indexes are built at a country level and then aggregated into regional and other composites.

The most famous of the MSCI indexes is the EAFE index (Europe, Australasia, and Far East index). For many years this index coupled with any major U.S. index provided a rough global benchmark for equities. The MSCI EAFE Index captures the performance of developed markets, excluding those of the United States and Canada. The index consists of 21 developed market country indexes, which include Australia, Austria, Belgium, Denmark, Finland, France, Germany, Greece, Hong Kong, Ireland, Italy, Japan, the Netherlands, New Zealand, Norway, Portugal, Singapore, Spain, Sweden, Switzerland, and the United Kingdom.

The MSCI ACWI (All Country World Index) is an index that covers equity performance of developed and emerging markets. It consists of 48 country indexes comprising 23 developed and 25 emerging market country indexes. MSCI has a series of Regional Equity indexes.

In Asia, the MSCI AC (All Country) Asia ex Japan Index measures the performance of Asia, excluding Japan. The index consisted of 11 developed and emerging market country indexes for China, Hong Kong, India, Indonesia, Korea, Malaysia, Pakistan, Philippines, Singapore, Taiwan, and Thailand. The MSCI AC (All Country) Far East ex Japan Index is the same but excludes Pakistan and India.

The MSCI AC (All Country) Pacific Index is an index that covers developed and emerging markets in the Pacific region, which is the same as the Far East ex Japan index but adds Australia, Japan, and New Zealand. The MSCI Asia APEX 50 Index contains 50 of the largest and most widely followed stocks from the MSCI AC Asia ex Japan Index. It is a subset of highly liquid securities that is optimized for tradability and serves as the basis for investment products such as exchange traded funds and other passive instruments.

The MSCI BRIC Index is designed to capture the performance of four emerging market countries: Brazil, Russia, India, and China. The MSCI Emerging Markets Index covers the 25 emerging market countries of Argentina, Brazil, Chile, China, Colombia, Czech Republic, Egypt, Hungary, India, Indonesia, Israel, Jordan, Korea, Malaysia,

Mexico, Morocco, Pakistan, Peru, Philippines, Poland, Russia, South Africa, Taiwan, Thailand, and Turkey. The MSCI EM (Emerging Markets) EMEA (Europe, Middle East, and Africa) Index extracts the 10 markets that focus on Europe, the Middle East, and Africa from the MSCI EM index. The MSCI EM (Emerging Markets) Latin America Index measures the performance of six emerging markets in Latin America: Argentina, Brazil, Chile, Colombia, Mexico, and Peru.

In Europe the MSCI Europe Index consists of the EMU (European Economic and Monetary Union) Index, which captures the performance of the 11 EMU countries. It includes Austria, Belgium, Finland, France, Germany, Greece, Ireland, Italy, the Netherlands, Portugal, and Spain plus five additional European countries: Denmark, Norway, Sweden, Switzerland, and the United Kingdom.

The MSCI KOKUSAI Index consists of 22 developed market country indexes, which includes all 16 countries in the Europe Index plus Australia, Canada, Hong Kong, New Zealand, Singapore, and the United States. The MSCI World Index measures all 22 developed markets of the MSCI KOKUSAI plus Japan.

The MSCI Global Standard indexes are divided into large-cap and midcap segments that cover around 85 percent of free float–adjusted market capitalization in each market. The large-cap indexes cover around 70 percent of free float, while the midcap indexes cover the other 30 percent. The MSCI Global Small Cap indexes cover companies that are in the Investable Market Index but not in the Standard Index in each market.

The MSCI Global Value and Growth indexes cover the stocks across all size segmentations. MSCI uses three variables to define a stock's value style weight and five variables to define the growth investment style weight. The methodology divides the constituents of an underlying MSCI equity index into respective value and growth indexes with each segment having 50 percent of the float-adjusted capitalization of the underlying market index.[4]

---

[4] A detailed description of MSCI's index construction methodology "MSCI Global Investable Market Indices Methodology: Index Construction Objectives, Guiding Principles and Methodology for the MSCI Global Investable Market Indices" (June, 2008) can be found at the MSCI Barra Web site, www.mscibarra.com/products/indices/equity/methodology.jsp.

MSCI also has price indexes that measure only the price performance of markets. Dividends are not considered in price indexes, but each index is free float–weighted price returns on a given day. The MSCI Total Return indexes measure the market performance, including both price performance and income from dividend payments. The MSCI Daily Total Return (DTR) Methodology reinvests dividends in the indexes on the day the security is quoted ex-dividend. The MSCI Total Return indexes are calculated with gross dividends and net dividends.

MSCI Barra also offers indexes based on GDP weights, indexes hedged to the various currencies, custom indexes, as well as sector and industry indexes based on the Global Industry Classification Standard (GICS).

MSCI provides a very comprehensive set of country and segment indexes.

DOW JONES GLOBAL INDEXES

The Dow Jones family of indexes has a long history, and this history permeates the approach that they take to building indexes. The set of indexes that most users will use to evaluate portfolios are subsets of the Dow Jones Global Total Stock Market Index.[5]

These indexes are based on a bottom-up aggregation of country-level total market indexes for 61 countries. The criteria for selecting countries are not just capitalization and trading volume but also include country risk using an economic freedom index. There are 28 developed countries and 33 emerging market countries in the indexes as defined by the international monetary fund. The countries are also grouped into regional indexes as well as global and regional subindexes. The stock list is also grouped into 10 industries, 18 supersectors, 39 sectors, and 104 subsectors using the ICB (Industry Classification Benchmark) [the sector classification system jointly owned by Dow Jones and the Financial Times and Stock Exchange of London (FTSE)].

The index construction procedures have methods for assigning stocks to the appropriate market universes and this can

---

[5] See the Dow Jones Web site, www.djindexes.com, for more information about the Dow Jones Global Total Stock Market Indexes.

be complicated. Investable universes of stocks in the global indexes must pass through screens for share class and liquidity. The object of the screens is to prevent thinly traded or inaccessible securities from being included in the indexes. The stocks included are all securities that have the characteristics of common equities and must be accessible to nonresidents. They exclude securities such as convertible notes, mutual funds, unit trusts, closed-end mutual funds, warrants, as well as limited partnerships. The one exception of course is real estate investment trusts (REITs).

The liquidity screen is used to identify a universe of securities that is tradable. To qualify, a stock must have had no more than 10 nontrading days during the past quarter. As mentioned, stock capitalization is float weighted. The indexes include 98 percent of the underlying free float in developed countries (excluding Europe). At the regional level, which includes Europe, they seek 95 percent of the capitalization within the region regardless of country. The breakpoints for the large-cap and mid/small-cap stocks are at the 85th percentile of market capitalization. Midcap stocks lie between the 80th percentile and the 90th percentile and overlap the large and small indexes.

The Dow Jones global indexes undergo a quarterly review process. The universe is reranked by free-float market capitalization and the size categories are established as outlined earlier. Bands are established at each of the capitalization breakpoints to control turnover at the quarterly reconstitutions. They do not move a stock unless its rank changes substantially.

One issue with the indexes centers around the coverage of the investment opportunities set. While they cover 98 percent of the capitalization in developed countries and 95 percent of the capitalization within regions, there is a substantial portion of the capitalization in countries that they do not cover.

S&P/CITIGROUP GLOBAL INDEXES

The S&P/Citigroup Global Equity indexes were created in 1989, when Salomon Brothers teamed up with Russell to create the Salomon-Russell Broad Market Index (BMI) and its large- and small-cap components, the Primary Market Index (PMI) and the Extended Market Index (EMI). From inception, the indexes have been rules-based, float-adjusted, capitalization-weighted measures of the global equity market. Salomon Brothers assumed sole ownership of the indexes in 1994, which became known as the Salomon Brothers World Equity indexes. After the merger in 1997 of Salomon Brothers with Travelers Group, which owned Smith Barney, the indexes were renamed the Salomon Smith Barney Global Equity indexes. Following the creation of Citigroup from the merger of Citicorp and Travelers Group in 1998, the indexes were renamed the Citigroup Global Equity indexes in 2003. S&P assumed operational responsibility, and the indexes were renamed the S&P/Citigroup Global Index series in 2004.[6]

S&P began to move into the global index arena in 1997 with the launch of the S&P Global 1200 Index, which combined the S&P 500 and six other country and regional subindexes. S&P had partnered with the Australian stock exchange, the ASX, and the Toronto Stock exchange, the TSE, to include their headline indexes in the S&P Global 1200. Prior to that time, both the Toronto Stock Exchange and the Australian Stock Exchange had teamed with Russell to create families of growth and value style indexes based on Russell's nonlinear style weighting methodology. After the creation of the S&P Global 1200, these indexes were discontinued and replaced with style indexes based upon the breakpoint methodology of the S&P/Barra Style indexes. The S&P/Barra Style indexes were replaced by the S&P/Citigroup Style indexes in 2005.[7]

The S&P/Citigroup Broad Market Index (BMI) is decomposed into two segments. The first segment is the large-cap component

---

[6] "History of the S&P/Citigroup Global Equity Index System," *S&P Citigroup Global Equity Indices: Index Methodology* (New York: Standard & Poor's, August 2006), p. 45. See the S&P Web site, www.standardandpoors.com/indices, for more information about S&P indices.

[7] "A Chronology of Standard & Poor's Global Indices," *S&P Global 1200: Index Methodology* (New York: Standard & Poor's, June 2007), p. 19. The S&P/Barra style index methodology was similar to Russell's original method, described in Chapter 25, using the cap-weighted median book-to-price ratio. Bill Sharpe, who had collaborated in 1987 with Russell on asset allocation in a venture called Sharpe-Russell Research, Inc., worked with Barra on its style indexes.

known as the Primary Market Index (PMI) and the second component is the Extended Market Index (EMI), which covers the smaller cap segment of the stock universe.

The S&P/Citigroup Global indexes include all companies with a capitalization greater than $100 million. A country and all its securities are eligible for inclusion in the S&P/Citigroup Global indexes if the available float capital within a country exceeds one billion U.S. dollars for the index-eligible companies. Buffer rules are used to prevent a country from being dropped from the index until the capitalization falls below $750 million U.S. These country buffer rules have proved unnecessary to date since no country has been dropped from the index.

The indexes are fully float weighted as accurately as possible. This means that the family of indexes covers nearly all securities that institutional investors would consider in both the developed and emerging markets areas. There is no sampling like there is in the MSCI family indexes. The free-float adjustment to capitalization ensures that a stock weight reflects what is truly purchasable. Free-float weighting helps avoid liquidity problems because index investors are not required to try to purchase a weight in a security for which there are no shares available. The float-weighting adjustments are similar to other float-weighting adjustments. Capitalization is adjusted for corporate cross holdings, for large private blocks of securities, holdings by government agencies, and shares that are legally restricted by government regulation or locked up as in IPOs.

The number of securities in the master list is over 9,000, and these companies are found in over 49 countries. Subindexes have been created for style indexes and capitalization substyles. The indexes have been maintained "as is" since 1989 and hence avoid survivorship bias in the holdings.

The distinction between developed markets and emerging markets is based on the purchasing power parity of the gross domestic product of the country. If the per capita GDP exceeds $10,000, it is considered a developed markets country. Again, there is a buffer rule so that only when the country's gross domestic product per capita falls below $7,500 is it removed from the developed country list. Emerging markets are those countries whose GDP per capita falls below $10,000. Of course, there are always difficulties with such rules. For example, Taiwan and Israel, while exceeding the per capita GDP threshold, are not considered developed markets because of the legal limitations imposed on nondomiciled investors.

The broad universe of securities in the BMI is split into the PMI and the EMI within each country by first ranking all the companies within a country by total capitalization. The capitalization rank is preserved. Then within each country, the available capitalization is cumulated to find the breakpoint of 80 percent. This method ensures that large-capitalization companies even if they have small float are included in the PMI. Any stock above the 80 percent breakpoint is placed in the PMI, and any stock falling in the bottom 20 percent is placed in the EMI. Of course, this means that the capitalization breakpoint between large-cap and small-cap securities changes from one country to the next so that near the breakpoint what is a large-cap company in one country is a small-cap company in another country. Problems can emerge when there is more than one stock class issued by a company. It is possible that one of the share classes might not have enough capitalization to be in the PMI when all the other classes of shares are.

FTSE INDEX FAMILY

The Financial Times and Stock Exchange of London (FTSE) created a series of indexes to track the UK equity market beginning with the FTSE All Shares Index back in the 1960s. FTSE expanded their index family to the All World Index series in 1987. It was only natural that they would seek a U.S. partner to expand coverage even further. In the 1990s they teamed up with the NASDAQ stock exchange, which published the NASDAQ-100 and the NASDAQ broad market index. The FTSE All World Index and the FT/S&P Actuaries World Indexes were folded into the FTSE Global Equity Index series.[8]

In the United States they created the FTSE NASDAQ 500 Index, which behaves like the NASDAQ 100 but is more widely diversified and more liquid, making it easier to trade stocks in the composite.

FTSE publishes thousands of indexes covering every group of assets imaginable. Their global equity indexes began with the FTSE All World Index series. This index series is meant to cover

---

[8] See the FTSE Web site, www.ftse.com, for more information about FTSE indices.

large- and midcapitalization securities and contains 2,700 stocks from the FTSE Global Equity Index series. As mentioned, the All World Index is a subset of the FTSE Global Equity Index series. This index has over 8,000 securities and 48 different countries and captures 98 percent of the world's investable market capitalization. It covers every equity sector and is divided into three basic groups of stocks from developed countries, stocks with advanced emerging countries, and stocks from the secondary and emerging countries. Indexes are calculated at the national and regional levels as well as the global level.

The total set of securities is divided into capitalization groups, some of which are grouped as in the old World Index, which covers large- and midcap securities, or the Global Index, which covers large-cap, midcap, and small-cap. However, they also provide single size indexes for large-cap, midcap, and small-cap. The index constituents are also grouped into regional and country indexes.

The global index master list construction process begins by rank ordering all companies that are traded on a global basis, and they retain stocks until they have acquired 98 percent of the capitalization. They drop any stocks that have less than $100 million in gross capitalization. Next they apply liquidity tests. Like most indexes the FTSE group of indexes have liquidity rules that they claim provide investors with a better representation of the true investability of global companies. The liquidity rule is more restrictive than other indexes because it requires that for a stock to enter the index, 0.05 percent of its free float must be traded in 10 out of the last 12 months and to remain in the index 0.04 percent of its free float must trade in 8 out of 12 months. The resulting list becomes the investable index, and each of the shares is free-float weighted. The free-float adjustments include cross-ownership, large blocks of securities that are never traded (like family holdings), restricted employee ownership, government ownership, foreign company or government ownerships, and restricted shares due to lock-in clauses.

For stocks to be eligible to be included they must be investable for nonnationals, and the data for them must be timely and available. And there should be no significant controls that would prevent the repatriation of dividends or capital. FTSE also includes unusual criteria, such as there must exist a demonstration of significant international investor interest. When FTSE classifies a country as developed, advanced emerging, or secondary emerging, they use a variety of factors such as the free flow of foreign exchange, gross domestic product per capita, the number of stocks available in the market, the number of industrial sectors in the market, and the ratio of stock market capitalization to gross domestic product. FTSE also includes subjective requirements such as an efficient settlement system, market maturity, and membership in an economic group or currency bloc. New countries are added to the index by the FTSE regional committees.

FTSE has procedures for determining a nationality of companies. They also have procedures for handling capitalization changes such as mergers and acquisitions.

The FTSE divides stocks into large-cap, midcap, and small-cap groups with about 72 percent in the large-cap group, 20 percent in the midcap group, and 10 percent in the small-cap group. However, the banding rules that they use for reducing turnover make it unclear exactly what percentage of the capitalization falls in each size class classification.

RUSSELL/NOMURA INDEXES

To underscore the complex issues when creating equity indexes outside the United States, we will delve into the Russell/Nomura indexes for the Japanese markets. The Russell/Nomura indexes were built using the same principles as were used in the Russell U.S. equity indexes but were adapted in several unique ways to reflect the complexity of the Japanese equity market.[9]

---

[9] The following discussion flows from the two papers that describe how the Russell/Nomura indexes were created: Jon A. Christopherson, Yasuyuki Kato, and Jeffrey A. Hansen, "Russell/NRI Japan Equity Style Indexes: Tools for Performance Evaluation and Plan Management," *Russell Research Commentary* (Tacoma, WA: Russell Investments, September 1996) and Jon A. Christopherson, Yasuyuki Kato, and Jeffrey A. Hansen, "Russell/NRI Japan Equity Style Indexes: Rulebook for Index Construction," *Russell Research Commentary* (Tacoma, WA: Russell Investments, April 1996). The current Russell/Nomura Index methodology paper can be found at the Nomura Web site, http://qr.nomura.co.jp/en/frcnri.

The Russell/Nomura Total Market Index represents approximately 98 percent of the investable Japan equity market. The indexes were the first float-adjusted indexes for the Japanese market. In 1996, this portfolio of securities comprised approximately 1,700 of the largest Japanese securities based on total available market capitalization. Over historical periods, the number of stocks included varies. All other indexes are subsets of this universe of stocks.

The Russell/Nomura Large Cap Index is designed to represent approximately 85 percent of the total market capitalization of the Russell/Nomura Total Market Index (rounded to the nearest 100th stock). This index is designed to measure performance of large companies and currently consists of the largest 350 securities in the Russell/Nomura Total Market Index. The "Top Cap" and Mid Cap Indexes are subsets of this index. The Russell/Nomura Top Cap Index represents approximately 50 percent of the Russell/Nomura Total Market Index. The Top Cap Index consists of the 60 largest securities in the Russell/Nomura Total Market Index as ranked by total market capitalization.

The Russell/Nomura Mid Cap Index consists of approximately the middle 35 percent of the Russell/Nomura Total Market Index remaining after excluding the Top Cap and Small Cap Indexes. The Mid Cap Index contains approximately 290 securities.

The Russell/Nomura Small Cap Index is designed to represent approximately 15 percent of the total market capitalization of the Russell/Nomura Total Market Index. This index is intended to measure the performance of small companies and currently consists of approximately 1,300 of the smallest securities in the Russell/Nomura Total Market Index.

The stocks in the Total Market Index are rank ordered by their adjusted capitalization within the index. The breakpoints for the cap tiers change over time as the number of stocks in the Japanese market changes. The indexes target capturing 98 percent of the total market, 50 percent in the Top Cap, 35 percent in the Mid Cap indexes, and 15 percent in the Small Cap indexes.

There are a number of peculiarities within the Japanese market that require attention. We will explore some of these issues to underscore the difficulties underlying the building of global indexes generally and style indexes in Japan. Similar complications arise around the world when trying to build accurate equity indexes.

Stock Index Membership Issues

- *"Seiri" Post Stocks, and "Kanri" Post Stocks:* Stocks that are close to bankruptcy, in bankruptcy, or in serious financial difficulty are moved to the Seiri and Kanri Post on the floor of the Japanese Stock Exchanges. Investors treat these stocks differently, and valuations, and so forth, are problematic. Such stocks trade differently than the rest of the stock market and hence are excluded from the index.

- *Non-Japan Domiciled Companies Trading on the Exchange:* Stocks traded on the different exchanges in Japan but domiciled in other countries (such as, Royal Dutch Petroleum, Schlumberger Ltd., Seagrams Co. Ltd., and Unilever N.V.) are also excluded from the indexes. The behavior of foreign stocks is heavily influenced by factors outside Japan. Hence, including such stocks would cloud the picture on the performance of the Japanese stock market.

- *Other Exclusions:* Preferred stock, convertible preferred stock, participating preferred stock, paired shares, warrants, and rights are also excluded. The Bank of Japan is also excluded.

Float-Adjusted Capitalization: Cross-Ownership Adjustments

- *Nonbank Companies:* Two sources of information on cross-ownership are used: (1) Toyo Keizai listing of large shareholders (usually the largest 10), and (2) Equity Index Group of Nomura Securities analysis of company annual reports. All nonbank stocks are adjusted for the sum of cross-held shares.

- *Banks:* A further adjustment is calculated for banks. Equity Index Group of Nomura Securities estimates the total number of corporate shareholders from interviews with selected banks to determine if the two sources listed earlier adequately represent the total stable shareholders. If this is inadequate, then Group 3 is added, which consists of the average number of shares held in the second source (Equity Index Group) times the estimated number of shareholders not listed in securities filings. The complexity and intense analysis by Nomura make these indexes unique and more accurate, in terms of float, than any other Japanese indexes.

Adjusting Book Value

Correct book value is critical for the price/book ratio (PBR) valuation measure because the PBR is used to determine the weightings of stocks in the growth and value indexes. The Russell/Nomura indexes are adjusted for two classes of assets—real estate and securities. These asset classes are typically not valued on the books at their current market prices; hence, they are underpriced.

The adjustments to PBR are not equally proportional for all industries, and some industries will move on the value/growth dimension because of the adjustment.[10] The general formula for adjusting a stock's PBR is[11]

$$\text{Adj. PBR} = \frac{\text{price} \times \text{outstanding shares}}{\underset{\substack{\text{equity} \\ \text{(BV)}}}{\text{shareholder's}} + \underset{\substack{\text{securities} \\ \text{(MV} - \text{BV)}}}{\text{marketable}} + \underset{\substack{\text{pension} \\ \text{liabilities}}}{\text{unrecognized}}},$$

where

BV = shareholder's equity

MV − BV = marketable securities change in value

UPL = unrecognized pension liabilities.

- *Real Estate Holdings:* The specifics for adjusting real estate and held securities were a major problem when the family of indexes was first created, but they are less so today since real estate assets have been marked to market for corporations since 2000. Prior to 2003, the adjustments for real estate were quite complex.[12]
- *Holdings of Securities:* Nomura estimates that the hidden assets of all TOPIX companies are about 56 trillion yen, or about 17 percent of the aggregated book value of all TOPIX securities. The book value of stocks is adjusted to reflect these assets. These hidden assets are disclosed each year (since 1991) by all listed companies and Nomura has this

---

[10] The Air Transport industry still remained high even after adjustment, but that is due to the franchise nature of the companies in this sector.

[11] Shares are not adjusted for stable holdings for this calculation.

[12] See Christopherson, et al., "Russell/NRI Japan Equity Style Indexes: Rulebook for Index Construction."

information in a database. For data before 1991, the hidden assets are estimated based on the historical price movements of TOPIX and each company's historical reported book value.

The foregoing demonstrates some of the difficulties in building style indexes in Japan to underscore the complications that arise around the world, not just Japan, when trying to build accurate equity indexes.

Particular attention was paid to the cross-ownership, complex ownership, and partnership structures unique to different markets. Float-adjusted capitalization-weighted indexes along with growth/value indexes require adjustments to the underlying stock characteristics in most cases. The adjustments and rules discussed earlier are very complex, and we have only scratched the surface.

RUSSELL GLOBAL INDEXES

The Russell Global Indexes are a family of global equity indexes that represent the institutionally investable equity market.[13] They are rules based and comprehensive. The Russell Global Indexes include 98 percent of the global equity market cap, with approximately 10,000 securities in 63 countries and 22 regions, and incorporate turnover management rules to balance transaction costs and market representation. As of May 2008 the Russell Global Indexes represented approximately $48.2 trillion unadjusted and $21.4 trillion float-adjusted market value. What makes the Russell indexes unique is a single global stock list that is independent of country membership and provides the basis of all subindexes.

The Russell Global Index family includes the Russell 3000 as its U.S. component and incorporates the main features of the Russell U.S. indexes, such as float-adjusted market cap weighting. Russell's company-based approach allows for quicker inclusion of new stocks as they emerge as part of the institutional opportunity set.

The Russell Global master list can be divided into myriad subcomponents by region, country, developed/emerging markets, capitalization size, sector, and industry to provide modular benchmarks

---

[13] The following discussion is based on the current construction methods paper *Russell Global Indexes Construction and Methodology*. Some portions are verbatim extractions from the paper. The paper can be found at the Russell Investments Web site, www.russell.com/indexes.

representing different opportunity sets within the Russell Global whole. All Russell Indexes are subsets of the Russell Global Index.

The following overview is a summary of the construction rules. For the complete rules, see the Russell Investments Web site, www.russell.com/indexes.

Defining the Total Stock Universe

The Russell Global Index is fundamentally constructed from a company-level perspective. Every publicly traded company around the world that meets minimum size and investability standards is included in the stock universe.

- *Total Universe Security Type:* Equity and equity-like securities are included in the Russell global equity universe, with some country-specific nuances. Equity-like securities are those that represent ownership of a company without an obligation for the company to repay invested capital in the form of coupon payments or lump-sum payments throughout the life of the investment.
- *Excluded Securities:* Certain security types are excluded from the total stock universe, such as warrants and rights, trust receipts and royalty trusts, depository receipts (with some exceptions), limited liability companies, bulletin board and pink-sheet stocks (some global exceptions occur), closed-end investment companies, limited partnerships, exchange traded funds (ETFs), and mutual funds.
- *Universe Minimum Size Requirement:* The minimum total market capitalization requirement for inclusion in the Russell stock universe is $1,000,000 USD. Total market capitalization is determined by multiplying total outstanding shares by the market price as of the last trading day in May.
- *Universe Country Eligibility:* Some countries with sizable stocks do not provide a stable environment for institutional investment and thus are not included in the Russell global indexes universe. Russell assesses the adequacy of investability conditions in a country based on a group of factors and references. These factors include the country's political stability, capital market policies, corporate

governance, competitiveness, de facto operating conditions, and trends in transaction volume and liquidity. Russell's primary sources for country risk ratings are the Economist Intelligence Unit (EIU) and the Organization for Economic Co-Operation and Development (OECD).

- *Universe Liquidity Screen:* Russell removes securities with inadequate liquidity by evaluating the average daily dollar trading volume (ADDTV) and the active trading ratio (ATR). ADDTV smoothes the abnormal trading volumes over short time periods and measures the actual transactions taking place in the market. ATR evaluation provides further refinement, due to the possibility that a few transactions across the year could distort the ADDTV for individual stocks. This two-step liquidity screen provides the most accurate representation of the market and its liquidity.

- *Capturing 98 Percent of the Eligible Universe:* Next Russell assigns stocks to individual countries according to a process described in the section that follows. The Russell Global Index is composed of the Russell 3000, which captures 98 percent of the U.S. equity universe, and the largest 98 percent of the remaining country equity universe.

Assigning Securities to Countries

As we mentioned earlier in our discussion of Pangaea stocks, country assignment is important and problematical. In most cases, country assignment is straightforward, but some differences and complexities in the global equity environment warrant specific attention and rules.

- *Home-Country Indicators:* For each security in the index, Russell utilizes three home country indicators (HCI) to determine index membership: (1) country of incorporation, (2) country of company's primary headquarters, and (3) country of company's primary stock exchange. If all the HCIs are consistent, a company is assigned to the country index in which it is incorporated. However, if there is divergence in the HCIs, Russell analyzes the three HCIs to determine appropriate country assignment. In this analysis country of incorporation is given greater importance.

- *Benefits-Driven Incorporations:* A group of countries/ regions offer benefits to incorporation—specifically, operations, tax, political, or other benefits. Russell identifies them as benefit-driven incorporation (BDI) countries/regions. These BDI countries/regions typically are not associated with active stock exchanges or direct strategic investment for asset allocation purposes. Companies choosing to incorporate in BDI regions are equity securities from other regions, such as the United States and China, that have elected to seek the tax and jurisdiction advantages available outside their domiciles. Russell evaluates all companies incorporated in BDI regions and will assign a company to a non-BDI country if the company meets one of the following criteria: (1) the headquarters is in a non-BDI region/country, or (2) the headquarters is in a BDI-designated region/country, and the primary exchange for the local shares is in a non-BDI country. In this case the primary exchange would be determined by the average daily dollar trading volume (ADDTV).
- *More Complex Countries/Regions:* Other rules apply to certain markets with unique characteristics such as China, Hong Kong, Macao, Russia, the Philippines, and Thailand, and to countries that lack domestic stock exchanges.

Russell Global Index Membership

Once the total universe has been screened, and securities have been allocated to their home countries, Russell determines cap tier and style index membership. Russell includes the top 98 percent of U.S. market capitalization, the Russell 3000, and the top 98 percent of the rest of the world's market capitalization. This index design preserves global equity market integrity and effectively relieves the overrepresentation of U.S. securities from the global perspective. Additionally, this design ensures consistency between the Russell Global Index and its U.S. subindexes as components.

Global Large- and Small-Cap Index
Construction Research Summary

The need for cap-size indexes is based on a well-documented phenomenon known as "the cap-size effect." Russell addressed this effect in the United States when it created the Russell 2000, and the effect has been observed in global markets as well. Much research has been focused on determining an appropriate dividing point between large and small stocks, but Russell's research has demonstrated that the division between large and small stocks should be established as a range or "band" around which representative large- and small-cap indexes can be created.

In addition, Russell research has found that the cap-size effect exists across regional boundaries; that is, *companies of similar size tend to behave similarly regardless of geographical location.* While this relationship is not equally strong in all regions (particularly in emerging markets), it does appear to be increasing as markets continue to globalize.[14]

As a result of this research, Russell implemented a *global-relative methodology with banding* when constructing the Global Large, Mid, and Small Cap indexes beginning with the June 2007 reconstitution. This approach differs fundamentally from the current industry practice of determining cap-size on a country-by-country basis, where companies with very different market capitalizations may be classified in the same cap-size index, or, alternatively, where companies with similar market capitalizations may be classified in different cap-size indexes simply because they are in different counties or regions. Cap-size indexes constructed by use of country-relative distinctions (whether banded or not) can generate substantial overlap when combined into broader indexes, and this reduces an index's usefulness in accurately representing what it was intended to measure.

Construction Rules of Size Indexes

At reconstitution, all companies in the Global Index (ex-U.S.) master list are ranked by their total market capitalization in descending

---

[14] Barry Feldman and Kelly Haughton, "Indexes Brief: Defining Global Small Cap," (Tacoma, WA: Russell Investments, May 2008).

order and the cumulative total market capitalization percentile for each company is calculated.

To determine the Global Large Cap and Global Small Cap indexes, all companies that rank below the 90th percentile are classified as small cap, and all companies that rank above the 85th percentile are classified as large cap. Companies that rank within the capitalization band between the 85th and 90th percentile and that are members of the current index retain their existing classification; that is, if a member of the existing Global Small Cap Index is within the 85th to 90th percentile band at reconstitution, it will remain classified as small cap. New companies being added to the Global Index are classified relative to the midpoint of the range; that is, new companies ranking above the 87.5th percentile are classified as large cap, and new companies ranking below the 87.5th percentile are classified as small cap.

To determine the Global Mid Cap index, which is a subcomponent of the Global Large Cap, all companies that rank below the 60th percentile are classified as mid cap, and all companies that rank above the 55th percentile are classified as megacap. Companies that rank within the capitalization band between the 55th and 60th percentile and are members of the current index will retain their existing classification. New companies being added to the Global Index are classified relative to the 57.5 percentile.

The use of a global-relative 5 percent band has been shown to create portfolios that are robust representations of large and small stock behavior and consistently provide better tracking results when tested against global and non-U.S. cap-tier mandated managers. Use of the banding approach also has the associated benefit of dramatically reducing turnover at reconstitution. Russell research shows that a 5 percent band provides an optimal balance between representing asset class return behavior and reducing turnover, which ultimately benefits investors using the indexes as passive vehicles or active portfolio benchmarks.

Table 28.1 displays these index capitalization tier membership rules.

Regional and Country Cap-Size Indexes

After every security in the Global Index has been assigned a cap-size classification, all other regional and country cap-size indexes use these classifications in their construction. As a result, any

T A B L E 28.1

Index Capitalization Tier Membership Rules

Index Name	Upper Range (percentiles)	Lower Range (percentiles)
Russell Global Mega Cap	NA	55%–60%
Russell Global Mid Cap	55%–60%	85%–90%
Russell Global Small Cap	85%–90%	NA

Note: Percentiles are based on descending total market capitalization. Large Cap = Mega Cap + Mid Cap.

combination of regional or country indexes across cap-size portfolios is based on a consistent methodology.

Emerging and Developed Market Indexes

Russell uses a combination of macroeconomic and investment market criteria to distinguish developed from emerging markets. Additionally, Russell Global indexes use a transparent methodology for recognizing countries that have become developed or that, conversely, have taken steps to be less accessible to investors.

Float Adjustments

Once index membership has been determined using total market capitalization, each security's shares are adjusted to include only those shares available for public investment—shares called "free float." The following types of shares are removed:

- Material employee stock ownership plans
- Large private holders
- Government and state-owned-enterprise (SOE) shares
- Corporate cross-owned shares
- IPO lock-ups
- American Depository Receipts (ADR) and Global Depository Receipts (GDR), with certain exceptions
- Treasury shares
- Minimum available shares—large-cap companies with 1 percent or less float and small-cap companies with 5 percent or less float are removed

Foreign equity ownership limits are common, especially in emerging markets. These ownership limits are imposed either by local governments or by regulation bureaus for political and economic reasons. Foreign investment is often restricted in business sectors considered to be sensitive by a country, such as automobiles or telecommunications. However, some of these heavily regulated sectors present substantial investment opportunities. Russell adjusts securities with foreign ownership limits (FOLs) and removes them from index weights.

Adjustments are made for restricted and unrestricted share classes, such as in Thailand, for foreign ownership limits by industry or sector, and for markets segregated via share classes as in China, where only three share classes can be owned by foreign investors with limited or no voting rights.

Sectors

The Russell Global Index is available in a variety of sector classification systems, including Global Industry Classification Standard (GICS) sectors and Russell Global industry sectors. Russell has been classifying companies into industries and sectors since the late 1970s. Russell's system has evolved over the years, and today Global Russell sectors encompass nine economic sectors and 160+ industries. Russell classifies a company into one of the economic sector categories based on its primary economic orientation. Multiple resources are used, including SEC filings, company Web pages, and stock exchanges, to obtain overall information about each company and its primary economic orientation. Many firms have multiple lines of business classified within different sectors. In such cases, the Russell industry classification is determined by the business with the highest revenue.

Index Maintenance

Russell applies corporate actions to the Russell Global Index on a daily basis to both reflect the evolution of securities and continue to be highly representative of the global equity market. In general, changes to the Russell Global Index are made when an action is final. The methods used are generally the same ones used for the

U.S. equity indexes where appropriate.[15] Initial public offerings (IPOs) are added each quarter in order to quickly reflect new additions to the global investment opportunity set. The Russell Global Index is reconstituted annually in June, based on market values and characteristics as of the last trading day in May.

CONCLUSION

As the reader can see, there are several competent providers of equity indexes for the global equity markets. Over time there has been a convergence of methods in two dimensions. Most of the indexes are now float weight adjusted to remove capitalization that cannot be purchased by the international or global investor. Secondly, the number of stocks and capitalization covered by the indexes has expanded and is quickly approaching 100 percent coverage, although 98 percent seems to be the current limitation on coverage.

As the methods converge, the performance of the indexes will also converge. However, there is still a divergence on how the indexes divide up the global investment pie into sections. Most index providers take a country-by-country approach and divide the countries in slightly different ways. Russell has recently taken a more global approach, and time will tell whether that proves to be more effective in measuring performance.

---

[15] There are many aspects of corporate actions that have specific procedures for handling that are beyond the scope of this book and the reader is referred to the Russell Global index methodology paper available at the Russell Investments Web site, www.russell.com/indexes.

CHAPTER 29

Fixed-Income Benchmarks

There are many fixed-income indexes offered by many vendors. There are so many, that we cannot do justice to all of them. We choose those index families that we think are most used by investors. We begin with a general discussion of the problems facing fixed-income benchmarks.

FIXED-INCOME BENCHMARK CONSTRUCTION DIFFICULTIES

Fixed-income benchmarks are a difficult topic because the assets in this class, apart from having a fixed payment schedule, differ on a wide variety of other characteristics.

Fixed-income assets are created and redeemed as they mature, which sets them apart from stocks. Some instruments such as U.S. Treasury securities are created and redeemed on fixed, predictable schedules, but commercial paper and municipal bonds, which also have fixed maturities, may be offered as needed. This means that the universe of assets from which to create indexes changes frequently. The number of individual fixed-income securities vastly exceeds the number of equity securities. Many of the bonds included in broad indexes trade infrequently.

The fixed-income market is very much a dealer market in which dealers buy and sell from their own inventory. As a consequence, the finite liquidity of bonds can make trading them quickly difficult. This tends to make price pressure effects substantial in the behavior of the bonds. This also means that for a variety of reasons obtaining timely prices is also fraught with difficulties.

All of this makes it difficult for bond traders to replicate any bond benchmark as well as they would like. There is a problem with the availability of bonds, so the bond indexes are not investable in the same way equity indexes usually are. When bond funds track their indexes well, they tend to be very large funds because there are a large number of bonds in most benchmarks. Also because it is a dealer market, large funds do better with large orders and get better prices on the trades. This is exactly the opposite of what is observed in the equity markets where large orders tend to be more expensive trades. It is also the reason why most bond index funds operate by statistical sampling and risk factor replication rather than by full replication.

Fixed-income assets have carefully specified cash flows and other properties that make them easy to distinguish into groupings. However, the number of observations in each group can become very small. A list of the different types of fixed-income assets in the United States is long. There are government-issued securities and government-backed securities. Treasury assets are backed by the full faith and credit of the U.S. government, but other assets sponsored by the government are not, though it is unlikely the U.S. government will allow them to default. Added to the government-backed securities is a variety of notes, bonds, and paper offered by corporate entities. There are also a large number of fixed-income instruments offered by states and municipalities. All these different fixed-income instruments specify the coupon payment, the currency in which the bond pays interest and principal, the priority of claims to be satisfied if the issuer defaults, and the terms and conditions for payment of the fixed income. Often various covenants and restrictions appear in the indenture agreement associated with the security.

Corporate bonds offered by corporations such as General Motors and Ford are rated as to their "quality," which is an indirect way of forecasting their probability of default. There are different companies or rating agencies that evaluate these bonds. The primary rating agencies are S&P (Standard and Poor's), Moody's, and Fitch. Each of these agencies has its own rating system. It is generally the case that the lower the quality of the bond, the higher the interest rates it must pay to attract investors. Corporations also offer what is known as "commercial paper," or short-term obligations of less than one-year duration.

As we mentioned in Chapter 11 on fixed-income risk measurement, each bond has certain characteristics that make it more or less attractive to investors with different sensitivities to changes in interest rates and investment horizons. Each bond can be evaluated in terms of these risk characteristics. The combination of issuing agency, terms of repayment, and other characteristics relating to the nature of the issuing agency plus the risk characteristics of each bond lead to a fairly long list of characteristics that can be used to classify bonds. Any grouping can be used to justify a particular bond index. There are simply too many of these possible classification systems to choose any one of them over the rest.

Building an index for any particular group of fixed-income securities raises additional index construction issues that must be dealt with. In equity indexes the value or weight assigned to each security return matters a great deal in the performance of the index. We have devoted an entire chapter, Chapter 22, to justifying capitalization and free-float weighting of indexes. With fixed-income securities this becomes a problem because companies who choose to finance operations through floating debt instruments may or may not be the highest-quality companies, but because they have floated a lot of debt, their debt receives a large weight in the index. The more debt they float, ceterus paribus, the higher the interest they must pay and the more sensitive any index that includes them becomes to interest rate changes. Hence, the financial behavior of these companies causes volatility in the behavior of the index. This is sometimes referred to as the "bums problem."

Another problem with fixed-income benchmarks is the "duration problem," which reflects the proportion of bonds in each term category (short, intermediate, or long term). The proportion of bonds in each of these categories depends upon the duration preferences of the issuers who in turn are seeking to minimize the cost of capital, not to build benchmarks. Investors who use benchmarks are seeking to maximize their returns. There is an inherent conflict of objectives between the issuers of fixed-income instruments and the purchasers of fixed-income instruments that does not exist in the equity markets. The preferences of the purchasers do not match the preferences of the issuers, and it is the preferences of the issuers that are reflected in the benchmark.

In equilibrium, the prices of fixed-income instruments must adjust until supply equals what investors want to hold. Investors such as pension plans have long-term liabilities and tend to view long-term government bonds as low-risk investments, particularly if they can match the duration of the bonds to their liabilities. Long bonds have higher durations and are more sensitive to interest rate changes; hence, their prices tend to be more volatile. Volatility is not something that individual endowments and foundations care for, and hence they view these government bonds as risky investments. These bonds are less attractive than other issuers' bonds even at the same yields.

As we saw in Chapter 11, duration is a factor exposure analogous to beta in the equity markets—it is an exposure to interest rates or the interest rate factor. Since the duration of a bond index is a weighted sum of the duration of each of its components, the investor has a clear idea of how sensitive the portfolio is to interest rate changes. Duration as a factor of investing does not provide much of the risk premium. Leading fixed-income index funds with different durations have Sharpe ratios that are roughly the same.[1]

Corporate takeovers and other acquisitions are often funded by the issuance of fixed-income instruments. This has led to growth in the size of the credit or corporate bond market while at the same time lowering the quality of these bonds and making them riskier. The composition of the Barclays Capital Aggregate Index is more risky today than it has been historically. Mortgage-backed securities and asset-backed securities have tended to displace corporate bonds. The end of the Clinton administration showed a budget surplus, and as the U.S. government reduced the size of Treasury debt, it retired a substantial portion of long-term government bonds. This has caused corporate debt to have a larger share of the Barclays Capital Aggregate. In the future, of course, this may change.

Let us now review some of the major families of fixed-income benchmarks. This survey is by no means exhaustive. As you will

---

[1] Laurence B. Siegel, *Benchmarks and Investment Management* (Charlottesville, VA: The Research Foundation of AIMR, 2005), p. 91. See www.cfapubs.org/toc/rf/2003/2003/1.

see, there is considerable variability in how the universe of securities is categorized, and given the complexity outlined here there is little wonder why. There is no one obviously correct method for grouping the data.

BARCLAYS CAPITAL FAMILY OF GLOBAL FIXED-INCOME INDEXES[2]

The best-known general index family is the family of global fixed-income indexes created by Lehman Brothers, which was rebranded as Barclays Capital indexes in November 2008. Their database of fixed-income securities has over 70,000 assets, which have a market value of about $32 trillion. Fixed income is an important part of the investable universe. By comparison, Russell's global equity master list has only about 10,000 equity securities, so the sheer number of securities in fixed-income markets vastly complicates index construction and management. Barclays Capital's global database covers all kinds of fixed-income securities including treasuries and sovereigns as well as government agency assets, corporate, asset-backed, mortgage-backed, commercial mortgages, CDs, emerging market debt, and U.S. municipal bonds. They also cover interest rate swaps, inflation swaps, and commodity-backed securities.

The best-known single Barclays Capital index is the Barclays Capital U.S. Aggregate Bond Index, which is composed of a wide range of government bonds, corporate bonds, mortgage-backed securities, and asset-backed securities. The return on this index is a total return, which includes price appreciation as well as income as a percentage of the beginning period market value.

The aggregate index encompasses three major subindexes, the Barclays Capital Government/Credit Bond Index, Barclays Capital Mortgage-Backed Securities Index, and Barclays Capital Asset-Backed Securities Index. All the bonds in the Government/Credit Bond Index are investment grade. The U.S. Aggregate Index is a subcomponent of the U.S. Universal Index.

To be in the index the bond must be U.S. dollar denominated and rated Baa3 by Moody. If they're not covered by Moody, then

---

[2] The information presented here was drawn from the Lehman Brothers Web site, www.lehman.com/fi/indexes/ssues in mid-2008.

T A B L E 29.1

Composition of the Barclays Capital U.S. Aggregate Benchmark (as of 12/31/2006)

Sector Composition	Percentage in Sector	Quality Composition	Percentage in Rating
Government related	14.1%	Aa	5.1%
Fixed rate	34.0	A	8
Treasury	23.5	Baa	7.1
Corporate	18.6	Aaa	79.8
Asset backed	1.1		
Commercial mortgage backed	4.9		
Hybrid ARMs	3.8		

Source: Barclays Capital, U.S. Aggregate Bond Index, www.lehman.com/fi/indices/factsheets.htm.

they must be rated BBB– by S&P or finally BBB– rated by Fitch. The general composition by quality of the types of securities in the Barclays Capital Aggregate is displayed in Table 29.1.

If a rating is reported for the bond by all the agencies, the median of all three ratings is used. If there are only two ratings, then the lower rating is used. If only one rating is available, then the eligibility for the bond to be in the index is reexamined. All the bonds must also have at least one year to maturity to be included. Bonds must also have a fixed rate, be taxable, and SEC registered.[3]

Fixed-income securities are not traded on exchanges like stock markets; rather they are traded among traders who represent

---

[3] Barclays Capital determines investment grade as follows: Investment-grade securities must have a minimum rating of Baa3/BBB+/BBB+. They choose the middle rating of Moody's, S&P, and Fitch, respectively as we discussed earlier. High-yield indexes have a maximum rating of Ba1/BB+/BB+ and choose the middle rating. Managed money indexes have a minimum rating of Aa3/AA–, and insurance mandate indexes have a minimum rating of A3/A–. The general principle is that when all three agencies rate an issue, a median or "two out of three" rating is used to determine index eligibility by dropping the highest and lowest ratings. When a rating from only two agencies is available, the lower ("more conservative") of the two is used. When a rating from only one agency is available, that rating is used to determine index eligibility.

different trading groups at different firms. The prices at which the trades take place are not quoted continuously because traders view this sort of information as potentially valuable in their trading activities. This makes pricing of securities very difficult. Obtaining correct prices is one of the major drawbacks of the bond market. Barclays Capital is known for its bond traders, so when it comes to the pricing of securities for its indexes, it turns to the information maintained by its own traders. Other bond index providers do the same thing.

Barclays Capital's traders price all index-eligible securities on a daily basis, but pricing varies by bond sector. For example, Barclays Capital's traders price Treasury bonds daily, but corporate bonds are priced in the middle of the month and at the end of the month. Up to 1000 actively traded corporate securities are priced by traders on a daily basis. Those bonds that are less liquid are priced daily based on the matrix of models showing the relationship between the prices of less liquid securities and the prices of the daily traded securities. There are a series of models that are used to relate these prices.

Other third-party sources of information are used to confirm these prices when that information is available. When there are discrepancies between the sources of information, the group providing Barclays Capital indexes researches the issue and adjusts the prices accordingly. The bonds are priced in terms of the bid price rather than the ask price.

Unlike most stock indexes, the interest and principal payments earned by the bonds in the index are not immediately reinvested in index shares. Rather, they are held in the index without the reinvestment return until the end of the month. They contribute to the overall return of the index for the month but are removed from the index capitalization for the beginning of the next month. During the month they remain in the universes. The composition of the returns universe is rebalanced monthly at the end of the month and represents the set of bonds used to calculate returns. The second universe, the statistics universe, can change daily to reflect capitalization changes that take place, that is, bonds that enter or leave the universe. At the end of the month this universe becomes the starting universe of securities for the next month.

Changes to index member securities, such as rate changes, sector classifications, amount outstanding, and maturity, are reflected in both the statistics and return universes on a daily basis, but they will affect composition of the returns universe only at month end.

New issues that qualify for inclusion in the index (but are not necessarily settled) by the end of the month before the rebalancing takes place can be added to the returns universe and hence be available at the beginning of the next month.

The Barclays Capital mortgage-backed security index includes all fixed-rate securitized mortgage pools by GNMA, FNMA, and FHLMC as well as GNMA graduated payment mortgages. To be included in the indexes each security must have a minimum principal amount of $50 million. Total return is calculated as the price change plus income divided by the beginning market value.

The Barclays Capital U.S. Corporate Bond Index includes all fixed-rate nonconvertible investment-grade corporate debt publicly issued by U.S. corporations. To be included, bonds must be investment grade. Collateralized mortgage obligations (CMOs) are not included in the index.

Barclays Capital U.S. Government-Related Bond Index includes all publicly issued nonconvertible bonds of the U.S. government and agencies of the U.S. government including quasi-government corporations, that is, any bond that is guaranteed by the U.S. government. Flower bonds and pass-through securities are excluded from the index. This inclusive governmental bond index is divided into two subindexes. The first is the Barclays Capital Government intermediate Bond Index, which includes all bonds with maturities between 1 and 10 years (actually 9.99 years). The second is the Barclays Capital Government Long-Term Bond Index, which includes all bonds with maturities of 10 years or longer. The Barclays Capital Treasury Bond Index includes all U.S. Treasury publicly issued debt. In addition, the Treasury Notes Index includes notes that have outstanding principal amounts of $50 million or more, a minimum 1 year to maturity, and a maximum of 5 years to maturity. There is also a Treasury Intermediate Bond Index, which is a subset of the Treasury Bond Index with maturities between 1 and 9.9 years.

The Barclays Capital Municipal Bond Index is based on information supplied by Kenny Information Systems Inc. and is computed twice monthly based on the prices of 1,100 bonds in the U.S. market. The index has roughly 40 percent state government bond obligations and 60 percent revenue bonds.

T A B L E 29.2

Composition of the Barclays Capital U.S. Universal Index (as of 12/31/2006)

Segment Composition	Percentage in Segment	Quality Composition	Percentage in Rating
144 – A (ex-Agg.)	3.1%	Aaa	69.5%
Eurodollar seasonal (ex-Agg.)	2.6	Aa	5.3
U.S. emerging markets (ex-Agg.)	2.0	A	8.9
CMBS and other (ex. high yield)	0.6	Baa	8.0
U.S. high-yield	6.3	Ba	3.9
U.S. aggregate	85.2	B	3.3
		Caa-C	1.1

Source: Barclays Capital, U.S. Universal Bond Index, www.lehman.com/fi/indices/factsheets.htm.

The Barclays Capital Global Aggregate Bond Index includes the most liquid portion of the government, credit, and collateralized securities universe on a global basis. The Barclays Capital U.S. Universal Index, which includes all U.S. denominated taxable bonds that are rated investment grade or below and are found in the combination of the U.S. Aggregate Index, the U.S. Corporate High-Yield Index, the Investment Grade 144A Index,[4] the Euro-Dollar Index, the U.S. Emerging Markets Index, and the Non-ERISA eligible segment of the CMBS Index. If the issue is found in more than one of these indexes, it is only counted once. The general composition by quality of the types of securities in the Barclays Capital U.S. Universal Index is displayed in Table 29.2.

Multiverse Index

The Multiverse Index is a broad-based global fixed-income bond market index and is the most comprehensive of the Barclays

---

[4] Rule 144A by the Securities and Exchange Commission has allowed firms to sell securities to qualified institutional buyers that are registered with the SEC. These securities can be traded between qualified institutional buyers but may not be resold to individual investors. See Miles Livingston and Lei Zhou, "The Impact of Rule 144A Debt Offerings Upon Bond Yields and Underwriter Fees," *Financial Management*, Winter 2002.

Capital indexes. The index includes all the members of the Global Aggregate Index and the Global High-Yield Index, which captures all eligible investment-grade and high-yield securities in the world. The Euro Floating-Rate ABS Index and the Chinese Aggregate Index are not included. The Multi-Verse Index is decomposed into a wide range of standard and customized subindexes on the basis of sector, quality, maturity, and country. The index is maintained in a manner similar to the other indexes and is rebalanced monthly.

U.S. Municipal Index

The Barclays Capital U.S. municipal indexes includes nearly all the long-term tax-exempt bond market. The index has four main subsectors of bonds, which include revenue bonds, state and local general obligation bonds, insured bonds, and pre-refunded bonds. The broad index is broken down into subindexes based on revenue source and maturity. Barclays Capital also has a non-investment-grade municipal bond index. It also created "enhanced" state-specific indexes for Arizona, Connecticut, Maryland, Massachusetts, Minnesota, and Ohio. The general composition by quality of the types of securities in the Barclays Capital Municipal Bond Index is displayed in Table 29.3.

T A B L E 29.3

Composition of the Barclays Capital Municipal Bond index (as of 12/31/2006)

Segment Composition	Percentage in Segment	Quality Composition	Percentage in Rating
Revenue bonds	22.9%	California	16.0%
Pre-refunded bonds	15.2	Florida	5.3
Insured bonds	45.9	Massachusetts	5.0
Local general obligation bonds	Via 20	New York	16.1
State general obligation bonds	10.1	Texas	6.8
		Other states	50.9

Source: Barclays Capital, Municipal Bond Index, www.lehman.com/fi/indices/factsheets.htm .

MERRILL LYNCH FIXED-INCOME INDEX FAMILY

Merrill Lynch fixed-income indexes also cover the broad spectrum of fixed-income markets, investment-grade to high-yield issuers, and bonds domiciled in developed to emerging markets.[5] Merrill Lynch provides over 3,000 bond indexes with each being delivered with many different price types. The scope and coverage of the indexes is prodigious. They contain over 10,000 bond price series, and the bonds are priced daily. The sources of the bond prices are from their own traders as reported daily. Their bond history goes back to 1970. They update their databases daily. The indexes are rebalanced on the last calendar day of the month. The total return calculations used by Merrill Lynch are complex and include not only daily prices but also accrued interest during the month.

The Merrill Lynch U.S. Broad Market Index is a well-regarded U.S. bond index. The index tracks the performance of U.S. dollar-denominated investment-grade government and corporate bonds that are available in the U.S. domestic bond market. It includes collateralized products such as mortgage pass-through and asset-backed securities.

One of the more widely used indexes is the Domestic Master Index, which is part of the U.S. Broad Market Index. The Domestic Master Index includes U.S. dollar denominated investment-grade public, corporate, and government debt as well as mortgage-backed securities, Treasuries, global bonds (but only that portion of debt issued simultaneously in the Eurobond and U.S. domestic bond markets), and some Yankee bonds (but only that portion of debt by foreign issuers issued in the U.S. domestic market).

The Domestic Master Index excludes asset-backed securities (ABS), tax-exempt municipal debt, 144-A bonds, and those bonds without a fixed coupon rate. It also excludes U.S. Treasury securities with less than $1 billion outstanding, those securities with less than $150 million outstanding, and securities with less than a year remaining to maturity.

Subindexes of the U.S. Domestic Master Index include the Corporate and Government Master Index, the U.S. Treasury Index, the Quasi and Foreign Government Index, the U.S. Corporate Master

---

[5] The methodology can be found at www.styleadvisor.com/support/download/merrill_bond_rules.pdf.

Index, the Mortgage Backed Securities Index, and the Fixed-Rate Asset-Backed Index. Additional indexes include the U.S. Government Index, the U.S. Agency Index, the Foreign Government and Supranational Index, the U.S. Financial Corporate Index, the U.S. Industrial Corporate Index, and the Yankee Index.

Another widely followed index is the Merrill Lynch Eurodollar Master Index, which includes dollar-denominated publicly available coupon-bearing Eurobond debt securities. There are approximately 1,000 issues in this index. To qualify, the security must have at least a term to maturity of 1 year and $10 million par amounts outstanding. The securities must be nonconvertible and have no equity warrants attached. Floating-rate debt is not included in this index. From this master list of securities a number of subindexes are calculated for several different maturities, including: 1 to 2.99 years, 3 to 4.99 years, and 5 to 6.99 years.

The Merrill Lynch Treasury Master Index contains publicly available, coupon-bearing U.S. Treasury debt. There are approximately 160 securities in this index. The securities have a term to maturity of at least 1 year and $10 million par amounts outstanding. Flower bonds are excluded from this index. A variety of subindexes are calculated for different maturities, including: 1 to 2.99 years, 3 to 4.99 years, and 5 to 6.99 years.

The country-specific Treasury indexes track the performance of local currency denominated investment-grade government and corporate public debt. Indexes include the Australian Government Inflation-Linked Index, Canadian Provincial & Municipal Index, and Japanese Financial Index.

The primary Pan-Europe Broad Market Index tracks the performance of the major investment-grade bond markets in the Pan-Europe region. The subindexes include the EMU Broad Market Index, Sterling Broad Market Index, and government indexes. Additional indexes include the Financial Corporate Index, Non-Financial Corporate Index, and Asset-Backed Index.

Merrill Lynch also offers a Global Broad Market Index, which measures the performance of investment-grade public debt issued in the major domestic and Eurobond markets, including "global" bonds. Subindexes of the Global Broad Market Index include the Global Government Index, Global Broad Market Non-Sovereign Index, Global Broad Market Quasi-Government Index, Global Broad Market Corporate Index, and Global Broad Market Collateralized Index.

The Global Large Cap Index tracks the performance of large-capitalization investment-grade public debt issued in the major domestic and Eurobond markets. The Global Currency and Money Market contains country-specific indexes of Spot Currency and LIBID/LIBOR. The Global High Yield & Emerging Markets Index tracks the performance of a number of investment-grade global debt markets, covering both sovereign and corporate issuers denominated in the major developed market currencies. Further subdivisions of the global high-yield indexes are available for the United States, Europe, and Canada.

Finally, emerging markets sovereign indexes and Brady bonds are available for a number of emerging market countries.

J.P. MORGAN FAMILY OF FIXED-INCOME INDEXES

The J.P. Morgan bond indexes also offer a complete set of indexes for analysis of the global bond markets. They offer extensive data history from 1985 to the present and comprehensive coverage of emerging markets. The indexes come with a wide range of statistics. There are over 30,000 bond return series in their database, which cover over 60 countries. The data are updated daily and monthly.

The J.P. Morgan fixed-income indexes contain capitalization-weighted current and historical market data for indexes and their constituents. The specific data for each of the indexes are extensive such as stripped or blended spreads, weights, market cap, average life, and face amount outstanding.

J.P. Morgan offers a Global Government Bond Index from which flow the country indexes. The Global Government Bond Index is a total return, market-capitalization-weighted index and is rebalanced monthly. The index includes government bonds from the following countries:

- Australia
- Belgium
- Canada
- Denmark
- Germany
- Italy
- Japan
- Netherlands
- Spain
- Sweden
- United Kingdom
- United States

In addition to the U.S. Treasury Index, the U.S. Government Agency Index includes bonds from government agencies such as Fannie Mae (FNMA), Freddie Mac (FHLMC), Federal Home Loan Bank (FHLB), Federal Farm Credit Banks (FFCB), and Tennessee Valley Authority (TVA). The Mortgage-Backed Securities Agency Index tracks the total return of fixed-rate GNMA, FNMA, and FHLMC bonds.

J.P. Morgan also offers the J.P. Morgan Asia Credit Index (JACI), which measures the performance of the Asian fixed-rate dollar bond market. JACI is a market-capitalization-weighted index comprising sovereign, quasi-sovereign, and corporate bonds.

The J.P. Morgan constant maturity indexes (CMI) measure the performance of bonds that are closest to their respective maturity sector. The yields are always for a single bond and are not interpolated. The actual maturity for some countries may differ from the designated maturity because of the infrequent issuance or a lack of issuance of bonds with a 30-year term, as occurred in the United States for a few years.

The J.P. Morgan EMU Bond Index measures the performance of local-currency-denominated fixed-rate government bonds issued by members of the European Monetary Union. Finally, there is the J.P. Morgan Russia Corporate Bond Index (RUBI CORP), which measures the performance of the corporate bond market in Russia. It is a capitalization-weighted index that includes 21 Russia corporate instruments representing four subindexes.

CHAPTER 30

Real Estate Benchmarks[1]

Benchmarks in the real estate asset class present problems because the assets in this class behave in a more diverse manner than those in other asset classes. In equities, the assets are traded almost continuously, so determining a correct price for a security—what the market is willing to pay for that security—is not difficult. In contrast, private market real estate assets, either individual properties or as a portfolio, trade infrequently. Because of infrequent trading, the market value of these assets has to be estimated between purchase and sale points. This makes real estate a unique asset class and presents several challenges for benchmark builders.

There are two basic classes of indexes for real estate assets. In simple terms, there are indexes that measure "private real estate" and indexes that measure "public real estate." Private market real estate portfolios are composed of assets purchased, held, and managed for a variety of investor types including individuals, corporations, insurance companies, pension funds, opportunity funds, endowments, foundations, and other similar institutions. The portfolios and/or their assets trade infrequently. The second type of real estate investments are owned by corporations either in the form of a real estate operating company (REOC) or in a real estate investment trust (REIT). These structures can be either privately owned or publicly listed on one of the stock exchanges. The shares of the REOCs and REITs that are listed on the stock exchanges are

---

[1] A substantial portion of this chapter is based on work by Russell Senior Research Analyst David Brunette.

common stocks; therefore, they trade like common stocks. Most real estate companies that are publicly traded prefer to use the REIT structure because of the tax advantages provided to long-term ownership of real estate. While the shares are essentially securitized real estate assets and can be viewed as large real estate assets being broken into shares, most REITs are self-managed; therefore, a portion of their share price includes a value for management. We will discuss private property indexes and REITS indexes after we discuss some theoretical issues unique to real estate benchmarks.

REAL ESTATE INDEX CONSTRUCTION ISSUES

Valuing Real Estate Assets

The market value of a real estate investment can be a complex matter. The value varies with the type of real estate asset and its cash flow. A residential home, a warehouse, or an apartment complex are quite different types of real estate assets. For each type of asset, there are appraisers whose profession it is to estimate the current market value of the real estate asset. Anyone who has ever purchased or sold a house is familiar with the role of the appraiser in determining value. For single-family residential real estate, the primary factors that are used to estimate value are the location of the house, the lot size, the size of the house, and its general condition. Since there are no cash flows to factor into the valuation, appraisals for single-family residential real estate are primarily determined using a comparable sales method in which homes of a similar type that have sold recently in the neighborhood are used to construct an estimated value. Since no two homes are exactly the same, appraisers use attributes from the comparable sales properties to create a valuation for the property being measured.

A warehouse has different characteristics that an appraiser must take into account. Again, while the location of the warehouse is critically important, the appraiser must also factor into the valuation the expected future cash flows of the property. For example, a warehouse located in an economically depressed area may have a reduced value because it is unlikely that the space in that particular warehouse can be leased at market rates comparable to warehouses in other, more vibrant locations, even assuming that the physical attributes of the spaces are nearly identical.

Real estate appraisers and analysts who are responsible for evaluating institutional quality income-producing real estate need to combine sophisticated quantitative analysis with a multitude of qualitative assessments, often in very ingenious ways, to determine a property's value. Even with all the tools and applications available to assist in the valuation process, there is an element of uncertainty in all these evaluations. For institutionally owned real estate, the National Council of Real Estate Investment Fiduciaries (NCREIF) has taken a leadership role in the industry to develop reporting standards for real estate.[2] These standards use industry best practices for accounting procedures, appraisal management, and performance measurement techniques in order to develop a database of property operating information, which has evolved into the NCREIF Property Index. At year-end 2007, this index tracked over 5,700 properties worth an appraised value of over $300 billion. Properties that are included in the index must be formally appraised at least once a year; as a result, the index has a rich history of purchase prices, cash flow data, and sales prices that can be use to evaluate the efficacy of appraisals during different market environments. While this is a large and growing database, NCREIF only measures a small portion of the several trillion dollars worth of properties in the United States.

The vast majority of properties owned in the United States are typically not appraised on a regular basis. As such, it is difficult, if not impossible, to compare private real estate investments that are not regularly appraised to private market indexes.

Valuing Properties Using Appraisal-Based Methods

There are three main appraisal approaches: the discounted cash flow approach, the comparable sales approach, and the replacement cost approach. The method that usually carries the most weight in the valuation is the discounted cash flow method. This approach values the asset by estimating its expected future price

---

[2] See the NCREIF Web site, www.ncreif.org.

and all the cash flows in between which must be discounted at the appropriate interest rate.

For example, suppose we are considering purchasing an apartment complex in an upscale neighborhood that has 30 apartments, all with the same size and features. Currently, 90 percent of the apartments are rented at an average rent of $2,500 per month. Table 30.1 illustrates the expected annual cash flows [net operating income (NOI)] over the next five years from the property's operations.

The next step is to determine an appropriate capitalization rate (commonly referred to as the "cap rate") to estimate a property's market value. Cap rates function similarly as bond yields do for the bond market in that when cap rates increase, values decline, and conversely, when cap rates fall, values will rise. Cap rates are used throughout the real estate industry as a quick way to estimate a property's value because they typically are based on valuations of properties that have recently traded. For many years, cap rate data were extremely difficult to obtain, partly because real estate transactions are privately negotiated, with final terms that can impact the final sales price kept confidential. While final terms remain confidential, there are now several industry research organizations that publish information on real estate sales that provide transparency to transaction-level data. As such, a significant amount of market research is conducted in the real estate industry regarding current trends in cap rate movements both at the national level and at the metro market level by property type.

With data on transactions more easily accessible, the key to successfully using a cap rate is to identify the most appropriate cap rate to use on a particular property. Similar to bond yields, there are

TABLE 30.1

Expected Annual Cash Flow Example

	Halland Hills View Apartments				
	Year 1	Year 2	Year 3	Year 4	Year 5
Cash flow from rents	810,000	858,600	910,116	964,723	1,022,606
Operating expenses	100,000	103,000	106,090	109,273	112,551
Net operating income (NOI)	710,000	755,600	804,026	855,450	910,055

many factors that influence the movement of cap rates, including the change in 10-year Treasury yields and the appetite for investors to acquire more real estate both nationally and at the local market level. In our example property, if we assume the first year's NOI is "stabilized" in that it represents how the property will normally perform going forward (i.e., the rent and occupancy levels are appropriate for this asset and the property is in sufficiently good condition that no capital improvements are necessary), then a reasonable estimate of its value would be as is shown in Table 30.2.

In this very simple example, if we assume the first year's NOI is a reasonable estimate of the property's stabilized earnings, then by applying a cap rate of 5.8 percent, we estimate this property's value to be $12,241,379. In this example, we used an industry source, the Korpacz Real Estate Investor Survey (www.pwcreval.com), for an appropriate cap rate to use for this type of property, given current market conditions.

However, since we have made cash flow estimates going out five years, we could employ another method to estimate the value of this property, the discounted cash flow (DCF) approach. To employ the DCF approach, an estimate needs to be made for the terminal value of the property at the end of year 5. A traditional method of estimating this terminal value is to employ the so-called

T A B L E 30.2

Capitalization Rate Calculations

Halland Hills View Apartments Cap Rate Calculation		
Cap rate	=	$\dfrac{\text{stabilized NOI (year 1)}}{\text{value}}$
Value	=	$\dfrac{\text{stabilized NOI (year 1)}}{\text{cap rate}}$
Assume:		
Cap rate	=	5.80%
Value	=	710,000
		$\overline{5.80\%}$
	=	12,241,379

Gordon model. This model converts perpetuity DCF analysis for a constantly growing cash stream into a simple cap rate approximation. Table 30.3 illustrates this calculation.

In the preceding example, we assumed that the NOI growth rate for this property is 3 percent; for the residual cap rate, we selected 6.5 percent, again using Korpacz as our source. The terminal value of our example property at the end of year 5 is calculated to be $14,420,879. The next step is to incorporate this terminal value into the DCF calculation as shown in Table 30.4.

In the example, we selected 8.15 percent as the discount factor. Typically, for more risky investments, a higher discount rate is used; for less risky investments, a lower discount rate is used. The estimated value of the property using the DCF method is $12,925,234, which is about $700,000 more than the value that we estimated in Table 30.2. Therefore, as a starting point for negotiating the acquisition price of this property, $12 million or below might be considered a good price, while $13 million or above might be considered expensive.

T A B L E 30.3

Discounted Cash Flow Approach

Halland Hills View Apartments Estimate of Terminal Value		
Forward year NOI year 6	=	NOI year 5 × (1 + growth rate)
	=	910,000 × 1.03
	=	937,357
Gordon Model		
Value	=	$\dfrac{\text{NOI}}{(\text{discount rate} - \text{growth rate})}$
	=	$\dfrac{\text{NOI}}{\text{residual cap rate}}$
Terminal value year 5	=	$\dfrac{\text{NOI year 6}}{(\text{residual cap rate})}$
	=	$\dfrac{937,357}{6.5\%}$
	=	14,420,879

TABLE 30.4

Terminal Value and Discounted Cash Flow Calculations

Halland Hills View Apartments

	Year 1	Year 2	Year 3	Year 4	Year 5
Cash flow from rents	810,000	858,600	910,116	964,723	1,022,606
Operating expenses	100,000	103,000	106,090	109,273	112,551
Net operating income (NOI)	710,000	755,600	804,026	855,450	910,055
Cash flow from sale	—	—	—	—	14,420,879
Net cash flow	710,000	755,600	804,026	855,450	15,330,934
Discount factor at 8.15% rate	$\dfrac{1}{(1 + 0.0815)}$	$\dfrac{1}{(1 + 0.0815)^2}$	$\dfrac{1}{(1 + 0.0815)^3}$	$\dfrac{1}{(1 + 0.0815)^4}$	$\dfrac{1}{(1 + 0.0815)^5}$
Discounted cash flow	656,496	646,009	635,610	625,300	10,361,819
Value of property	12,925,234				

393

Sophisticated investors will use this basic framework and develop multiple models using different assumptions (for example, perhaps a new roof will be required in year 3 resulting in higher operating expenses) in order to fine tune their analysis. Further, with larger properties, for example a 50-story office tower with over 100 tenants with different lease terms and many operating costs and expense items, the amount of data necessary to accurately estimate cash flows needed to do a DCF is quite substantial. This can be additionally complicated with the addition of partnership structures and complex debt financing that are often used in the real estate industry. Today, virtually all data used in an appraisal are maintained in electronic form using special software like ARGUS. Most professionals in the real estate industry consider ARGUS to be an industry standard for cash flow analysis. ARGUS can be used to model commercial real estate across all segments of the property life cycle, from development, to initial acquisition, through lease-up, and disposition as well as incorporate different financing and ownership structures.[3]

Calculating Return and Return Attribution for Real Estate Assets

The calculation of return for real estate assets is the same as it is for equity or bonds assets, which we covered in Chapters 3–5. It involves beginning market value, ending market value, and the contributions to return of intermediate cash flows. Typically the real estate industry calculates an income return and a capital appreciation return, which are then summed together on a quarterly basis to obtain the total return.

Income return measures the portion of total return attributable to each property's net operating income (NOI). It is computed by dividing NOI by the average quarterly investment for the quarter:

$$\frac{\text{NOI}}{\text{Beginning market value} + \dfrac{1}{2}\,\text{capital improvements} - \dfrac{1}{2}\,\text{partial sales} - \dfrac{1}{3}\,\text{NOI}}$$

---

[3] For more information on the intricacies of real estate valuation, we suggest as a good starting point Peter Linneman, *Real Estate Finance & Investments: Risks and Opportunities* 2nd ed. (Philadelphia, PA: Linneman Associates, 2004).

Capital appreciation return measures the change in market value adjusted for any capital improvements or partial sales for the quarter:

$$\frac{\text{(Ending market value} - \text{beginning market value)} + \text{partial sales} - \text{capital improvements}}{\text{Beginning market value} + \dfrac{1}{2}\text{ capital improvements} - \dfrac{1}{2}\text{ partial sales} - \dfrac{1}{3}\text{ NOI}}$$

As you can see, the denominator is the same in both formulas. The formulas are based upon the modified Dietz method of return calculation. The usage of one-third weight for the NOI assumes that net operating income is distributed at the end of each month. There are strict definitions that constitute capital improvements. Typically they are broken out into tenant improvements and leasing incentives; clearly one improves the physical structure and the other is essentially a cost of doing business that needs to be spread out over the life of the lease. Partial sales rarely occur; this is a "placeholder" in the formula in case a large property like a regional mall is subdivided into multiple properties. We note that this formula is for unleveraged properties; the formula for leveraged investments is substantially more complex. Those interested in additional information should refer to NCREIF performance measurement documents for specifics regarding performance calculations for different types of real estate investments.

As we noted earlier, NCREIF standards are employed by only a small fraction of real estate owners. For many investors, the costs involved in having their properties appraised on a regular basis are expenses that are usually avoided. As a result, those investors would not have the beginning and ending market values on a quarterly basis to input into the NCREIF formula. This makes comparing infrequently appraised assets to the NCREIF Property Index problematic. As a result, there would be a high degree of uncertainty regarding the performance of these investments.

For the properties that are regularly appraised, performance attribution for real estate faces the same problems that equity or bond performance attribution faces. One can use the excess return attribution methods described in Chapter 18 to determine how much of the return of a portfolio of real estate assets is due to allocation, asset selection, and the interaction of the two. Of course, benchmark portfolio return series are necessary for the calculation of attribution.

It is also possible to do a factor model decomposition of real estate assets, but the data requirements for the assets make this difficult. That said, organizations such as Investment Property Databank (IPD) from the United Kingdom have made substantial progress in developing a framework in decomposing private real estate returns and offering such a product to the industry.

Calculating the Risk of Real Estate Assets

As exhibited in our simple example earlier in this chapter, calculating the value of an asset in terms of discounted cash flow can become very complicated. In our example, there were several risks that we have assumed away. For example, we assumed that no financing was required to acquire the property and therefore there was no interest rate risk in this investment. As in bond analysis there is always default risk. Default risk shows up slightly differently in real estate in the form of tenants and others partners not fulfilling their contractual obligations. Other risk factors can impact real estate such as changes due to an unexpected increase in operating costs or a decrease in the building's net cash flows as well as property tax changes, insurance cost changes, maintenance costs, utility costs, and other costs that can fluctuate over time.

Vacancy rate risk is always a problem for commercial real estate and tends to move with overall economic conditions. The time horizon valuation problem occurs due to the pattern of contract expirations such as when leases run out. Of course, one of the biggest risks is always liquidity risk or the inability to sell the property when you want for an appropriate price. The length of time to sell a property can vary significantly in different parts of the real estate cycle. Given all these issues and risks, it is imperative that real estate assets be appraised as frequently as possible in order to incorporate the impact of a changing economic and real estate market environment.

The aspects of real estate risk we have outlined are very difficult to assess when estimating risk. Setting aside the valuation problems, one can view real estate risk in exactly the same way as equity risk. Assets are priced; the value of the assets changes over time, which is reflected in the volatility of the prices over time; hence, standard deviation is a good measure of the riskiness of real estate assets and standard deviation can be calculated in the normal way.

Problems emerge when the analyst compares the standard deviation of real estate assets with the standard deviation of asset classes with more frequent pricing like equities. There is no easy way around this comparability problem. The problems associated with the more traditional measure of risk, standard deviation of asset returns, also present difficulties for fund management. Most private market real estate benchmarks and indexes, which we discuss later, have historically contained stale prices because of the infrequent pricing of assets in real estate.

The infrequency of pricing and the reliance on appraisals leads to depressed volatility in real estate asset prices when compared with the volatility of other assets. The volatility of the U.S. equity market is around 15 percent annualized, while volatility of the NCREIF Property Index is only about 3 percent annualized (using quarterly returns). This lower volatility would indicate that real estate is a much safer investment than equities. While one can argue that these returns should be lower risk because the properties have no debt, they are income-producing, and they have no exposure to development risk, most industry observers view this risk level to be inappropriate. An easy adjustment is to use annual returns to calculate risk for private real estate. This has some merit in that until only a few years ago most properties in the index were only appraised once a year. The result of using annual returns places the risk of unlevered real estate to be about 6.5 percent. Even at this low level of risk, problems remain when including real estate in asset allocation studies. Mean-variance optimizers have a tendency to allocate a large proportion of the assets to real estate investments when they are included in asset allocation studies because of their low variance and low and/or negative covariance with other assets.

Index Philosophy for Real Estate Benchmarks

The benchmarks and indexes we discussed in earlier chapters have been created to represent an asset class or subsets of securities within an asset class. The object of these benchmarks is to track the occurrence of market trends and to be used as benchmarks against which to measure risk and financial performance.

One of the criteria outlined earlier for a good index is that it should be representative of the investable universe from which portfolios are formed. It should include all the assets that can be bought or sold. Including all assets that can be purchased allows for the measurement of performance indicative of the investable market as a whole. But what about real estate that has not sold in years and is not likely to be sold—should that be included in the index? An index should also be unbiased, simple to construct, use transparent methodologies, and be investable. None of the criteria are easily obtainable for real estate asset benchmarks.

The development of real estate indexes did not begin in earnest until the 1970s. Prior to that time, the "market-place [had] been characterized by developers and investors who built, developed and/or transacted using money borrowed from a financial institution . . . and paid back in level installments. The passive institutional investor was content to be in a secured position through a bond-like instrument."[4]

With the passage of the Employment Retirement Income Security Act (ERISA) in 1974, an incentive for the development of real estate indexes was created. The act required that retirement plan assets be adequately diversified in order to protect the plan beneficiaries from being overexposed to any single investment class. The resulting increase in institutional investment in real estate led to a demand for an accurate performance measurement benchmark. While there was an intuitive belief "that equity real estate constituted a superior hedge against high rates of unexpected inflation, that real estate returns were competitive with returns to other asset categories over time, and that real estate could lower overall portfolio volatility,"[5] methods of quantitative measurement were not available at that time. Although meaningful and accurate real estate performance measurement data were not readily available prior to the 1970s, considerable progress has been made constructing benchmarks during the past three decades. An ever-growing flow of information provides greater understanding of the performance of the asset class and how to build benchmarks. Despite this

[4] Blake Eagle, "The Challenge of Performance Measurement and the Choice of Management Techniques," in Tom S. Sale III, ed., *Real Estate Investing* (Homewood, IL: Dow Jones-Irwin, 1986), pp. 43.

[5] Eagle, "The Challenge of Performance Measurement and the Choice of Management Techniques," pp. 44.

dramatic growth, there are few blended indexes that report both private and public real estate investment performance, and none that report private investment performance on a global basis. This gap will ultimately be filled as the growing trend toward globalization makes such indexes necessary.

There are various ways that one could go about creating the private market real estate indexes. The ideal approach would be an index composed of all real estate assets, regardless of ownership (REITs, REOCs, private owners, etc.), and with prices estimated by assuming constant trading in the securities under the assumption that one could buy and sell them any time one wished; that is, there is constant liquidity. However, as we pointed out, real estate markets tend not to maintain constant liquidity over time, let alone trying to obtain even basic data on the entire universe of properties. Therefore, it is not possible to estimate empirically a constant liquidity private market index based on observed prices in the private market.

Another approach is a transaction-based index created using the prices of private market values over time. David Geltner, a well-respected real estate researcher, has published, both individually and with other researchers, numerous studies on appraisal bias, liquidity, random noise, temporal lag, and other data challenges in measuring periodic returns for real estate.[6]

A third approach is to base an index on appraised values of a large collection of private property. We have discussed many of the difficulties with appraisal valuations including the difficulty with the frequency and sequence of appraisals. To overcome some of these difficulties, it is now common practice among institutional investors that their external appraisals are being rotated among different appraisal firms and these external appraisals are staggered to happen at different times during the year so the number of external appraisals per time periods is more even. Further, especially among real estate open-end funds, internal appraisals are conducted more frequently (as often as quarterly for their largest properties) to be more closely aligned to current market conditions. Appraisal-based index returns are the most widely used even though some feel they

---

[6] For more information, a good starting point is David M. Geltner and Norman G. Miller, *Commercial Real Estate Analysis and Investments* (Upper Saddle River, NJ: Prentice-Hall, 2001).

must be adjusted for staleness of the appraisals, especially in the early historical returns, in order to use them properly.

PRIVATE REAL ESTATE INDEXES

Investment in private real estate properties generally falls into one of five main property types: apartment, hotel, industrial, office, and retail. Indexes often stipulate that properties represented are fundamentally past the development stage, have a high occupancy rate, and are generating a substantial percentage of operating income from real estate activities. Private real estate indexes typically measure the capital appreciation and operating income growth of privately held individual properties. The index constituents are not easily traded; therefore, these indexes are typically not investable.

Private Real Estate Indexes—United States

NCREIF Property Index
The National Council of Real Estate Investment Fiduciaries, formed in 1982, is an association of institutional real estate professionals who share a common interest in their industry. The difficult task of uniting a highly competitive industry began in the late 1970s. Blake Eagle of Russell Investments (then known as Frank Russell Company) led several meetings resulting in 14 real estate investment managers agreeing in principle to form a nonprofit organization to foster research on the asset class. This effort led to the development of a database consisting of property operating information and an index published by Russell, known at the time as the Russell/NCREIF Property Index.[7] On January 1, 1995, 13 years after its inception, NCREIF assumed full responsibility for the index, its publication, and distribution. The index became the NCREIF Property Index (NPI).

---

[7] See Blake Eagle, "The Challenge of Performance Measurement and the Choice of Management Techniques," in Tom S. Sale III, ed., *Real Estate Investing* (Homewood, IL: Dow Jones-Irwin, 1986), pp. 43–51.

The NPI is a capitalization-weighted, total return (income return plus capital appreciation return) index. This index shows real estate performance returns for direct property investment submitted by contributing members.

The members contributing data are primarily pension plans and their investment advisors. Each data contributor is a tax-exempt entity with a minimum of $50 million invested in commercial real estate. This composition of information providers leads to a sampling bias toward large property holders, but there appears to be little material biases in the index content or performance given the purpose of the index.

The index is currently composed of 5,976 apartment, hotel, industrial, office, and retail properties with a market capitalization of the index at $328 billion as of March 2008. At inception, the database consisted of 233 properties covering the retail, industrial, and office sectors of the private real estate market with a value of $580 million. There has been significant growth in the scope of the NPI, and it is the industry standard. While the NPI includes both leveraged and unleveraged properties, performance is calculated quarterly on an unleveraged basis. Properties are evaluated for inclusion and compliance on a quarterly basis.

NCREIF also produces a number of other indexes and reports such as the NCREIF Timberland Index, NCREIF Farmland Index, MIT Transaction Index, NCREIF Fund Index—Open End Diversified Core Equity Fund Index (NFI ODCE), and NCREIF Property Index Trends.

The NFI ODCE is a fund-level index rather than a property-level index. It is a capitalization-weighted, time-weighted return index and includes property investments, ownership share, cash balances, and leverage (i.e., the returns reflect the fund's actual asset ownership positions and financing strategy). This index was released in May 2005. Performance at the fund level is reported both gross of fees and net of fees on a quarterly basis. The NPI ODCE reports performance on 14 funds with a market capitalization of $102 billion at March 31, 2007.

NCREIF continues to develop new indexes including Value Added and Opportunity Fund Indexes. It developed these specialty indexes based on data supplied by the Townsend Group. NCREIF has continually maintained a policy of working in partnership with academia and members of the professional real estate investment community to improve market knowledge and transparency.[8]

S&P/Case-Shiller Home Price Index

The S&P/Case-Shiller series of home price indexes measures the residential housing market, tracking monthly changes in values in 20 MSAs (metropolitan statistical areas) across the United States. The metropolitan regional indexes are aggregated to form two composite indexes: one comprising 10 major metro areas and a second index comprising all 20 MSAs that is designed to serve as a proxy for the national residential real estate market. In addition, the S&P/Case-Shiller U.S. National Home Price Index is also available. This quarterly index is a broader composite of single-family home price indexes based upon the nine U.S. census divisions.

The main benefit of these indexes is that they measure changes in housing market prices given a constant level of quality, using the "repeat sales method" of index calculation. This method draws on data from properties that have sold at least twice in an "arms-length" transaction, in order to capture an estimate of appreciated value of the individual asset. Changes in the types and sizes of houses or changes in the physical characteristics of houses are specifically excluded from the calculations.

Some criticisms of the S&P/Case-Shiller indexes are: (1) the monthly reports are based on repeat sales and exclude new development; (2) the index offers only partial coverage of the national U.S. housing market, because many states and markets are excluded; and (3) because the index weights transactions by value, it would give eight times as much weight to the sale of an $800,000 home as it does to a $100,000 home. As such, it is particularly sensitive to what is happening with high-priced homes in the largest, most expensive markets, and therefore may not be representative of what the average U.S. resident is experiencing.[9]

---

[8] For more information, see the NCREIF Web site, www.ncreif.org.

[9] For more information, see the S&P Web site, www.standardandpoors.com/ indices.

Private Real Estate Indexes—Global

Investment Property Databank (IPD)

IPD provides independent market indexes and portfolio bench-marking to the property industry. Formed in 1985, and headquartered in London, IPD produces real estate market indexes from over 43,091 properties in 20 countries, including a pan-Europe combined performance report. In addition, IPD produces sector indexes for UK Forestry, UK Let Land, a Pooled Property Fund Index, and a Multinational Index Spreadsheet.

Indexes are designed to show market trends of stabilized (held) properties, with active portfolio management effects of property development and transactions excluded. Property assets are examined for inclusion and compliance on a monthly basis.

IPD indexes are published annually with the exception of the IPD UK Quarterly, UK Monthly, and SCS/IPD Irish Quarterly Indexes. Performance is calculated by chain-linking 12 monthly returns. Real investment returns are reported on a total (time-weighted) basis and broken down into return components such as gross income, net income, operating costs, capital growth, market rental value growth, and changes in yields.

IPD produces or maintains indexes in the following non-European countries: Australia, Canada, Japan, and South Africa. IPD developed a Global Index in 2007 in partnership with NCREIF in the United States and KTI in Finland.[10]

PUBLICLY TRADED REAL ESTATE SECURITY INDEXES

There are a number of vehicles for publicly traded real estate investment, including equity securities, real estate investment trusts (REITs), real estate operating companies (REOCs), commercial-backed mortgage securities (CMBS), exchange traded funds (ETFs), structured debt products, and derivatives. Most indexes of these securities can be replicated with passive investment strategies.

---

[10] For more information on IPD indices, please see the Investment Property Databank Web site, www.ipdglobal.com.

Free-float adjustment is considered the industry best-practice for public real estate like REITs. Float adjustment involves market capitalization decrements to reflect only the proportion of issued stock that is readily available for public investment. Examples of shares that are excluded from the calculation are those held by governments, strategic partners, owners, and other company insiders.

Publicly Traded Real Estate Security Indexes—United States

Dow Jones U.S. Select Real Estate Securities and REIT Indexes

The Dow Jones Select Real Estate Indexes are complete market coverage capitalization-weighted indexes that were introduced in 1991 (with historical data back to 1977). They provide total returns. The movement from full market capitalization reporting to float weighting was completed on December 31, 2006. The origin of the index begins with the Wilshire Real Estate Security Index and the Wilshire REIT Index that were maintained by Wilshire Associates until April of 2004, when Wilshire and Dow Jones began co-branding all the Wilshire indexes. As part of the joint venture agreement, Dow Jones assumed responsibility for calculating and maintaining the indexes.

The Real Estate Securities Index (RESI) represents all equity real estate investment trust (REIT) and real estate operating company (REOC) securities listed on the Dow Jones U.S. Total Stock Market Index meeting minimum market capitalization and liquidity criteria. The REIT Index represents all REITs within the RESI Index. Dow Jones Wilshire also produces indexes for the global publicly traded securities market and domestic indexes for the Australian market.[11]

FTSE NAREIT Equity REIT Index

The FTSE NAREIT Equity REIT Index represents most of the publicly traded REITs listed on the New York Stock Exchange, the American Stock Exchange, and the NASDAQ National market list. NAREIT stands for the National Association of Real Estate

---

[11] For more information, see the Dow Jones Web site, www.djindexes.com.

Investment Trusts. FTSE assumed responsibility for the calculation and dissemination of this index from NAREIT in 2006. Under FTSE's direction, this index is now screened for size of market capitalization, liquidity, and adjusted for free-float. However, the monthly historical index data, which date back to January 1972 (daily index data are available back to January 1999), was not computed in this fashion.

The REITs in each index are examined for inclusion and compliance on a quarterly basis. Both total return and price return calculations are reported on a real-time basis. There are a large number of subindexes produced by FTSE NAREIT as well as composite indexes that include hybrid REITs, mortgage REITs, as well as the smaller REITs.[12]

MSCI US REIT Index

The MSCI US REIT Index is a capitalization-weighted, total return index of all the equity REIT securities included in the MSCI U.S. Investable Market 2500 Index. The securities are screened by market capitalization and liquidity. REITs that do not generate a majority of their revenue and income from real estate rental and leasing operations, such as mortgage REITs and subindustry REITs, are excluded from this index.

On June 20, 2005, MSCI assumed responsibility for calculation and dissemination of this index from Morgan Stanley. It previously was known as the Morgan Stanley REIT Index and was calculated and maintained by the AMEX. Historical data date back to 1994.

Float adjustments for available shares to the index weights are made on a quarterly basis. Securities are examined for inclusion and compliance on a semiannual basis. Index performance is calculated in real time and distributed by the American Stock Exchange.

IPOs and newly listed securities are considered for inclusion on a semiannual basis. Securities are eligible for early entry into the index on the close of the first trading day after the market capitalization is ranked as one of the top 750 largest companies in the current Broad Market Index and all other inclusion criteria are met.[13]

---

[12] For more information, see the NAREIT Web site, www.reit.com.

[13] For more information, see the MSCI Barra Web site, www.mscibarra.com.

Publicly Traded Real Estate Security Indexes—Global

Dow Jones Global Select Real Estate Securities and REIT Indexes

The Dow Jones Global Select Real Estate Securities and REIT Indexes are capitalization-weighted indexes that were introduced in 2006. Historical data date back to 1993 for the RESI and 2005 for the REIT index.

The Global Real Estate Securities Index (RESI) represents all publicly traded REIT and REOC securities in 24 countries meeting minimum market capitalization and liquidity criteria. The Global REIT Index represents all REITs within the Global RESI Index.

The indexes exclude mortgage, net-lease, timber, hybrid REITs, real estate finance companies, home builders, large landowners, and subdividers. The indexes are calculated and distributed every 15 seconds during U.S. stock exchange trading hours. Securities are examined to meet the inclusion and compliance criteria on a quarterly basis. Dow Jones Wilshire also produces both the Global REIT and Real Estate Securities indexes excluding U.S. securities.[14]

FTSE EPRA/NAREIT Global Real Estate Index

The FTSE EPRA/NAREIT Global Real Estate Index is a total return capitalization-weighted index designed to represent real estate stocks worldwide. FTSE and NAREIT joined the European Public Real Estate Association (EPRA) to create a family of indexes.[15] The index currently represents securities domiciled in over 20 countries.

To be included, companies must provide audited annual reports in English and are screened for size and liquidity relative to their geographic region. Each must meet minimum size and liquidity targets for two consecutive quarters prior to inclusion. Stocks are examined for inclusion and compliance on a quarterly basis. Total return and prices return performance is reported on a real-time basis. The index was launched in 2000. FTSE assumed responsibility for the calculation and dissemination of this index from EPRA/NAREIT in 2005. Historical data date back to 1990.

---

[14] For more information, see the Dow Jones Web site, www.djindexes.com.

[15] For more information see the FTSE Web site, www.ftse.com/Indices/FTSE_EPRA_NAREIT_Global_Real_Estate_Index_Series/index.jsp.

The index is calculated using the official closing share prices from the home exchange of all securities included. The exchange rates applied are the official closing prices for the trading day. Calculations are performed every business day a market is open for trading. Three values are calculated: a price value, total return based on gross dividends, and a total return based on net dividends.

S&P/Citigroup Global Property Index

The S&P/Citigroup Global Property Index includes securities from property companies located in 31 developed and emerging countries. All securities included are classified under the Global Industry Classification Standard (GICS) Real Estate Industry Group in the S&P/Citigroup Global Broad Market Index (BMI).

Companies are screened for free-float capitalization and liquidity. This index excludes real estate agents, brokers, appraisers, and companies that build residential units for the purpose of selling to homeowners. The index was launched in 1989, with historical data dating back to June 30, 1989.[16]

---

[16] For more information, see the S&P Web site, www.standardandpoors.com/indices.

CHAPTER 31

Hedge Fund Universes

Hedge funds are not like traditional investments. They are investment funds or portfolios that reflect the manager's view of how to exploit mispriced assets. Hedge funds are not an asset class like stocks or bonds—they are investment vehicles. Investors provide money to the hedge fund manager, and the manager in turn invests the money in anything, but usually in publicly traded securities like stocks, bonds, and derivatives. However, hedge fund managers have the freedom to invest any way consistent with their mandates. There is a wide variety of hedge fund types. They are distinguished by the strategies they pursue. The construction of benchmarks must therefore take a different approach.

HEDGE FUNDS AS ABSOLUTE
RETURN STRATEGIES

Hedge funds fall into the category of "absolute return investment strategies." While individual stocks, mutual funds, and other stock funds can be evaluated in comparison to a basket of securities like the Russell 3000, hedge funds are evaluated relative to zero, the risk-free rate, or LIBOR, plus a prespecified alpha. Their return goal might be stated, for example, as "5 to 10 percent regardless of market condition" or "the LIBOR rate plus 5 percent." They seek to perform positively regardless of the market condition, index performance, asset class, or sector performance. The strategies are typified by using combinations of long positions in assets as well as short selling; trading in derivatives (put options, call options, and futures) as well as using leverage—all in the pursuit of positive return.

One should bear in mind that hedge funds have other unique risk characteristics. Hedge funds in general are not required to register with the SEC because the hedge fund normally limits the number of investors in their funds. The fund requires that their investors be accredited (i.e., they meet an income or wealth criteria). Sometimes the hedge fund asset management team invests its own money along with its clients' money to emphasize its commitment to the investment strategy and to share the risks.

This "partnership-like" investment structure exempts hedge funds from SEC registration. Consequently hedge funds are prohibited from advertising. They do solicit investments at capital introduction events where they describe for potential accredited investors the opportunities they seek to exploit. Otherwise, their attractiveness is passed by word of mouth from one investor to the next. Hedge funds have certain other unusual features such as lockup periods in which investors cannot remove their money from the fund under any circumstances.

Hedge funds also are known for charging relatively high fees for their services. Investors are charged an annual management fee such as 2 percent of assets managed, and they also agree to give to the asset management team 20 percent of the investment gain above a certain floor or "hurdle rate." Goetzmann, Ingersoll, and Ross calculate that this option-like structure can effectively grant as much as 33 percent of the portfolio value to the manager.[1]

The fairness of size and structure of hedge fund fees has been the subject of some debate. Leola Ross demonstrates that hedge fund fees have actually been quite similar to the fees charged by long-only mutual funds if we use the intensity of active management as a

---

[1] William Goetzmann, Jonathan Ingersoll, and Stephen Ross, "High Water Marks and Hedge Fund Management Contracts," *Journal of Finance*, vol. 58, no. 4, August 2003, p. 1689.

scaling factor.[2] The argument for reasonableness of hedge fund fees is that beta exposure, the portion of a fund's returns that is tied to "being in the market," is very inexpensive and can be obtained through index funds or futures. On the other hand, alpha, the portion of a fund's returns that comes from skillful (or lucky) decisions made by investment managers, is expensive and not guaranteed. Traditional mutual funds provide both alpha and beta in one package. Hedge funds can provide pure alpha, and most often can leverage this alpha; hence, the cost per unit of alpha for hedge funds may not be out of line with the fees charged by long-only managers. The reasonableness of this argument varies by strategy, and not everyone subscribes to the notion. Of course, the problems with estimating betas and therefore alphas, as we discussed before, make it easy to underestimate beta and overestimate alpha. Many of the early studies of hedge funds likely overestimated their alphas.

Historically, hedge fund performance varies by strategy. Many strategies provide strong, positive alphas in trending markets or bull markets. Hedge funds as a group tend to do well in down markets or markets where things are uncertain, that is, during periods of volatility. During the bull market from 1994 to September 2000, the Russell 3000 index outperformed every major hedge fund strategy by over 5 percent annualized. However, during the same time period, certain hedge fund strategies did quite well such as the market neutral strategies that take balanced long and short positions in equities. In fact, during this period market neutral strategies delivered about the same return as the broad market—with considerably less volatility. Therefore, not all hedge fund strategies are equal in all environments, which emphasizes the importance of diversification among funds.[3]

---

[2] Leola B. Ross, "Hedge Fund Fees: Do You Get What You Pay For?" *Russell Investments Practice Note,* No. 60 (Tacoma, WA: Russell Investments, 2003). See also Leola B. Ross and Meena Lakshmanan, "One for You, ONE for Me . . . One for You, TWO for Me . . . One for You, THREE for Me . . . Deciding What's Fair in Hedge Fund Fees," *Russell Research Viewpoint* (Tacoma, WA: Russell Investments, March 2006).

[3] William Fung and David A. Hsieh, "Empirical Characteristics of Dynamic Trading Strategies: The Case of Hedge Funds," *Review of Financial Studies,* vol. 10, 1997, pp. 275–302.

HEDGE FUND INDEXES

For equity or bond indexes, the smallest unit of analysis is a stock or bond. For hedge fund indexes the smallest unit of analysis is the entire hedge fund, which itself may be composed of stocks and bonds as well as derivatives and leverage liabilities. For these reasons two hedge funds following the same general strategy often have portfolios of long assets, short contracts, and all kinds of derivative instruments that do not resemble each other at all. This makes building an index in the normal way, as a basket of assets, impractical.

The hedge fund indexes that have been created are viewed as universes of hedge fund managers, and like all universes of managers, they have certain shortcomings. Hedge fund universes are composed of self-reported returns and can be backfilled to provide history. This creates a backfill bias of positive returns since managers are less likely to report negative information voluntarily. As we discussed in Chapter 20, the two most prominent problems of universes are herding behavior (the tendency of group members to do the same thing as everyone else in the group) and survivorship bias (only the successful members tend to survive). We will discuss these issues a little later.

The creation and liquidation of hedge funds is a continuous process. There are almost 7,000 hedge funds in existence, and funds are liquidated every day for a variety of reasons. There are almost as many hedge funds in the United States as there are stocks in the U.S. equity market. Not all these hedge funds are represented in all the hedge fund indexes. Like pension funds, hedge funds self-report their performance at their discretion to data vendors. Nevertheless, hedge fund indexes have proliferated and are currently the most widely used benchmarks to evaluate hedge fund managers.

BUILDING A GOOD HEDGE FUND INDEX

When we discussed the creation of good equity benchmarks, the general principles espoused could also be applied to hedge fund benchmarks where appropriate. For example, we would expect that any good index would have a complete representation of the hedge funds available in the public marketplace, that is, the opportunities set. The index should provide an undistorted picture of the performance of available hedge funds that follow a particular strategy.

The ideal index should represent what happens to a dollar invested in a style of hedge fund. This means that the index should take into account both the performance of the hedge fund and the relative number of dollars invested in that hedge fund by the market participants. This is similar to the capitalization-weighting argument for equity indexes. "Assets under management" (AUM) weighted indexes are superior to equally weighted indexes because they more accurately reflect what happens to a dollar invested.

Arguments against AUM weighting in favor of mean return or equal-weighting return focus on the behavior of the typical hedge fund manager. The proponents of equal weighting argue that the asset flows in and out of particular funds are very large and can yield a distorted view of what the typical hedge fund manager is providing. They argue that the funds should not be weighted by the quality of the fund's marketing department (i.e., the firm's ability to attract AUM). The difference in return between an asset-weighted index and an equal-weighted index can be substantial, as we saw in earlier chapters.

Advocates of equal weighting also argue that by focusing on capital invested in the funds rather than on the behavior of the group of funds, asset-weighted indexes ignore the performance of about 70 percent of the hedge funds. This, some contend, undermines the representativeness of the index return. Furthermore, those indexes that transform the returns in local currency by converting all the returns into U.S. dollars take a very U.S.-centric position. The effect of currency returns may be one of the key hedge fund decision variables.

The investor is usually more interested in what happened to the average dollar invested in hedge funds rather than how well the average hedge fund performed, so an asset-weighted hedge fund index would be more useful than an equal-weighted hedge fund index. However, the equal-weighted argument is not without merit.

A well-built hedge fund index should have a set of clear selection criteria and rules for the construction of the index. These rules should be specified in advance and be publicly available so that anyone with the same underlying data could produce exactly the same result. There should be no committees arbitrarily interpreting the rules. The index should be transparent, which means that any changes to the index should be published, should be consistent with the rules, and where possible should be announced in advance. It should be managed by an organization whose objective is to provide information to users and not strictly to advance its own business.

INHERENT PROBLEMS WITH
UNIVERSES OF HEDGE FUNDS

As mentioned earlier, herding behavior and survivorship bias are problems for hedge fund indexes. The herding behavior of managers in equity universes tends to lead to those managers taking bets similar to others like a herd of buffalo. These bets are often inconsistent with passive index weights for securities (where such passive indexes are available). The equivalent of this herding behavior for hedge funds would be for many or most hedge fund managers within a given hedge fund style to take the same bets on the same hedge fund components such as buying the same stocks or shorting the same assets. Since taking unusual bets is what investors pay the hedge fund managers to do, it would seem to be highly undesirable for herding behavior to cause the funds to behave the same way.

Survivorship bias is a more problematic issue. The effect of survivorship bias is to remove the universe managers who, for example, perform poorly thereby ensuring that only winners survive and the universe median and average returns become inflated. This is a problem in evaluating past performance and estimating future performance. The effect of this kind of survivorship bias is to overestimate the future returns and underestimate the risks. Clearly, selection bias (the criteria for inclusion in the index) affects the universe membership and hence risks and returns. The success bias makes the index more difficult to beat.

Survivorship bias is a serious problem with hedge fund indexes. First, managers who drop out of the universe do not provide data and hence the returns cannot negatively influence the index return if the reason they drop out is related to poor performance. Sometimes, managers drop out with good performance because they are no longer interested in attracting new investors. Their missing data tend to bias the index in the other direction. Second, when managers are added to the universe, their past history is often added to the universe returns, which creates the backfill bias we mentioned. Again this bias may inflate historical universe returns because the managers entering the universe tend to be managers who have had recent success. This means that adding manager returns to the database changes the historical returns.

There is no known easy way to deal with this survivorship problem. The most common approach is to analyze only frozen universes. In this procedure the analyst picks an arbitrary date such as five years before his current research date and examines returns of only those managers that were in the universe five years ago and in the universe today. One problem with this approach is that the return for the current or recent past periods does not reflect the currently available investable universe. If the universe was in a "steady state," this might work reasonably well, but if the universe is growing over time, it can lead to unrealistic performance estimates. This of course interferes with one of our desirable characteristics mentioned—comprehensive coverage. There is no good method for dealing with the absence of data from managers who drop out of the universe. We do not know nor can we estimate what their true returns might have been because we really do not know why they dropped out. Hedge funds can be shut down because the management team may want to pursue other interests or the clients want their money back for some reason, or it can be because of poor performance. Most of the time, it is unclear why a fund disappears from the universe.

Finally, there's the problem of unreported data. Managers of hedge funds, unlike those of companies or mutual funds, are not required to report their returns to anyone or even the structure of their portfolios. Hedge fund managers are notoriously secretive. There is no easy way to gauge the extent to which hedge fund managers refuse to report their returns. Hence, there is no way to estimate the effect this absence of information has on hedge fund index returns.

To see what the effects of these biases are in hedge fund returns Ibbotson and Chen[4] analyzed the performance of a universe of about 3,500 hedge funds from January 1995 through March 2004. They found that both survivorship bias and backfill bias (i.e., filling in back history when a fund is added to the universe) were serious problems in hedge fund returns. The equally weighted performance of the funds that existed at the end of the sample period had a compound annual return of 16.64 percent net fees. Including dead funds (no longer reporting) reduced this return to 13.90 percent. Excluding backfilled data reduced the return to 9.06 percent, net of fees. In the adjusted data set, they estimate a pre-fee return of 12.8 percent, which they decompose into fees of 3.8 percent, an alpha of 3.7 percent, and a beta return of 5.4 percent. Overall, they found that the alphas were statistically significantly positive. The alphas were approximately equal to the fees, which means that the excess returns were almost equally shared between hedge fund managers and their investors.

AVAILABLE HEDGE FUND INDEXES

The list of hedge fund indexes is extensive and continues to grow.[5] We cannot hope to cover all the indexes in this chapter, but we provide a partial list of all the major indexes and the Web sites for each listed index in Table 31.1. Note, that some of the index providers are forthcoming in the description of how their indexes are created, while others are less so. As we pointed out, openness is a highly desirable criterion for indexes.

The major index families like MSCI, Standard & Poor's, Dow/Jones, and CSFB/Tremont offer asset-weighted indexes, while most of the others are equal weighted. HFR is the major index provider that uses both an equal-weighted and AUM-weighted composite methodology to compute returns. HFR uses quantitative methodology to assign funds to indexes.

---

[4] Roger G. Ibbotson and Peng Chen, "Sources of Hedge Fund Returns: Alphas, Betas, and Costs" (Yale University ICF Working Paper No. 05-17, August 2005), Yale School of Management, and Ibbotson Associates. This paper can be obtained from the Social Science Research Network at http://ssrn.com/abstract=733264.

[5] See the Hedge Fund Marketing Alliance at www.hedgefundmarketing.org/hedgefundindexes.htm.

T A B L E 31.1

Indexes Available for Hedge Funds and Their Sources

Source of Hedge Fund Index	Internet Web Site for the Index
Barclay Hedge Fund	www.barclayhedge.com
CISDM	http://cisdm.som.umass.edu/index.asp
CSFB/Tremont	www.hedgeindex.com
Dow Jones	www.djhedgefundindexes.com
Edhec Alternative Indexes	www.edhec-risk.com
Eurekahedge Indexes	www.eurekahedge.com/indexes
FTSE Hedge	www.ftse.com/hedge
HedgeFund.Net (Tuna indexes)	www.hedgefund.net
Hedge Fund Intelligence	www.hedgefundintelligence.com
Hedge Fund News (Bernheim Index)	www.hedgefundnews.com
Hedge Fund Research	www.hedgefundresearch.com
Hennessee Group	www.hennesseegroup.com/indexes
MondoHedge (Italy)	www.mondohedge.com
Morningstar Hedge Fund	http://global.morningstar.com/ hedgefundratings
MSCI Hedge Fund Indexes	www.msci.com/hedge
Standard & Poor's	www2.standardandpoors.com
TalentHedge (Now Portable-Alpha-Index)	www.portable-alpha-index.com
Greenwich Alternative Investments	www.greenwichai.com
Hedge Fund Consistency Index	www.hedgefund-index.com

Things are constantly changing among the players in the hedge fund index providers, so the user must check the Web sites and providers to clarify their methodology. To obtain a feel for what hedge fund indexes are like, we will examine the CSFB/Tremont family of indexes in a little more detail.

CSFB/Tremont Hedge Fund Indexes

One of the best-known and widely followed family of hedge fund indexes is the CSFB/Tremont hedge fund index family. The hedge fund industry's first asset-weighted hedge fund index was the CSFB/Tremont hedge fund index.

The CSFB/Tremont Index LLC is a joint venture of Credit Suisse First Boston (CSFB) and Tremont advisors, with CSFB being the majority owner. CSFB is a major international investment bank with worldwide offices offering a broad array of financial services including hedge funds. Tremont Advisors is a subsidiary of Oppenheimer Funds, which has been heavily involved in the alternative investment advisory business.

The index has 12 styles. The CSFB/Tremont hedge fund indexes are drawn from the Tremont Pass database, which covers over 3000 hedge funds. For a fund to be a member of the hedge fund universe a firm must meet the following criteria:

- It must report net asset value (NAV) every month in a timely and accurate fashion.
- The fund must have at least $50 million under management.
- The fund must have audited financial statements.
- The fund must have at least a one-year track record with the exception that funds with more than $50 million under management can be included without the track record.

The 12 sector indexes or hedge fund styles covered include the following:

Convertible Arbitrage   These are strategies seeking to exploit price inefficiencies between convertible securities and the underlying stock. They tend to be long on convertible bond and short the common stock for the same company. They generate income from the fixed-income security return as well as from profits from the short sale of stocks. The option to convert the bond to stock protects the principal from market moves.

There are a variety of variations on the convertible arbitrage strategy including cash-flow arbitrage, volatility trading, option gamma trading, credit arbitrage, skewed arbitrage, the carry trade, and multistrategy.[6]

---

[6] For coverage of a variety of hedge fund strategies in more detail, see Filippo Stefanini, *Investment Strategies of Hedge Funds* (Hoboken, NJ John Wiley & Sons, 2006).

Dedicated Short Bias   These strategies take more short positions than long positions, so on average they maintain a net short exposure in equities. The decisions on which companies to go short are based on extensive company research. Typically these funds focus on companies with weak cash flow. The short sale involves borrowing the stock and selling it in the market. Short positions can also be achieved by selling forward. Offsetting long positions and stop-loss strategies provide risk management.

Emerging Markets   These are strategies that exploit inefficiencies in equity and fixed income in emerging markets worldwide. These funds take only long positions because most emerging markets do not have short-selling vehicles. (Those funds that do short selling tend to be expensive.)

Market Neutral Equity   These are strategies that use matching to offset long and short equity positions that yield beta neutral and/or currency neutral portfolios within the same country. Leverage is often used to enhance returns.

Event Driven   These are strategies that focus on capturing the price movements that are likely to result from major corporate events. Strategies that fall under this rubric risk arbitrage, distressed securities, and combinations thereof.

Event-Driven Multistrategies   These strategies typically invest in a combination of event-driven equities and credit. Within the equity market the substrategies include risk arbitrage, holding company arbitrage, equity special situations, and value equities. Within the credit-oriented market the substrategies include long/short high-yield credit, leveraged loans, capital structure arbitrage (debt versus debt or debt versus equity), and distressed debt.

Event-Driven Distressed   These are strategies that invest in the debt, equity, or claims of companies in financial distress or bankruptcy. They expect the prices to rise when these companies turn around. They may take arbitrage positions in the company's debt structure.

Event-Driven Risk Arbitrage   These are strategies that exploit expected price movements of companies involved in a merger or acquisition. They take long positions in the company being acquired and short positions in the acquiring company.

Fixed-Income Arbitrage   These are strategies that exploit the inefficiencies in price between related debt securities. These involve strategies that arbitrage interest rates between U.S. and non-U.S. bonds, forward yield curve arbitrage, mortgage-backed securities arbitrage, and credit. The strategies also include credit yield and curve relative value trading using interest rate swaps, government securities, and futures. They also exploit volatility opportunities using options and mortgage-backed securities arbitrage.

Global Macro   These are strategies that seek to exploit macroeconomic inefficiencies between countries on a global basis. They take long and short positions in any of the major capital markets around the world depending upon which market they find most attractive and/or least attractive. They use both cash and derivative instruments to take positions in stocks, bonds, currencies, and commodities.

Long/Short Equity   These are strategies that use equity derivatives to take directional equity positions (as opposed to equity neutral strategies). They use options and futures to establish positions in different regions of the world or economic sectors.

Managed Futures   These are strategies that exploit inefficiencies in the futures market between assets or among contracts within the same assets. The managers of these funds are usually referred to as commodity trading advisors (CTAs).

Multistrategies   This approach uses multiple strategies including risk arbitrage, distressed securities, and other opportunities or combinations of the previous 12 strategies. This is also the residual category for strategies that do not fall under any of the previous categories.

CHAPTER 32

Determining Investment Style

Historically, consultants and plan sponsors have used several ways to determine a manager's investment style. The sequence of logic underlying style identification is as follows: return patterns of groups of managers are observed, and clusters of managers are identified. Managers are interviewed to determine the orientation of their investment philosophies, and their portfolios are examined to determine if there are common portfolio characteristics or factors. If there is sufficient commonality in manager philosophies, portfolio characteristics, and subsequent returns, then the type of investing can be labeled a style.

Managers with similar investment philosophies or "styles" will, on average, produce performance that is more similar to each other than to the overall market or to managers pursuing other styles (otherwise we would have a distinction without meaning). This is because they share similar investment philosophies that lead to similar portfolio characteristics and factor exposures that are priced or rewarded in the market.

Equity style classifications provide a variety of benefits to investment practitioners. Not only is equity style an important ingredient when designing and maintaining an aggregate portfolio strategy, but style classifications can also serve as a useful guide when searching for managers to fulfill a particular role in a multiple-manager context. Style classification can provide a framework for appraising the extent to which managers are adhering to their investment disciplines and, therefore, fulfilling the roles for which they were hired.

Despite these perspectives, the manager classification process is an imprecise science because investment managers do not think in terms of style per se. They are focused on how to find under-priced securities and build them into portfolios. Because classification fundamentally involves the naming and categorization of things, there is an element of arbitrariness or lack of precision in any classification system. There is no infallible, unambiguous method for classifying managers because manager styles, in reality, are a continuum, as opposed to discrete "boxes."

APPROACHES TO THE STYLE CLASSIFICATION PROBLEM

Traditionally, equity manager analysts have used a variety of statistical methods to identify styles of investment management. An analysis of portfolio characteristics relative to both the market and to other managers over time has been the prime tool for assigning managers to styles. Verbal descriptions of the investment process (key security selection criteria and portfolio construction principles) are key elements in determining investment style. The verbal description and the portfolio characteristics should match. As a final check, performance correlations are usually computed to confirm that the appropriate style index and/or universe is similar to the manager returns.

There are a number of traditional quantitative methodologies for classifying observations into groups. These include

1. Discriminant function analysis
2. Cluster analysis
3. Factor analysis
4. Logistics regression (logit)
5. Neural networks

All these multivariate techniques have certain features in common. First, they are quantitatively empirical. This means that the classification process and coefficients are based upon specific observations rather than on general principles or theoretical assumptions.

All but neural networks have inherently linear mathematical models. They all suffer from the "simultaneity" and training-set problems.

The Simultaneity Problem

The forced inclusion of all classification variables in the model to classify managers in situations where they are not relevant is a central problem shared by all multivariate techniques when applied to the classification task. This is the simultaneity problem.

Equity characteristics are often conditionally dependent. For example, a dividend yield of zero is common for growth stocks, but it also occurs for very low priced value companies in distress. Consider a manager who has a low price-to-book ratio, low dividend yield, high sector concentration, and very high price/earnings ratio. A simultaneous consideration of factors could lead to a conclusion that this is a growth manager. However, this menu of characteristics is also common among contrarian value investors who typically invest in companies with depressed earnings (thus, high P/E ratios and no dividends). In these cases the simultaneous consideration of portfolio characteristics will lead to a classification error. If we could somehow capture the fact that the very high P/E ratio is misleading in this case, we could classify more accurately.

Analysts who classify managers by style tend to focus on a few key variables in a manager's portfolio because they know from experience that these variables drive returns. They then use other variables as supporting data to refine their classification. Analysts do not simultaneously consider all information because portfolio characteristics should be judged in context.

Training Set Difficulties

Most multivariate classification techniques begin with training sets or groups of observations that are "known" to be in specific groups and different across groups. These sets are used to calibrate the model, that is, to calculate the model's parameters. Training sets must be accurate so that the model coefficients are accurate. Unfortunately, training sets are difficult to create and maintain, and they can contaminate the classification process in unintended ways.

One chooses a training set to maximize the purity of the style of its members, but this is, in fact, difficult to achieve. It is not an easy empirical task to judge the purity of style when you think you know the managers. It is even worse when you are unsure about the purity of the manager's style or if the purity changes and the analyst fails to notice it. A manager's degree of style purity may wander over time. Among the most common reasons for unstable portfolio characteristics are

- Changes in portfolio strategy in response to market conditions and sector/stock/factor exposures. These bets may be short or long term in nature.
- Changes in the investment philosophy, process, or personnel. New members of an investment team may have different definitions of what constitutes value, which may fundamentally alter portfolio traits.
- Major changes in assets under management. Manager size affects portfolio characteristics in areas such as market capitalization, diversification, and the number of holdings.[1]
- Substantial periods of underperformance, which jeopardize the firm's business. Managers sometimes lose their nerve and begin changing investment strategy in an effort to improve short-term performance.

From an end user's point of view, multivariate techniques are problematic. Getting timely portfolio characteristic data is difficult especially for prospective managers that you have not dealt with before. Also, there is no easy way to describe why a manager was classified in a particular manner. Discussions of factor loadings and discriminant function scores are obscure for even the experienced methodologist and present obstacles to the analyst and sponsor.

The preceding observations about multivariate techniques do not mean they are not useful for classification, but only that their use in the equity manager style application has limitations. The simultaneity and

---

[1] Jon A. Christopherson, Zhuanxin Ding, and Paul Greenwood, "The Perils of Success: The Impact of Asset Growth on Small-Capitalization Investment Manager Performance," *Journal of Portfolio Management*, Winter 2002, pp. 41–53.

training-set problems, along with the demanding data requirements of these methods, contrast with the simplicity and low data requirements of correlational methods for determining style.

Portfolio Characteristics and Style Membership

Christopherson and Trittin proposed an approach to style classification that focuses on the insights of equity analysts regarding equity characteristics of the portfolios.[2] On average about 70 percent of the value portfolios in Russell's large-capitalization value universe have a P/B lower than about 1.7 standard deviations below the market. Consequently, it is reasonable to say that for a portfolio that has a P/B equal to +0.3 sigma, the probability that the portfolio manager is a value manager is very small. In other words, the lower the P/B, the higher the probability the manager is a value manager.

From the cumulative frequency distributions of P/B in the Russell style universes the relationship between portfolio characteristics and the probabilities of a style membership seemed to be inherently nonlinear. The probability of value classification does not increase 5 percent as the P/B drops 5 percent below market. A curved line represents a more realistic probability of membership function than a straight line. In a sense, then, the nonlinear probability functions that are used in the Russell indexes methodology can be seen as a "fuzzy" interpretation of classic screen, or hurdle, methodology.

The Christopherson and Trittin approach uses these nonlinear probability notions and classifies managers through a structured, sequential examination of equity portfolio characteristics. The system uses nonlinear probability functions to assign probabilities to paths in a decision tree, which produces style classifications. When compared with Russell analysts' classifications, the manager classification system was found to be largely coincident. The virtue of systems like this is that, because the analysis is cross sectional for individual points in time, it allows for quick detection by the analyst of major shifts in strategy or portfolio characteristics.

---

[2] Jon A. Christopherson and Dennis J. Trittin, "Equity Style Classification System," in T. Daniel Coggin and Frank J. Fabozzi, eds., *The Handbook of Equity Style Management* (Philadelphia: Fabozzi and Associates Publishing, June 1995).

EFFECTIVE MIX: A RETURNS-BASED METHODOLOGY

Effective mix analysis is currently the most widely used method for assessing the equity styles of a portfolio. This method assigns style based on return pattern analysis or correlational analysis. William Sharpe proposed a complete system of plan management and performance measurement based upon the analysis of covariance structures in manager returns. In Sharpe's approach, style analysis is the determination of a manager's "effective asset mix" of asset class returns.[3] In this sense it is an asset class factor model.

The objective of effective mix analysis is to develop a set of weights that when multiplied by asset class or index returns will closely replicate the observed portfolio returns. "Effective mix" implies that the observed portfolio may or may not be composed of elements of the asset classes involved. The methodology seeks to minimize the squared differences between the portfolio return and a weighted combination of index returns. As a result, effective mix is very much analogous to an ordinary least squares (OLS) regression where the dependent variable is the manager return and the independent variables are the style index returns. Quadratic optimization methodology is necessary to obtain a set of coefficients that are all greater than zero, less than 1.0, and sum to 1.0.

Sharpe's effective-mix methodology assumes a general factor model formulation that portrays a portfolio's return as a set of exposures to style indexes.[4] The relationship is R,

$$R_{it} = \sum b_{ij} I_{jt} + \varepsilon_{it},$$

(32.1)

---

[3] William F. Sharpe, "Determining a Fund's Effective Asset Mix," *Investment Management Review*, December 1988, pp. 59–69.

[4] Sharpe justifies this by asserting that manager returns "effectively deliver" the weighted combination of asset class returns, in "Determining a Fund's Effective Asset Mix." Of historical note, see Kenneth Winston, *Predicting Portfolio Returns with Style* (New York: Balch, Hardy, Scheinman, & Winston, Inc., 1993), and David Tierney and Kenneth Winston, "Using Generic Benchmarks to Present Manager Styles," *Journal of Portfolio Management*, no. 17, Summer 1991, pp. 33–36.

where

j = asset class indexes used in analysis[5]

R_{it} = manager i's portfolio return at time t

I_{jt} = returns for index j at time t of asset classes

b_{ij} = sensitivities of manager i's returns to asset class j's return

ε_{it} = manager i's non-factor-related return (residual or error) at time t.

The b_{ij}'s are estimated over a rolling window. As specified by Sharpe (1988), effective mix has two inequality constraints on the b_{ij}. The optimization constrains the weights or index sensitivities, so they sum to 1.0 (100 percent), and each must be positive or zero.[6] The rationale for the constraints on the effective mix solution is that they ensure that the weighted combination of investable indexes can serve as an investable alternative to purchasing the managed portfolio. As such, the effective mix solutions make reasonable benchmarks. While constraints can be applied in standard ordinary least squares (OLS) regression, it is difficult to impose inequality constraints (i.e., all coefficients being positive or zero). Quadratic optimization can handle both equality and inequality constraints.

Choice of Asset Class Proxies

In Sharpe's 1992 article he analyzes Delaware Investment Advisors' portfolio.[7] The set of asset class factor portfolios included U.S. indexes, international equity indexes, fixed-income instruments, and international bonds. The effective mix solution for Delaware Investment Advisors' portfolio included a substantial weight on international bonds. Delaware Investment Advisors is a U.S. equity

---

[5] Asset class returns and style index returns are used interchangeably in this exposition, which can be confusing. However, Sharpe's original work and all subsequent work assumes that like high-grade bond returns, large-cap growth returns are legitimate candidates for effective mix analysis.

[6] Mathematically: $\Sigma_{j=1}^{j} b_j = 1$ and each $0 \leq b_j \leq 1.0$.

[7] William F. Sharpe, "Asset Allocation: Management Style and Performance Measurement," *Journal of Portfolio Management*, Winter 1992, pp. 7–19.

value manager and has not had an international bond in its portfolio for years. In other words, effective mix presented the analyst with a result that was simply not true.

This example highlights one of the issues that a user of effective mix must consider carefully. The choice of indexes to use in the effective mix solution is a matter of choice. In Sharpe's defense, one could say that this result is exactly what you would expect. Delaware Investment Advisors return portfolio "behaves as if" it had a 12 percent allocation to international bonds. For [delete for agreement] plan sponsors considering whether to use Delaware Investment Advisors in their portfolio, the tendency of the portfolio to historically produce returns that look similar to international bonds may be a risk characteristic they should be aware of.

For consultants seeking to identify the style of investment manager so that they can know how to classify the manager, this result is unacceptable. Their objective in determining a manager's style is to correctly assess the factor exposures to which the manager is subjected so that the fund manager can correctly control the factor risks of their aggregate plan.

This example underscores the importance of the asset class indexes that one includes in the analysis. The common practice among analysts today is to choose indexes that span the investment universe of the portfolio being evaluated. If one is evaluating an equity portfolio, that means equity indexes should be used. Few analysts would include international bonds in evaluating a U.S. equity manager. Some users of style analysis want to include a large number of indexes—generally equity indexes. Sharpe's only admonition on the choice of indexes was to choose asset class indexes that are mutually exclusive; that is, the same assets should not be in more than one of the asset class indexes.

There is a danger in choosing too many indexes. In the same way that specific risk may correlate with the wrong index, if one includes enough indexes in the analysis, there is a strong likelihood that the analyst will find some combination of indexes that explains nearly all the manager's returns. The problem is that the weight on some of the indexes might be spurious and not meaningful, and there is no way for the analyst to know if this is true or not. This is essentially the same problem as putting too many independent variables in a regression, especially if the variables are correlated.

Evaluation Window

The user of effective mix next has to determine the evaluation window. Analysts normally use between 36 and 60 months of return data. However, Christopherson has shown that you can obtain different weighting results by choosing shorter or longer windows.[8] Why 60 months? This choice is purely arbitrary but is usually justified on the basis of the business cycle lasting on average about five years. The assumption is that five years is a sufficiently long time series for the style to have gone through different economic environments and analysis is likely to be more accurate. Of course, if the manager's style is to change risk exposures over the business cycle, five years could be too long.

The argument against shorter windows is that 24, 36, or 48 months will yield weights that are more volatile as you roll the evaluation window and the proportion of return due to specific risk is larger; that is, specific risk has less chance to cancel out. Given the volatility of the underlying return distributions it can be shown that the weights will change to a greater degree with a shorter evaluation window. The argument for shorter windows is that managers are dynamic and sometimes change styles or take bets in such a way that their factor exposures change. Longer windows tend to mask short technical bets and dynamic style shifts. If the style changes for any reason, the longer window will be slow to notice this and correctly estimate style exposure.

Current observations presumably have more information about the manager's factor exposures than do more distant observations. Such logic would argue for some sort of declining weighting scheme with the most recent observations receiving the most weight and the more remote observations receiving less weight. The user must choose how to weight the observations within the evaluation window.

Presentation of Style Analysis Results

Once all the decisions about indexes, window length, and weighting of observations have been made, then the analysis can be completed.

---

[8] Jon A. Christopherson, "Equity Style Classification: Adventures in Return Pattern Analysis," *Journal of Portfolio Management*, Spring 1995, pp. 32–43.

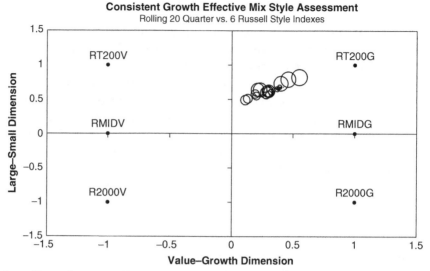

Source: The graph is produced by the FactSet SPAR system.

Figure 32.1 Effective mix analysis for the consistent growth ISP

In Figure 32.1 we show an example plot of effective mix solutions for a consistent growth investment strategy portfolio (ISP). The portfolio was created by Russell U.S. equity research analysts and is designed to have very specific equity characteristics.

This portfolio was constructed to mimic the behavior of consistent growth investment managers who focus on securities with above-average historical growth and low variability in growth. There are no small-cap stocks in this portfolio by construction. All stocks are drawn from the Russell 1000 Index list.

The analysis uses 60-month windows for calculating effective mix solutions and uses six Russell style indexes: the large-cap Russell Top 200 Growth and Value Indexes, the Russell Midcap Growth and Value Indexes, along with the small-cap Russell 2000 Growth and Value Indexes. This set of indexes spans both the growth/value dimension and the large/small dimension. Users of course, can choose any family of indexes they wish, but they should choose indexes from one family of indexes so that there is no overlap in the growth/value or small-cap/large-cap dimensions.

On plots like Figure 32.1 there are normally two scales corresponding to the strongest factors in U.S. equity returns: growth

versus value and large versus small. In Figure 32.1 the style locations of six indexes used in the style analysis are portrayed along
the two dimensions with the midcap indexes lying at zero on the
size dimension and with zero being halfway between the growth
and value indexes on the growth/value dimension. The effective
mix solution weights are manipulated to provide a single value on
each dimension. In this way any particular effective mix solution
can be plotted as a single point somewhere in the scatterplot. The
point where the two axes cross is midcap market oriented.

The circles for the portfolio appear to migrate toward the Russell
Top 200 Growth Index over time. The size of the circle denotes
remoteness with the smallest circle being the oldest analysis and the
largest circle denoting the most recent analysis. We can see that the
portfolio migrated toward the center of the style space and began to
move toward the Russell Top 200 Growth Index more recently.

Another way to portray the time series of effective mix solutions is shown in Figure 32.2. This figure is an area chart that shows
the effective mix values that sum to 1.0 by color or pattern.

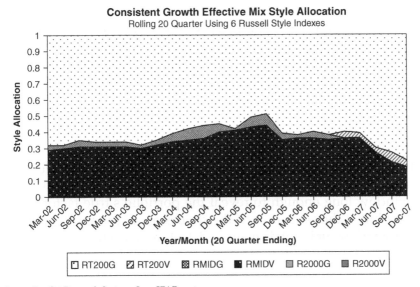

Source: FactSet Research Systems Inc., SPAR system.

Figure 32.2 Area chart of effective mix solutions for the mixed-weight
consistent growth ISP

Note the appearing and disappearing of minor contributions for some indexes. From the nature of the portfolio underlying the consistent growth ISP, that is, the rules of construction, we know that all these minor positions are wrong. No stocks in these indexes found their way into the consistent growth ISP, so the effective mix solution that says the ISP behaved as if it had 5 percent of its securities in small-cap value, that is, the Russell 2000 Value Index, is unambiguously wrong. We return to this issue later.

Confidence Intervals for Style Weights

Lobosco and DiBartolomeo[9] and others have attempted to generate confidence intervals for style weights produced by effective mix. The difficulty with doing this is analogous to the confidence intervals for correlation coefficients that, like effective mix weights, are constrained to lie between –1 and +1. Unfortunately, the weights in an effective mix solution are not correlation coefficients and do not follow the same sampling distribution patterns as correlations. The problem lies in the constraints, which require that the weights must sum to 1.0. Any one effective mix weight is jointly dependent upon all the other effective mix weights through these constraints and so are their distributions. There is no direct solution for calculating confidence intervals.

So while the Lobosco and DiBartolomeo methods for estimating confidence intervals look appealing at first blush, they can at best only be an approximation.

Style Drift Scores

Style drift and style change have been a consistent problem for effective mix methodology. As mentioned earlier, the analyst needs a window long enough to reveal the portfolio's true factor exposures, but at the same time, if the style changes for any reason, the long window makes it difficult to detect this change.

---

[9] Angelo Lobosco and Dan DiBartolomeo, "Approximating the Confidence Intervals for Sharpe Style Weights," *Financial Analyst's Journal,* July/August 1997, pp. 80–85.

Idzorek and Bertsch[10] attempt to develop a methodology for detecting style drift and change over time. The method uses some of the ideas we have already mentioned regarding the changing of window lengths and weighting schemes to develop the style drift measures.

EFFECTIVE MIX LIMITATIONS AND MAXIMIZING USEFULNESS

The effective mix methodology has found wide use in the investment management community despite its shortcomings. Often, return data is all an analyst has and effective mix is the only tool available for determining investment style. For these reasons, it is doubly important to understand the shortcomings of effective mix and to adjust for as many of them as possible to obtain the most accurate analysis.

Problems with the effective mix methodology fall into two general categories. The first is data characteristics such as noisy data[11] and investor behavior that confounds the methodology. The second set of problems has to do with the nature of the methodology itself and the practical problems of using it effectively. We will begin with the problems associated with noisy data and manager behavior.

The Confounding of Specific Risk and Style in Manager Returns

Firm-specific risk causes managers with identical investment strategies but different portfolios to obtain dissimilar return patterns. Managers pursuing a given style can be viewed as selecting samples of stocks from the style index distributions. Given the variability of returns within one style, managers pursuing the same style are likely to have returns that vary from the index and from other managers employing the same style.[12] Furthermore, a manager's

---

[10] Thomas M. Idzorek and Fred Bertsch, "The Style Drift Score," *The Journal of Portfolio Management*, vol. 31, no. 1, Fall 2004, pp. 76–84.

[11] "Noisy data" refers to data that have a high degree of random variation or noise surrounding the true underlying signal.

[12] Jon A. Christopherson, "Equity Style Classifications: Adventures in Return Pattern Analysis," *Journal of Portfolio Management*, Spring 1995, pp. 32–42.

portfolio average return will approach the underlying style index return the longer the window of measurement. This means that on average, the manager's long-run returns will be closer to its style index return than to some other style index return—but not in every case and perhaps not in the short run.[13]

We often see large-capitalization behavior of some small stocks because in any single time period some small-capitalization stocks will *just happen by chance* to correlate more highly with a large-cap stock index than they do with a small-cap stock index. If we relied only on the correlations, we could be led by the methodology to believe the stocks have factor exposure they do not have.

The Effects of Noise

In the real world, portfolio managers must deal with portfolio alpha, noise, and style dynamics that are confounded, all of which makes style determination difficult. To investigate the effects of noise on effective mix solutions, Christopherson and Sabin[14] created simulations based on the returns from existing indexes, combined in different ways to which noise, alpha, and betas were added. The simulated portfolio return series was subjected to effective mix analysis to see how well the methodology correctly estimates the underlying known a priori parameters in the presence of noise. Thousands of simulations were conducted.

Portfolios were created that combined two index returns at prespecified style weights. A random return or noise was added. In the first set of portfolios, added noise was equal to 100 basis points (bps) and in the second set of portfolios, 200 bps of noise was added.[15] The average excess return and the mean of specific risk were

---

[13] Christopherson, "Equity Style Classifications," and Charles A. Trzcinka, "'Equity Style Classifications': Comment," *Journal of Portfolio Management,* Spring 1995, pp. 44–46. Angelo Lobosco and Dan DiBartolomeo, "Approximating the Confidence Intervals for Sharpe Style Weights," *Financial Analyst's Journal,* July/August 1997, pp. 80–85.

[14] Jon A. Christopherson and Frank C. Sabin, "How Effective Is Effective Mix?" *Journal of Investment Consulting,* vol. 2, no. 1, 1997, pp. 23–45.

[15] As mentioned previously, the choice of 100 bp is based on typical levels of specific risk for a manager. The 200-bps scenario shows how a more aggressive manager or small-cap managers are likely to behave.

both assumed to be zero. If the effective mix method successfully dealt with noise, we would expect the time series graphs of style weights from rolling windows to show a horizontal line at the pre-specified style weights. Similarly, we would expect that the median values of the style weight time series would be at the prespecified weights. The larger of the two prespecified style index weights was set at 0.70 and the smaller style index weight was set at 0.30.

For the noise level of 100 bps, the effective mix solutions suggested that the portfolio was exposed to small-capitalization stocks with a weight of 0.08 or greater 5 percent of the time. For a noise level of 200 bps, the weight on small-capitalization stocks was 0.15 or greater 5 percent of the time. Since the underlying portfolio weights were prespecified and the portfolio had no exposure to small-capitalization stocks by construction, these results show that effective mix is prone to errors and style estimates.

When estimating weights for the large indexes, the study found that 90 percent of the time (for the 100-bps noise level scenario) effective mix estimated the large weight to be between a low of 0.57 and a high of 0.79—a weight range of 0.22. For the cases with 200 bps of noise, the study found that 90 percent of the time the smaller weight was estimated to be between a low of 0.43 and a high of 0.89 for a weight range of 0.46.

Our conclusion from this analysis is that levels of noise typical of most managers will produce substantial variation in the style weights generated by the effective mix method. It is clear that the greater the specific risk of a particular return series, the greater the likelihood that the style weights will be incorrectly estimated. This makes sense since under OLS estimation the standard error of regression estimates are, ceterus paribus, related to the size of the regression residuals.

Blindness to Style Dynamics

Style changes are important to managing plan risk. Fund structures that assume a manager will continue to invest in the same area of the stock market in the future can be very wrong when styles shift or drift or when cycles occur thereby increasing fund risk. Effective mix style analysis tends to be blind to style dynamics. The reasons for this follow inexorably from the nature of the method, which assumes that the effective mix weights are constants.

Investment managers are businesspeople who seek to recruit and retain clients. When an investment strategy does not perform well, they are likely to "adjust" the process to improve performance. Sometimes the changes can have a significant impact on the underlying investment style and the factor exposures associated with it. Style changes should be monitored.

In effective mix analysis, correlations are computed over a window—usually 60 months. Unless you differentially weight each of the values in the windows, the most recent time point is as important as the most remote time point. If a style shift occurs, this shows up in the most recent time point. As the effects of the change in style cumulate over time, a larger proportion of the observations reflects this new style and a smaller portion reflects the old style. Gradually the proportion of points reflecting the old style becomes smaller, and the effective mix solution changes. *Inevitably, there is a delay in the recognition of a style change.* The length of the delay will be a function of the severity of the style shift and the extent to which the styles are correlated.

Therefore, when styles are stable and you have enough information about the equity characteristics to know this is true, effective mix is unnecessary. However, it tends to fail when you really need to know if risks have changed, that is, when styles are dynamic.

Methodological Problems with the Effective Mix Model

The effective mix model uses a quadratic optimization to find a set of weights that minimizes the differences between the weighted indexes and the observed return. In this sense effective mix is a cousin of ordinary least squares (OLS). To the extent that effective mix is similar to OLS regression analysis, the effective mix model should be consistent with the assumptions of classical regression theory to generate accurate results. Among the OLS assumptions are[16]

- The equation should be accurately specified—relevant explanatory variables are included and irrelevant variables are excluded.
- No exact linear relationship exists between one or more explanatory variables.
- Coefficients are fixed over time.

---

[16] Good discussions are found in P. S. Pindyck and D. L. Rubinfield, *Econometric Models and Economic Forecasts*, 3d ed. (New York: McGraw-Hill, 1991).

An examination of the effective mix model shows that it can violate all these assumptions producing the predictable result that the parameter estimates—or style weights—will be biased.

The list of problems that afflict effective mix include:

- Choosing the wrong set of indexes for the analysis
- Making the window lengths either too short or too long
- Choosing a family of indexes that does not match the manager's choice set
- Assuming that the portfolio's alpha can be captured in the unexplained return from the effective mix solution
- Assuming the portfolio's style beta is constant when in reality it is dynamic

If beta is dynamic for any reason, then the effective mix methodology can at best estimate the average beta and at worst get it completely wrong. As Richard Roll has pointed out, when you get the beta wrong, then the alpha is wrong.[17]

For all the preceding reasons, claiming that the average of the residuals of an effective mix solution is an estimate of a manager's stock-picking ability should be viewed with a healthy dose of skepticism. Let us more closely investigate some of these problems in a little more detail.

The Effect of Including Irrelevant
Indexes Variables

Sharpe (1992) provides a 12-asset class model for effective mix that includes U.S. equity returns, U.S. fixed-income returns, international equity returns, and international bond returns.[18] Since few, if any, investment products are invested across 12 asset classes, the introduction of one or more irrelevant variables is guaranteed. As we said, it does not make much sense for U.S. equity analysts to use

---

[17] Richard C. Roll, "Bias in Fitting the Sharpe Model to Time Series Data," *Journal of Financial and Quantitative Analysis*, vol. 4, no. 3, September 1969, pp. 271–289.

[18] Sharpe justifies this by asserting that manager returns "effectively deliver" the weighted combination of asset class returns. William F. Sharpe, "Determining a Fund's Effective Asset Mix," *Investment Management Review*, December 1988, pp. 59–69, and "Asset Allocation: Management Style and Performance Measurement," *Journal of Portfolio Management*, Winter 1992, pp. 7–19.

bond returns or international equity returns in evaluating U.S. equity portfolios. It is important for users of effective mix style analysis to consider carefully which indexes or asset class proxies they choose. A widely used set of equity indexes is the Russell family of U.S. style indexes, but most other families that we mentioned earlier will work as well. To the extent all equity index families tap the same drivers of return, they should produce nearly the same sets of results. However, different families of style indexes usually produce different results.

As Buetow et al.[19] demonstrate, one can obtain different and inconsistent results by choosing different families of style indexes. This is reinforced by Christopherson and Barton[20] who show why the returns of different style indexes can behave so differently. Buetow, Johnson, and Runkle[21] show that sometimes conflicting results can result from different definitions of style and style's many dimensions. The result of including irrelevant variables in an effective mix analysis is to undermine the efficiency or precision of the weight estimators. While including more indexes usually improves the tightness of fit or R^2 of the solution, the confidence the analyst can have in the precision of the estimates tends to be reduced. This is so because the weights are required to sum to 1.0, and including irrelevant indexes, while explaining some of the unexplained return, inevitably also absorbs the explanatory power of one or more of the other indexes. In the context of style analysis, index redundancy could lead you to believe that you have less of an exposure to some style(s) and a positive exposure to a style when in fact you do not.

---

[19] Gerald W. Buetow, Jr., Robert R. Johnson, and David E. Runkle, "Inconsistency of Returns-Based Style Analysis," *Journal of Portfolio Management*, Spring 2000, pp. 61–77.

[20] For example, in 1997 Russell's Large Cap Growth and Value indexes performed quite differently than did the S&P/Barra style indexes—they diverged 11.24 percent. In an effective mix context, these differences could lead to different style weights. Jon A. Christopherson and Amy Barton, "Comparing Style Index Performance: How Can the Russell and S&P Indexes Behave So Differently?" *Journal of Performance Measurement*, vol. 5, no. 3, September 1999, pp. 33–45.

[21] Buetow, Johnson, and Runkle, "Inconsistency of Returns-Based Style Analysis."

Multicollinearity

Even if all indexes in the model were relevant, another issue that could potentially plague the analysis is multicollinearity, or correlation among the independent explanatory variables. All the index portfolios are large, broadly diversified portfolios, so all style indexes share common broad market return factors and exhibit common return patterns. As a result, the style indexes typically used in an effective mix analysis tend to be highly correlated with one another.

Multicollinearity in OLS reduces the precision of the model estimators because when the independent variables are correlated, the standard errors of the corresponding regression coefficients increase. To the extent that the two methods suffer from the same estimation problems they should have the same estimation characteristics. If so, then in the presence of multicollinearity the style weight estimates would have larger standard errors, which in turn mean that the weights are likely to vary considerably from one analysis to the next so that the style weights "jump around" over rolling windows. LaRoche shows that changes in index multicollinearity can lead to coefficient unreliability.[22]

Fixed Coefficients

The effective mix methodology assumes that a manager's style weights, or style coefficients, are fixed throughout the estimation window. However, in practice, this assumption is probably not true—style weights do vary over time. Indeed, recognizing shifts in style as they occur is important. For example, if a U.S. equity manager changes style from a large growth style orientation of 0.70 and 0.30 large value to a market-oriented style of 0.50 large growth and 0.50 large value, investors would clearly want to know this because such a shift changes their fund's factor exposures.

In such style change circumstances where managers change their style and their style coefficients remain fixed, the estimators will lose precision *and* be biased. Since all observations are weighted equally in a linear regression and the coefficient is assumed to be constant, a style change will appear to be an error or noise around

---

[22] Jeffrey P. LaRoche, "Returns-Based Style Analysis: The Squirrelly Duck," *American Century Investments* (Kansas City, MO: Research Report, 2006) p. 3.

the average of the window. The rolling window framework of effective mix was implemented to mitigate this issue, but problems remain. As we pointed out, if we assume a 60-month window, and a style shift occurs at the start of the window, the shift would remain in the window for the full length of the 60 months. The coefficient of the new style will gradually grow to its proper weight, but until it reaches that point, the weight will be in error. The point is that during the slow adjustment period the style weights are wrong and produce errors in style estimation and, as we shall see, errors in alpha estimation, and so forth.

To make this slow adjustment quicker a smaller rolling window, like 24 months, can be used to hasten the recognition of style shifts. One might also turn to using daily or weekly return series in the analysis to increase the number of observations; however, the noisy nature of the data may overwhelm the gain in precision. While shorter windows do make it quicker to detect the style shift, the trade-off is that the estimators become more volatile.

Beta Greater or Less Than 1.0

Some managers are higher beta than others. They choose assets within their normal range of securities that have a higher price volatility than the rest of their normal stock universe or normal portfolio. Some managers have more concentrated style portfolios relative to the style indexes used in effective mix. Either of these selection behaviors can lead to a style index beta other than 1.0.

It is also true that a primary constraint of effective mix is that the sum of weights must be equal to 1—not more or less than 1. Each and every weight must be equal to or greater than zero and also less than 1. If a true weight is greater than 1.0, that is, the beta versus an index is greater than 1.0, the methodology cannot correctly estimate it due to the constraints. For the same reason it is also true that if the true beta is less than 1, effective mix cannot correctly estimate the style weight. If the true weight versus an index is 0.8 and all other weights are truly zero, then the effective mix methodology will have to assign a 0.2 weight to one or more other asset class returns because the weights must sum to 1.0.[23] This is an

---

[23] If one of the asset classes used in the analysis is "cash," this distortion can be reduced, but the problem still fundamentally remains.

obvious error, but effective mix must generate imaginary weights for one or more of the other asset classes because the methodology must find a home for the missing weight. This leads us to this observation: When the sum of true betas is not equal to 1.0, effective mix must incorrectly estimate the weights because the methodology allows no sum of weights to be greater than 1.0 or less than 1.0. The less pure the style mix, the greater will be the spread in errors. Also, the lower the beta against the true style components, the more biased and the wider will be the distribution of weight estimation errors.

The inability of the methodology to find a high enough or low enough beta leads to weights that leave unexplained or specific risk in the solution. In other words, the poorer the average fit, the larger the "stock-picking ability" or average residual return.

Unfortunately, the analyst usually does not know what the true effective mix weight should be and is led to an erroneous conclusion about the manager's ability to add alpha or to believe the portfolio has an exposure to an asset class that it really does not have.

Measuring Alpha as the Average
of Effective Mix Residuals

Before we leave effective mix there is one more issue that should be addressed. The purveyors and users of effective mix have argued that like other factor models the unexplained return in the target portfolio is specific risk or the return that cannot be explained by the model. If they left it there, there would be no problem. Unfortunately, Sharpe laid the groundwork for excessive claims for the methodology when he said the average of the specific risk (the residual component) from a factor model can be viewed as an asset selection, which has be interpreted to mean stock-picking ability.[24] Although the statement is technically correct, it can lead to unwarranted statements about a manager's ability or lack thereof.

---

[24] "For expository convenience, the sum of the terms in the brackets can be termed as the return attributable to *style* and the residual component ($\tilde{e}_j$) as the return attributable to *selection*." William F. Sharpe, "Asset Allocation: Management Style and Performance Measurement," *Journal of Portfolio Management*, Winter 1992, p. 8.

There is a belief by some that you can use effective mix analysis to discover the true style-adjusted alpha by examining the residual average return from the effective mix benchmark.[25] We will show that this is a risky belief.

Earlier we pointed out many of the shortcomings and limitations of effective mix. The groundwork has been laid for all the reasons why one should be very careful in assuming that the unexplained variance in portfolio return can be attributed to stock-picking ability. At the risk of being repetitive, let us point out the reasons why one should exercise such caution.

As with regression analysis, the quadratic optimization procedures will attempt to assign weights or explanatory power to only those explanatory variables included in the analysis and by extension cannot assign explanatory power to variables not included in the analysis. If for any reason analysts are unable to find the appropriate index, they can rest assured that the methodology will assign the explanatory power that should go to the missing index to whatever indexes happened to be there. This inevitably leads to errors in return explanation, both positive and negative, so the analyst is never sure exactly what is contained within the unexplained return—much less that it is alpha.

Correlational analysis will attribute stock-picking ability to available index behavior. Appearing and disappearing factors (i.e., oil shock exposure) may be priced for a certain period of time and then disappear. These factors may produce systematic positive or negative shocks to a style index return for a reasonable period of time, which cannot be separated from a manager's alpha.[26]

---

[25] As Hardy says, "The information we can't get (the difference between 100 and 94.8 percent) can best be attributed to the manager's stock selection." (p. 54) and "It is this excess return over the style benchmark that warrants active management fees." (p. 58). Both quotes from Steve Hardy, "Return-Based Style Analysis," in T. Daniel Coggin and Frank J. Fabozzi, eds., *The Handbook of Equity Style Management* (New Hope, PA: FJF, 1995) pp. 51–67.

[26] Barr Rosenberg, "Choosing a Multiple Factor Model," *Investment Management Review,* September 1987, pp. 33–35, and Nai-fu Chen, Richard Roll, and Stephen A Ross, "Economic Forces and the Stock Market," *Journal of Business,* vol. 59, 1986, pp. 383–403.

Behavior of Effective Mix in the Presence of Dynamic Alpha

Time-varying alpha is a problem area for effective mix. If it is likely that alpha is a time-varying series with a nonzero mean that changes with economic conditions, effective mix will run into difficulties. There is reason to believe that alpha behaves this way as we saw in Chapter 15. Christopherson, Ferson, and Turner provide evidence that manager alpha and beta appear to be time-varying for institutional portfolios.[27]

Maximizing the Usefulness of Effective Mix

Earlier we explored the limitations of effective mix methodology as a way of determining manager style and estimating manager stock-picking ability. However, because effective mix is easy to do, requires so few inputs (only portfolio returns and index returns), requires a quadratic optimizer that is increasingly available,[28] and may be the only tool available to determine style (i.e., the analyst may only have returns for the portfolio), the methodology is likely to remain widely used and misused. Here we will try to provide guidance on how to get the most out of effective mix methodology and to avoid its pitfalls. Throughout we will assume that the analyst is primarily concerned with trying to determine the style of an investment portfolio within an asset class rather than the combination of asset class indexes that mimics a fund or plan portfolio return.

Choosing the Right Benchmark Indexes

As we have mentioned, choosing the right benchmarks for effective mix analysis can make all the difference in the world. Few people follow Sharpe's original recommendation of including a wide variety of asset classes when one is analyzing equity portfolios. Most users of effective mix are concerned with identifying the style within an asset class and hence confine themselves to indexes for that asset class.

---

[27] Christopherson, Turner, and Ferson (2000) is reviewed in Chapter 15 when discussing conditional performance evaluation methods.

[28] Quadratic optimization can now be done within Microsoft Excel using the Solver Add-in.

Presumably if the analyst is spending the time to correctly determine the style of a portfolio, the analyst has some idea of what asset class that portfolio belongs to. The choice of indexes should be confined to indexes that span that asset class.

We have spent considerable time discussing the benchmarks for different asset classes in previous chapters, so the analyst should first be familiar with the index choices available for the asset class in question. We noted that within each asset class such as equities or bonds, there are families of indexes created by index providers. It is our opinion that the analyst should choose within a family of indexes rather than choosing indexes from different families. This of course assumes that the manager actually confines his or her investments to within the asset class. Most of the index families seek to span all the investment opportunities within an asset class. Some index providers do a better job of spanning the asset class than others. The reason for staying within one family has to do with the provider treating the data and handling the data in consistent ways across all securities in the asset class. This consistent approach in index construction should help to ameliorate noise that the idiosyncrasies of index construction can introduce. For example, the breakpoints between size groups will be consistent across all indexes rather than being different for each index.

A convenient choice among Russell indexes is reflected in Table 32.1. The analyst could do the same thing using other index families. On the capitalization dimension we have chosen the Russell Top 200 for large-cap, the Russell Midcap for midcap, and

T A B L E 32.1

Russell Indexes That Span the Equity Asset Class

	Value	◄——►	Growth
Large Cap	Russell Top 200 Value		Russell Top 200 Growth
↑↓	Russell Midcap Value		Russell Midcap Growth
Small Cap	Russell 2000 Value		Russell 2000 Growth

the Russell 2000 for small-cap as our indexes. On the growth/value dimension, we have chosen style indexes within each capitalization group. One could just as easily have chosen the Russell 1000 Index and its embedded style components.

This framework is often referred to as the six-box framework that spans the U.S. equity universe of securities. MSCI, S&P/ Citigroup, and the Dow Jones families have sets of indexes that would allow a user to create a similar six-box framework. All these indexes span the growth/value dimensions to a greater or lesser degree and should provide similar results for the analysis of the same portfolio.

Sensitivity Analysis I: Drop Biggest Weight Index

A relatively simple technique for determining how stable the style weights are for effective mix analysis is to perform a preliminary analysis, note the index with the highest weight, and then redo the analysis but eliminate that index from the solution set.

Pay attention to the changes in the weights on the other indexes that result. To the extent that a weight does not change very much, the lack of change indicates orthogonality of that index to the other indexes in the solution. It helps you to identify which of the indexes is making an independent contribution to the solution. You can perform a similar analysis by dropping each of the other indexes in your solution. If the weights on an index gyrate wildly when you include or exclude other indexes, this is a good indicator that the index in question is highly correlated with the other indexes. It could be explained by a dynamic alpha or a dynamic beta or some other poorly modeled return stream. The analyst should exclude the suspicious index or try an instrument that is less correlated with the other indexes than the suspicious index.

Sensitivity Analysis II: Change Window Length

Another relatively easy way to develop understanding of the effective mix solution weights is to perform effective mix analysis using different window lengths. This is useful in two dimensions.

First, it helps answer the question of whether a style change has happened in the portfolio over time, as we mentioned earlier. Shorter window lengths will reveal the style change more quickly than longer window lengths. Higher frequency data such as weekly or daily return data might help. Second, if a style exposure is strong and fundamental to the portfolio return, the weight on that index should be about the same regardless of the window length. As you shorten window lengths, style weights will become more volatile. Ceterus paribus, we would expect that the stronger more fundamental style factor exposures would have smaller variability than less fundamental style factor exposures.

We would also expect to see that regardless of window lengths, the average exposure to an index should show greater random variation around the long-term average the shorter the window length. We would not expect to see trends in the style weights that would indicate style dynamics or style shift. If such dynamics exist, we would expect to see the same general pattern over different window lengths.

Sensitivity III—Aggregate Beta
Greater or Less than 1.0

We have pointed out that the structure of the effective mix model precludes an index having a beta greater than 1.0. This can be a serious problem in particular for growth portfolios, small-cap portfolios, and microcap portfolios. Not only is the effective mixed solution incorrect, which can lead to errors in assessing the true styles factor exposures, but it makes the assessment of average excess return or alpha misleading.

There is a method for determining the extent to which this might be a problem in the portfolio under analysis. The simplest solution is to inflate the volatility of each of the indexes in a solution opportunity set by taking each of the indexes, one at a time sequentially, multiplying by an arbitrary amount such as 1.1 or 1.2. Using the inflated indexes, perform effective mix analysis in the normal manner and note carefully the changes in the overall fit of the effective solution measured in terms of the pseudo-R^2. If the explanatory power of the model improves, this suggests that the aggregate beta is above 1.0.

To test for a true beta less than 1, the analyst can use a similar heuristic by deflating each of the indexes by an arbitrary amount like 0.80. Each of the returns of the indexes would be multiplied by the arbitrary amount and then an effective mix analysis would be performed in the normal manner. Again, note carefully the changes in the overall fit of the effective solution measured in terms of the pseudo-R^2. If the explanatory power of the model improves, this suggests that the aggregate beta is below 1.0.

Purified Return Analysis

The work by Christopherson, Ferson, and Turner on CPE analysis showed that for many manager portfolios detectable dynamic alpha and beta can be estimated.[29] We also know that most equity indexes owe over 70 percent of their return to the common market factor that drives all equity returns. We know from the Barra factor model research that a substantial portion of cross-sectional equity return and aggregate portfolio return can be explained in terms of equity factors. All this leads us to the conclusion that determining equity style can benefit from other widely available information.

The easiest adjustment is to work with the residuals from a CPE analysis of the portfolio and the selected indexes. The only information required above and beyond the index returns is the time series of macroeconomic information such as market dividend yield, the yield curve tilt, and the corporate bond quality spread. The residuals from a regression that includes the market portfolio and the macroeconomic environmental portfolios for the portfolio in question and each of the indexes can be used as "purified proxy" inputs to the effective mix analysis.

Using the residual return series implies that the return series, which had a dynamic alpha and dynamic beta due to macroeconomic factors, has been linearly purged of these explanatory factors. This is an approximation, but the resulting effective mixed weights could more accurately measure the style exposures of the portfolio.

---

[29] If you suspect style dynamics related to macroeconomic variables z_{t-1}, you could perform a CPE analysis and check the significance of the coefficients on the interaction terms, $(r_{st}z_{t-1})$, for example, with an F test that compares the R^2 of regressions with or without the interaction terms.

CONCLUSION

Taking the factors mentioned here into account in estimating the effective mix weights may get you closer to an accurate style assessment. However, there is no perfect way to do effective mix that avoids all the pitfalls that we have mentioned. Effective mix should be used with care and caution, and remember, "Caveat emptor."

CHAPTER 33

GIPS: Global Investment Performance Standards

THE REASON FOR GIPS

The Global Investment Performance Standards (GIPS) are a set of ethical and professional standards for the presentation of performance results that emerged from the work of the Association for Investment Management Research (AIMR), now known as the CFA Institute, and its European counterparts. The genesis of the standard were the AIMR-PPS standards in the United States, which were put together largely due to the widespread abuse of the presentation of statistical information in ways that were just short of illegal. We will not regale you with case studies of performance presentation abuses, but without the standards that did evolve money managers who were honest and ethical were at a distinct business disadvantage to those who played fast and loose with the truth. The investment management business is highly competitive and the temptation to fudge the numbers to get the business (assets under management) is very strong. Without a globally accepted standard, who is to say what presentation of statistics and information is fair and accurate?

For example, an investment management firm that combines recent past performance with a simulated more distant past performance and then obscures where one left off and the other began is obviously at a competitive advantage over a competing firm who reports only its realized returns over the same time period. However, until GIPS came along to level the playing field, there were no rules against this. The bottom line was that many firms recognized the shortcomings of the best practice current at that time but were at a loss to do anything about it especially when it placed them at a competitive disadvantage. It was in the best interests of both the clients and the providers of investment management services to have a workable standard and to mutually ensure that the standard was enforced.

Once the AIMR-PPS standards were established, a network of informal arrangements developed between the United States and countries such as Japan and Switzerland thereby establishing sets of international standards. While these multiple national standards were a vast improvement, they also posed real practical problems for global firms that were marketing across multiple countries. The need for a truly global set of standards was part of the impetus for formulating a global standard that evolved into GIPS.

The establishment of GIPS sought to accomplish several things. The first objective was to create a level playing field across markets for sellers of investment services. The standards also sought to create clear and unambiguous standards of best practice that could be applied to all firms in all markets.

Since these standards do not have official legal status, that is, they're not part of the U.S. code, for example, the method for enforcement had to rely upon a network of key stakeholders (led by the CFA Institute) who could promote, update, and develop the standards. While the standards do not have the force of law, a service provider who fails to observe standards that are widely accepted within the investment community and consistent with most national laws regarding fraud and deception would be at a considerable disadvantage in a court of law. The threat of suit for failure to comply with the standards has considerable enforcement power. As a result of the standards, there has been an increase in the levels of confidence investors can have in the information on which their decisions were based.

The community has long recognized the need for one global set of standards that would guide all investment management companies on how to calculate and present performance to their clients. The GIPS provide a comparable format for the full, accurate, and consistent disclosure of information.

OVERVIEW OF GIPS

The GIPS are long and complex, and we cannot cover all aspects of the standard in this chapter. For a firm to claim compliance with the GIPS, the firm must implement the standards over the entire firm. Exactly what constitutes the firm when it has many divisions or is a subsidiary of a larger organization can be ambiguous, but the basic idea is that the firm must be a distinct business entity held up to potential clients as an investment management firm.

There are a number of general points about the GIPS that help illustrate the role that they play and the general ethos of the standards. The fundamental guiding principles of the GIPS are to achieve a framework of "full disclosure" and "fair representation." These two principles provide a foundation for virtually all aspects of the GIPS and are fundamental to most of the standards.

The GIPS are intended as a set of ethical standards (as opposed to prescriptive rules), so in practical terms these two guiding principles serve to guide practitioners when dealing with situations (of which there are many). In addition, there are a series of guidance statements available on the GIPS Web site, www.gipsstandards.org, which deal with certain aspects of the standards such as "the definition of the firm" or "the creation of composites."

Standards must be applied "firmwide," which means that there is no bias or selectivity in the calculation of representative performance. There is some flexibility allowed in the definition of the firm (see the guidance statement), but it must broadly reflect how a business "holds itself out" to the marketplace. The underlying principle is that the general standards of best practice should apply to all performance calculations across the firm and not just to the representative track records that are provided to prospects.

The GIPS require that compliant firms combine similar accounts into "composites." There is much discussion about the methodology involved (and some criticism about complications that can arise), but in simple terms this is just a way of ensuring that a firm most effectively communicates its aggregate skill in a particular asset class or market segment. Firms must provide lists of composites on request—but it is not necessary for a firm to maintain hard-copy, pro forma, written, historical performance track records for all composites. The requirement is simply (1) that a firm has undertaken exercises to evaluate all mandates and group those that are similar together and (2) that (as stated earlier) the firm exercises a consistent approach and applies the same standards of best practice when calculating all returns.

The GIPS provisions are divided into sections reflecting various aspects of presenting performance information: fundamentals of compliance, input data, calculation methodology, composite construction, disclosures, presentation and reporting, real estate, and private equity. The themes of fairness, accuracy, consistency, and disclosure are woven throughout the standards.

In addition to the provisions, the GIPS covers procedures for verification, which is the review of an investment management firm's performance measurement processes and procedures by an independent third-party verifier. The goal of verification is to establish that a firm claiming compliance with GIPS has adhered to the standards.

The verification procedures for calculating returns can be very time consuming and complex. That is why an entire industry has grown up around providing investment firms with verification. The verification procedures document and adjust for the timing of information, the actual flow of funds from custodian to brokerage houses, and specify when and where fees are assessed. Getting these values right and their recognition at the proper time is critical to accurate calculation of realized returns. This is a specialized business and requires expertise in systems normally not available in investment management firms.

The GIPS document is a living document and is subject to modification and addition, so readers should consult the latest version to ensure they are up to date. We urge everyone in the business to be familiar with the full GIPS.[1]

---

[1] For the complete standard visit the GIPS Web site at www.gipsstandards.org. The companion book *GIPS: Global Investment Performance Standards Handbook*, 2d ed. (Charlottesville, VA: CFA Institute, 2006) elaborates on the standard and provides some useful examples.

INDEX

Jon A. Christopherson, Ph.D.
Research Fellow, Investment Policy and Research
Russell Investment Group

Ph.D., University of Washington
Jon A. Christopherson is Russell Investment Group's first research fellow on the basis of his record of intellectual innovation at Russell and the significant impact this has had on Russell's businesses. Jon has performed extensive research in style analysis and style index construction and is currently engaged in exploring methods for improved manager evaluation and performance forecasting in U.S. equity. Jon helped create Russell's equity styles indexes in the United States and Japan. He has published on the subjects of normal portfolios, manager return predictability, and small capitalization stock returns, as well as the methods of performance measurement and equity style classification. His paper on equity styles is a CFA III reading. Prior to Russell, Jon was an associate professor of government specializing in methodology, national security policy, international relations, comparative government, and political theory. Jon is a member of the advisory board of the *Journal of Investment Consulting* (the IMCA journal) and was on the board of the *Journal of Portfolio Management.*

David R. Cariño, Ph.D.
Research Fellow, Investment Management & Research
Russell Investments

David Cariño is a research fellow at Russell Investments, where he conducts research on indexes, performance measurement, and rebalancing. He has assisted numerous clients with multimanager portfolio strategies and has served as director of investment strategy for Russell's office in Sydney, Australia.

David has published several influential articles on asset allocation and performance measurement since joining Russell in 1987. He was the architect of the Russell–Yasuda Kasai model, an asset/liability management model using multistage stochastic programming, which received a 1993 Franz Edelman Award by The Institute of Management Sciences. His 1999 article "Combining Attribution Effects Over Time" received a Dietz Award by the *Journal of*

Performance Measurement. He currently serves on the advisory board of that journal.

David earned engineering degrees from M.I.T. and a Ph.D. in engineering-economic systems from Stanford University.

Wayne Ferson, Ph.D., M.A., M.B.A., B.S.
Wayne Ferson specializes in investment performance evaluation, mutual funds, asset pricing, and empirical methods.

Curently, he holds the Ivadelle and Theodore Johnson Chair in Banking and Finance, Marshall School, University of Southern California (2007–present) and is a research associate, National Bureau of Economic Research.

He also held the Collins Chair in Finance, Boston College, between 2001–2006. Wayne was a Pigott PACCAR Professor at the University of Washington (1992–2001), a visiting professor at Stanford University, Arizona State University, the University of Miami, and the University of South Carolina, assistant professor at the Wharton School (1981–1983), and an assistant and associate professor at the University of Chicago (1983–1992).

He was the President of the Society of Financial Studies (2006–2008) and the Western Finance Association (2000–2001), editor of *Journal of Empirical Finance* (2005–2007) and *Review of Financial Studies* (1996–1999), director of the American Finance Association (1997–1999), director (1993–1996) and vice president (1998–1999) of the Western Finance Association, and associate editor for various journals.

Wayne received the Berstein Fabozzi/Jacobs Levy award for *Journal of Portfolio Management* paper (2000), the Dean's Research award at the University of Washington Business School (1997), the New York Stock Exchange award for the best paper on equity trading at the Western Finance Association meeting (1993), and the Graham and Dodd Scroll for *Financial Analysts Journal* paper (1991).

CPSIA information can be obtained at www.ICGtesting.com
Printed in the USA
LVOW01*2007280915

456070LV00008B/38/P